# OUT *of* TIME

## THE VEXED LIFE *of* GEORG TINTNER

TANYA BUCHDAHL TINTNER

FOREWORD BY RICHARD GILL

UWA PUBLISHING

First published in 2011 by
UWA Publishing
Crawley, Western Australia 6009
www.uwap.uwa.edu.au

UWAP is an imprint of UWA Publishing
a division of The University of Western Australia

THE UNIVERSITY OF
WESTERN AUSTRALIA
Achieve International Excellence

National Library of Australia
Cataloguing-in-Publication entry:

Tintner, Tanya Buchdahl.
Out of time : the vexed life of Georg Tintner / Tanya
   Buchdahl Tintner.
ISBN 9781742582566 (pbk.)
Includes index.
Tintner, Georg 1917–1999.
   Conductors (Music)—Biography.
784.2092

Typeset in Bembo by J&M Typesetting
Printed by Griffin Press

This project has been assisted by the
Australian Government through the Australia
Council, its arts funding and advisory body.

'Georg Tintner's unforgettable performances and recordings place him alongside Bruno Walter, Wilhelm Furtwängler and Arturo Toscanini. All who worked with this lyric giant will remember his Mozart, Beethoven and Bruckner, as well as his modest nature, whimsical humour, blazing integrity and profound devotion to the great masters in a rare and exalted music making. It was ecstasy to perform with him concertos by Mozart, Chopin, Brahms and, on several occasions, the five Beethoven piano concertos.

'*Out of Time* balances the tragic and tender with some extremely funny moments that constituted the life and work of the true musician.'

Roger Woodward

Tanya Buchdahl Tinter, Georg's third wife and widow, is a freelance writer and classical music reviewer. She has also managed a professional development program for orchestra conductors for almost twenty years, and served as concerts officer at the Queensland Conservatory. She lives in Halifax, Canada, and Sydney, Australia.

# Contents

## Foreword

'Jews are just like everybody else, only more so,' quoted Georg
Tintner to an audience of parents and students, prior to conducting
a Bruckner symphony at the National Music Camp in Geelong,
Victoria, in 1979.

Anton Bruckner, Catholic peasant, and Georg Tintner,
Austrian Jew, are linked forever in the minds of many music
lovers here and elsewhere in the world, based principally on the
extraordinary Naxos recordings Tintner made of the Bruckner
symphonies towards the end of the last century. Bruckner's music
is inextricably linked with Tintner's life.

Tintner, at the age of eight, joined the Vienna Boys' Choir.
History records that he was the first Jew to do so. His anti-Semitic
experiences in the Vienna Boys' Choir were somewhat amelio-
rated when he discovered the music of Bruckner which, according
to Tintner's own accounts, touched him more directly and spoke
to him more powerfully than the other Viennese masters. Indeed
the music of Anton Bruckner turned out to be Tintner's salvation
in so many ways.

These early years in Georg Tintner's life introduced him in a
powerful and frightening way to the concept of man's inhumanity
and to the concept of music as a source of nourishment for the
heart, mind and soul; the *sine qua non* of life – a phrase I heard
Georg Tintner use in rehearsals and which has stayed with me.
In fact most of what I observed of Georg Tintner as a man and
musician has stayed with me throughout my musical life. I can say
without fear or favour that I have worked in close collaboration
with an enormous number of conductors. Two with whom I have
worked have made a seriously profound impact on me: Carlo
Felice Cillario and Georg Tintner. Although Tintner never really
knew it, he was my first and probably only mentor.

I met Georg Tintner for the first time when we worked together on a production of *Carmen* at the then New South Wales Conservatorium of Music in 1975. I had heard of him but had not encountered him directly. I was a comparatively young Conservatorium teacher whose job it was to prepare the chorus for *Carmen*, cobbled together from voice students, music education students and any other student who was interested enough to sing in this production which was to be directed by Ronal Jackson, at that time Head of the Opera School.

Tintner's profound knowledge of the score had such a powerful impression on me, it changed the way in which I examined music. He seemed to be so certain about all musical matters and every musical detail, but at the same time was always looking for extra musical truths – as if one could never know enough about the music. It was clearly the approach of a composer, not a conductor, and in his conducting it was as if he was actually composing the music. The intensity with which he worked was palpable and the ownership of the work he was conducting was never in question. He never put himself above the score and one never heard him use the phrase 'my interpretation', although it was as clear as crystal that he had very fixed views and very strong opinions. His work on *Carmen* was exhilarating, refreshing and, to use a very over-worked word, exciting – genuinely exciting.

I also discovered that Tintner was never afraid to express a view and was not celebrated for his tact in dealing with bureaucracies. He was not a diplomat, he was not a bureaucrat, he was not a politician and he was not a public servant. For all of these ostensible failings and his inability to deal with the political side of music in countries which were, and indeed still are, learning how to be civilised, he suffered unfairly, not securing musical directorships or other positions that often fell to less worthy people.

Tintner came to Australia bringing with him an incomparable background in music. He had been a part of that great epoch of music-making which was flourishing in Europe post–World War I and was to change irrevocably post–World War II.

This background is directly attributable to the rare and special insight he brought to everything he did, not simply because of his extraordinary, natural musical talent but also because of his astute and highly evolved powers of musical observation which he had been developing from his earliest years as a chorister, coupled with the fact that he was passionately curious about all things musical and never musically satisfied.

This passionate curiosity kept him eternally youthful as a musician and contributed to his monomaniacal pursuit of excellence in musical performance. It also distinguished him from his so-called colleagues who often found his eccentricities amusing at best and disturbing at worst. How interesting that a parochial, under-educated, musically unaware society in which Georg Tintner found himself when he arrived in New Zealand and Australia, would have the knowledge to be able to pass musical judgement on this extraordinary human being; but pass judgement it did. Often the judgement was ill-informed and frequently biased. He was, in many ways, a fish out of water. Had he been a European guest conductor who flew in occasionally for concerts, his treatment in New Zealand and Australia might have been very different. As it turned out he was a prophet without honour and frequently treated as such.

Tintner was interested in all things musical, from composition to interpretation and had well-developed opinions on every musical matter known to mankind and was not afraid of sharing them. Tintner was afraid of no-one and could never understand why everybody else didn't share his feelings about the music he was conducting. He knew his players and singers very well and was aware of the range of mental acuity and musical comprehension in every group with which he worked.

I have no knowledge of Georg Tintner's work as a composer other than that he was one and that, as I have said before, he conducted as if he had written the work. It is patently clear that in everything Tintner did of a musical nature his profound knowledge of composition informed his approach.

Tanya Tintner's biography is not only a detailed and compassionate study of a musician but is simultaneously a rich history of music, especially in New Zealand and Australia. This book is replete with musical, historical and personal detail and is a significant literary landmark in the recording of this country's musical heritage.

Georg Tintner was not like everybody else; he was not like anyone else; he was his own man, his own musician and his own master – a musical Diogenes.

I'm not able to speak of Georg's work elsewhere, but New Zealand and Australia owe him an extraordinary debt and I shall never forget him. *Out of Time* is a reminder to us all that we once had living amongst us a true musical giant.

Richard Gill

# Prologue

Instantly recognisable by his cloud of white hair, Georg was sitting nearby with an old friend of mine at a concert in the Sydney Opera House. I joined them at interval. 'I understand you are an authority on Bruckner,' I said to him. 'I must confess I have absolutely no idea what Bruckner is about.' He beamed at me and said politely, 'That's quite all right.' We chatted for a while, in spite of that inauspicious beginning, and when he heard I was leaving shortly for the Bayreuth Festival he asked me to deliver his regards to the singing teacher there, Dr Clemens Kaiser-Breme. In Bayreuth I tried at the stage door to see Kaiser-Breme, but the guard allowed me only to leave a brief note. I was just twenty-two and he clearly thought I was a pushy singer. I sent Georg a report by postcard and forgot all about it.

Some weeks later I went again to an Opera House concert, and as I left I saw on a poster that Georg was conducting *Jenůfa* in the theatre next door. Stage Door's information board showed that it was just finishing. It was late and I was tired, but I owed him an explanation; rather reluctantly I decided to wait. After twenty minutes or so he came out of the loading bay, with dishevelled hair and wearing scruffy, ill-matching clothes. His jacket was a couple of sizes too small and his trouser legs were fastened with bicycle clips over skinny ankles. He was pushing a bicycle even shabbier than his clothing. 'Hullo!' he said with a big smile. I was surprised he remembered me. I told him I had done my best with the message but he brushed the explanation aside, saying instead, 'I would like to meet you tomorrow.'

A little puzzled, I met him the next day in the city and we went for a long walk. He stood slightly shorter than I and he stooped a little. His eyes were pale blue-grey and very expressive, his mouth wide and a little lop-sided. His forehead was high and wide, his skin pink and slightly translucent. He was no better dressed than the evening before. He looked to be in his seventies, but he moved and spoke with youthful vigour. He insisted on walking on my left – an Austrian mark of politeness, he explained, which he simply *must* observe. A gentleman always walked on a lady's left because if she were insulted he could draw his sword from his scabbard without risk of injuring her.

At the end of our walk he said he would like to meet me the following day. Again we walked again through the city and Georg questioned me about my life, wheeling his bicycle all the way. It grew late, and there were few buses to where I lived so I hurried him along to the stop. A bus was on the point of leaving, and as I leapt inside Georg stopped me on the steps. 'I don't want this to spoil our friendship,' he said nervously, 'but I would like to ask you something. I want you to marry me.' The bus driver rolled his eyes, slammed the door shut and drove away before I could say a word.

Marry him? I hardly knew him. Who was this impulsive creature? He had said little about himself; I only knew that he had been a member of the Vienna Boys' Choir – how enchanting! – and he had flourished in the long-gone artistic hothouse of Vienna until forced to flee from Hitler. He seemed weighed down, perhaps with disappointments suffered, and out of place in his surroundings. He was exotic and courteous, nothing like unpolished Australians – he had even farewelled me with '*Küss d'Hand, gnädige Frau*' (I kiss your hand, gracious lady).

Eventually I did marry Georg, and we spent twenty-three years together. When it was over I realised that I hadn't known him nearly as well as I had thought and I set out to find him. It has taken me many years to piece his life together. He himself left few clues. He used no appointment books or diaries, kept few concert programs and reviews, and only a handful of letters. He had no secretaries to preserve his business correspondence, all handwritten, and very few of his friends kept (or were willing to show me) his personal letters. Almost all I had were the fragments he had told me over the years. At least I had the priceless advantage of knowing that – apart from dates, about which he was reliably unreliable – everything he said was true. I interviewed about 200 people and surprisingly many said: 'Marvellous musician, Georg. One of the finest musicians I ever knew. He wasn't treated well – never received his due…Mind you, I never really *knew* him.'

*Part I*
*1917–1954*

# One

On a beautiful spring day in 1917, in a pretty suburb of Vienna, Mizzi Tintner sat in the garden with her newborn son Georg. Her husband Alfons, a lieutenant in the Imperial and Royal Air Force, was away at the war, floating high above Bosnia in a hot-air balloon. He had just been granted his dearest wish: a son, who would follow him into the army and become an officer like him. He had already converted to Lutheranism to ensure Georg could climb higher than he kept to the lower ranks because he was a Jew.

Officially speaking, Jews were not excluded from anything – Emperor Franz Josef had decreed so half a century earlier. For the first time in 700 years Jews had equal rights: they could own property, live where they pleased, attend university, and join the civil service and the army. And so they flocked to Vienna from all corners of the Austro-Hungarian Empire – from Krakow and Dubrovnik, Bregenz and Brasov, Trieste and Lvov – to partake of German culture, which they considered superior to all others, and to make hay while the sun shone.

Young Bernhard Steinhof, Georg's great-grandfather, came from Mattersdorf (then in Hungary) in the 1860s. He set up a linens business directly opposite Vienna's main synagogue, and as soon as he was established, he found himself a wife. On 28 June 1868, aged thirty-three, he married nineteen-year-old Adele Horowitz, a Jewish immigrant from the east.

Less than a year later the first of their children was born, on 31 May 1869: Helene Therese, always known as Therese. Three boys followed: Friedrich Karl in 1874, Robert in 1876, and Eugen Gustav in 1880. Mathilde came last in 1882, but she died of meningitis the following year. Bernhard diversified into general fabrics and linings, and by 1876 he was doing so well that the family could move to Praterstrasse 15, the most magnificent residence in the Second District – the Jewish ghetto of Leopoldstadt.

*Therese Horowitz, Georg's grandmother, in an undated photo around 1914.*

Therese grew into a beautiful girl, her strong face graced with full lips, large, heavy-lidded black eyes and bold eyebrows. By all accounts she was a charming and happy girl, with a liberal outlook on life. She studied the piano, and became accomplished enough to play for the middle-aged Johannes Brahms. 'Miss, I like your playing,' he said. 'But I like you much better!'[1] Then Therese fell in love with her uncle Moritz, her mother's much younger brother, and was determined to marry him. Although marriages between cousins were relatively common, this bordered on incest and required permission from the highest governmental authorities. Eventually it was granted, and twenty-one-year-old Therese married Moritz Nathan Horowitz, a bank official, on 12 October 1890, the day after Moritz's thirty-second birthday. Moritz immediately joined the Steinhof firm.

Bernhard and Adele owned a substantial villa in Baden, the fashionable spa near Vienna, in the most elegant part of town next to the Kursalon. It was here that Moritz and Therese's first child was born, on 6 September 1892: Marie Elisabeth, always known as Mizzi. A year and a day later their second and last child,

Clothilde, was born. They became the very picture of a cultured and happy – and completely assimilated – family. There was money for governesses who taught the girls an assortment of languages, and money for sojourns in fashionable places: the Dolomites, the Italian lakes, the Tyrolean mountains. Therese often went to the opera, and maintained that not even the greatest conductors came near to Mahler's utter fascination.

The Steinhof sons Friedrich Karl and Robert joined the family company,* and as Emperor Franz Josef built up the army the firm prospered. Bernhard's materials were used to line and insulate the soldiers' greatcoats, and in recognition of his services he was made a *Kaiserlicher Rat* (Imperial Councillor). By the time he died in 1906, he had made a fortune, and his partner and brother-in-law (also his son-in-law) Moritz had made one as well. By 1909 Moritz and Therese had moved to one of Vienna's best addresses, a splendid new building on the Stubenring, the eastern end of the Ring. Life was good – as good as any Jew could expect. But it did not mean freedom from anti-Semitism. The Jews' very success fanned its coals, and the installation of Dr Karl Lueger as Mayor of Vienna in 1897 added fuel. In his thirteen years in power the enormously popular Lueger played on the fears of the working and lower middle classes, who resented Jewish domination of Viennese life and feared losing their jobs to industrialisation, which was undertaken overwhelmingly by Jews. Before emancipation began in 1848 there were 179 officially 'tolerated' Jews in Vienna, whose usefulness as bankers and merchants outweighed their undesirability as Jews. Fifty years later that number had increased to 147,000, just under 9 per cent of the population. Lueger railed against Jews in commerce, the arts, finance, law and medicine, and especially against Jewish liberals. Many of his friends were Jews, but when questioned he gave his famous reply: '*Wer ein Jude ist, bestimme* ich' – '*I* decide who is a Jew'. Lueger's anti-Semitism was politically expedient; he knew his demagogic declamations fell on fertile ground. Adolf Hitler, who lived in Vienna as an impoverished student from 1907 to 1913, learned much from him.

---

* Eugen ignored the family firm and became a sculptor, architect and structural engineer instead. He studied with Otto Wagner, Josef Hoffmann and in France with Henri Matisse. He also created stage designs for his friends Arnold Schoenberg and Maurice Ravel. He taught at Vienna's Kunstgewerbeschule before moving to America in 1931, where he taught at various universities, consulted for Lockheed, and advised Walt Disney on Technicolor.

*Mizzi Tintner, in a photo shortly after her marriage in 1914.*

*Mizzi (left) and Thilde in a Tyrolean meadow.*

Around 1912 Mizzi fell in love with the Austrian writer Stefan Zweig. He was eleven years older, but they had much in common: Zweig was the son of non-religious Jews, and his father was a wealthy textiles manufacturer. Mizzi had only a middle school education but she was intelligent, a liberal thinker, she loved literature and was well read. She was also 'a very charming, truly lovely person', according to her niece Elisabeth, and loved by everyone who knew her. Though short of stature, not much over five feet tall, her appearance was striking. She had thick dark hair and a round face dominated by huge black eyes with a sweet and gentle expression. She and Zweig came as far as contemplating marriage. But when Mizzi consulted her doctor, he warned her against it. They both came from rarefied, artistic families, he said, and Zweig, moreover, suffered from depression. With the inbreeding in Mizzi's family he could not guarantee how their children would turn out. One or both of them called it off. Zweig moved to Salzburg in 1913 and a year later married a fan of long standing, Friderike von Winternitz. Mizzi found herself a man who was anything but a *littérateur*: Alfons Tintner, a first lieutenant in the *K. u. K. Luftfahrtruppen*, the Imperial and Royal Balloon Corps.

The Tintners had been in Moravia, mostly in Austerlitz (now Slavkov u Brne), since the 1300s. Georg's grandfather Ignaz developed a new stock feed that made him a rich man. He married Rosa Tauszky, a notary's daughter from Holič, and they lived in Brno, where six children were born. Around 1879 they moved to Vienna and settled in Leopoldstadt, where their last two children were born. Although their five boys and three girls all did well, Georg was dismissive of his father's family, referring to them variously as 'peasants' and 'much more of a lower social order' (than his mother's family) – a curious view given that the Horowitzes were Jews from the east, seen even by other Jews as inferior.

Klara, the first-born, married Wilhelm Brünner, who was the director of the Dorotheum, the famous Viennese auction house. Camilla, the youngest, married a factory director but died of diabetes aged thirty-eight. Bertha, the second daughter, married Leopold Weinberger who owned the Weinberger und Fischer Schirm- und Spazierstockfabrik (Umbrella and Walking-stick Factory). One of the Tintner brothers, Arthur, joined the firm, eventually took it over and became very rich. Leopold (Onkel

Poldi) became the Consul for El Salvador. Rudolf (Onkel Rudi) became an architect and the town surveyor for the city of St Pölten, the capital of Lower Austria. Early in 1911 he married Johanna Ludwig and converted to Catholicism. Their first daughter, Elisabeth, was born on 12 September the same year, suggesting they had married in some haste. Their second daughter, Rosa, was born in 1917, but the marriage failed. It was only in the Nazi time, when people pointed out such things, that Elisabeth and Rosa discovered to their considerable shock that their father and his family were Jewish.

Friedrich, Onkel Fritz, did best of all. He became a *Generalstabsarzt*, a military surgeon with the rank of general, an almost impossibly exalted position for a Jew. He made a number of medical inventions during the Great War, most notably a stretcher that could be bolted easily into railway carriages and ambulances for speedy evacuations. It was used all over Europe by the armies of many countries, including those of Germany and Great Britain.

*Alfons Tintner, shortly after his marriage to Mizzi Horowitz in 1914.*

Alfons was born in Vienna on 20 January 1881. He was educated as far as middle school, and at nineteen, after a few years working for the Weinberger umbrella firm, he joined the army, as many younger sons did. Photographs of him in his thirties show a handsome man, moustached and completely bald despite his youth, standing proudly in his uniform oozing charm and sex appeal. He was also an elegant dancer, and had a reputation as *der Löwe in der Tanzschule* – the hot number in the dance academy. He was such a success with women that the army had to transfer him more than once because of his affairs with actresses and the like. His face was covered in scars from duelling over them.

He met Mizzi Horowitz by chance. Mizzi was resting on a bench during a promenade along the Danube when Alfons and one of his brothers walked by. She thought, 'That is the most handsome man I have ever seen', and burst into tears. Alfons walked over to her, and Mizzi did something unthinkable for a lady – she stood up.

There was trouble when they decided to get married. Both families were strongly opposed, but despite their best efforts they failed to stop it. A few months after the war began Alfons took leave from Mostar, where he was posted, and he and Mizzi were married on 1 December 1914. They were an unlikely couple, but they loved each other deeply, and according to Georg it was an idyllic marriage. Alfons gave up philandering forever, and if Mizzi ever regretted not having an artistically minded husband, she never let on to anyone.

Mizzi was soon pregnant, and Alfons was convinced the baby would be a boy, who would follow in his footsteps as a professional officer. He was now a lieutenant, but he knew that, as much as Jews had equal rights according to the law, the implementation in those post-Lueger days was often very different. He and Mizzi, neither of them religious, converted to Lutheranism. It was very much a minority religion in Austria, but many Jews converting for practical reasons could not quite bring themselves to join the Catholic Church, the primary source of Austrian anti-Semitism.

Alfons guessed the sex of his child wrongly. On 21 March 1916 Mizzi gave birth to a girl, Annemarie Rosa. It was not until the following year that Alfons was given the son he hoped for. Georg was born on 22 May 1917 at the upscale Loew Sanatorium,

*Annemarie and Georg Tintner in 1919.*

*Stubenring 6, the luxury building where Georg grew up. The family occupied the middle floor.*

and baptised at the Garrison church three months later. His name, Georg would later point out gleefully, meant 'country bumpkin'.

Emperor Franz Josef died in November 1916 after a reign of sixty-eight years. He was replaced by his grandnephew Karl, who tried to save the empire by withdrawing from the war. He failed, and both monarchy and empire collapsed in November 1918. Vienna was left presiding over a small, remnant country of just 6.5 million people. Alfons was such a devoted monarchist that he felt he could not serve a republic, and resigned from the army on the first day of 1919. At least that is what Georg always believed. In fact this much-reduced Austria simply retired surplus officers. Alfons was granted a pension and the rank of captain, and was promoted to the rank of major in 1924. In November 1919 the family moved in with now-widowed Therese and Thilde* at Stubenring 6. It was not until the middle of 1921 that Alfons found a steady job, as a salesman with the Adolf Popper oil firm.

At first Georg seemed to develop slowly. He was three before he began to talk, but when he finally did he spoke in complete sentences. At the age of six he began piano lessons with his grand-mother, who discovered he had absolute pitch. And then, a little later, his life changed for good. 'My rather artistically minded mother took me once to a suburban church where the Vienna Boys' Choir, plus an orchestra – I forget whether it was the Philharmonic or not – performed *Christus am Ölberg*, and the whole performance and the atmosphere made a tremendous impression on me. I was eight years old then. And I said to my mother, "I want to do that too".'[2]

The Vienna Boys' Choir was formed in 1498 to sing in the Hofburgkapelle, the Imperial court chapel. Josef Haydn was a member, as was Franz Schubert. With the collapse of the monarchy in 1918 the choir was suspended, then revived in 1924 by Rektor Josef Schnitt. Georg remembered:

> The monarchy was totally discredited after the war, and of course the Hofburgkapelle and the boys were all part of the establishment of the monarchy, and I'm sure as a reaction they abandoned all that. But the Austrians are naturally very conservative people and I think they gradually went back

---

* Thilde never married. Georg's explanation was that 'she was too intelligent' (for any man to want her).

to the idea of having them. And Rektor Schnitt was a very enterprising businessman...This Vienna Boys' Choir thing suited him very well.[3]

He should never have become a priest. He was *totally unsuited* to be a priest. When he was in the womb, his mother was very ill, desperately ill, and she vowed to the Almighty that if she survives, if it's a daughter it will be a nun, and if it's a son it's a priest — which is one of the most wicked things to do. You can make plenty of vows for yourself, but not for somebody else. So he felt obliged to fulfil his mother's vow, though he would have been a marvellous entrepreneur.[4]

Georg auditioned with about a thousand other boys. One of the examiners was Franz Schalk, the 'feared and famous' music director of the Vienna State Opera and director of the Hofburgkapelle, who was sufficiently impressed by Georg to admit him. A later inscription on his (very incomplete) file card noted: '*Stimme mittelmäßig, musikalisch hervorragend begabt, absolutes Gehör*' ('Average voice, musically exceptionally talented, absolute pitch'). Georg joined the newly formed preparatory class probably early in 1927, and on 15 September he was formally admitted to the main choir as a First Soprano.

The Vienna Boys' Choir now comprises four choirs, but then it was only one group of between thirteen and seventeen boys. They lived in spartan conditions in the Hofburg palace, though because Georg lived hardly more than a kilometre away he was allowed to sleep at home. The boys worked very hard. With private tutors they did the usual schoolwork expected of Austrian children. They were given the Classical education offered in the elite *humanistische Gymnasien*, comprising eight years of Latin and five years of Greek, and as well they rehearsed extensively.

Voice training in that sense didn't exist in the Vienna Boys' Choir, and I think that was one of the best things about it. The choir in my time sang with their natural voice. That doesn't mean that they could sing as they liked, that was not so. But there was no vocal tuition in the narrow sense of the word. Mind you, we rehearsed for three hours every day at least, and we took it very seriously. But we sang with our natural voice, and that is so different from the English idea

of boys' voices where they make all boys sing treble whether
they have low or high voices, and therefore they have this sort
of – to me – unnatural nasal sound, which is a different sound
ideal...We were taught to breathe properly. But there was not
much emphasis even on that, because you know that children
do things naturally which adults have to learn. I remember,
for instance, when people told us, how do you sing these
horribly difficult things like the beginning of the E minor
Mass by Bruckner, which is divided into eight parts and very
chromatic – only then did we realise there was anything
particularly difficult about it.[5]

The choir sang for the Mass every Sunday morning in the
Hofburg, with the men of the State Opera chorus and the Vienna
Philharmonic. They sang in the top gallery at the back of the
chapel, as they still do, sounding like angels on high.

> The choir sat in the balcony, facing the altar, but it would
> have been blasphemous for the conductor to face the players
> because in this case he would have been with his back to the
> altar. So these world-famous conductors sat facing the altar,
> and we could just see their hands the wrong way and we
> couldn't see their facial expression. Now that may have been
> very pious, but it certainly made it very much more difficult
> for us.[6]

They also sang small operettas and operas, fully costumed.
Mozart's *Bastien und Bastienne* was a perennial favourite wherever
they went. Other regulars were Johann Schenk's *Der Dorfbarbier*
(*The Village Barber*) and Schubert's *Der Vier-Jährige Posten* (*The
Faithful Sentinel*), in both of which Georg took the part of a serving
girl in wig, skirts and apron. They sang the masses of Mozart,
Schubert and Haydn, and it made a great impression on Georg
when he found in the back of his Haydn part a comment scribbled
by Schubert when his voice broke: '*Zum letzten Mal gekräht*' –
'crowed for the last time'. They participated in outside concerts
where boy choristers were needed: Hector Berlioz's *Damnation
of Faust* under Felix Weingartner, Mahler's Third Symphony
under Oswald Kabasta and Bach's St Matthew Passion under both
Wilhelm Furtwängler and Willem Mengelberg. When he was

about eleven Georg met Erich Korngold. He also shook hands
with Richard Strauss, and didn't wash his hand for a week.

By the time Georg joined the choir in 1927, Rektor Schnitt had
realised the financial and publicity value of touring, and the choir
travelled the length and breadth of Europe for several months each
year. In his four years in the choir Georg visited every European
country except the Baltic states, Belgium and the Netherlands.
The boys travelled by train, Georg sitting by himself devouring
the Wild West novels of Karl May. On one trip across Poland there
were no free seats and they spent the night sitting on their suitcases
in the corridor before giving a concert the next day. In Sweden
they sang for the king, who slept through the performance. In
Athens, in March 1930, 'we were invited to one of these socialites.
There was a mandarin tree, and we were allowed to pick our own
fruit. Mandarins don't grow in Vienna, and to eat a mandarin
from the tree! – that was one of my greatest joys.'[6] On their first
visit to Italy, in April 1929, there was an earthquake in Bologna
and Georg was awakened by women screaming in the streets.
The high point of that tour was an audience with Pope Pius XI
at the Vatican, an immensely significant event for the devoutly
Catholic choir. All the boys kissed the Pope's ring except Georg,
who refused. The consequences of this action are unknown, but it
must have enraged Rektor Schnitt – something Georg should have
avoided at all costs.

## Two

A musical boy could have no better education than in the Vienna Boys' Choir, but for Georg it was far from an unqualified blessing. 'My parents converted to be Lutherans in order to save trouble for their children – they *thought*,' Georg said. 'As a matter of fact it made it much worse for me, because we were rejected from *all* sides.' On his first day one of the boys accused him of being a Jew, and from that moment his life was a misery. He was the first Jewish boy ever admitted to the choir; even Lutherans would have been rare enough. Georg had not even been aware that he was Jewish – the closest he came to Judaism was a handful of Yiddish words gleaned from Therese, who used the language when she didn't want the grandchildren to understand. 'My greatest disadvantage was that I was the most musical and the most intelligent among these boys,' he said, 'and that of course was the worst thing that could have happened to me.'[1]

For the entire four years he was in the choir Georg was persecuted, principally by Rektor Schnitt. Georg was so frightened of him that on swimming excursions to the Danube he hid from him in the gorse bushes. He became ashamed of his 'Jewish looks', what he thought of as his 'African' appearance: his thick lips, which he tried to make thinner by pressing them together, and his mass of thick, crimped hair. 'I felt like a hunted animal,' he said. 'In the end they made me ashamed of my parents. It is a terrible thing, but I believed them. They destroyed the innocence of a child. He loses his spontaneity and naturalness, and that is a terrible thing.' But he said nothing to his parents, for they would have removed him immediately, depriving him of the music. In all the surviving photographs of Georg as a choirboy he appears unsmiling and anxious.

*Georg in the Vienna Boys' Choir in 1930 (back row, second from left). Rektor Schnitt stands back row, centre; Robert Kuppelwieser, a Kapellmeister who befriended Georg, stands behind Schnitt. Herbert Hnatek (back row, second from right) was the boy who accused Georg of being a Jew on his first day. Walther Tautschnig (seated, second from right), later director of the choir, remained on friendly terms with Georg.*

*An anxious Georg standing on the balcony at home.*

By 1930 the choir had acquired Dr Georg Gruber, a Nazi sympathiser, as *Kapellmeister*. Georg came into conflict with him almost immediately, in an event he remembered as a musical crisis.

> We were part of a benefit concert* in the *Konzerthaussaal*, and we rehearsed away – I still remember even the piece we did, by Conradin Kreutzer it was. Gruber played away and we sang, and I stopped and I said, 'It is very hard for me to sing that because the piano is over a quarter tone too high.' He said, 'Always you with your cleverness! In the second most famous concert hall in the world they would have a piano that is wrongly tuned!' I immediately thought I had made a mistake, but I persisted in my mind that it is wrong. The next item on the program was a famous lady fiddler. She came out with a beaming smile onto the stage, asked the accompanist to give her the A, and as soon as he gave her the A she walked off the stage and said, 'I cannot play with this piano. It is much too high!' To the end of my days I will be grateful to this lady because had she not said that, I would today believe that I had made a mistake.[2]

At the end of his four years there was the ceremonial awarding of certificates. Each boy was called out in alphabetical order, but the official, probably Rektor Schnitt, passed Georg over. At the end he said: 'And of course there is nothing for the Jew.' Georg remembered it as one of the worst moments of his life. In an interview more than sixty years later he stated:

> Anti-Semitism is endemic [in Austria], and when you said it was civilised I had to smile to myself because it was *all but*. I have since my earliest childhood been subjected to this kind of persecution and I say that without any self-pity. And in a way it was probably good for me…But when that started, then I stopped being a child.[3]

Of his time in the choir, Georg in later years would say only that it had afforded him a wonderful musical education. He didn't mention his persecution except to a tiny handful of people, mostly other refugees, and he refused to go into detail. When I mentioned

---

*    The concert was on 26 January 1930; the soloist was Hilde Rings.

20

his difficulties to Dr Walther Tautschnig, a fellow chorister Georg had been friendly with and who later spent almost three decades as the choir's director, he brushed my comments away saying that Georg was likely complaining about the spartan physical conditions they endured. Anti-Semitism was so much a part of life in Vienna that those who were not on the receiving end of it simply did not see it. The only time Georg is known to have broken his silence on what actually happened was an occasion not long after we were married. A colleague from my university days came to visit, a writer who had once been a trainee Jesuit priest. He was also, as I warned Georg, an unrepentant anti-Semite. He had hardly sat down when Georg came into the room and quietly poured out a long and detailed description of what Schnitt had done to him. It was an appalling tale of sadism, petty intimidation and terror. On our visitor it made no impression at all.

When in 1984 historian Byron Riggan asked Georg for his choir-time reminiscences, he replied:

> My four years with the Wiener Sängerknaben were musically extremely important and formative, but in every other respect those four years with them were traumatic in the extreme so I have forgotten all of it except the music. The most intriguing question of the lot is: Why was Rector Schnitt not a Nazi? His anti-Semitism, which ruined and poisoned my childhood would have been worthy of the best of them and was perhaps more virulent than of Dr Georg Gruber, who dethroned him in the name of the 'Führer'.* The world is a strange place.[4]

It was as a choirboy that Georg discovered the music of Anton Bruckner, with which he fell instantly and permanently in love. As much as he adored the music of the other Viennese masters – Mozart, Haydn, Schubert and Beethoven – it was Bruckner's music that meant the most to him.

---

\* The Nazis removed Schnitt and installed Georg Gruber as director only days after the Anschluss in March 1938. Gruber had also formed his own choir, the Vienna Mozart Boys Choir, in 1936. They toured worldwide until the outbreak of war trapped them in Australia. He was arrested as a Nazi in Melbourne in March 1941 and interned at a prison camp at Tatura before being deported to Austria in November 1947. He was later cleared by a de-Nazification tribunal.

It is I think the feeling of peace and contentment in some way, that sort of cosmic feeling that in spite of every horrible thing the world can be a good place. Mind you, when I was nine years old I wouldn't have put it in those words, but I think that's what it was.[5]

A person who deals with eternal things has plenty of time. There is no hurry, no hurry whatsoever. Bruckner was an ardent Catholic, and he was an upper Austrian peasant. Therefore you may think that you have either to be an Upper Austrian or an ardent Catholic to love and try to understand his music. This is not the case. The peasant side to Bruckner, that sort of rustic side, the heavy scherzos and the heavy-footed dances mean *comparatively* little to me...I, a heathen, gained more comfort from this music not because of the particular denomination, or *any* denomination, but because of that feeling which transcends all these little labels and which addresses itself to all Man.[6]

Bruckner was the salvation of a boy chronically under siege who had nobody to turn to. It is likely that this is when Georg first realised that music (and not just Bruckner) could be a refuge. In later years, as events threatened to overwhelm him, it was music he clung to, music that kept him going. In a world he found increasingly discouraging, increasingly chaotic, music was his one certainty. He understood it intimately; it was the rock on which he could depend.

On 15 August 1929 the choir sang Bruckner's Mass in F minor at the Salzburg Festival, under the direction of Bruckner's student Franz Schalk. Georg often recounted the story of this event, for him a life-altering experience.

Franz Schalk was a truly nasty piece of work. We were absolutely terrified of that man. He was very thin and he had a goatee beard and his eyes stared behind his glasses and we were terrified. He was what we call an *Intrigant*, and very much a man of this world: cynical, and very clever, cruel, ruthless – the lot...It was the final rehearsal of Bruckner's F minor mass with the Vienna Philharmonic Orchestra. When it came to the Benedictus (this piece, incidentally, might have inspired Mahler for the slow movement of his Fourth Symphony. It is very similar. He was a great admirer, and in a way a pupil, of Bruckner), we suddenly noticed – you know children are very observant – we noticed that his beat, which was a very good and very clear beat, got less and less clear and less and less good, and suddenly he stopped altogether and he went to the window and he started to cry. Just to cry. He was terribly ashamed of it, of course. I would say these tears were the most important tears in my life. It may be that they made me into a musician. I felt…what music can do, to this dreadful man, and…and then the rehearsal went on, I [have forgotten] everything about it, the performance, nothing of that matters. But this sentimental, perhaps slightly ridiculous, story was *terribly* important to me. But it would have meant nothing had I not loved [Bruckner's] music as intensely as I did. But there was a man so infinitely greater than that little boy of eleven [*sic*] who felt the same way, and suddenly all his mask and his front dropped, and the *real* man, the great artist, with his great soul, was laid bare.

There it is.[7]

As he told the story Georg's voice would waver. To the end of his life he couldn't tell it without tears coming to his eyes.

At the end of each year, following the official school examinations, the boys went as something of a reward to the choir's summer home at Hinterbichl, in an isolated corner of the eastern Tyrolean mountains. Schnitt began the retreat in 1925 and it was at first quite basic. Despite having to work at jobs such as tending the garden, it was fun for the boys. Georg soon turned himself into a virtuoso table tennis player, and he also became a passionate mountaineer, climbing to the top of the Grossvenediger every year.

Soon Hinterbichl became fashionable for guests, including the choristers' families, to come from all over Europe to spend summer with the choir. It became a meeting place for international celebrities and artistic people. 'I suppose it was rather cute – these little boys waited at the tables and at the weekends they assembled and entertained their distinguished visitors with their supposedly angelic voices.'[8] One such guest was Aldous Huxley; another was the composer Hans Gál, whom Georg met in 1928:[*]

> I sat quietly in a barn where we used to rehearse – there was a piano – and studied one of the lesser known string quartets of Haydn's. I was just in the middle of the development section when I felt somebody bending over me from behind and saying, 'Oh, Opus so-and-so, Number so-and-so', and he proceeded immediately to the piano, without the score of course, and played vast stretches of this comparatively unknown piece. I gaped at him – I'd never seen anything like it, and I must say I've never seen anything like it since. This man is the most educated and erudite musician I have ever met. There is just one limitation to his erudition, that is, he is not interested in contemporary music, but from Bach to, let's say, 1905 he knows *everything*, and everything from memory. It is fantastic. He is a brilliant pianist *still*, but he played also practically every orchestral instrument – not that well, but he played it. And he also conducted – not that well, but he conducted.

Though Georg was twenty-seven years younger than Gál, he had found a musical soulmate and lifelong friend. He was by this time writing music of his own – apparently without any training in composition. He wrote choral pieces for his colleagues to sing and himself to conduct, including a Missa Brevis. At Hinterbichl in 1928 or 1929 he premiered his 'Herr, Schicke was Du willt', performed one Sunday between sections of the Mass. He and his cousin Elisabeth sang the first and second soprano parts with two altos from the choir. 'Liesl!' he protested to her afterwards, 'you were a quarter-tone flat the whole way through!'

There is nothing quite like being the only son in a Jewish family, especially if he is gifted. There was nothing musical in either side of Georg's immediate family apart from Therese and her piano. His mother wrote stories for her children, but the closest Alfons came to culture was playing chess with the Court Opera bass Josef von Manowarda at their local *Kaffeehaus*. Georg attributed his talent to the inbreeding in his grandmother's generation.

---

[*] Hans Gál (1890–1987), Viennese composer and musicologist. He taught at the University of Vienna and then from 1929 at the University of Mainz, until the advent of the Nazis in 1933. He emigrated to Great Britain and became professor at the University of Edinburgh.

'I'm the freak of the family. I would say people who are tone deaf are rarer than people who are intensely musical, but it so happened that my father and my sister were of this category. They were not able to sing two notes in tune.' Alfons was disappointed to find himself with a son determined to be a musician when he had hoped to produce an army officer, but he put no obstacles in his way. Georg respected his father, but they had little in common and contact between them was mostly casual. Alfons was much closer to Annemarie, whose immoderate swearing he found enchanting.

Georg was the darling of his grandmother, mother and aunt, who regarded his abilities with unlimited admiration and indulgence. It instilled in him a boundless sense of his own self-worth, a classic example of Freud's observation: 'I have found that those persons who consider themselves preferred by or favoured by their mothers manifest in life that confidence in themselves, and that unshakeable optimism, which often seem heroic and not infrequently compel actual success.' Or as Georg put it, 'Most geniuses are close to their mothers.' One day in the middle of winter he was practising the piano, sitting in front of an open window dressed only in his underpants. Alfons came into the room and said, 'Put some clothes on, you silly boy, you'll catch your death of cold!'

'Leave him alone,' said Mizzi. 'He's an artist.'[9]

Georg's voice broke when he was thirteen and a half, around the end of 1930. For the remainder of the school year he transferred to the Amerling Gymnasium in the Sixth District, a conventional *humanistisches Gymnasium* where he took Greek, Latin and German, plus science, mathematics and religion. Annemarie had been sent to the most progressive school in the city, run by the visionary educator Dr Eugenie Schwarzwald. She believed that girls should also have access to a superior education, and at her school at Herrengasse 10 the girls, two-thirds of them from liberal Jewish families, learned from the likes of Oskar Kokoschka, Adolf Loos, Egon Wellesz and Arnold Schoenberg. 'I'm sure it was completely wasted on Annemarie,' Georg said. She lasted only a year before transferring to a conventional school. She was a striking girl with her mother's black eyes and long red hair of a most unusual colour: chestnut with a blue tinge, as Georg described it, which made her much in demand by Vienna's young portraitists. In her mid-teens she cut it to a bob and it immediately turned dark brown. 'Served her right for cutting her hair,' Georg said to me.

At the Gymnasium he immediately made friends with Heinz and Franz Röhr, non-identical and very different twins from a well-to-do Jewish family. Heinz was talented at everything intellectual, musical and sporting; Franz was talented at nothing, but he had a compassionate heart and it was to him that Georg remained close all his life. Franz was impressed by the breadth of Georg's reading, which included Rilke and Theodor Storm, Shakespeare in translation, and most of Goethe and Schopenhauer. Georg admired Freud's work and often worshipfully waited all day outside Freud's house at Berggasse 19, even in the rain, hoping for a glimpse of the great man, but in vain. Even more important to Georg were the writings of Friedrich Nietzsche, from whom he derived much of his view of creativity – indeed his view of life. He concurred with Nietzsche's view of Christianity and democracy as moralities for the weak masses; he preferred the Platonic idea of a benign dictatorship of learned men. Such moralities should be replaced by the values of the 'superman', who is interested in life on earth rather than the rewards of an afterlife. He is courageous and willing to 'live dangerously' (as Georg claimed to do); he is motivated by the 'will to power': power over oneself that leads to creativity and originality – willpower. This became a fundamental guiding force of Georg's life, for good and ill.

Together Franz and Georg discovered the novels *Niels Lyhne* by Jens Peter Jacobsen and *Jean-Christophe* by Romain Rolland, both of which remained among his favourite books, together with Dostoevsky's *The Brothers Karamazov* and Thomas Mann's *Der Zauberberg*. Georg strongly identified with the composer Jean-Christophe:

> Every real musician lives in a world of sound, as other men live in a visible world, and that his days are lived in and borne onward by a flood of music. Music is the air he breathes, the sky above him. Nature wakes answering music in his soul. His soul itself is music: music is in all that it loves, hates, suffers, fears, hopes. And when the soul of a musician loves a beautiful body, it sees music in that too. The beloved eyes are not blue, or brown, or grey: they are music: their tenderness is like caressing notes, like a delicious chord.[10]

Georg loved these portraits of the development of the single-minded artist, the Romantic creative hero inspired by adoring and supportive women – the superman for whom the normal rules and conventions did not apply. And why not? Vienna was full of artist-supermen. Yet if such an existence was possible in the artistic hothouse of pre-war Vienna, it had currency in few other places. Georg would cling to this frame of reference all his life, even when it failed him time and time again.

In March 1931 he completed a nine-minute Kyrie for eight-part choir, inexplicably dedicating it to Rektor Schnitt. He followed it with a song for tenor and piano, 'Die Stadt' ('The City'), in the month in which he turned fourteen. He showed his compositions to the Staatsakademie für Musik und darstellende Kunst (State Academy of Music and Drama, now a university), which was sufficiently impressed to admit him for a diploma course. Georg took piano with Berta Jahn-Beer, music history and instrumentation courses with the famous oboist Alexander Wunderer and others, and Music Theory II–V. He had long wanted to study with the great Austrian composer and director of the Academy, Franz Schmidt, but it was too late. Robert Kuppelwieser, a *Kapellmeister* who had befriended Georg in the boys' choir, took him to meet Schmidt, but he was on the point of retiring and was no longer accepting new students. Georg was too much in awe of him to ask for private lessons. Instead he was admitted to the theory class of Josef Marx.

Largely forgotten today, Marx was at the time a highly regarded composer of more backward-looking music.

> To be honest, he was not a good teacher but he was an important composer so we all looked up to him quite humbly. His music was a little bit like himself and like his contemporary Korngold. He was very fat and his music is a little bit in that line – Korngold also was fat. But there was a certain attractive sensuality both in the man and in his music, and some of his works really were quite important: two piano concertos, the second of which was performed often by Gieseking, and chamber music. But it is really the songs that made him famous. Whoever has heard Lotte Lehmann or Elisabeth Schumann singing Marx's songs, sometimes with

the composer at the piano, will know that these songs have great quality. They are not very profound, and perhaps he is a better Austrian version of Roger Quilter or something like that. But they have their place and are beautifully crafted. He also orchestrated quite a few of them brilliantly, as he did songs of Hugo Wolf. He was a very good orchestrator, and pieces like his *Northland Rhapsody* are really very effective and also beautiful...

Before the Nazis occupied Austria there was a sort of clerical dictatorship and Marx, who had no religious affiliations at all, was nevertheless, as one of the most prominent musicians of his day in Austria, appointed as what they call *Staatsrat*, State Councillor. They structured then the political spectrum a little bit like the Fascists in Italy, according to professions, not to unions or anything, and so when the Nazis came – though Marx was not a Jew – he was banished and rather badly treated. I corresponded with him after the Nazi thing was over and he was full of complaints about the time, but actually he had a much better time than many others. But that is why he looked elsewhere [and went to Turkey to advise the government on music education]. I believe Hindemith also went to Turkey and advised on music education there. But Josef Marx was also a very clever music critic, and his volume of essays on music is remarkably astute and clever.[*] But then when all that was over he settled in Vienna (and again could eat a lot, because he complained all the time that he had not enough to eat in the bad time).[11]

So impressed was the Academy with Georg's compositions that he was immediately placed in the second year. Georg, seven or eight years younger than his classmates, was completely intimidated: 'I came home and I said, "I can't do this, they know everything and I know nothing!"' Marx, evidently, did not agree; he soon made Georg tutor the others.

How much music Georg actually wrote in his Academy years is impossible to know, for much of it is lost, a combination of his own carelessness and the peripatetic nature of his later life. He

---

[*]    *Betrachtungen eines romantischen Realisten. Gesammelte Aufsätze, Vorträge und Reden von Joseph Marx über Musik.* Hrsg. von Oswald Ortner. Gerlach & Wiedling, Wien, 1947 (*Reflections of a Romantic Realist. Collected Essays, Lectures and Speeches on Music by Joseph Marx,* edited by Oswald Ortner).

certainly wrote songs, short chamber pieces, an orchestral sinfonia, and works for piano. A sonata in F minor that did survive is a fully tonal and youthfully passionate work in one movement that owes much to Chopin, Brahms and Scriabin.

At sixteen Georg met Piroska Pinter, an American piano student with a vague but very romantic background. She was flirting her way through Vienna, casting coquettish eyes on eminent musicians including her teacher Eduard Steuermann, and keeping them all in her thrall by the time-tested expedient of waxing hot and cold. She played this game with Georg for at least two years, and although they were never actually lovers she caused him exquisite pain. But she also inspired him to write several songs for her: 'Die Geige' ('The Violin') in 1933, and two more in 1935: 'Der Vogel' ('The Bird'), and 'Dämmerstunde' ('Twilight'). The latter he brought to Piroska's apartment to present to her, but she wasn't there. As he waited for hours with his precious gift, full of longing, she was in the arms of the principal trumpet of the Vienna Philharmonic, Helmut Wobitsch. Like Jean-Christophe's Ada, she may have been flighty and unworthy of the attention of a serious and single-minded person, but she was important in the development of the artist. Though Georg was still a teenager, his 1935 songs are fully mature and very beautiful. Years later, when he had written a few more love songs inspired by lovely women, he collected them as a cycle of five songs and called it *Junge Liebe* (*Young Love*). He considered them among his finest works.

From 1931 to 1935 he was a full-time student at both the Gymnasium and the Academy, and was also earning money by coaching singers. His grades at the Academy were mostly As, with a few Bs; his high school grades were less impressive. They were sometimes 'good' but mostly only 'satisfactory', especially in the sciences. But he loved his Greek and Latin lessons, especially the works of Plato and Sophocles and the stories of the heroes, which he quoted all his life. In addition to all this the Sängerknaben hired him for a year as accompanist and trainer of one of its new training choirs, probably 1933–34, and likely as a result of his work preparing them for two performances of Mahler's Eighth Symphony* under Bruno Walter in April 1933. Certainly by 1935

---

\* Georg was never particularly fond of this symphony. 'I think I am a minority view when I say of all his big works it is the weakest, because it depends much more than any other on effect…Mahler was

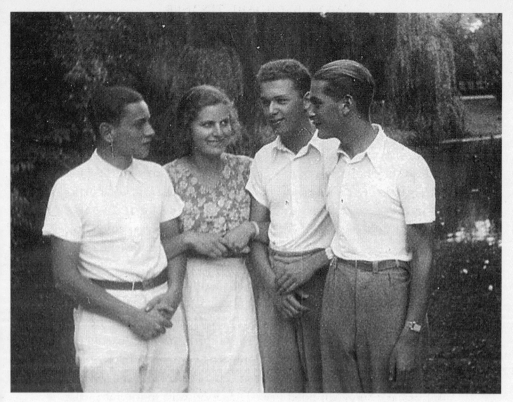

*Georg with (left to right) Piroska Pinter, Heinz and Franz Röhr, autumn 1935.*

his own 'Steht Auf!' (for alto solo and four-part choir) was in the standard repertoire of the main choir, and it was probably this work that he included in a program he conducted at the time for Radio Vienna.

In his rare free time he went to Buster Keaton movies and enjoyed them hugely. At least once a week he went to the opera, buying the very cheapest standing-room ticket. Franz would save a place for him, and at the last minute he would arrive eating an orange for his dinner. Up in the third balcony he conducted along with the performance, orange pips in his hand. He attended the Viennese premiere of Richard Strauss's *Arabella* on 21 October 1933, where Strauss expressed his gratitude to Lotte Lehmann who sang that evening though her mother had died the same day. On 10 January 1934 he attended the first performance of Franz Schmidt's Fourth Symphony, given by the Vienna Symphony Orchestra

a man of the theatre, and the Eighth Symphony is full of theatre. But at his greatest he *transcends* the theatre.'

under Oswald Kabasta,* and recognised it as a great work. Ten days later he went to the premiere of Lehár's operetta *Giuditta*, which he thought a poor piece except for one or two 'reasonable bits' such as *Meine Lippen, sie küssen so heiss* (*My lips, they kiss so hotly*).

In one three-week period Georg heard Beethoven's Seventh Symphony conducted by Erich Kleiber, Wilhelm Furtwängler,† Arturo Toscanini and Otto Klemperer. 'We were so lucky – we didn't realise it,' he said. 'It was like a different work each time, and yet it was *totally valid* each time.' On 23 January 1932 he went to the premiere, given by the Vienna Philharmonic Orchestra under Clemens Krauss, of the Lyric Suite for string orchestra by Alban Berg, who was 'tall and had a very beautiful suffering face a bit like Oscar Wilde, without Wilde's frivolous expression'. When the jubilation after the performance had finished, Georg was horrified to see Schoenberg, Webern and others of the circle depart before Bruckner's Eighth Symphony was played; only Berg stayed. On 10 October 1936 Otto Klemperer conducted Bruckner's Fifth Symphony and his Adagio from the Seventh with the Vienna Philharmonic, to commemorate the fortieth anniversary of the composer's death. Georg went to the rehearsals in the Musikvereinssaal. 'In the organ loft there was a big bust of Bruckner for the anniversary. Klemperer went on, and went on… and suddenly he stopped and said – he *shouted* – "Take him away! He's looking at me and I can't bear it!"'[12]

Wilhelm Furtwängler, Arturo Toscanini and Bruno Walter were the conductors he admired most, although for very different reasons.

> Bruno Walter was to me the ideal of a conductor in his handling of the orchestra. [He] never raised his voice, never got angry; he was patience itself. And what I think was the greatest about him, he didn't try to make his orchestra play by terror, but by love. Not only was it obvious that he loved the musicians but he loved the music, as all other conductors do, I suppose, but he was able to convey that love to others. And so, not as an interpreter necessarily, but as a conducting

---

* Oswald Kabasta was born in 1896 and studied at the Academy in Vienna, later becoming one of its conducting professors. During the war he was music director of the Munich Philharmonic. An ardent Nazi, Kabasta did not recant after the war and committed suicide in February 1946.
† Georg told me that the intervals at Furtwängler's concerts were always very long, to allow time for a pretty young lady to help him change his shirt.

personality, he is my ideal – because he did it all with *love*, that's all I can say. I think he was very much better in the idyllic pieces of music than in the heroic ones. For instance, to hear Bruno Walter conduct the first symphony of Schumann or the second of Brahms was unique. I think in the Eroica and the Ninth Symphony there were greater people. But the Pastoral, or things like that, it was just like he was. His Mozart was also very beautiful. But one must however admit that occasionally there was perhaps a slightly sentimental streak in him, in certain modifications of the tempo which nowadays would be totally unacceptable but which he really felt that way; and therefore one must respect that. But he was a fine man, there's no doubt about it.[13]

[He gave a lecture] entitled *Das Ethos in der Musik* – ethical thought in music. That was something for him because he obviously thought of music as an ethical force in the universe. This is a very unfashionable view nowadays but he held it sincerely and he talked very cleverly and very long... and everybody thought it was very good. Then he says, 'And now I am going to show you what I mean.' He went over to the piano and sang a Mahler song – he didn't sing, he crowed, 'Ich bin der Welt abhanden gekommen', Mahler's greatest song: 'I have got lost to the world.' He could have talked for *twenty years*, and he wouldn't have conveyed one per cent of what he did when he crowed that song. It was one of my great musical experiences.*[14]

Stravinsky's preferred conductors were at first Weingartner and late in his life Bruno Walter, surprising though that may seem, as Walter and Stravinsky lived in opposite musical worlds. He didn't think anything much of the great Furtwängler.[15]

The god of the new generation of conductors is not Toscanini but Furtwängler,† who was the most subjective of

---

*   At the age of eighty Georg gave a conducting masterclass at Yale University. 'When the maestro went to the piano and began to [sing] the Benedictus from Bruckner [Mass in F minor]', said one of the students much later, 'it was one of those moments where you really feel that you are a part of something more important than oneself, even greater than music and art itself. It felt like we were a part of the collective unconscious, nothing could have been more important and more true than just a few bars on a bad piano. I felt it as a kind of mystical experience.' (Denis Segond, letter to author, 12 March 2001).

†   Once Georg spotted Furtwängler at the Beethovenplatz, standing motionless and staring up into a tree. He watched him from a distance for twenty minutes but never found out what interested him so much. Furtwängler was a curious person. He loved escalators, and spent hours riding on them in the London Underground.

all conductors I have ever experienced. When he stood there, mind you, you believed him. I must confess to you that when I was in the hall when the great Furtwängler conducted, I was *utterly spellbound*. But when you hear it now you find it very hard to take. [Taking Furtwängler as a model] is, I think, a very dangerous thing to do because there are artists who cannot be imitated. And I think Furtwängler was one of them.

I heard him in the flesh do Bruckner's Seventh Symphony, which was one of the greatest performances of all time, for me. But there is also something else about Furtwängler, to do him justice: many of his recordings were made after the war when he was on the decline. In the end Furtwängler was very deaf, and the podium on which he [stood] had to be wired with electrodes, or how one calls it, so he could hear what is going on, and under these conditions no artist can do his best. For instance, I could have cried the other day – I heard the Manfred Overture conducted by Furtwängler. Now, it was like a *pale shadow* of what it really was like. But I heard Furtwängler conduct the Manfred in the early Thirties, and *it was tremendous*. That sort of wilfulness doesn't do the Manfred Overture any harm. It was one of the greatest things, but when Furtwängler did it on the recording, it was still very good, but no more than that. So it is a pity that some of these very great conductors who have absolutely no equal nowadays came a little bit too early as far as recording technique is concerned, that many records of Toscanini and Furtwängler came later than they should have done in their lives.[16]

I was fortunate enough to attend all the concerts Toscanini gave with the Vienna Philharmonic Orchestra. The balances and beauty of sound and architecture of *La Mer* or the Brahms symphonies or his Wagner excerpts were unattainable by anyone else.[17] He was the greatest Brahms conductor who ever lived, in my opinion.

It was quite true that Toscanini had a lot of drive, and he never dragged, but this is not in my opinion his greatness. There are some other conductors who conduct fast, all the time fast, and others who conduct slowly – and it might interest you that when Toscanini conducted *Parsifal* in Bayreuth it was the slowest *Parsifal* that was ever recorded, either before or after. So it is not good to say, 'Oh well, Toscanini raced everything'. But first of all, you know he was a cellist, and whenever he conducted he still sort of played the cello. It was so *beautiful* to watch. I thought he was a *giant* when I saw him on the podium because he was so perfectly proportioned. Yet when I stood beside him he reached to *my* shoulder, giant that *I* am as you know.* So he can have been hardly five foot tall. But it shows everything is relative. On the podium he looked enormous, and what does it matter anyway. But the body and the movements were utterly in balance, in perfect sort of movement, and I only mention that about the cello because I think that sort of movement had a very great bearing on the sound he achieved...And that, I think, brought about this utter perfection of pace. It was *not* metronomical – in fact the story is told that Toscanini said once to a colleague, 'Now *this* section in a Beethoven symphony must be taken *strict* in time', and in order to endorse his point he reached for the metronome and put it on and started conducting. Within three bars he was out with the metronome. That speaks very much for him, because we are not machines, and we shouldn't *try* to make music like machines. But he had this sort of *flow*, the music sort of flowed on and on and you felt that it just couldn't go any other way. The other even more remarkable thing was his sense for orchestral balance and texture. That has *never* been reached again. He knew *exactly* what the relationship between the various instruments should be in any particular bar. And he didn't have to *say* anything, that was the miracle. He didn't have to say *anything*, he just stood there and did this, and they played.[18]

I have the greatest adoration for Toscanini...he was perhaps the greatest executant, next to Casals, I have ever heard. But perhaps his psychology was not as great as his music. And I think it can be said that some of the people he dealt with couldn't give of their very best, especially singers, because he frightened them so much.[19]

There was yet something else. There was in spite of all this drive, which is sometimes more of a negative quality really, there was that inner spiritual fire that inspired

---

* In his youth Georg stood 165 cm (five feet six inches), considered average in Vienna. He was not pleased later to find himself to be short by New World standards.

everything. And perhaps such a thing cannot be reproduced on a mechanical toy like a record; it is possible. There was that inner fire, I can only call it like that...but it was an *unselfish* fire that was dedicated to the great work he was conducting. And that made him, to those who were fortunate and old enough to have heard him in the flesh, what he was.[20]

In the interval of one of those wonderful Toscanini concerts with the VPO I went to the toilet, which was also used by the performers. I heard two elderly players talk to each other. One said, 'What does this man do to us? We haven't played like this since Mahler conducted us!' This was in 1936, and Mahler had died in 1911![21]

Although Georg's recollection of dates was always sketchy, his memory of musicians and their performances was faultless. He went to everything and forgot nothing. One day in 1980 I teased him by playing an old recording of a Mozart violin concerto and asking him who the conductor was. After only a few bars Georg said, 'Dobrowen'. Issay Dobrowen was a conductor he could have heard only a few times at most, and not at all for almost half a century. 'How did you know?' I asked. He replied, 'I recognise his emphatic style.'

Instrumentalists no less illustrious than these conductors lived, or performed often, in Vienna: pianists Artur Schnabel and Rudolf Serkin, and Vladimir Horowitz who was said in Georg's family to be a distant relative. Georg once observed him chatting to a lighting assistant in a concert hall 'while practising double octaves faster than most pianists play single ones'. He heard the Kolisch, Rosé and Busch Quartets; and the violinists Adolf Busch and Bronislaw Hubermann – his favourite – who suffered such extreme stage fright that he had to be pushed onto the stage. Now-legendary singers were regulars in opera and recital: Leo Slezak, Richard Tauber, Alexander Kipnis, Kerstin Thorborg, Jarmila Novotná; but the singers he loved most were the sopranos Elisabeth Schumann and Lotte Lehmann.

Lotte Lehmann, the greatest singer I ever heard, sang not only with her very beautiful voice but with her *soul*...her superlative art, and the three Bruckner masses, made me into that bit of a musician I became. Later after my voice had broken I heard Lotte Lehmann again, this time in *Fidelio*, under Toscanini. This (I attended all three performances) was the greatest opera performance I ever heard. (The great Lotte Lehmann was not quite as young as she had been and Toscanini agreed to transpose her great aria down a semitone. That would have been acceptable, but what was totally unacceptable was the fact that he started the Recitative in the original [key] and then by a truly horrible modulation went down the semitone. That shows that even a great master can do a silly thing.)

These two things, Toscanini's conducting and Lotte Lehmann's singing, though two so very different things (because Lotte Lehmann was by no means one for regular meters and so on), meant more to me, I would say, in music making than anything else. One thing excepted perhaps: I heard Casals's playing as a little boy, which made an indelible impression on me. But how deeply that *Fidelio* under Toscanini moved me is clear from the fact that there are places when I conduct *Fidelio*, which I do often, I don't hear what I do but I hear what he had done, and envy him that he could do it. The sound that he could achieve in certain woodwind chords is *absolutely unique*, and I have heard the Vienna Philharmonic Orchestra very often in *Fidelio* with other conductors, but it just wasn't a patch on it. As far as Lotte Lehmann is concerned, she had a beautiful voice, but the voice wasn't it. There are other singers who have better voices than Lotte Lehmann but I always say a great singer doesn't sing with his voice, he sings with his soul, or her soul, and that's just what she did. When at the end of the *Rosenkavalier*, when she has given up her young lover, the father of the little girl says, 'That's how it is, that's how young people are' – the father has no idea that she was the mistress of Oktavian – she has to say, '*Ja, ja*'. I *swear to you* that these two *Yes* meant more to me than many a symphony concert.[*] And that is where human personality comes in. You saw and

---

[*]   Georg told me, 'When I heard Lehmann sing "*Ja, ja*", I cried because it was so beautiful, and when I heard Schwarzkopf sing it I cried because it *wasn't* beautiful.'

heard the whole tragedy of the aging woman in these totally irrelevant two *Yes, yes*. One cannot explain it but one can feel it. Therefore I will never cease to be grateful to Lotte Lehmann for giving me what no-one else has.[22]

## Three

By 1933 the Tintner family was in financial trouble. Like all good Austrians they had bought war bonds in the Great War only to see them become worthless in the hyperinflation that followed. The Baden villa was sold in the early 1920s, and a succession of disasters had finished off the once-illustrious Steinhof firm in 1932. Robert Steinhof, who had run the firm with his older brother Friedrich Karl, died of renal failure in July 1929, aged only fifty-two. The Great Crash came four months later; then in June 1931 Austria's largest bank, the Creditanstalt, collapsed, setting off a European banking crisis. Finally Friedrich Karl committed suicide on 2 June 1932. The Tintners were left only with Alfons's modest army pension and his salary from the Vacuum Oil Company. No longer able to afford their luxurious apartment on the Stubenring, in November 1933 they moved to a walk-up flat in a much less salubrious part of the First District: Schellinggasse 6. Thilde, working as an office assistant, took a flat on the top floor with Therese, who at sixty-four could barely manage the six flights of stairs.

Far from lamenting these reduced circumstances, socialist-minded Georg rejoiced. 'My people lost ALL THEIR MONEY (in WARLOANS; served them right for being so "patriotic").'[1] In order to supplement the family's income he took on still more work, giving private lessons in harmony and theory. Heinz Röhr was one of his students, and another was Richard (Dickie) Hoffmann,* who came once or twice a week. On the recommendation of Josef Marx, Richard Hoffmann Snr hired sixteen-year-old Georg to teach Dickie as a present for his ninth birthday in April 1934. Georg, looking 'tennis-sporty' dressed all in white, paced up and down as he instructed, talking quickly and energetically while

---

* Richard Hoffmann later wrote twelve-tone music and became the assistant of Arnold Schoenberg (to whom he was related) in Los Angeles. From 1954 he was Professor of Composition and Music Theory at Oberlin Conservatory.

Richard scribbled as fast as he could. So animated was Georg
that the chairs had first to be removed so he didn't fall over them.
After some months of tuition Richard produced an orchestral suite
called *Goldene Jugendzeit* (*Golden Youth*), which was broadcast on
Radio Vienna. He was hailed as a *Wunderkind*, though it was
Georg who had written and orchestrated most of it. Dickie's les-
sons ended in 1935 when his Jewish father, with foresight unusual
for Austrians at the time, emigrated with his family to New
Zealand. Not so very long afterwards, the Hoffmanns would save
Georg's life.

In June 1934 Georg completed a piano work for his own
use, *Variations on a Theme of Chopin*, based on the Prelude in
A major, and dedicated it to 'My friend Robert Kuppelwieser'.
Renée Gärtner performed it at the Konzerthaus on 5 April 1935,
in a concert of contemporary Viennese music celebrating Bach's
250th birthday, and again in a radio broadcast on 25 March 1936.
Describing Georg as a 'rising talent', an unnamed critic in Radio
Vienna's magazine wrote:

> The young composer was endeavouring in this piece to
> approach the style of Chopin and thereby to show the naïve
> theme and its dancing mood in new lights. So it appears vari-
> ously as a chorale, as a brilliant miniature, then as nocturne;
> in short, with its form, key and rhythm always changing,
> giving interest to both the performer and the listeners.[2]

In June 1935 Georg graduated from high school. At the same
time he completed his diploma course at the Academy, graduating
in music theory 'with special distinction'. He immediately enrolled
in a two-year graduate program, continuing in composition with
Josef Marx and joining a conducting masterclass taught by Felix
Weingartner. He greatly respected the famous conductor, but afterwards felt he had not benefited much from his lessons.

> We took turns playing these masterpieces on eight hands, four
> hands on each piano – we went to the orchestra but not nearly
> often enough – and he judged us conducting our colleagues
> and gave his advice...But what he tried to teach us was how
> he personally saw these masterpieces, and with all due respect,
> though he was an infinitely greater man than I ever could

be, I didn't always take to his way. He wanted to make little Weingartners out of us.[3]

I suppose when you have conducted Beethoven for fifty years and practically nothing else, or not much else – he was of course also an opera conductor, not as good as many others – then your ideas how Beethoven should go are so much identified with the music itself that you begin to think that your way is the only way. And in fact Weingartner was aided and abetted by publishers who published the Beethoven symphonies already with Weingartner's changes *without saying so*, so that became really the standard way of playing Beethoven. It isn't any more, I'm glad to say. So he expected of his pupils to do the same and I strongly objected to that, because I didn't want to learn his interpretations, I wanted to acquire his skill. I could never claim that I did, but I wanted to. But I don't think he was aware of it. I saw him once fail a pupil in an examination because he did not make the same *ritenuto* in the first movement of a Beethoven symphony [No. 5] which is *not* in the score and which I don't do either…I think that's disgraceful, actually.

Weingartner did it all with the wrist – in his later days. People who knew him earlier thought he conducted with every limb of his body, but when I knew him he had the most flexible wrist and he had an obsession. You know most conductors have an obsession about something. He spent *hours and hours* explaining that it must come all from the wrist, and only in the *highest climaxes* should it come as far as the elbow and never the whole arm. Who says? Some of the *greatest* conductors don't do that. Although I must say his stick technique was tremendous…But I think that wrist business had more to do with his elegance than with anything else.[4]

I remember his incredible stamina at the age of seventy – although he was always seventy. He conducted Beethoven's First and Ninth symphonies for a morning concert whilst standing and then in the evening he conducted *Tristan and Isolde* for five hours, standing once again. The next morning he stood to repeat the Beethoven symphonies, and after all that he didn't appear to be the least bit tired. When I asked him how he managed to achieve this great feat of physical endurance, he replied: 'It's all in the wrist.'[5]

It was only in summer that Georg had any leisure time, and he spent it composing. In July 1936, most likely while at Hinterbichl with his family, he completed two of his finest works. The first was a short Scriabinesque work for piano: *Prelude*, also known as 'Sehnsucht' ('Longing'). Eight days later he completed a song for mezzo-soprano and piano, 'Frühling' ('Spring'), to words by Hermann Hesse – the same poem Richard Strauss used in his *Four Last Songs*, written thirteen years later. 'He was over eighty and I was nineteen,' Georg wrote when he himself was seventy-nine. 'I have great admiration and respect for Strauss but (not very modestly!) I claim mine to be better.'*6

'Frühling' was Georg's second wonderful song in 1936; the other was 'Schliesse mir die Augen Beide' ('Close Both My Eyes') to a poem by Theodor Storm. It was around this time that he found a new girlfriend, possibly somewhat older than he, a Yugoslav singer called Ljerka. They were together until Georg left Austria two years later.

In the autumn of 1936, at the start of his last year at the Academy and aged just nineteen, he began working part-time at the Volksoper. The Municipal Opera, Vienna's second opera, was founded in 1898 to celebrate Franz Josef's jubilee. One of the conditions signed by the first director was that there was to be 'no Jewish influence' – a singularly shortsighted stipulation, for it was Vienna's Jews who created, produced, financed and attended much of the city's performing arts. It took only five years for the Volksoper to go bankrupt. It was restarted with a new director, a new program of opera and operetta, and without a 'No Jews' clause.

Georg was very fortunate to get the job, because 'it was quite obvious that the provincial theatres would not take me on *even before* Hitler's arrival.'7 It was almost certainly arranged for him by Weingartner, who had been the Volksoper's music director from 1919 to 1924. Many years later Georg recalled:

[To be alive in the 1930s] was marvellous and alarming at the same time. I often wished I had been born just a little earlier than that, because the greatest period of that time was when I was too young to appreciate it. But it was the

---

*    Georg altogether did not think much of the *Four Last Songs*. He felt Strauss 'had said it all much better before', notably in *Rosenkavalier*.

*politics* that ruined everything. For instance, [for] the circle
around Schoenberg and Alban Berg and Webern – though
Alban Berg and Webern were not Jews, but Schoenberg was –
the movement against them was already *before* the Nazis
came into Austria so strong that these composers had to be
performed in private houses* because they were frightened
of terrible lack of peace in the concert hall. And so, being
a Jew myself, it was not an unmixed blessing to grow up
in this time. But we all felt the tremendous creativity and
ferment that was going on. But how the politics came into
it...Pfitzner came to Vienna from Munich to attend both
the performance of his *Von Deutscher Seele* and his new opera
*Das Herz*. In the last moment he was forbidden to attend
[the opera] because Bruno Walter conducted it, who was a
Jew.† And he was cowardly enough, one *must* say, the great,
the wonderful Pfitzner, was cowardly enough to stay away
because the Nazis wanted it.[8]

On 24 June 1937 Georg's six years at the Academy ended
with a graduation concert at the Musikvereinssaal, and his final
conducting grade was B. In September he resumed working at the
Volksoper, now full-time, as répétiteur and rehearsal conductor.
He was now a handsome young man, still with the thick, sensual
lips and tightly curled thick hair he wished he didn't have. The
beautiful Czech soprano Jarmila Novotná made eyes at him across
the piano, but he was too shy in those days to avail himself of the
opportunity. He enjoyed good food and coffee, and went out for
the odd beer with his friends, most of whom were foreigners 'who
treated me like a human being'.

A photograph taken at the Hinterbrühl villa of the von
Motesiczkys, an influential Jewish family, shows a Georg quite
unrecognisable to those who knew him even a few years later:
neatly and stylishly dressed, wearing a tie, drinking coffee, and
enjoying an afternoon's conversation. He looks cheerful and full
of confidence, well on his way to a brilliant career. Because of
his 'untiring enthusiasm' and 'exemplary diligence' the Volksoper

---

*    Many performances were under the auspices of the Wiener Verein für Musikalische Privataufführun-
     gen (Viennese Society for Private Musical Performances). One such house was at Graben 20, where
     Georg heard Berg's works.
†    Pfitzner himself conducted *Von Deutscher Seele* at the Konzerthaus on 17 December 1937.

*Summer 1938, at the Lieben family villa in Hinterbrühl: (left to right) Karl von Motesiczky, the pianist Erna Gál, Georg, Astrid Liljeblad, and friends.*

had already scheduled him – 'a positively remarkable occurrence among young Austrian musicians'[9] – to conduct an opera in the 1938–39 season.

Yet even with Georg's earnings the family could hardly manage. Alfons had lost his job as a salesman for the Vacuum Oil Company on the last day of 1935 and (as Georg told the story) just before he qualified for special benefits. An immensely proud man, Alfons continued setting out as if for work every day for several weeks. When the truth was revealed Georg conceived a deep hatred of business and its heartlessness that he maintained to the end of his life. Much of the family's furniture and valuables had already been sold off piece by piece at the Dorotheum, and in October they moved to a slum in the centre of town at Wildpretmarkt 8.

On 19 February 1938 Georg attended the first Vienna performance, conducted by Bruno Walter, of the 1878/80 version of Bruckner's Fourth Symphony. It had recently been edited and published by Robert Haas, replacing the much-altered first-publication version by Ferdinand Löwe in use since the previous century. Such a concert was of enormous interest to him, but it was overshadowed by the events overtaking Austria.

There was a terrible feeling of insecurity and also political *ineptitude* because the Austrian government thought it could fight both the Socialists and the Nazis for their own cleri-cal–monarchistic ideals, which had practically no following in Austria. So it is sad, but politics did play a terrifying and absolutely negative part. For instance the composer Anton von Webern was an ardent socialist and he created concerts for the workers, which he himself *very ably* conducted. That was all either stopped or frowned upon. So everybody was in difficulties, [for example composer Wilhelm] Kienzl, whom I knew personally. He was not a Jew, but at that time he wasn't very pleased with what was going on. But it must be said, later on he wrote a hymn of welcome to Adolf Hitler.[10]

Everybody knew, *everybody*, that the situation in Austria was untenable, and it couldn't go on like that. And I'm afraid many people thought it was so bad that the Nazis couldn't do much worse. But they learned better. So the political situation was dreadful, untenable…Yet this Schuschnigg for instance, [Chancellor] Dr Kurt von Schuschnigg – I knew him personally a little bit – was a very artistic and totally upright man; he just was a very rotten politician. I still see him there when Bruno Walter performed Bruckner's Fourth Symphony…perhaps *days* before the Nazis came in, and he sat there entranced. He was an artistic, lovable man but he should have never entered politics.[11] He left the concert early – an ominous sign, if such was still needed.*[12]

Three weeks later, on 12 March, life as Georg knew it ended.

I still remember that fateful day when I had a chorus rehearsal in the Volksoper, and suddenly we heard the most amaz-ing sound I have ever heard. There were millions of people welcoming the Nazis. So I want to say that 'innocent little Austria was ransacked by the evil invader' is unfortunately quite untrue. They were welcomed like heroes. Not by

---

\* The following day Hitler announced he would protect all Germans outside the Reich, thereby threat-ening Austria's sovereignty.

everybody – I can't say whether it was the majority or not, but it certainly was a very large proportion of the population. One must know that Austria was in a terrible state economically, and so [some of it] was that 'anything was better than what we have now'. So there was this choral rehearsal that was very short…

Four days later Hitler himself made a triumphant entrance into the city. As he passed by, young women screamed hysterically, '*Führer! Führer!* We want to have your baby!' At the Volksoper Georg had to endure speeches by Goering and Goebbels broadcast every night before the performance. People he had thought were his friends donned swastika armbands and refused to have anything to do with him. The one good thing about the Anschluss, he said later, is that he stopped smoking immediately. He knew he would no longer be able to afford such luxuries, but more importantly the tobacco industry was then state-controlled, and he refused to finance the Nazis.

The day after the Anschluss Jews, among them Annemarie, began losing their jobs. Nazi sympathisers rushed in to fill the vacuum. The Viennese singer Anton Baumann wrote to the Volksoper proudly stating that his father had been 'a great friend of Dr Lueger (see *Mein Kampf*)', that Hitler himself had appointed him a Kammersänger in Berlin, and that he had been a member of the Nazi Party since 1932. Within weeks he was installed as Intendant. On 28 April Georg's career collapsed: the Volksoper directorate had found a replacement for him and he was fired. Not realising how much danger he was in, Georg sued them.

> After I lost my job six weeks after the 'glorious' Anschluss I found an 'Aryan' lawyer who was prepared to sue the Volksoper in my name for breach of contract. He wrote to the Volksoper to begin the proceedings. A few days later the Director of the Volksoper called me (I believe his name was Fritz Köchel* [*sic*]) and invited me to a conference. I accepted. Mr Köchel was *no* Nazi and for him the whole story appeared to be very embarrassing. *Despite that*, when I arrived at the appointed time he greeted me most friendly BUT beside

---

\*    Fritz Köchl was the Deputy Director.

him was an SA officer, probably to intimidate me. Köchel explained that 'because of the "changed circumstances"' it would be completely pointless if I were to continue with this complaint and as a gesture of 'good will' the Volksoper offered me 100 Schillings. I stood up, shook Mr Köchel's hand, ignored the SA officer and marched out with the words, 'You can keep your 100 Schillings'. And so ended my 'relationship' with the Volksoper.

Please, do NOT believe that I was *courageous*. I was simply crazy.[13]

Georg made his lunatic protest because 'I thought the Nazis were a joke. I just didn't take them seriously. I had seen it all before.'[14] It has sometimes been asked: Why did Viennese Jews take so long to flee? Why did so many wait until they saw the devastation wrought by Hitler's arrival, unlike German Jews who began emigrating in 1933 or even earlier? Some, like Alfons, had loyally served Austria as army officers and believed their country would look after them. And then, 'Wien bleibt Wien' (Vienna is always Vienna), said one popular song, and 'Wo ist der Himmel so blau wie in Wien?' (Where is the sky as blue as in Vienna?) asked another, written by the Jew Emmerich Kálmán. Jews were so intimately bound into every aspect of the city's life, and its cultural and intellectual plenitude, that they couldn't imagine living anywhere else. Some Jews never did try to leave, and paid for it with their lives. Anti-Semitism remained so firmly rooted in Vienna that Jews simply accepted it as part of daily life. Therefore many at first saw the German variety as nothing new, and nothing particularly worrisome.

Austrian Nazi bullies immediately began tormenting Jews, and so enthusiastically that German Nazis were taken aback at their viciousness. Alfons, who Georg described as 'the most honourable man I ever met', was among those rounded up and humiliated by being made to scrub the streets with a toothbrush. Those responsible were not Germans but Austrians.

On 15 June Georg risked his life to attend the premiere of Franz Schmidt's oratorio *Das Buch mit Sieben Siegeln*, conducted by Oswald Kabasta, the only concert at which he dared show his face after the Anschluss. Jews were prohibited from attending entertainments and to contravene the order was to invite arrest and deportation, but he couldn't resist. At the end Schmidt came to the front of the stage and acknowledged the tumultuous applause with his arm outstretched in the Nazi salute. For Georg it was a terrifying moment. That his hero could do such a thing! He did not think that Schmidt was a true sympathiser, but that he could bring himself to accommodate the Nazis even to this extent was for him 'one of the greatest agonies of my life.'[15]

Georg finally realised the Nazis were far from a joke. Within three weeks of the Anschluss the Nazis had arrested thousands of political prisoners and sent them to Dachau. In July Jews were ordered to lodge a statement of their belongings and their value, from apartment buildings to the last tie-pin, to facilitate their confiscation. He now saw that escape was imperative – but his family no longer had money or property for buying their way out.

> The strange thing is that the Nazis *said* they were only too *anxious* to get rid of these bloody Jews, but they did *everything* in their power to make it difficult for us to leave. It's just one of these perversities you can't understand. We sometimes stood for three hours in the rain queuing up for one of these innumerable exit permits and things. After three hours in the rain they would come and say, 'No service today, Jews can go home.'[16]

Georg tried to gain entry to America, Canada, Australia and many other countries, but the answer was always the same. He had no money, no reputation and no connections.

He had just one way out. His young student Dickie Hoffmann was in New Zealand. His father was able to arrange for Annemarie and Georg to immigrate there, guaranteeing for them with a surety of £200 each – the annual average wage. The idea was that Georg would resume teaching Dickie. Annemarie, however, wanted to remain in Vienna. She had a lover, Dr Franz Wilhelm, whom she met for assignations at her parents' flat – 'Better here where it is clean than in a seedy hotel,' said Mizzi, in a remarkable display of liberal thinking. But Wilhelm was a Nazi, distributing propaganda and probably using Annemarie as unwitting cover; in the five years before the Anschluss the Nazi Party was illegal in Austria. Passionately in love, Annemarie had to be pushed into leaving. As the danger closed in, Georg met Wilhelm at the entrance to the Stadtpark metro station and told him he must decide at once whether he would leave with her. Wilhelm stayed, breaking Annemarie's heart. She kept his photo all her life; on the back he had written, '*Bleib dir selber treu*' – stay true to yourself. After the war Georg's wife heard that he was wanted as a war criminal. Annemarie was never told.

During those months of trying to obtain an exit permit, Georg was called to the police headquarters.

> Such an invitation usually meant at *least* concentration camp, sometimes death. I can still see my poor parents coming with me to that Praesidium. They sat down on a bench…it said on the bench, 'Jews not allowed to sit here', but they sat down, terrified, absolutely *terrified*…after waiting about two hours, the man in charge said, 'What is your profession?' I said, 'I'm a musician: conductor and composer.' And suddenly he changed. He was a musical person. He said, 'I can see on your application to leave the country there is a twenty cents stamp missing.' I said, 'Oh yes? Here's twenty cents.' He said, 'Oh no, I made a mistake, it is not really missing.' I waited for the real thing to come, and I said, 'What else?' He said, 'Nothing else. You can go.' I still see my parents – it was like a ghost would have…They thought they would never see me again, you see. And when I landed in New Zealand I met a doctor there who came from Vienna too, and he was also called to the Police Praesidium the day [after] me, but he was not a musician, so they tore up his application and beat him unconscious and threw him into a concentration camp. Now I was just as guilty or as innocent as this doctor was. I was just lucky and he was unlucky.[17]

On 2 September Georg finally obtained a passport, a swastika-emblazoned German document with a large red 'J' for 'Jew' stamped on the front. A week later he obtained a three-month tourist visa for Yugoslavia, and left by train the same night, crossing the frontier at Spielfeld and Maribor on his way to Novi Sad. Annemarie followed six days later, heading for Belgrade. Five weeks later she went on to London, for England had need of her nursing skills; she was given a job at London Hospital in the East End. Georg, with no such useful profession, remained behind.

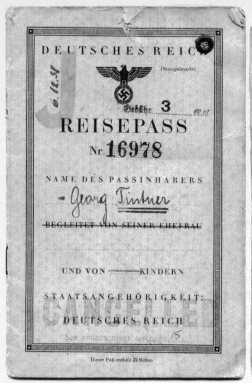

*After much difficulty Georg acquired a passport on 2 September 1938 and left Austria the next day.*
*The document was issued by the 'German Reich' and bore a large red 'J' for 'Jew'.*

Georg would have been destitute but for another piece of luck: Alfons had been posted to Novi Sad before World War I and had made friends with the city pharmacist and his family, who were not Jews. They now had an unmarried pregnant daughter, and she was sent to Vienna to have the baby. Georg's parents arranged to support her there – they sold their last possessions and jewellery to do so – and in exchange her family would give Georg money. When he arrived at their house, however, the maid told him that the family was on vacation. Until they returned he was in desperate straits. But without the girl's illegitimate child he would likely have starved in Yugoslavia.

He also went to a Jewish aid organisation for refugees in Belgrade.

There was a very dignified gentleman who received me and he said, 'What is your profession?' I said, 'I'm a conductor.' He said, 'Oh marvellous, we will see to it you get employed, and everything is all right, we look after you'…Just as I went out of the door he said, 'By the way, I take it you are a member of the Jewish faith.' I said, 'I must confess I am not.' And his face became like granite…He said, 'In this case I can't do anything for you.' I said, 'But I am here not because my parents converted to Lutheranism, but because of my Jewishness. That is why I am here!' He said, 'I'm very sorry, but we have to look after our own people. *Of course* – if you revert to the faith of your fathers everything will be all right.' I said – I had to say – 'I can't do that because it would be for the wrong reason. It would be to save my skin, not from any conviction. I can't do that.' So he said, 'I'm sorry.' I said, 'What can I do? *What can I do?*' He said, 'As a Lutheran, go to the Lutheran community.' The Lutherans were the headquarters of the Nazis in Yugoslavia…In the end I could get to England and get away. And you know, that was one of the best things that happened to me, because then the Nazis came and occupied Yugoslavia and I would have been killed. And I respected that man. He acted according to his narrow view of what was right and what was wrong.[18]

And I am very sorry to say that the gentleman in Belgrade perished when the Nazis came in. So it was *good* for me that he couldn't do anything for me. But you never know these things. When they happened it was a big blow. But it was good because, because of that I moved on, otherwise I would have been caught.[19]

To go on to England, from where he could travel to New Zealand, he had to obtain a permit, and he applied at the British Consulate in Belgrade. He would be allowed into Britain only on condition he left it again, and the Consul refused to issue a visa until he had seen proof of permission to enter New Zealand. Georg made several ever more desperate journeys to Belgrade, to an ever more suspicious Consul, to find out if the evidence had arrived. The trips put him in extreme danger; he spent at least one in the train toilet hiding, terrified, from armed guards checking identity papers. His peasant landlady was becoming suspicious of his lack of money, and what was worse, his tourist visa was due to expire on 7 December and could not be renewed.

On Friday 2 December the statement from New Zealand finally arrived.* 'The English [Consul] in Belgrade was a horrible man and he thought I was making it all up and I don't expect any [permit]. He was very rude and nasty to me…But when that permit finally arrived the Consul nearly *embraced* me he was so happy. I said to him, "*Now* I don't need your support. I needed it when everything was bad!"' Georg was given a visa good for three months. He immediately booked his travel and obtained a Swiss transit visa, but when he went to pay for his tickets the travel agency demanded more money. Georg threw the only screaming fit of his life, and the agency supplied them at the original price. The next day, as his Yugoslavian visa expired, he left by train for Italy, travelling overnight to Zürich where he was to take his flight to London. But there was an enormous thunderstorm, and all flights were grounded. The Swiss police told Georg that if he didn't leave the country within the hour he would be arrested and thrown into prison, refusing to listen to his frantic protestations that it wasn't his fault he was still there. Yet Providence looked after him one more time. Just one flight left Zürich that day: Georg's flight.

---

\*     There is some reason to believe that Richard Hoffmann sent the papers by surface mail to save money on the postage.

## Four

What happened after Georg reached England is unclear; he rarely spoke about it. He seems to have spent his first four months in Newcastle-on-Tyne with Eric Blackall, a friend from Vienna. He met Sir Charles Fergusson, a former governor-general of New Zealand, who was a prominent member of a refugee organisation. Sir Charles was interested in his military connections, and his wife, Lady Alice, took such a liking to Georg that he stayed for a week at their estate in Ayrshire. Because Fergusson also knew of Uncle Fritz's stretcher, which had benefited the British Army in World War I, he arranged to bring Alfons and Mizzi to England. They arrived in January 1939, followed by Therese two months later, and not a moment too soon. The Nazis had confiscated Alfons's army pension in December, leaving him and Mizzi destitute. And Alfons's brother Rudolf had moved in with them after the Nazis confiscated his apartment in St Pölten. Whatever money they lived on probably came from the other brothers.

In England Alfons and Mizzi depended on refugee organisations, for which Georg seems not to have been the least grateful. At the same time, the British had no idea of what it was to be a refugee, or what it was they were fleeing. When Georg's parents arrived in London his father was called aside by an Army officer. 'Major Tintner!' said the well-meaning man to a terrified Alfons. 'An *officer* does not live in Camden Town.' Georg told the story with scorn. To see his family reduced to fear and bewilderment was acutely painful. So was the sight of Therese, completely disoriented, driving furniture movers to distraction by endlessly asking them to rearrange pictures she had somehow spirited out of Austria.

By the time Georg moved to London in April, Annemarie had left for New Zealand. With a permit obtained by the YWCA she had sailed on 11 January and arrived in Auckland seven weeks later. Georg moved into 28 Sunnyside Road, N19, with Thilde, who had arrived in England on 16 November, a week after Kristallnacht. As a certified translator in four languages she was sponsored by the Commercial Union Insurance Company, of 24 Cornhill, where to Georg's undying displeasure her boss never let her forget how fortunate she was to have a job. With no desirable skills Georg 'was allowed to breathe the air in England but I was not allowed to work, so I depended on charity to keep alive'.[1] But he clandestinely coached Covent Garden singers, gratis, on a piano in the theatre basement.

It is not clear why Georg spent so long in England, almost a year, extending his British visa every few months. He may have been waiting for the YMCA to send his New Zealand permit, which was eventually expedited by Fergusson. He volunteered twice for the armed services but was rejected as an Enemy Alien. He went to whatever concerts he could afford, including one of Beethoven by the London Symphony, which he thought a marvellous performance spoiled (in the days before pitch was standardised) by being terribly sharp. At a recital by Myra Hess at the National Gallery the Queen left before the end, obliging Hess and the audience to stand in the middle of a movement – an unforgivable affront to composer and artist.

For the most part English music meant little to him, and he was appalled to find that Bruckner and Mahler were rarely performed. 'It was no-one less than my beloved Delius who said, "These English, now they make a fuss about Sibelius – in a few years they will even sink as low as Mahler and Bruckner."' They were considered, as musicologist Cecil Gray put it, 'Continental aberrations'. Georg never forgave the English for this either.

There is no doubt he was miserable, living in a culture he neither understood nor liked. 'I know better than most how terribly lonely one can be in London,' he said later. He continued composing, however, and in those eight months he completed several works, all fugues. One was dedicated to eighteen-year-old Peter de Francia, later the eminent painter and portraitist, whom he probably met through a pianist acquaintance. Another was dedicated to his school friend Heinz Röhr, who also fled to England and had to abandon his dream of becoming a concert pianist. He went to Oxford University, and despite beginning with little English he was said within a year to be the most brilliant law student they had ever had. He joined the British establishment and became the eminent lawyer Sir Henry Rowe QC. He became more English than the English, and never spoke of his Austrian past, even to his children.

In the 1940s Georg said he wanted his music to be like Scriabin – a curious comment given that this can be said of almost nothing he wrote after the 1936 'Sehnsucht'. During the rest of his compositional life Georg wrote many fugues, and extremely complicated ones at that. There is hardly an extant piece that is not, or does not incorporate, a fugue. It is something of a mystery, given that he always wanted to write music that is beautiful and full of feeling, and the fugue does not readily lend itself to either. Such a strict and uncompromising form was not in keeping with his nature, which was far more instinctual. My surmise is that he turned – subconsciously – to a rigorous form to give order to his mind as his life became more disordered. Besides, the fugue had no structural problems, unlike sonata form and especially finales, which (as Georg often pointed out) gave Romantic composers endless trouble.

On Saturday 11 November 1939 his passport was stamped with his New Zealand visa, and an exit stamp from Britain endorsed 'No return to United Kingdom'. He rushed to obtain a berth on a ship, and found one sailing on the coming Tuesday. All this took so long that he was late for a party given by a friend called Mercy. As she waited for Georg she rhapsodised to her friend Muriel about the wonderful young man she had found. But when he finally arrived it wasn't Mercy he noticed but Muriel. He saw her across a crowded room and was instantly smitten. 'You will come to New Zealand with me!' he announced to her brightly.

Rosa Muriel Norman, aged twenty-one, was an outstanding beauty. She had a wide-eyed look, a strong jaw and a high forehead. She was well made up and had long hair she coloured reddish with henna. She was about the same height as Georg, and her figure was of the type he favoured then, buxom and with powerful broad shoulders. She came from the landed gentry; her family had come to England in the Norman Conquest and had lived around Leighton Buzzard in Buckinghamshire ever since. Muriel's father, an engineer, went to Shanghai to install the city's new waterworks; Muriel was born there in 1918, and returned with her family to England when she was about seven. She attended high school in Oxford but was denied a university education because her family considered it unsuitable for girls. According to Georg, she was 'intelligent but uneducated'. She fed her mind by attending debates at the Oxford Union, and went to work in London as a bank clerk. She was beautifully spoken and had been brought up to have perfect poise, although those who knew her well knew she was not as confident as her manner suggested. She was also a very unconventional girl who did what she pleased (she had already had a number of lovers), and despite being a member of the Hooray Henry set she had no interest in marrying into it. She wanted someone exotic; not specifically a musician, as she was quite unmusical, just someone exotic, and in Georg she found exactly what she was looking for. She was also pleased to find a way of escaping the stuffiness of her class and her family.

Much later she told her children that her first impression of Georg was that he was rather full of himself. The impression cannot have lasted long because she agreed to meet him again the day after the party at Piccadilly tube station. Each arrived at the appointed time and waited increasingly desperately for an hour, until it occurred to Muriel that there was more than one entrance. In the two days they had left they met each other's families, finding approval on both sides. Muriel's mother, far from being horrified at her daughter's choice, encouraged her, despite Georg's being a penniless foreigner with negligible prospects who was heading to the farthest colony in the Empire. 'You will never meet a more honest man,' she said. According to Muriel, the rest of her family disowned her for running away with the enemy.

Georg told her he didn't like the name Muriel, so she told him to call her Sue, as her father for some obscure reason had called her; thereafter it was the only name by which she was known. On 14 November Georg sailed alone from Tilbury on the *Largs Bay* and arrived in Fremantle, Australia, on 20 December. Although he was heading into the unknown, and despite being kept under constant surveillance, he enjoyed the trip. He gave piano recitals, provided handwriting analysis as a self-styled graphologist, and was alto-gether a great success with the other passengers. He also avoided washing his underwear by dividing the number of scheduled days at sea by the number of pairs he had brought.

The ship was delayed in Fremantle and arrived in Sydney late, on New Year's Day 1940. Georg's connecting ship to New Zealand had already sailed, and he was told he would have to buy another ticket. He flatly refused on the grounds that it was not his fault he had missed the boat. An immigration officer asked him if he had any money. Georg, whose English was still limited, misunderstood him to ask if he was going to hand over his money and he replied 'No!' Apart from his clothes and manuscripts he had only £5, and he had no intention of parting with it. The officer searched him, found the note, and arrested him as a spy. How it was sorted out is not recorded; he sailed a day or two later on the *Mariposa*, swearing he would never set foot in Australia again.

## Five

Georg arrived in Auckland on 8 January 1940, sixteen months after leaving Vienna. Alerted by the Hoffmanns, both Auckland newspapers recorded the event, although he may have wished they hadn't; one of the journalists asked him if he had personally known Wagner.

The Auckland Georg came to could not have been more different from Vienna. It had 250,000 inhabitants but there was no opera, no conservatory and no professional orchestra, except the part-time radio orchestra at station 1YA. There were occasional concerts by music teachers and their students, such as the Zillah Castle String Orchestra.* Amateur societies produced Gilbert & Sullivan, and *Chu Chin Chow* was a staple. There were occasional tours by international celebrities such as Gladys Moncrieff, Gracie Fields, New Zealander Oscar Natzke, and Isobel Baillie, who freely admitted she was fed up with rationing and came to New Zealand for some decent food. There were choral societies and church choirs, and the preferred repertoire was always English, no matter how indifferent the quality. Those were the years when third- and fourth-generation New Zealanders who had never been out of the country referred to Great Britain as 'home', and all things British were, ipso facto, better than anything else.

For refugees, happy as they were to be away from the terrors of Europe, life was very strange. Confronted with tea and toast, and lamb with three veg, they longed for the foods they knew in Europe: hearty dark breads, strudels and schnitzels, coffee with cream. Auckland teahouses boiled up 'coffee' from chicory on

---

\* Something of the flavour of such concerts can be found in a 1944 review from the *Temuka Leader*. 'The concert given by the Norman Concerto Company was a veritable musical treat – indeed we feel sure that a more evenly balanced combination has not yet toured the Dominion. Miss Nellie Black plays the violin with a fine broad tone full of feeling and expression. The Bolero movement was played with a vivacity and grace that was delightful. Miss Black also showed her capabilities as a vocalist by her very fine rendition of Allitson's beautiful song *The Lord Is My Light*.'

*Georg and Annemarie captured by a street photographer in his early days in Auckland in 1940, before Sue arrived.*

Wednesdays; coffee houses were unknown. Georg often sighed over the fine coffee and cakes and cream that Dickie's mother had served him in Vienna. He gave the impression that he had been, if not exactly a hedonist, certainly fond of his creature comforts.

In his first weeks he lived in a room at the YMCA, in the centre of town. It was basic accommodation, but had a common-room piano on which he could practise. On his second day he met Les Thompson, a year younger than he, who came to play billiards in his lunch-hour. He was a technician at the telephone exchange next door but had always wanted to study music. Georg took him on immediately as his first piano student, refusing, however, to charge him any fees – he was only too happy to find a music-lover who wanted to learn.

An official at the YMCA soon found him a job as choirmaster at the Presbyterian Church in suburban Mount Albert, at a salary of £30 a year. He started on 4 April and was welcomed with a morning tea after the service. He worked the choristers hard, improving them to the point where they could give occasional small concerts. 'It was a post which must have been torture for him,' recalls a friend. 'Such choirs were rarely of a high standard, however he never spoke disparagingly of it – in fact one could almost believe it afforded him a mild degree of pleasure – occa- sionally! He wore the mask well.'

Georg wasn't allowed to play for the National Broadcasting Service, in case he might send coded messages in the music. But he began to get a little work around Auckland as a recitalist, mostly in private homes. He was asked to play at a charity function at the town hall, and he programmed substantial pieces by Chopin and Beethoven. 'The ladies had wanted flowery miniatures of just a few minutes, like *Träumerei*,' recalls Les Thompson's wife, Marjorie, 'and after looking at their watches and getting restive they finally started to clap in the middle of Georg's playing to stop him. He was bewildered, and very upset – he was like a child who doesn't understand what is happening to him. I think this is where he realised what he was up against.'[1] He also played for the Travel Club, a snobbish organisation restricted to persons who had been overseas: 'home' was best but even Australia would do. The Union Jack flew at every meeting, flapping in the breeze created by a fan directed at it.

On 2 May he completed the last in a set of four piano fugues and dedicated it to Sue, who, with the help of an uncle in the Foreign Office, was on her way. On 20 May, two days before Georg's twenty-third birthday, she stepped off the *Aorangi* looking so glamorous that people waiting at the docks asked who the film star was. There had been no second thoughts in the intervening six months; the two were much in love and overjoyed to be reunited. Sue moved in with Georg and Annemarie in a house they had rented in Spring Street, Onehunga – a plain house in a plain street in an outer working-class suburb. Annemarie stayed for the sake of appearances, for unmarried cohabitation was socially quite impos- sible, but word got around all the same. Richard Hoffmann was offended that Georg should so cavalierly abuse his guarantorship; Ella was horrified and was only placated when told that Annemarie lived there too. She was very jealous of Sue and, after her arrival, Dickie's family faded from Georg's circle of friends.

Before Sue arrived Georg told Annemarie that she had agreed to his three conditions for their life together: they would not get married, there would be no children, and there would be free

*Les and Marjorie Thompson, among Georg's closest friends, in 1953, not long after they moved to Oxford.*

love for everyone. Annemarie's only comment was 'I don't believe it.' Yet Sue agreed wholeheartedly, not only to please Georg but because she was almost defiantly unconventional; thirty years later she would have been a hippie.

All the same, it was accepted by both of them that Georg was the important person. Sue hung off his every word, uttered no opinion that was not Georg's, and for a while adopted a German accent. She wore her hair long and loose to please and inspire the artist, and she wore clothes of blue and green together because he liked the combination. She would do anything for him, and she continued to do so long after the marriage began to fail. But in the beginning there was nothing in the world more wonderful than Georg. In their first few months together Georg wrote a song, 'Liebeslied' ('Love Song'), for Sue's twenty-second birthday on 11 September. He considered this and 'Frühling' his two finest.

In October the three of them moved to 61 Marine Parade, Herne Bay, a middle-class suburb just west of the city centre. Sue bought the house with money she had inherited from her father. It was an old and small weatherboard cottage, but it had a lovely garden of which Georg was proud. It sat atop a steep slope on the waterfront, with an attractive view over Coxs Bay from the back verandah. Dickie's cousin Frank (Feri) Hoffmann built them a chicken coop, and Georg installed a rooster to keep the hens (although probably not the neighbours) happy. Sue worked in a canning factory to support the war effort, and Georg cycled all over Auckland to teach piano to schoolgirls. The couple kept to themselves, socialising mainly with refugees: the Hoffmann brothers Paul, Feri and Carl, Karl Wolfskehl and Margot Ruben, Wolf and Alice Strauss, Maja Blumenfeld and her brother Konny from Berlin, and Ernst Reizenstein (brother of the composer Franz Reizenstein) with whom Georg played violin sonatas. Georg was particularly close to Paul Hoffmann, who became one of his closest lifelong friends. He was a poet and scholar of German literature, but there was not much use for that in New Zealand. He went share milking with his brother Feri at Runciman, forty-seven kilometres south of Auckland, and in his little spare time cycled into Auckland to pursue a Master's degree.

It became clear that Georg and Sue could not continue living in sin, even with Annemarie as chaperone, especially as Georg was working for a church. As well, Sue detested Annemarie, not least because she was loud, lusty, forthright and tactless – all the characteristics the British found most intolerable about 'foreigners'. Sue was so unpleasant to her that Annemarie either threatened to kill herself or actually tried to do so. Thus, although neither Georg nor Sue wanted to get married, they did so on 10 January 1941 in the small town of Te Kauwhata, close to the Hoffmanns' dairy farm. Sue went to stay there before the wedding for the statutory minimum residence requirement of three days, and when she arrived she startled everyone by falling into a chair and bursting into tears. 'We have to get married!' she sobbed (a performance she repeated for the Thompsons). Georg was more sanguine, announcing that he was marrying 'the most beautiful woman in the world'. He loved her, he told Feri Hoffmann, 'in my own way'. They were married at the local registry and all-purpose office, with Paul Hoffmann as witness. The proceedings were constantly interrupted by the noise of telegrams arriving on the telegraph machine, which they found hilarious.

Everyone saw that Georg and Sue were much in love. They were always holding hands, and their faces lit up when the other walked into the room. The lone doubter was Maja Blumenfeld, who was certain from the start that the marriage could not work.

> Sue was a bit overpowering – to anyone. You couldn't put her in a corner and forget about her. They were probably very helpful to each other in the beginning, but I couldn't see it as a life to go on and on. Sue was quite a person, but she wasn't on his wavelength, really. There were too many sides to her that were not included in this set-up. A talented person like Georg should have had someone to guide him along, a person of knowledge and musicality who would know 'where to apply'. He needed guidance. Maybe he had too much pride and independence. If he hadn't had that, he would have sought out somebody.[2]

Georg talked openly about relationships and sex, though these were topics New Zealanders would never dream of mentioning in polite society. It was very different from Vienna, where married men visited prostitutes as a matter of course (Georg recalled that Josef Marx 'used to visit the whores of Vienna') and where sex was an open preoccupation of artists. Exploring the psyche à la Freud was utterly contrary to the New Zealand practice of keeping a stiff upper lip and just getting on with it. Georg applied his 'knowledge' to his friends, thinking he knew what was best for them. For those who were writers or artists, he was sure he knew just the right muse for them, or which woman would be poison for their art. Mystified as to why one of his friends had no girlfriend, Georg decided he must be homosexual and (at a time when homosexuality was illegal) tried to fix him up with a gay hairdresser he knew. He also knew who was 'suitable' for marriage and who wasn't: when another friend announced he was marrying someone in another town, whom Georg didn't even know, Georg thought he had gone mad and tried to talk him out of it. He interfered with only the best of intentions, but he caused embarrassment and sometimes did real damage, though he likely never realised it. In spite of his interventions, all of his New Zealand friends created happy, lifelong marriages. The only one who did not was Georg.

About two months after his marriage Georg completed a piano work he had begun in London, significantly called 'Trauermusik' ('Musica Tragica'). He translated the title blandly as 'Sad Music', but it is full of grief and anguish. He took two and a half years to write it, though it is less than seven minutes long. He thought well of this piece, and made a private recording of it (played by himself) on 78s in March 1946; he orchestrated it in 1958, and considered using it twenty-five years after that, for a threnody (on South African racism) which was never written. Mysteriously, it is dedicated to 'XXX', whose identity is unknown. It is unlikely to be Sue because he had no need to disguise her identity. It would be strange if XXX were a woman, given his marital happiness, but it cannot be ruled out. It could just possibly be Annemarie.

On 7 July 1941 Georg and Annemarie appeared before the Alien Review Board. As Enemy Aliens their way of life was circumscribed by the Aliens Emergency Regulations, introduced in 1940. Their mail was censored. A police permit had to be obtained to travel more than 32 kilometres from home, or for longer than twenty-four hours. Aliens could not own or operate a car, and were not allowed to work on ships or on the docks. They could not own a camera, telescope, binoculars or a shortwave radio, and ordinary radios had to be soldered shut at the local police station in case anyone should convert them into transmitters. As it turned out, the Board's interviewing official, Mr West, was sympathetic. After noting that 'Georg is a music teacher and appears to be quite harmless', he placed brother and sister in Class D, which meant 'it is felt there is really no capacity for mischief at any stage'.[3]

In spite of the dearth of professional musicians in Auckland, Georg was not without artistic contact. In his first few years he came to know many of the poets of New Zealand, including A. R. D. (Rex) Fairburn, Allen Curnow and James Baxter, and often attended their readings. Perhaps through Paul Hoffmann, he met the German writer and Jewish refugee Karl Wolfskehl. Not even the fact that Wolfskehl's family had been German for over a thousand years was good enough for Hitler, and he fled to New Zealand, chosen more or less for being as far as possible from Germany. Although he was befriended by some of the leading New Zealand writers he never came close to adapting to his new country, nor vice versa.

*The great German poet Karl Wolfskehl, one of Georg's refugee friends in Auckland.*

Wolfskehl often came to visit Georg in Herne Bay to discuss music and German poetry, walking the six kilometres from his home in Mount Eden, although he was by then nearly blind. They spent hours discussing the language and culture they both loved. Unlike many refugees who chose never to speak German again, Georg adored it and used it whenever he could – it was an important part of his identity. Although he spoke English eloquently (though grammatically imperfectly) he was never entirely comfortable with it. He always thought in German, and counted bars in it. To his mind it was the language of Goethe, Heine and Schiller, and it could not be held responsible for Hitler. He spoke *Burgtheaterdeutsch*, the clear and beautiful High German of the Austrian National Theatre, with a faint Viennese inflection but no trace of the suburban dialects. It was used by many of the city's Jews in order to signify: 'I know you do not consider me one of you, so I shall not speak as you do.'

Sue sat with them in the kitchen, understanding not a word, but transfixed by Wolfskehl. He was very tall, six feet two inches but appearing even taller, and although he was in his seventies his hair was still black and long to his shoulders. He wore thick glasses on a big nose, a black hat and cape, and a scarf knotted in a huge bow under his chin. He declaimed poetry in a curious far-away monotone; slow, quite high-pitched and falling away a little at the end of each line, in the manner of a prophet. All his admirers adopted the style, including Georg, who retained it all his life. It was beautiful, and like an incantation from a distant time and place, which in a way it was. Antipodeans found it a little affected. The relationship between Wolfskehl and Georg cooled a little after a two-week visit Wolfskehl made to the Tintners in July and August of 1943, not long after they had moved to their farm. Frantically busy with fencing and construction, they did not pay Wolfskehl the attention he felt was his due. He is supposed to have said, 'You have looked after Wolfskehl the man, but not the poet.'

On the face of it Georg was leading a reasonable existence, with a small income, secure living arrangements and a devoted wife he adored. But musically he was starving. His only musical soulmate was Les Thompson, but he soon joined the Army. His only real source of music was from his static-ridden radio, with silences every few minutes while the record was changed. Early in 1942 he began writing down his thoughts on what he heard, 'because I have no-one to talk about music with'. Giving piano lessons to largely talentless young girls with difficult parents was not how he had envisioned his life – and teaching was a precarious existence. One mother withdrew her daughter when he refused to teach her Addinsell's Warsaw Concerto on the grounds that it was bad for her musical development. He had to listen to the teenage troubles of his students, and one of them developed a rich fantasy life about him that caused him considerable embarrassment. Conducting a church choir was hardly a future either. He considered, and rejected, giving up conducting and becoming a concert pianist instead. He did not show his disquiet to anyone, probably not even Sue. The extent of his misery can be seen in a piece he wrote in his exercise book (in German) on his twenty-fifth birthday.

Today I am twenty-five years old. I have achieved almost nothing. How the time flies. I know that I must improve my piano playing, I sacrifice quite a lot of time in my life, I need it for everything else. And my arms constantly hurt and hinder me…nevertheless I *know* there is something exceptional in me. How it will go on, I think so often that I don't make the most of this mercy of living in peace. But what shall I do? I don't often waste time, I don't read much, and nevertheless I achieve almost nothing…I hate acting, but I continue to be forced into a role. I hope I can soon tear myself away from all that. My parents' life fills me with shame, the poverty of the world overwhelms me in my impotence. I have *everything* I can wish for (except a better way of earning a living…) I must not be unfair to myself, my experiences could have completely broken me.

It is so difficult to do what one must in times like these.

My church concert went well yesterday. These good people really do what they can. But how laughable the whole thing is! How unnecessary for them, what a waste of energy for me…

To a considerable degree I have the talent to push away the things that are unpleasant or dreadful; if I did not I would long ago be dead or mad, but for sure with the bad things many good ones also get pushed aside, and for those things it is a pity…I owe thanks to *too* many people, the result is that I more or less neglect them all, or it would overwhelm me. – So many people (and good ones) believe in me, do I have the right to doubt myself?…

It may have been shortly after this that he began working on a sonata for violin and piano, perhaps because he had begun taking violin lessons to improve his conducting. Three months later he wrote another note into his exercise book, sounding a little brighter:

I have injured my finger, just now when I need it, so as a consequence my whole being is depressed. It is getting better (injured when I spent an hour in pouring NZ rain in the Parnell Rose Gardens taking cuttings for us). This is not as poetic, but compare it with Rilke's end.* I have everything *but* thoughts of death, and before anything else I must finish my Violin Sonata.

---

\*    Many people believe the poet Rainer Maria Rilke (1875–1926) died of blood poisoning after prick-
     ing his finger on a rose thorn.

The exercise book finishes at the end of October 1942. Les Thompson was invalided out of the army after suffering a life-threatening case of meningitis, and as he recovered Georg had someone with whom to discuss music again. He also began teaching Les harmony and theory, which cheered Georg up and changed the direction of Les's life.

At last Georg and Sue had the Herne Bay house to themselves. Because Annemarie's nursing qualifications were not recognised in New Zealand she had worked in an assortment of menial jobs, and it was while waitressing at Cooke's Café in July 1942 that she met Francis William Tett, then serving in the air force as a flight instructor. Frank was English, and almost forty-one, fifteen years older than Annemarie. He had been widowed only nine months earlier and was still recovering from his loss. Annemarie saw an honourable and kind man who could provide her with security and a home of her own, and they responded to each other's loneliness. They were engaged within a week. Georg was always fond of Frank, but Sue never took to him. She told Marjorie Thompson that the reason she had left England was to get away from nineteen uncles just like him.

Frank and Annemarie were married on 27 July 1942 at Georg's church in Mount Albert. When Frank left the army he became the art teacher at a boys high school in New Plymouth, considered by the locals not a job for a real man. Though Franz Wilhelm remained the love of Annemarie's life, she was a good wife to Frank. She became a housewife and took pride in her housekeeping ('She has the best-polished chairs in New Zealand', Georg sniffed). One of only two non-British foreigners, she adapted as best she could to the quiet and conventional life of small-town New Zealand. She never spoke of her early experiences, even to her family, and when films or documentaries about the war appeared on television she silently left the room.

## Six

When France fell in May 1940 the British decided it was too risky to leave their enemy aliens at large and began rounding up all men aged sixteen to sixty. Alfons, aged fifty-nine, was sent to an internment camp on the Isle of Man, where he was imprisoned for three months. Georg was desperate to bring his parents to the safety of New Zealand, away from one squalid tenement after another, but he could do it only by providing Alfons with a job. The only possibility was farm work.

At about the same time Sue's mother died. Too late, Sue discovered that her mother had almost certainly known she had cancer when she encouraged her to follow Georg to New Zealand. Heartbroken, Sue said had she found out earlier she would have returned immediately, and had she known before she left she would never have gone at all.

With her inheritance, and Alfons in mind, Sue decided to buy some land that could be turned into a farm. Georg knew nothing about farming and was very doubtful ('I'm a child of the asphalt'), but they found a forty-six-acre property in the Waitakere Hills, about twenty-two kilometres west of the city. It was near the top of Forest Hill Road, with a beautiful view of Auckland. The land was partly cleared and the rest was covered in ferns and vibrantly green bushland. Nearby there was a waterfall, on a neighbour's property. 'I covet this waterfall,' Georg said. 'I'm ashamed of myself because I don't believe in private property. But I wish it were mine.'[1]

Georg and Sue moved there in February 1943. The farmhouse had bare floors and few comforts, and apart from Georg's upright piano their furniture was basic and sparse. Sue had some made, and had it lacquered red with pale blue upholstery; Marjorie Thompson made blue curtains to match. It was nothing like the well-stuffed sofas, carpets, net curtains and blinds of the time and was considered rather shocking. Neither of them cared in the least.

*The farmhouse in the Waitakere Hills.*

*Sue with Ferdinand on the farm in 1943.*

*Georg and Astrid on the farm around 1944.*

Although Sue preferred a cropping farm they decided on eggs – it seemed more profitable and it would suit Alfons better. Everything had to be built from scratch. They hacked out the needle-pointed gorse, the scourge of the North Island, and fenced the property by slinging posts across the valleys on a wire pulley. Sue designed a water system and they irrigated the property from natural springs. They built large henhouses for 1200 birds; Georg sawed wood for the framing, mixed the concrete and laid the floors. When the hens were installed he created his own poultry feed that included wheat sprouts, mash, and watercress grown in a pond created for the purpose. In an effort to breed the best layers he made a serious study of Mendelian genetics, which Sue thought a little silly, but in later years their eggs won many prizes. They did not, however, generate better profits.

They brought in milking cows, and a magnificent bull Georg called Giovanni after Mozart's operatic Don. They acquired a dog they called Ferdinand because he smelled the flowers. When he was killed by a car shortly afterwards they replaced him with two German Shepherds – Astrid for Sue and Percy for Georg – and began breeding them. Marjorie Thompson thought that Sue, with Astrid by her side, looked like Diana the Huntress.

These early days on the farm were perhaps the high-water mark of happiness in Georg's life. He soon came to love the brilliant blue skies and his spacious, verdant surroundings, so different from the artificial apartment life of Vienna. He found that he enjoyed hard physical labour, and was good at it. He loved milking the cows ('the closest thing to heaven I can think of') and was particularly fond of scything, both restful activities that allowed him to think about music. Les Thompson came for lessons and he and Georg strode over the property happily discussing music, a much-needed tonic for both of them. 'It must have been 1943 when my parents took me along to see Georg and Sue Tintner at their Waitakeres hideout,' remembers Carl Hoffmann:

> They were very much in love. I watched them holding hands during most of the time of our visit…I was very young then and only vaguely remember details of the conversation that seemed to alternate between music and chickens. But I have a clear recollection of the house, the mud surrounding it, the simplest of furniture, as well as the very, very plain

cookies offered us along with fruit juice and herbal tea. Georg
Tintner's clothes could well have been castoffs from a farmer
and Sue's overalls did nothing to enhance her lovely features.
They certainly did not dress for our visit. On the contrary,
they seemed to take pride in being different from the norm.
Did Sue also rebel against society's conventional concept of
*Woman*? I remember feeling rather uneasy and wasn't sorry
when we left.[2]

Though Sue could have kept them both in comfort, Georg
insisted on paying half of the household expenses:

> I was then and still am of the opinion that but for very
> exceptionable [sic] circumstances it is the duty of the *man* to
> support his family. Therefore I resisted quite a while when
> Sue suggested to buy a house, but I relented because it was
> so much more economical, but from then on and especially
> when she bought the Farm she spent all her money (which
> she had not earned, it is true) on ME and the children.[3]

Because he earned so little they often went without. When
Georg's only pair of shoes needed repair he went barefoot, even in
the city. And they ate a large amount of porridge. They had a Ford
car so decrepit that Georg drove with one hand and held the door
shut with the other. It had an egg crate instead of a front passenger
seat and no floorboards in the back, and it smelled so badly that
those who rode in it were convinced hens roosted in it.

Alfons never made it to New Zealand. He died in London of
heart failure, aged sixty-three, on 14 October 1944. Family lore has
it that he collapsed while peeling an apple, and died the following
day. Georg told me it was all because his father was made to sleep
on a cold stone floor in a school on the Isle of Man. 'He never had
a day's illness in his life, but three weeks after they let him out he
was dead.'[4] Georg had confused the dates – Alfons died four years
after his release – but he never stopped despising the English for his
father's treatment. Though he had little in common with Alfons,
he was grief-stricken when he died. He recognised his father as an
honourable man and for the rest of his life regretted that he had not
known him better. On the very rare occasions he made a nostalgic
remark about a relative, it was not about his beloved mother but

his father: that he was colour-blind and was always put out that he couldn't find the cherries on the trees; that he would eat all of an apple including the core and pips; that he loved gadgets and to Mizzi's despair would often come home crying, 'Look, Mizzi, look what I've found!'

Shortly after his father's death Georg completed the Sonata for Violin and Piano in A. He dedicated it to Karl Wolfskehl, with the inscription: 'If this, my best, but a trifle by your standards helps to slightly balance an uneven friendship I shall be happy.' With a duration of over twenty-five minutes it is his longest work. Fifty-five years later he said that the four movements deal with, respectively, love, defiance, sorrow and triumph, but there is no such indication on any of the manuscripts. They were themes – autobiographical themes – that occupied him always, returning more than a decade later in his other most important work, *The Ellipse*. More exactly, the first three did; triumph was by then long gone.

The piece, especially the piano part, is difficult to play. Georg told Keith Jacobs, a composition student and acolyte he took on around 1946, that he was interested in 'the emotional possibilities of the larger interval'.[5] He described the work as 'what you might call late Romantic, or post-Romantic', although the third (*Lentissimo*) movement is atonal. Nevertheless, melody is still important, particularly in the first movement with its soaring first theme and its second tune that was inspired by Sue's long hair. With this work he began his lifelong search for a suitable compositional language.

After completing the sonata Georg decided to compose an opera based on the Restoration play by John Ford, *'Tis Pity She's a Whore*. He thought the play ideal for operatic treatment: everything was already there, even the recitatives. The play concerns incest between brother and sister (Giovanni and Arabella) that ends in tragedy. It is easy to see how he would have found it appealing; it questions the laws of religion and society. Georg also thought there was nothing whatever wrong with incest 'if the genes are good' – after all, there was near-incest in his own family. His friends were aghast. If merely living in sin was unacceptable in New Zealand, how could he think to create an opera about brother-sister incest? But Georg was unmoved, even by the opinion of Wolfskehl, who suggested strenuously he find another topic.

In November 1945 Georg resigned from his church position. He had been frustrated for years over the choristers' unreliable attendance, and there was growing discontent over his choice of repertoire. He had decided to do one of his great loves, Mozart's *Ave verum corpus*, but he was thwarted by a senior church official, a rigid Scotsman, who told the minister they would refuse to sing it. According to a friend, 'They were shocked out of their corsets to discover Georg expected them to sing in *Latin*. The Devil himself wore Latin, Popish dress.'[6] The church elders began insisting that the repertoire 'be harmonised as much as possible with the address.'[7] Georg likely tried passive resistance, but this only resulted in more pressure. When he finally gave up, the choir issued a heartfelt little note in the annual report: 'Mr Tintner was greatly respected by all members of the Choir, and was most faithful and exceedingly considerate. We miss him very much indeed.'[8] The minister, Mr Young, wrote Georg a reference, stating that:

> [He] has given service to the Choir that will be long remem-
> bered by those who were privileged to receive tuition under
> his leadership. The Choir, though not numerically strong,
> was able to render Anthems of singular merit with very great
> acceptance to the Congregation. Mr Tintner was held in high
> esteem both for his exceptional gifts as Musician and for his
> humility, graciousness and tact.[9]

Late in 1945 Sue decided that she wanted children after all. Turning her mind to it was learning that Annemarie was pregnant (her son Michael was born on 15 July of the following year). She couldn't bear the idea that Annemarie would have a baby and she wouldn't; and she was convinced that Annemarie would be a terrible mother and that she could do it much better.[10] Georg, however, remained adamantly against having children. There was the matter of his limited earnings, and the fact that the farm was only starting out. More importantly, he had long been certain that the life of a musician as he intended to live it was not compatible with children. A composer's life required peace and dedicated concentration, and a conductor's career would keep him constantly away. It would not be fair to them. 'But I have my children!' he argued, referring to his compositions. Sue replied: 'But they're not *my* children.'[11]

For Georg, Sue's demand was a betrayal, a breach of their original agreement. This was the first time Sue put her foot down.

It may not have occurred to Georg that a muse might want something more than just to support and inspire her man. In very short order she told Georg she was going to have a baby, and if he wouldn't provide it she would have one with someone else. He capitulated. When Sue told Marjorie Thompson, she thought, 'Oh Sue – you don't know what you've done!'

> It must have shaken Georg to his core when she delivered her ultimatum, and he could never have felt the same about her afterwards…Of course he loved Demas and all his children, but he had his reasons for not wanting to be a father and Sue had gone along with them. However much he came to see her point of view, such a crisis must have been earth-shattering to him.[12]
>
> He had the pictures of an idealistic young man and Sue helped to destroy this, in a way. He discovered she had clay feet.[13]

The baby was born on 10 August 1946, and Georg was delighted. He said to Keith Jacobs, 'I felt quite unworthy of the honour'.[14] Beginning a tradition of giving his children names guaranteed to invite ridicule at school, he named the child Franz Demas, the first for Franz Röhr, the second for the disciple who turned against St Paul, a saint Georg disliked. The boy would be, however, always known by his second name.

'Demas may have been worth it,' says Marjorie Thompson, 'but Sue paid a very high price for him.'

Demas was a small, premature baby, weighing under six pounds (2.7 kilograms). Georg attributed his early arrival to Sue's continuing heavy farm work during her pregnancy, though he had begged her not to. Indeed, some of her friends had begun to notice that she was given to making life unnecessarily hard for herself. She became self-sacrificial, and she may have begun martyring herself to show Georg that what she did was also valuable, an equal contribution to the marriage. In the end it took on a life of its own. Georg's view was that running the farm was necessary and important but it could not be compared with his artistic endeavours. Nobody, least of all Sue, would have thought that in the greater scheme of things feeding hens was as important as writing great music. But a marriage is not the greater scheme of things; it is a partnership in which such comparisons should never be made. That was what Georg could not understand, and never did.

Shortly after Demas was born Sue went to rest on the Hoffmanns' farm. Mrs Hoffmann, the mother of Paul, Frank and Carl, began advising Sue about how she should deal with Georg and stand up for herself, and Sue burst into tears. Marjorie Thompson went to comfort her, and she said, 'Everyone tells me what to do but I can't defend myself! I love Georg, but he's very difficult to live with.' She went on to say she couldn't divorce him – evidently something she had contemplated – because the scandal would ruin his career, and that she would never allow.[15] But Marjorie saw that Sue had lost her all-absorbing interest in him. 'There was nobody else but Demas. He was the sun, the moon and the stars. If Georg had been a jealous person he would have been jealous of Demas.'[16]

The showdown over having a baby had struck at the foundations of Georg's confidence. His difficulties with composing, already on shaky ground as he searched for a stylistic way forward, truly began about this time.

In January 1946 Georg applied for naturalisation, and citizenship was granted that October. His naturalisation certificate states his occupation, uniquely, as 'composer, conductor, poultry-farmer'. His application also noted that he was attempting to bring his mother to New Zealand. Sue needed help; Demas was walking and she could no longer leave him alone in the house while she worked outside. On 25 August 1947, Mizzi finally arrived, leaving only Thilde behind; their mother, Therese, had died five days after the birth of Demas. When Sue saw her at the docks she was shocked. Mizzi had greatly aged. She had two slipped discs and was stooped and frail – an old woman at fifty-four.

Sue had only met Mizzi once before leaving England and she had liked her. On further acquaintance, and under very different circumstances, she quickly turned against her. Not only was Mizzi like the detested Annemarie but it was soon clear that she couldn't provide the help Sue needed. Mizzi did her best, but her housekeeping skills were indifferent and shovelling coal and lifting firewood were beyond her. Demas was a big, strong boy and Mizzi was unable to get a nappy onto him when he resisted. She found it difficult to pick up the clothes Georg dropped on the floor – behaviour Sue excused by saying he was an artist. Mizzi's cooking also caused trouble. 'Sue had a British reaction to ethnic food,' recalls one of her sons. 'Plainness was a virtue. Salt was a European excess.'[17] She took offence that Mizzi disliked eggs and did everything she could to disguise them in her cuisine. 'Mizzi was a lackadaisical and absent-minded cook. Georg would have seen food as fuel, so wouldn't have noticed,' says Feri Hoffmann. Mizzi thought farming life was too arduous for Georg and Sue and begged them to give it up, but they wouldn't hear of it.

Georg began meeting concentration camp survivors. Helen Adler, a survivor from Bergen-Belsen, joined the choral society and sang with tears streaming down her cheeks. Another was Joe Burstein, the doctor who had not been as lucky as he at the Police Praesidium in Vienna in 1938. He had spent a year in Dachau before being rescued by the philosopher Karl Popper, a Viennese friend, who had come to New Zealand in 1937 to teach at Canterbury University in Christchurch. Georg's response to the terrible stories he heard was to develop an interest in healthy eating, possibly precipitated by Sue's telling him he was becoming plump. Marjorie Thompson recalls:

> When we first knew him, Georg used to talk about the wonderful luscious meals he had in Vienna, the coffee with chocolate and cream on top, the comfortable feather beds. He became much more of a puritan after the war, after he heard the awful things that had happened.[18]

Georg never did anything by halves. He made Sue plant large quantities of rhubarb, which they ate unsweetened because he deemed sugar unhealthy. They gave it up only when the oxalic acid eroded their tooth enamel. Cabbages came next, and even a whole one eaten raw gave Georg's iron digestion no trouble. They made European-style dark bread with rye and honey, which was so successful that the pianist Lili Kraus* asked them to send her some whenever she was in New Zealand. Over the years Sue developed the bread with ever more healthful ingredients but no salt, until almost everyone found it inedible.

---

\* After spending three years in a Japanese prison camp in Java, the striking Hungarian pianist Lili Kraus (1903–1989) came to New Zealand in 1946, and gave many concerts there. Georg told her that as a young child he had attended one of her recitals and she was his first experience of beauty. She replied, 'Then I was beautiful. Now I can play the piano.'

By this time the de-Nazification trials had started in Germany and Austria and Georg watched sceptically as Austria, at least, classified its artists according to who was useful and who was expendable for show purposes. One of those he thought unjustly treated was Robert Haas, the editor of the Bruckner Collected Edition. His feelings about Wilhelm Furtwängler, who spent the war in Germany and performed for Hitler and his henchmen, but who also helped Jews, were more equivocal. While he thought Furtwängler's Nazi associations more a matter of naïveté than conviction, Georg never bought recordings he had made during the war. Furtwängler was merely a recreative artist, however, in whom principle should have prevailed over expediency. In the case of creative artists Georg was more conciliatory. What was important was that their works were written, and on these grounds he defended all composers – such as Richard Strauss and Hans Pfitzner – who had compromised themselves. In the draft of a letter to an unknown publication, in 1946 or 1947, he wrote in still-imperfect English:

> Sir: Whoever was responsible for the writup [*sic*] of this com-
> posers artistic achievments must have mixed him up with
> his namesake Oscar of *Chocolate Soldier* fame of whom much
> more fittingly could be said: His compositions especially his
> lilting waltzes are widely known. Richard Strauss, however
> is one of the if not the greatest living composer, whose
> profound influence can also be felt in English music (Elgar,
> Bax etc). Poor old master he would deserve a bit better of
> an ungrateful world. He was never a Nazi his magnificent
> *Salome* was even banned on the German Operastage. Would it
> not be fitting to leave him in peace at eighty-two even should
> he have made minor concessions in order to be left alone. The
> over zeal of the German and Austrian Denazification courts
> is truly a sorry spectacle. To hide their own feeling of shame
> and inferiority could they not choose objects more worthy of
> their belated sense of justice than [the] Master Strauss?[19]

Over fifty years later he wrote to a choral conductor:

> You asked me whether Franz Schmidt was a Nazi or not. In
> difficult times many things are not either black or white.

I try to answer this question as well as I can. The doctor of Franz Schmidt, who was also a brilliant violinist, was perhaps his best friend for many years. They played chamber music together and Dr Adler[*] looked after him till he died. This man was a Jew. I also know that Franz Schmidt helped some of his Jewish students and friends to get out of Austria. These are the positive sides. But unfortunately Franz Schmidt wrote a cantata in homage of Hitler [*Die Deutsche Auferstehung* (*German Resurrection*)]. It is very fortunate that he died before finishing this piece. The Universal Edition holds the manuscript of the unfinished work and refuses (in my opinion wisely) to publish it. So what can you say? One thing is clear to me, that he certainly did not expose himself more incriminatingly than for instance Hans Pfitzner, whom I also adore.

After all, we judge the works of these great men and not their human failings.[20]

When Georg at last heard the fate of his relatives, several of whom were murdered, he was overcome by survivor guilt. He may, as he claimed, have had no sense of *meshpoche*[†] nor much liking for some of them, but the stories he heard shocked him so deeply that he always believed it was 'all of them' who had perished. But some survived the same way Georg did: through blind luck. One Horowitz relative in northern Germany survived because the official ordered to arrest and transport all Jews was so lazy that he pushed him across the Danish border rather than complete the paperwork.

Georg's aunt Klara Brünner escaped to Santiago. Her daughter Martha Brunner-Orne was given a fellowship to the Mayo Clinic in June 1938 and used it to get her husband and children out.[‡] But Georg heard with impotent rage that Uncle Arthur, the umbrella factory proprietor, had used his considerable means not to save himself and others but to import Kosher food. He and his wife Elsa were deported to Theresienstadt in September 1942, where Arthur

---

[*]  Dr Oskar Adler (1875–1955): musician, physician, Schoenberg's first music teacher. He escaped to England in 1938.

[†]  Family, both close and extended.

[‡]  Cousin Martha became a leading Boston psychiatrist, the first psychiatrist of the poet Anne Sexton. It was Martha's son, Dr Martin Orne, Sexton's next psychiatrist, who encouraged her to take up writing poetry.

died of heart disease two years later. Elsa was immediately sent to her death at Auschwitz, on one of the last transports.

Uncle Fritz, at least, had been left alone. Hitler, as respectful of honours and decorations as any Austrian, noted Fritz's splendid array and chose not to have him arrested. But Fritz died of a heart attack in January 1943 and his Hungarian wife Margit was left without protection. Uncle Rudi tried to help her by taking her to Budapest, but it was useless; when the Nazis invaded in 1944 Margit was sent to the Sarvar concentration camp and killed. Rudolf was also arrested and sent to Theresienstadt where he died of a heart attack a few months later. Though his ex-wife Johanna sent him daily food packages, she maintained to the end of the war that Hitler was a wonderful person who would do much for Austria.

Aunt Bertha Weinberger and her daughter Grete also escaped to South America, but her other daughter Fritzi was deported with her husband and children via Theresienstadt to Auschwitz. Fritzi was murdered, but some of the children survived, although nobody knew quite how. The story Annemarie told was that Fritzi and her daughter were among the last prisoners to be sent to the gas chamber as the Nazis tried to exterminate as many as possible before the Russians arrived. The prisoners were packed in so tightly that the gas could not penetrate far enough down to reach a small child, and when the troops opened the gas chamber they found her still alive, clinging to her dead mother's hand. Georg's version was that, as the prisoners were herded into the gas chamber, one of the guards was struck by a pang of compassion and pulled the child out. When he heard Annemarie's version he became angry. He wanted to believe – he *had* to believe – that one of the guards had just that once found some humanity within himself.

## Seven

Late in 1946, aged almost thirty, Georg found an opportunity to lead a significant musical organisation. Along with several dozen others, all in England, he applied for the position of music director of the Auckland Choral Society. The choir of 200 was founded in 1855 and had had only five music directors, all English; the most recent, Colin Muston, had been there for thirty years. Something of a stuffed shirt, he resigned over a minor issue expecting to be begged to return, and was shocked and offended when he wasn't.

At his interview Georg was asked if he knew any English composers. 'Such as whom?' he asked. 'Such as Handel.' 'But he's German!' he exclaimed. The interviewer then asked him if he knew Coleridge Taylor's *Song of Hiawatha*. 'No,' he said, 'but I will know it note- and word-perfect in a week, if that is your wish.' His audition comprised half an hour of selections from the *Messiah*, and he impressed everyone by conducting from memory. The choir appointed him in April for the remainder of 1947. Two weeks later the choir's chairman, John Black, reported to James Shelley, the director of the National Broadcasting Service, 'Our choice seems to be a happy one – the Committee and Choir are unanimous and enthusiastic about the appointment. His ability is undoubted, and his manner and graciousness very pleasing, so we look forward to a very successful season.'[1]

Such enthusiasm was in fact by no means unanimous. The conductor of the Royal Auckland Choir, Harry Woolley, asked John Black, 'Why do you want to pick a bloody foreigner?'[2] One of the choral society's board members, H. G. Staley, voted against Georg and insisted that the committee consider any applications still arriving from England. He went to the trouble of writing to the Prime Minister, Peter Fraser, to push for an Englishman. 'Mr Colin Muston, our late conductor, resigned last December. He gave us no warning and we have had to appoint a man for this

season who happened to be in Auckland.'[3] He spent the rest of the
year doing everything he could to undermine Georg, and when
that failed, he resigned.

In the choir there was a small group of men who tormented
Georg, not as a Jew but as a foreigner and a German. He simply
accepted that, once again, he didn't fit in. Anti-foreigner sentiment
reached a zenith in the years just after the war – surprisingly, given
that even in 1945 New Zealand had fewer than 27,000 immigrants
from non-Commonwealth countries, just 1.5 per cent of the population. In 1947 the Dunedin branch of the Returned Servicemen's
Association moved a motion that all enemy aliens be sent back to
the countries they had come from, and with only the possessions
they had arrived with. Some New Zealanders felt that refugees
had led a charmed life setting up businesses and getting rich
while 'our boys were over there'. Under the title 'Aliens Quietly
Dig In', a March 1947 issue of *Truth* claimed to have 'unearthed
sensational evidence' that at least 500 aliens had become naturalised since VJ Day:

> Throughout the war years there was nation-wide evidence
> that stealthily, but inexorably, aliens from enemy countries
> who for one reason and another had left theirs for this,
> insinuated their money and trading knowledge into New
> Zealand's business life, and piecemeal here and there acquired
> controlling interests. Glove-making, women's mantles and
> underwear, children's clothes, toys, hats, small lending librar-
> ies, shops, dairies [corner shops], and a host of other things,
> were scooped up gradually into the alien maw while the
> country's youth was away on the fighting fronts.[4]

What was worse, the anonymous writer argued, aliens were
sponsoring their relatives and friends. He went on to speculate
whether aliens might not be a Nazi fifth column, ready to destroy
New Zealand by spreading diphtheria, typhus and foot-and-mouth
disease.

In 1951 Yehudi and Hephzibah Menuhin made a keenly
anticipated tour of New Zealand. The latter, as she left the country,
remarked that the Welmar concert grand piano in Christchurch
was so stiff she could hardly play it, because it was normally kept
locked away. She was only one of many visiting pianists to complain

about the execrable state of the country's concert pianos, but she was taken to task by Dr Vernon Griffiths, professor of music in Christchurch and an Englishman, who said: 'In my opinion it is a gross impertinence for a visiting musician of another race – to which Britain has been a good friend – to come here and criticise adversely a piano of high grade made by British workmen and fully approved by British musicians of high standing.'*5

Georg's first performance was *Hiawatha*, a staple of choral societies, on 12 July 1947. His debut went well and the reviews were friendly. The *Star*'s Arthur Fairburn thought Georg created 'a most favourable impression with his well-defined beat and general all-round musicianship',[6] and L. C. M. Saunders in the *New Zealand Herald* concluded that 'Mr Tintner, who was warmly received by his audience, has begun well'.[7]

The reviewers, however, criticised the poor intonation of the Broadcasting Service's 1YA Studio Orchestra, attributing it to insufficient rehearsal time – just two rehearsals were all Broadcasting would allow to outside organisations. Fifty years later the concertmaster Felix Millar recalled Georg as

> a loveable and slightly mad eccentric, arriving on his push-bike in full evening dress, covered in chicken shit and feathers, to conduct a performance of Coleridge Taylor's choral work *Hiawatha* (not his choice). Somehow he was able to make this boring second-rate music sound almost acceptable. He was a musician of impeccable taste, extraordinary energy, with musical integrity of a rare order.[8]

His opinion at the time, however, was less cordial. With such limited rehearsal time Georg worked the musicians very hard, and they resented it so much that all sixteen of them submitted a petition to their resident conductor, Harold Baxter, stating that 'after our experiences with the Choral Society's *Hiawatha*, we wish it were possible that we do not, in future, have to play under the conductorship of Mr G. Tintner'.[9] Baxter then reported to Andersen Tyrer, the conductor of Broadcasting's new National Orchestra in Wellington: 'They had a trying time at the last

---

\*  The next year when Broadcasting gave in and bought four Steinways the Member for Petone, Mr Moohan, asked in Parliament why Broadcasting had found it necessary to spend £10,000 on German pianos when he was reliably informed that British pianos were just as good, and cost less.

*A rather plump Georg rehearsing the ladies of Auckland Choral Society.*

Choral Society's performance of *Hiawatha*, and as is customary, the orchestra received an unfavourable criticism in the press. However, after registering their protest, they will carry on.'[10]

The choristers were most put out to discover that the choir was no longer a social club. They were upset when Georg outlawed knitting, reading, gossiping and arriving late. They were to sing new and difficult works, not the same, largely British, repertoire.* The old ways were gone, which was evident from Georg's 6 December performance of the *Messiah*. Previous (much abbreviated) performances traditionally began with the audience's rendition of 'O Come All Ye Faithful', and finished with the 'Hallelujah' chorus done as an audience singalong. Georg eliminated all this and announced the work would be performed more or less complete, for the first time in New Zealand.†

---

\*      Vincent Wallace's *Maritana* and Edward Germain's *Merrie England* were favourites. Until Georg conducted the Peasant Cantata at the end of 1947 the choir had sung nothing by Bach in its ninety-two years.

†      To be sure of getting a ticket Les Thompson slept in the doorway of the booking office the night before tickets went on sale. In the middle of the night a policeman asked him what he was doing, and he replied from the depths of his sleeping bag: 'I'm waiting for the Messiah'.

The reviews were good but not glowing. Both critics found many of Georg's tempi too slow. Both commented on the deficiencies of the orchestra. But many remembered this performance half a century later, so different was it from what had gone before. Most novel of all was that Georg conducted from memory.

While rehearsing the *Messiah* Georg was invited to become the conductor of the Auckland String Players, an amateur group of thirteen. It was founded in 1940 by Owen Jensen, a pianist, concert presenter, critic, columnist, publisher of the magazine *Music Ho*, and the founder (in 1946) of the Cambridge Music School. Though sometimes criticised for never sticking at anything, his influence on New Zealand music was enormous.

It was a propitious time for Georg to inherit the orchestra. With peace there came a new hunger for culture, supported by the Labour government's social programs that gave New Zealand the world's highest standard of living by the early 1950s. Broadcasting set up its National Orchestra in 1946, and the 1947 tour by the British Boyd Neel Orchestra showed New Zealand what a first-rate string group could sound like. Alex Lindsay* used it as his model for the string orchestra he founded in Wellington the following year. People flocked to recorded music societies where they could listen to the collections of others. Georg lectured occasionally for the Auckland Recorded Music Society, which had 1000 members attending over 100 meetings annually. In 1947 the Auckland Music Council was formed to oversee music in the city, and in 1949 it began an annual festival. According to tenor Peter Baillie, 'There was a feeling that things were starting to get going again after the war, a feeling of optimism. We were on the ground floor now, laying the foundation for later. It was a good time.'[11]

Georg trained the String Players for a year (using an egg crate as a podium) before he thought them good enough to give concerts. He seated the Second Violins on his right, a disposition he used all his life because it gave the antiphonal sound familiar to the composers he loved. On 2 April 1949 they gave their first official concert at the town hall. The orchestra now numbered nineteen players, including Sir Edmund Hillary's first wife Louise Rose, and several refugees: Otto Hubscher, Joe Spring (Josef Sprinz), and

---

* Alex Lindsay (1919–1974), concertmaster of the New Zealand Symphony from 1967 and, as founder and conductor of the Alex Lindsay String Orchestra (1948–74), one of the country's most important musicians.

Frank Hofmann ('the one-F Hofmann'), a professional photographer who became one of Georg's closest friends. The program included relatively easy but stylistically varied works by Purcell, Boyce, Handel, Mozart, and his friend Hans Gál's Serenade for Strings. L. C. M. Saunders wrote that the Auckland String Players was 'a vastly improved and very competent group of instrumentalists' and credited Georg

> for the notable improvement in playing standards, and incidentally for a most happily chosen programme. We are still discovering new facets to this talented conductor's work, which is characterised above all else by painstaking preparation and a sincerity that puts the music before all else. Only on matters of tempo, where his preferences tend occasionally to a slower speed than seems appropriate, may one question his readings.[12]

On 19 August they gave the first Auckland performance of Douglas Lilburn's* *Diversions*, written for the 1947 Boyd Neel tour. Lilburn came to one of the rehearsals, and wrote afterwards to a colleague that he 'was amazed at Tintner's memorised knowledge of the score. He's a real conductor.'[13] Georg and Lilburn became lifelong friends, despite their very different backgrounds and sexuality. Georg considered Lilburn the best composer in Australasia, and he made it a lifetime crusade to promote his music. In a country where musical knowledge fell far short of what could be found in Vienna, Douglas was an important discovery. 'He knows as much as I do', he said admiringly to Keith Jacobs.[14]

Demas grew into a big and active child who was being brought up according to Freudian theories – or what Georg took to be Freudian theories. He believed children should be allowed to express themselves freely, at least in their early years. Discipline was inhibiting. Sue knew nothing about the theory; she was simply so besotted with her baby that she allowed him to behave as he pleased. Georg also subscribed to the view that children should not

---

*     Douglas Lilburn (1915–2001) is regarded as New Zealand's most important composer. He studied in England with Ralph Vaughan Williams, whose influence (with that of Sibelius) can be heard in his music. He returned to New Zealand in 1940 and from 1947 taught at Victoria University in Wellington. He wrote three symphonies and other orchestral works, piano and chamber music, as well as electronic music.

be shown affection, nor should they see affection between their parents, because it would sexualise them too early. Sue agreed with this too. On one occasion Paul Hoffmann's wife Eva tried to hug Demas, then a toddler, and Sue said sharply, 'Are you a kisser too? We don't approve of that.' Georg added, 'His first kiss should be from a girl.'[15] Sue also maintained that one must never indulge in sex for its own sake but only if there is some affection. She gave this lecture to Demas when he was about five.[16]

Sue and Georg's relationship had not, however, recovered from the showdown over Demas, and Sue found Mizzi's presence as trying as ever. She no longer gazed at Georg with admiration but wore only a look of resignation; she was no longer the adoring and beautiful woman Georg had married. Time and hard work had not been kind to her, and she had aged so much that she looked fifteen years older than she was. After Demas was born her figure never recovered. The elegant black evening dress and fur coat of her first year in New Zealand had disappeared, and so had the henna and make-up. She was generally seen, even when visiting friends, in dungarees with straw in her matted hair and poultry feed under her fingernails. Some suggested she should take greater care of herself, not least for Georg's sake, but she said she had no time. To Eva Hoffmann she said frostily, 'No woman would do as much for Georg as I do.'[17]

She had never been conventionally feminine; Wolf Strauss, another refugee, remembers Sue as 'a sort of man-wife. She was very robust and very strong, physically and psychologically.' Not long after Demas was born she startled Georg and the Thompsons at lunch one day by saying, quite out of blue, 'I think there are no men left. Perhaps in Russia…' Disillusionment had set in. 'Sue wanted a he-man,' says Marjorie Thompson. 'Someone more masculine than she was.'[18]

Sue began to speak as if she did all the farm work herself and was solely responsible for the success of the venture. Strangers who went there assumed Georg was just the farm boy, which rankled with him to the end of his life. According to Marjorie Thompson:

Once Georg showed he was good at practical work on the farm, some of this awestruck admiration went away and a little sense of competition set in. Somehow his being practical lowered him in Sue's eyes. She had seen him as awe-inspiring –

*Sue and Georg working on the farm in 1947. Visitors thought Georg was just the farm boy.*

certainly exotic and special. She didn't seem very happy that Georg and Paul [Hoffmann] could do farm work. They were artists. The farm was *her* thing and she was slightly resentful that Georg could do it too. She gloried in being the practical one, who could do things for him. When Sue saw him carrying bags of cement, he became an ordinary person, and she couldn't look up to him in the way she had any more. I remember being uneasy about this even at the time.[19]

By this time Georg was sleeping with other women, his 'illegal friends' as he called them, utilising the library table in the Choral Hall in Airedale Street. Despite his championship of free love – he talked approvingly of 'free love colonies' to Keith Jacobs – there is no evidence that he was unfaithful to Sue before the birth of Demas. As the handsome conductor with charming Viennese manners in charge of a large choral society and an orchestra, he found himself besieged by women both young and middle-aged. He bragged to Keith that he could have had any of the women in the String

Players. He told Sue about his affairs, because to do otherwise would have been dishonest. She found it very painful, and Georg apparently did not understand her feelings. Keith Jacobs recalled, 'There were many moments when it was clear things were not all right. The grand romantic passion had *long* gone.'[20] Sue found that free love was just as impossible in practice as Georg's other two stipulations. According to Feri Hoffmann:

> He was set on the idea that he deserved to be elevated onto a pedestal (late nineteenth century thinking) and in need of special privileges to facilitate creativity. The 'womanising' was part of the same romantic notion…He liked to quote from Ernest Dowson: 'I have been faithful to thee, Cynara, in my fashion.' Recognising his genius most of us were willing to overlook the weaknesses of his personality, even when he declared that, as an artist, he had to satisfy his needs in order to give his best.[21]

There was more to it than artistic licence, however. Georg's confidence had been undermined and, conscious or not, his method of reasserting himself was sexual profligacy.

Early in 1949 Mizzi went away for a long-overdue operation on her back, and Georg sent Sue and Demas to stay with friends. It was odd that he chose these particular friends, for he had long suspected one of them of having an unwelcome interest in Sue. Georg was convinced that every man who ever met Sue was in love with her and – free love notwithstanding – was extremely jealous. Reg (not his real name) had indeed long desired Sue, but as she was his friend's wife he considered her out of bounds.

One evening Sue rushed out of the house, apparently dis-traught at the thought of what Georg might be doing at that moment with a young soprano he was coaching. She reappeared some time later with her legs bleeding from climbing through a barbed wire fence. Reg was surprised, because Sue had plenty of experience in avoiding such injuries. He tended her wounds, and later that night went to her window to see how she was, perhaps a little hopefully. To his surprise Sue seemed to be expecting him. She climbed out of the window and led Reg to his room at the back of the house. He was hesitant, but she said that Georg was sleeping with other women and that it would be all right. The

second night Sue came to him again, and stayed until she heard
Demas crying. Feeling deeply guilty, Reg put a stop to any more.
He begged Sue not to tell Georg, and she agreed.

He was, therefore, unconcerned when, some time after Sue
had gone home, Georg asked to meet him on his way to a rehearsal.
They met on the roadside; Sue and Demas were in the car. Georg,
in a terrible rage, began by saying that he had slept with their
farmhand because she was upset at the recent loss of her boyfriend
and he had done it 'for the sake of her emotional health'. He then
went on to say that Sue had told him about what she and Reg
had done, in retaliation. It occurred to Reg that Georg's pride
was wounded; he couldn't imagine that Sue could possibly have
preferred someone he considered so obviously inferior to himself.
Stricken with remorse, Reg said that Sue had told him it would
be all right, and that he would never find out, and Georg replied
that this would have been living a lie. He went on to say that he
had saved Sue from being a whore in London, but it seemed she
had gone back to her promiscuous ways. He was full of self-pity,
saying 'When Demas cried during Sue's absence that night, it was
I crying.' He told Reg he should take Sue home with him: 'You
make up your mind. If you want her, you can have her.' But Reg
didn't want her. She had betrayed him, and he was too angry even
to greet her when she came to his car, 'apparently ready to be
traded'.[22] He drove her and Demas to the farm, and never went
there again. It was twenty-seven years before he and Georg healed
the rift.

Some time after this Georg illogically announced to Reg that
he couldn't bear the idea that Sue might have any child that was
not his own and he had set about making sure that she didn't. He
added that he had worked very hard at it. Their second son, Boris
Norman, was born (also prematurely) on 16 December 1949.

Reg's mother had guessed what had transpired between Reg
and Sue when she heard her rush through the back door to comfort
Demas. Adding fuel to Georg's rage, she told him he should look
after Sue better or he would lose her.

Georg's Violin Sonata was given its first performance in 1949,
apparently the only one in his lifetime. It was broadcast on 15 July
from a studio concert by two members of the Musica Viva Players

from Australia, violinist Robert Pikler* and pianist Maureen Jones. On 12 December at the town hall Georg performed five of his songs – four from Vienna and Sue's 1940 'Liebeslied' – that he had gathered into a cycle titled *Young Love*.† The soprano was Lesley Daykin, aged nineteen or twenty, who may well have been the singer causing Sue so much distress at the beginning of the year.

---

*     Robert Pikler (1909–1984), a student of Jenö Hubay and Eugene Ormandy, was a Hungarian refugee who had been interned in a Japanese prisoner of war camp in Java. He had an illustrious career as Principal Viola of the Sydney Symphony Orchestra, conductor and teacher (and was a virtuoso chess player). He and Georg were lifelong friends.

†     A recording of this performance shows Georg playing with extreme, almost incomprehensible rubato, which he always used when playing his own works. Over forty years later he suggested to cellist Paul Andreas Mahr that he record these songs in a version for cello and piano. Mahr recalled, 'He really attacked the piano with gusto; he played it like an orchestra from a sonority perspective. That being said he had a very jerky sense of rubato, something which was never in evidence in his conducting…I was reminded of something Artur Rubinstein once said about Paderewski: his rubato in other music was terribly exaggerated but in his own compositions it was marvellous; this was the reverse.'

*Eight*

The National Orchestra, founded in 1946, was run by Broadcasting and based in Wellington. It was a rough and ready outfit of whose excellence Broadcasting had a greatly over-inflated opinion. Some musicians had never even heard an orchestra before they joined it; some played instruments for which they hadn't been trained. For years there was no cor anglais, and all the bassoonists were self-taught for the want of a teacher anywhere in New Zealand. As late as 1960 the Fourth Horn parts were still played on the bassoon. Andersen Tyrer, the first conductor, was a pianist, a touring examiner from the Trinity College of Music in London (New Zealand had none of its own), and conductor of the short-lived Centennial Orchestra in Wellington. He was handed the job by his friend James Shelley, the director of Broadcasting. When questions were asked in parliament the prime minister, not knowing the famous Beecham wit, replied that Sir Thomas considered Tyrer 'was just the man for the job.'[1]

When Tyrer retired in 1949 the conductorship was advertised throughout the Commonwealth, and Georg applied. The process was supervised by the new director of Broadcasting, William Yates, an accountant. Donald Munro, who founded the New Zealand Opera in 1953, remembers him as 'a self-righteous and difficult man who disliked foreigners...Bill Yates was first and foremost a civil servant, inflexible to the last and devoid of personality. He was also religious: a bad combination.'[2] The conductors recommended by the Australian Broadcasting Commission were examined with moderate interest, those from New Zealand with virtually none. After disqualifying non-Commonwealth citizens the BBC interviewed applicants and recommended Michael Bowles from the radio orchestra in Dublin. He was hired immediately, and took over the orchestra in April 1950.

By this time Georg had enlarged the String Players to a group of nearly thirty. He was on the point of creating a full orchestra for Auckland when Owen Jensen founded the Little Symphony Orchestra, with Felix Millar as concertmaster. Not a few people felt that Jensen was jealous and had done it to spite Georg. After resigning from the String Players in 1947 he had discreetly left for England to pursue a woman and, he hoped, to become a BBC announcer. Neither ambition worked out and he returned to Auckland in 1949 wanting his orchestra back. Georg refused to give it up, and thereby made a dangerous enemy. 'If you weren't a friend of Owen', says Suse Hubscher, whose husband, Otto, was in the String Players, 'you were practically lost in Auckland. He masterminded musical life here.'[3]

Jensen's musicians, unlike the String Players, were paid. Georg had opposed paying his musicians on the grounds that once money was involved they would no longer play for the love of it, and he would no longer be interested. Unsurprisingly, the musicians saw it differently and began defecting. On 11 May 1950 John Proudfoot, the new station manager at 1YA, reported to Yates that there had been a showdown at a meeting of the Music Council, 'at which Mr Tintner and his supporters expressed the deepest concern that Mr Jensen was taking all Mr Tintner's string players, with the result that the String Players would not be able to maintain their commitment to take part in the opening function of the Music Festival next month.' Jensen was persuaded to abandon his premiere concert until after the festival, 'at which time Mr Tintner has offered to place his resignation from conductorship of the String Players.'[4]

Georg was persuaded not to resign and the String Players was incorporated in July to ensure its permanence. Jensen's Little Symphony lasted only a couple of years, but Georg's plans to create a full orchestra were ruined. Jensen changed his attitude toward Georg a couple of years later after hearing him conduct opera; a quarter of a century later he was moved to express regret for his behaviour. After a performance of the opera *Jenůfa* in Wellington Georg wrote to me:

I went by train to my former enemy Owen Jensen ('superb conducting'). He was very gracious and as much as apologised

for his actions thirty years ago. ('I always knew you were a
conductor of world class and behaved very silly towards you').

In June 1950 the National Orchestra was to present the first
Auckland performance of the Brahms Requiem, with the Choral
Society. The choir and the Music Council requested that Georg
conduct it, but William Yates refused. Georg had not minded
ceding Elgar's *Caractacus* to Andersen Tyrer at the 1949 festival
because he had little sympathy for the work, but the Brahms
Requiem was very dear to him.* Despite strenuous efforts by
the choral society and Music Council, neither Yates nor Bowles
relented. They were in no mood to accommodate the Music
Council, because they were also squabbling over whether the
National Orchestra would begin the concert with the *Mardi Gras*
overture by the young Auckland composer Edwin Carr. It was
the prize-winning entry in a competition for a festival overture,
and the Music Council maintained the orchestra had undertaken
to perform it; the orchestra claimed they had only agreed to consider it. The real reason for Broadcasting's resistance was that the
orchestra – or in Ted Carr's opinion, Michael Bowles – couldn't
play it. 'Bowles was a hopeless conductor,' said Ruth Pearl, an
English violinist who moved to New Zealand in 1949. 'One of the
wretched people one wants to get rid of and sends to the colonies.'[5]
    Prevented from conducting the Requiem, Georg acted as
rehearsal accompanist, and found it excruciating. Keith Jacobs recalls:

> He was sitting at the piano and Bowles was rehearsing. At
> one point Bowles said, 'This is a difficult bit; there's no-one
> playing here to help you.' Georg got up and said, 'Yes there
> *is* someone playing there', and went to the score to show him.
> 'Oh well, only a flute then.'

By the time the concert came Georg was in torment. According
to clarinettist Ken Wilson:

> When Bowles did the Brahms Requiem, he didn't really
> know it. It wasn't his thing – works like [Elgar's] *Dream of*

---

*      Georg trained the choir for *Caractacus*, but Tyrer 'made it very difficult for Georg,' says chorister Enid
       Evans. 'He was unduly and overly critical of the choir. Georg said, "He didn't forget my race either".'
       (Author's interview, 31 May 2004).

*Gerontius* were more his thing. Georg sang in the chorus, and stood in the front row, making loud comments like 'No, no!' and 'Not like that!' And the choir was in Georg's spell – his thrall. I must say I was very annoyed with him for doing this.

The Auckland critics righteously sided with Georg; Arthur Fairburn's review in the *New Zealand Observer* was titled 'A Fine Requiem: Thanks to Tintner, Michael Bowles on Easy Wicket'. Nevertheless, the Music Council engaged the National Orchestra to appear with the Choral Society at the following year's festival, in Berlioz's *Damnation of Faust*, and Broadcasting moved immediately to ensure Georg was shut out. Proudfoot reported to Yates on his meeting with the Music Council (at which Georg was present):

> The indications are that the National Orchestra…is not likely to be given to any but a professional conductor. I have already asked the Executive to refrain, while I am a member, from the cheap sneers at Andersen Tyrer who, whatever his faults, left a more favourable mark on New Zealand music than the Council collectively, or its members individually, are ever likely to do…The same feud is likely to develop with Bowles and for much the same reason, if we allow it to, so if we could make it clear…the National Orchestra is not available for amateur conductors…

Proudfoot's sour tone had much to do with a concurrent dispute – the customary dispute, which Georg this time won – over the number of musicians and rehearsals the 1YA orchestra would provide for the Choral Society's next performance: Elgar's *Apostles*. 'I knew I would be nagged to do Elgar', Georg told his friends, 'so I might as well get it over with.' He was no admirer of Elgar: 'All those sequences!' he complained. He told Les Thompson, 'When I heard the *Enigma Variations* on the radio in Vienna I thought, "Poor fellow! It must be his worst piece", and when I got here I found it was his best.'[6]

The argument over the Berlioz dragged on for months until a compromise was reached: Georg would conduct the choral concert, but with the String Players augmented by National Orchestra musicians. Because Bowles claimed the choir couldn't manage *The Damnation of Faust* Georg substituted Haydn's *Seasons*, receiving its

first complete New Zealand performance 150 years after its composition. The performance on 14 June received glowing reviews, and
on 22 September Georg finally conducted the Brahms Requiem,
in a performance that 'was able to restore dignity and tenderness'.[7]

Despite the favourable reviews Georg was frustrated by the
poor quality of the choir. He told Michael Bowles in 1950 that
when he had taken it over 'then it was shocking, now it is just fairly
bad'.[8] There was a chronic shortage of men, especially tenors, and
the choir was full of people whose voices were long past being
fresh. It had only recently lost its oldest member, a bass aged
ninety-two who had joined the choir in 1879. Georg asked for
permission to audition the members, which had never been done
before. Musical standards had risen so much in Auckland in recent
years, he argued, that nothing else would result in an acceptable
standard of performance. The board rejected the proposal. Seeing
no alternative, Georg resigned.

> What I had in mind was not just the retesting of the Choral
> members but a completely new start from scratch combined
> with a vigorous propaganda campaign that it is a *new* Choir
> that is being formed with all the assets of the old Society
> without its considerable liabilities. I would have offered (and
> sincerely so, not with the object of being refused) my whole
> salary of next season (£150) except an allowance for petrol
> perhaps, for an effective drive in Press and Radio...
>
> There are situations where the surgeon's knife is more
> kindly than 'milder' but ineffective remedies. My work with
> the Choir has reached a dead end...
>
> The sad truth is that quite a few insults I had to swallow
> both of Mr Tyrer and Mr Bowles regarding the Choir were
> justified. Is it not time that a new good choir emerges out of
> the ashes of a bad old one?[9]

What Sue thought of Georg's offer to throw away a sizeable portion
of his very limited income for artistic principle is not recorded. But
the board reconsidered, and Georg stayed. He spent the next few
months auditioning the choristers, meeting considerable resistance
from the older women, many of whom had been in the choir for
half a century. Some sopranos were offended to find themselves

demoted to alto, and some altos were even more insulted to find themselves in the tenor section; a few resigned from the 'strain'. But when Georg conducted *Elijah* the following May with his renovated choir, 'The illusion that the tenor tone was wholly male was complete,' said the *Herald*. 'This, with a thinning out of the women's ranks, brought a balance that one rejoiced to hear.'[10]

## Nine

Georg had won his battle to transform the choir, but his composing life was anything but successful. His letter of resignation was written on 28 July 1951, and its miserable tone may have had much to do with a crushing event of the day before. On 14 July Yehudi Menuhin arrived in New Zealand on his much-anticipated second visit. Georg knew that Menuhin championed contemporary composers and he gave him his violin sonata to consider. Menuhin played through it, and rejected it. Georg's despairing reaction was to have sex with one of his admirers on the Choral Hall's library table. Years later he told me that Menuhin's rejection was 'one of the worst moments of my life'.

Five years had passed between the violin sonata and his next completed work, 'My Love in Her Attire', a six-voice choral work dedicated to Hans Gál. Using old and new fugues, Georg then completed a four-movement suite for string trio he called 'Fugal Moods', which he thought 'a good piece', although not one of his best. It was performed the following year at the 1952 Auckland Festival.* The *Star*'s Dorothea Turner remarked that they were 'clever, argumentative little pieces'.[1] 'They're clever all right,' said a puzzled Georg, 'but I don't think they are argumentative.' Ruth Pearl, however, thought it 'an ugly piece, and not like the man I knew'.[2] On hearing it again fifty years later, she said, 'To me he seemed to be a musician who knew where he was at and where he was going. This piece was and still is a cry for help, which at the time in New Zealand was unforthcoming.'[3]

Georg followed it with an overture for full orchestra, which he dedicated to Arthur Fairburn, 'an *All*-weather *F*riend'. His initials were enshrined in the work, which Georg punningly titled *Lafa's Ardour* (A–F is *la–fa* in solfège). He sent the piece to an unidentified

---

\*    On 3 July 1952, with Alex Lindsay, Winifred Stiles and John Hyatt.

competition in Australia and was disgusted when it was returned with a judge's comment remarking disapprovingly on 'the sixths leaping all over the score'.

The opera, however, was progressing only very slowly. Georg had never composed quickly but this was something new, and it was undoubtedly related to his exterior life – difficulties with Sue, stagnation in his career, and too much work, both professional and agricultural.* But there was more to it than the shortage of time that would plague him for the rest of his life. He was suffering from cultural alienation, and he never stopped suffering from it. Much later he said:

> For me as musician the transfer into such a totally alien musical environment – or non-musical environment as New Zealand then really was – was certainly not helpful. In some ways it *was* helpful because I was a sort of pioneer, but I talk of my own humble creative efforts. That was a body blow, because I was suddenly taken out of – what really mattered to me.[4]

Georg *was* pioneering music, and with missionary zeal. In April 1951 he took over the forty-strong Amateur Orchestral Society, where they worked on sections of Bruckner's Fourth Symphony. A few professionals joined in because they knew how badly he wanted to conduct it. Every fortnight he drove to Katikati, over five hours from Auckland, to help with a choir run by Joe Burstein. By 1953 he had added a Maori choir formed by the Mormon Church. It was a strenuous schedule for someone who farmed all day: Maori Choir Mondays, Choral Society Tuesdays, Orchestral Society Wednesdays, String Players Thursdays, Choral Society Saturdays and String Players Sunday mornings. He also offered private harmony and theory classes gratis to anyone who was interested.† Composer and pianist Brent Parker still remembers the lessons as 'the purest musical experience I have ever had'.[5] At the time he tested Georg's absolute pitch 'with the insolence of

---

* · Although he was able to think about music while working on the farm, he needed a piano to compose. Two years after he died, his 1936 song *Frühling* was performed at the Festival Hall in London (by baritone Christian Immler and pianist Erik Levi). Marjorie Thompson was in the audience, and when it was over she said, deeply moved, 'If only he had never gone on that farm!'

† Georg willingly coached or accompanied anyone, also gratis. He helped Feri Hoffmann, a good amateur flute player, rehearse one of the Mozart flute quartets, and although Georg didn't know the piece he was able to reconstruct and play it on sight from the cello part.

*Georg's 1951 publicity photo.*

*Mizzi and Sue with Boris (left), Demas (right) and the twins Ariadne (obscured) and Tulin, in 1954.*

youth by playing at least seven chromatic notes simultaneously at the bottom of the keyboard which [he] duly named'. For Keith Jacobs the lessons were a revelation: 'Chords came alive, they were not just mathematical rules. Chords became wonderful magical things.'[6]

On 18 March 1952 Sue gave birth (prematurely) to twins, to everyone's surprise but her own. Georg was delighted to have a daughter, who was named Ariadne Georgina for Richard Strauss's operatic heroine. The boy was named Tulin Paul; his second name honoured Paul Hoffmann and the first was an invention by two-year-old Boris. While Sue was in hospital the cellist Betty Fenton, sister of the String Players' new concertmaster Moira Fenton, came to help on the farm. One day she was in the kitchen trying to chat with Mizzi over the noise that Boris was making. She tried to stop him, but he was unaccustomed to being told to behave and took no notice. Finally Betty gave him a good spanking. 'Good for you!' Mizzi said. 'I've been wanting to do that for a long time!' Visitors felt very sorry for Mizzi, suffering from back pain and trigeminal neuralgia, trying to cope with a household that was manifestly beyond her.

'From my conventional New Zealand viewpoint the house was chaos,' recalls Moira Fenton's husband, Graeme Craw, who occasionally helped with farm work:

> Dogs and kids running around, twins with no pants or nappies doing their thing on the floor. Mizzi shovelling coal with kids running around her. She seemed incapable of doing it, seeming always on the point of tears. And Georg with his own agenda, which was very powerful.[7]

Georg and Sue were still raising their children according to their principles of free expression, even allowing them to damage books and scores. Nevertheless, when Demas wanted a toy gun, Georg flatly refused. He gave in only when Annemarie pointed out that if he didn't Demas would steal one from someone else, and theft was worse. Demas was now at school and proving uncontrollable, prompting his teacher (and music lover) Margaret Hoyle to tell Georg he was a very bad father. Almost anything went, although Georg's principles were sorely tested when the children broke his batons in sword-fights, and when Demas set fire to the

cat. He would sit them down and give them long, earnest moral
lectures about their transgressions; Boris wished 'he would just
give me a bashing like every other kid and get it over with'.[8] Georg
once told me the story of a couple he knew, both psychologists,
who subscribed to similar theories of childrearing. The child asked
the parents if he might saw the legs off the piano and, in order not
to stunt his development, they agreed. 'That was taking things a
bit *too* far', he conceded.

In 1951, in an attempt to raise standards, Broadcasting created
the Auckland Radio Concert Orchestra from the 1YA Studio
Orchestra and the 1ZB Salon Orchestra.[*] They were therefore put
out when the Music Council ignored their orchestra and invited
the String Players to open the 1952 Auckland festival. 'The Music
Council…thought Mr Tintner's appeal as an established conductor
of serious works [sic] would be superior to that of Mr Cheesman,'
John Proudfoot wrote acidly to Bill Yates. 'Therefore the String
Players (amateur) will provide the concert…I hope that in this
festival, Mr Tintner among local conductors may enjoy undivided
Dorothea Turner's partisan plaudits.'[9] The concert took place on
1 July, with a program both difficult and lengthy: the Herbert
Howells Elegy, Elgar's Serenade, Beethoven's First Piano Concerto
with Tessa Birnie, his Eighth Symphony, and Schoenberg's
*Transfigured Night* – the last three receiving their first Auckland
performances. Georg had conducted the Schoenberg for the first
time in a studio broadcast on 20 April, as a trial run, and by the
end the musicians were so moved they were all in tears. Although
he was sure they would never play it as well again, the concert was
a sensation, and a turning point in his career. Under the headline
'String Players Achieve New Triumph – Standard Set for Festival',
the *Herald* said:

> From the moment the Auckland String Players opened
> their concert at the Town Hall last night it was obvious that
> the months intervening between this and their last concert
> have seen another rung passed on the ladder of our musical

* Julius Hogben told Yates in 1950: 'Last year there were two combinations of players in Auckland, one at 1YA and one at 1ZB. Neither of them could be honestly said to make any contribution of value to music or entertainment; neither was any credit to the Broadcasting Service. I know of nobody in Auckland who differs from this statement.' (Letter to John Schroder, Deputy Director of Broadcasting, 16 January 1950. Archives New Zealand, NZBC archive, AADL 793 Box 3 pt. 1).

progress. By the time the interval had been reached one was
certain that Mr Tintner and his players had not only achieved
their greatest triumph to date, but that they had set for the
music festival a standard of distinction which is the more
satisfactory because it comes from local musicians.[10]

Rex Fairburn wrote to Georg the next day that 'I haven't been
so musically uplifted for years. I salute you – incomparably the
finest musician in New Zealand.'[11] Also in the audience that night
was the respected composer Alfred Hill, born in New Zealand,
resident in Australia. His wife Mirrie recalls:

He was very taken with the conductorship of this semi-
amateur orchestra, so they asked him to speak after the
concert. He didn't know the conductor, only by name, and
asked about him and was told that this conductor was a
foreigner and very interested in conducting, but he lived
out of Auckland, where he and his wife kept a poultry farm.
So Alfred got up and addressed this crowded audience…He
began, 'I want to tell you that my wife says the silliest thing
on two legs is poultry. I think there are some people that are
sillier. They are the people of this city that would let a man
keep a poultry farm instead of conducting an orchestra.'

At a luncheon the following day Hill announced that Georg
was a genius, and that he should be made conductor of the
National Orchestra when Michael Bowles went on leave in April
1953. The *Herald* reported: 'There was no need to scour Europe
for a successor to Mr Bowles, said Mr Hill; Mr Tintner could
take the post. He should at least be given the chance.'[12] Antony
Alpers, Katherine Mansfield's biographer, wrote to the *Listener*,
the national weekly broadcasting magazine:

I should like to add my voice to Mr Hill's. Mr Tintner's
musicianship is outstanding, and he has the force that can
accomplish remarkable things; what he has done here with
the largely amateur talent of the Auckland String Players
has already given proof of this. His background is European,
and yet he has the energy of the new world. Moreover he
can evidently respond to a wide range of composers, an

important point in a country where a conductor may not
specialise; although he has taste, he is versatile. To come down
to particularities, his musical ear is impeccable; no false note
ever escapes it. And his beat (I speak from a few months'
observation as a humble member of the choral basses) is always
clear and meaningful, and never a means of showing off...
I have noticed that Mr Tintner inspires a quite extraordinary
personal loyalty in amateur musicians who have worked
with him.[13]

L. D. Austin, the conductor of Wellington's De Luxe Cinema
Orchestra and an indefatigable writer of caustic letters to editors,
complained: 'I have never been able to understand the fervour of
certain New Zealanders for foreign domination of our musical
scene when native talent as good, or better, is available,'[14] and
he recommended New Zealander Warwick Braithwaite for the
position. The discussion continued in the local and national press
for weeks. But to the suggestion that Georg take over the National
Orchestra, Broadcasting responded with stony silence.* After years
of conflict over the studio orchestra, compounded by the disputes
over the Brahms Requiem and Haydn *Seasons*, they cordially
detested him. According to Rewa Bissett, a violinist in the String
Players, 'He was ostracised a bit by the bigwigs in Wellington.
They treated him a bit as if he was lucky to be here.'[15] Their
hostility extended even to Les Thompson, who found his listening
privileges at the 1YA record library withdrawn because of his
'friendship with a certain Austrian gentleman'.[16]

On 18 October Georg performed a work he had long wanted
to do: Beethoven's *Missa Solemnis*, its first New Zealand performance. It had taken him five years to build a choir capable of doing
it, and this time he used his String Players augmented by wind
and brass from the Radio Orchestra. He taught the choir Central
European Latin pronunciation instead of that of Anglophone
countries: *de-tsendit de tsoe-lis*, *genitum* with a hard *g* (and also *quem*
as in 'qvack'). He had only three two-hour rehearsals with an
undersized orchestra, but the performance was judged a triumph,
if a somewhat flawed one.

---

\*     Broadcasting hired Warwick Braithwaite as interim conductor.

Less than a month later he returned to opera for the first time in fourteen years. At the end of November he presented a ten-night season of Smetana's *Bartered Bride* with the Amateur Opera Company, with Betty Spiro as Mařenka, Ramon Opie as Jeník, and with nineteen-year-old Auckland mezzo Heather Begg* singing a minor role. 'There was, first of all, the satisfaction of a production that was wholly local [for the first time in New Zealand], and then, as the opera proceeded, the thrill of discovering that ambition and venture had not outrun capabilities, but instead abundantly justified themselves.'[17] It was, said a *Herald* editorial, 'a milestone on the road of the city's musical development'.[18] Georg was the toast of musical Auckland.

---

\* Heather Begg (1932–2009) had an illustrious career, which included many years at the English National Opera and Covent Garden. 'Do you ever think of the days when I arrived practically daily at your place in Auckland,' Georg wrote to her twenty years later at a dark time in his life, 'and said "Have you practised today?" We had interesting sessions together and I still hear your lovely voice and great musical feeling and understanding singing my *Frühling*. Like from another world.'

*Ten*

Georg had come to the conclusion that he had achieved all he could in Auckland and was contemplating a change, encouraged by his friend Robert Pikler, who thought he should get off the poultry farm and go to Australia. He had also lost his closest musical friend, Les Thompson, who had gone to England in the middle of 1952 to study with Edmund Rubbra in Oxford. Les consulted Egon Wellesz, also living in Oxford, who recommended Georg move to America. Both Georg and Sue were against it; Sue said she could never live there because 'where could I get my cup of tea?'

There was no prospect of advancement anywhere in New Zealand. It still had no opera company or conservatory, and the National Orchestra in Wellington remained the sole (non-studio) professional orchestra. Georg also had difficulties with local musicians, who found him too demanding. George Poore, Auckland's leading flute player, complained, 'Tintner is difficult to work with. He insists we play softly [in the flute chords at the beginning of Mendelssohn's *Midsummer Night's Dream* Overture] but when we do it goes out of tune!'[1] In the words of Ken Wilson, 'Georg made musicians uneasy because they saw his knowledge, his ear and his dedication, and thought, "If *that* is a musician – then I'm not".'[2]

According to Dickie Hoffmann, 'Georg had the typical Central European arrogance towards the cultureless New Zealanders who were "imbeciles" – people like Owen Jensen, who didn't know an up-bow from a down-bow. But justified or not, it was not appreciated.'[3] 'Unfortunately Georg told everyone what he thought of them,' says Suse Hubscher. 'They weren't very good in those days – people who could play five tunes on the piano thought they were experts…You couldn't tell people they sang out of tune, you had to say, "How very nice".'[4]

Georg's womanising was no secret – some thought he was happy to have it known – but he didn't realise that what was acceptable in Vienna was considered extreme moral turpitude in New Zealand. He was also a known Communist sympathiser at a time when the Cold War was at its zenith. 'Unconventional, that was the word – unconventional,' says Graeme Craw. 'People said to me: "That silly little man".'[5]

Sue was considered no less strange. To please Georg she still wore her long hair loose, and what was worse, she did it at concerts, the only woman to do so apart from the poet Helen Shaw, Frank Hofmann's wife. She believed in conventional behaviour for everyone but Georg and herself, who were special. Despite having gone to New Zealand partly to escape her family and upbringing, she was very British, and in a way some of their refugee friends understood to mean 'not Continental'. She spoke in a manner some thought snobbish (about to make a new acquaintance, she asked Georg, 'Are they frightfully pukka, darling?'), though she spoke with the accent Broadcasting's announcers affected in order to sound like the BBC. She stayed in the background at post-concert receptions, seeming puzzled by artists, surly and almost defiant. She dressed in a manner as unconventional as Georg's, often in sandals and a long gypsy skirt or dirndl. Ruth Pearl recalls:

> She was rather beautiful, wore a black dress, and had bare feet with hen shit between the toes. At least that's how I remember her. She seemed deliberately unkempt. She hadn't a clue what Georg was about. She gave the impression that the musical life was all rather weird, rather foreign to her. She looked like a farmer's wife. I thought, what a funny couple. They seemed mismatched. She didn't do the conductor's wife thing very well, and Georg hadn't enough experience to tell her how to do it.[6]

Even with more experience Georg would not have given Sue instructions, for he didn't care about how a conductor's wife, or even a conductor, should behave, especially at public functions. Post-concert receptions were a necessary evil, nothing more.

'Sue didn't know how to cope with such a single minded egocentric,'[7] says Ruth Pearl. But Sue remained loyal to him and always looked after him to the best of her ability. Their friends regarded her as a tower of strength, even noble, and she was admired by everyone who knew her except Annemarie. Despite working hard on the farm all day, she found time to write out some of Georg's compositions for him, though she didn't even read music. She copied even his most complicated works in a neat and careful script, and one can only marvel at the results. But this was loyalty, not adoration. She hated his affairs with other women, which she saw as the behaviour of 'these volatile Europeans'. She once thanked Marjorie Thompson for helping out at the farm by saying, 'I'm not one of these bloody Austrians who can be all over you, but I'm very grateful all the same.' She never gave up the attitudes of the huntin', shootin' and fishin' set, and was offended when Georg criticised them. She was growing less tolerant of his views, just as his dietary restrictions became more severe. He was convinced she was addicted to tea and tried to stop her from drinking it, to which she replied that she fed the tea leaves to her plants so it couldn't be all that bad. When she brought Demas to tea at the Thompsons she would feed him chocolate cake with a conspiratorial look.

Marjorie Thompson believes that had Sue not thought it would do irreparable damage to Georg's career, she would have left him by the time the Thompsons moved to England in 1952.

In January 1953 Georg made a visit to the Cambridge Music School to perform Bruckner's Mass in F minor in the original version, published in 1944. It was enormously important to him.

> Fortunately the Choralparts are almost the same except for the dynamic and Tempodirection which being in German the Choir fortunately does not understand anyway. The Stringparts are just usable with a lot of additions and omissions (some parts had to be written again) and the whole Windsection I had to rewrite (much more than 100 pages). I don't feel sorry for myself in the least, I enjoyed it immensely but the old timefactor! What is incredible is not that the score is utterly different…what is so frightening is that after seeing the Original anybody can immediately see the patchwork of the usual one and yet it was accepted and loved (by me for instance) and no one of these Brucknerlovers saw these conductors retusches for what they were; I believe, it shows our limitation of perception! It also shows that it is hardly

possible to ruin a wonderful work of Art (with misguided love at any rate). Strangly to say the choir and Orchestra seems to love it…

This work made me into a musician and the little I am (no false coquettery here!) I thank mainly the wonders that singing this work did to me.[8]

Georg rehearsed and conducted the complete work from memory, in its first New Zealand outing.* 'I never tried harder in my life,' he said later. 'I conducted the Kyrie and the Benedictus as though my life would depend on it, and in a way I suppose it did.'

On 30 May the String Players participated in a concert celebrating the coronation of Queen Elizabeth: Vaughan Williams's *Flourish for a Coronation* and, more oddly, his *Tallis Fantasy*, a contemplative work ill-suited to such an occasion. Sitting in the festive Town Hall audience was Harold Williams, Australia's leading baritone, who was so impressed by Georg's conducting that he told him he would recommend him to the National Opera of Australia. Perhaps encouraged by this, Georg wrote to Alfred Hill, who had just been awarded the Order of the British Empire:

> May one who does not usually think overmuch of orders and honours express his unqualified joy on the long overdue recognition of your sterling personality. What a pleasure it was for me to have met in you, Mr Hill, a man who just says what he feels, is enthusiastic and straightforward! And as I told you before: you have been the first important musician who has been very kind to me ever since I came to NZ 13 years ago; and I will never forget it…I am toying with the idea of travelling abroad next season should my affairs not prosper here. If I go over† Australia may I pay my respects in person?[9]

Hill replied immediately with some suggestions and stated: 'It does not surprise me that you wish to seek a larger field for your talents and I will do everything I can to help you, should you

---

*    In the middle of the performance the bassoon player's reed broke, so Georg sang his part.

†    This is a mistranslation of the German *über*, here meaning 'via'. Although Hill spoke German, he may have assumed Georg meant 'over *to* Australia'. It is interesting to speculate whether one mistranslated word resulted in Georg's spending decades in Australia instead of going further afield as he clearly intended.

come to Sydney.'[10] Hill was as good as his word. Having already heard about Georg from Harold Williams, the National Opera of Australia offered him work within a few weeks, hiring him for its tour of New Zealand to take place in the first few months of 1954. He was to select and train a New Zealand contingent of singers and musicians and conduct some performances, and if all went well the company would offer him a job in Australia. Early in October Georg resigned from both the String Players and the Choral Society, effective at the end of 1953, and announced his new position. At the same time he received word of an engagement with the National Orchestra, for the week of 23 November. Broadcasting had found itself with six weeks free between Braithwaite's first and second interim terms, and they filled the time with studio broadcasts.

On 17 October Georg conducted his penultimate Choral Society concert: Beethoven's *Christ on the Mount of Olives* (a work he loved and promoted at every opportunity) and the first New Zealand (public) performance of Bruckner's Mass in F minor. He used the String Players with extras, and the country's best soloists: Mina Foley, Heather Begg, Ramon Opie and Ashley Pollock. The *Herald*'s L. C. M. Saunders wrote:

> But for one man's fervent enthusiasm for one of the 19th cen-
> tury's most neglected great composers, Auckland would have
> missed a choral performance that for an hour touched off a
> mood of spiritual feeling rarely created in the concert hall. It
> was not surprising that this was in every way Mr Tintner's
> night. Both before and after the concert he received ovations
> whose warmth indicated that the very large audience realised
> how great a blow will be dealt to Auckland music by his
> departure at the end of the year.[11]

As a parting gift the choir presented Georg with a recording of the performance on four open-reel tapes. Three of them were among the very few possessions he owned at the end of his life.

He conducted his final Auckland String Players concert on 14 and 16 November, and the following week went to Wellington where, from memory, he conducted a live-to-air broadcast that included the original 1878/80 version of Bruckner's Symphony No. 4. The broadcast ran a little longer than expected, and when it came time for the news the studio cut it off, obliterating the last six

*Georg in 1953. The position of his left hand was characteristic and earned him the nickname 'The Claw' in Australia.*

minutes or so. Georg, not seeing the red light go out, continued to the end.

His conducting of the Bruckner made an enormous impression on one of the National Orchestra's horn players. Many years later he would be responsible for another turning point in Georg's life.

The National Opera of Australia, Sydney's first permanent opera company, was formed in 1948 by Clarice Lorenz, the independently wealthy wife of a rich Sydney optometrist, and was first known as the National Opera of New South Wales. It gave its first performances in 1951, and in 1952 it added Melbourne performances in conjunction with the National Theatre Movement, a Melbourne opera company begun by Gertrude Johnson in 1939. But Lorenz and Johnson didn't get on, and they never again collaborated. So little did they like each other that Lorenz planned her 1954 tour of New Zealand to score a competitive advantage.

The season began in Auckland with 102 artists including some of Australia's best singers: Tais Taras, Ronald Dowd, Gladys

Mawson, Margreta Elkins, Betty Prentice, Geoffrey Chard and Neil Easton, plus conductors Dimo Galiungi and Warwick Braithwaite. Georg also hired twenty-one-year-old Heather Begg to sing Azucena in *Il Trovatore*, her professional debut. In addition to *Trovatore* the season included *Faust*, *Il Tabarro* and *Gianni Schicchi*, *La Bohème*, *The Barber of Seville* and *Il Seraglio*, the last three conducted by Georg. Early reviews were mixed, which was no surprise given that the full company had been together for hardly more than a weekend and the Australians had arrived under-rehearsed. One Australian musician was so inadequate that Georg insisted he be paid off and sent home.

A week after the Wellington season began the *Dominion* critic penned an editorial:

> After seeing a superb performance of *The Barber of Seville* by the National Opera, of Sydney, I would like to pay a tribute to the conductor, George Tintner…Mr Tintner's performance caused some to express surprise at the necessity of the NBS to go outside New Zealand to find a conductor to succeed Warwick Braithwaite as director of the National Orchestra (assuming the services of Mr Tintner were available). He conducted this opera without a score – an extraordinary feat of memory – and never missed a beat. Moreover, there was something magnetic in his energetic, yet unobtrusive manner on the podium, for he was in complete charge throughout. What share he had in producing the orchestra's lovely string tone I do not know, but throughout a lengthy experience I have never heard an operatic orchestra used with such delicacy and effect in accompaniment as was the case in *The Barber*.[12]

If Georg saw the item, he can only have smiled sadly. He had already applied for the National Orchestra job when it was advertised the previous November. As in 1949, British applications were solicited and screened by the BBC; they noted that one applicant, Lionel Salter, was 'Jewish probably, which is not said either in his favour or against him.' There were several applicants from Australia, and four from New Zealand including Georg and Alex Lindsay. William Yates did not bother to forward the New Zealand applications to the selection committee. The job was given to the BBC's selection, the Englishman James Robertson. Georg received his rejection letter in February.

Despite enthusiastic reviews the Wellington season sold poorly until the final few days, and the same happened in Christchurch. The company was now in serious financial trouble. The singers had not been paid for three weeks and some refused to continue. They gave lunchtime concerts to raise money, and the tour continued to Timaru, Dunedin and Invercargill – but only after Clarice Lorenz had flown from Australia with the unpaid salaries, apparently her own money, in banknotes in her handbag. She announced at the same time that Warwick Braithwaite would become the artistic director of the company after his National Orchestra term expired in August. The company returned to Australia at the end of May, leaving behind £1800 worth of unpaid bills.[13]

Georg spent a few last days at the farm, and departed for Sydney on 31 May to become resident conductor of the National Opera. Attached to New Zealand – where 'I felt for the first time, in practice, the equality of man' – Georg did not want to go to Australia at all. Some of his friends were horrified that he was going to 'that horrible, vulgar place'. But Sue had persuaded him that if he didn't take the opportunity he would never forgive himself. He would try it out, and if all went well the rest of the family would follow as soon as possible.

*Part II*
*1954–1965*

## Eleven

The Sydney season began in early June 1954 at the Empire Theatre in Railway Square. Georg conducted *The Barber of Seville*, *La Bohème* and, for his Australian debut, *Il Seraglio* – all from memory. Most critics agreed that under Georg's direction the orchestra, a scratch band, was much improved, but there was extensive criticism of the singing, acting and production. The first night of *Seraglio* was marred by a production disaster. As Osmin climbed an enormous tree, comprising the entire set, it toppled slowly onto the stage, to reveal four stagehands in shorts and singlets sitting around a table drinking beer and playing cards. Audience and stagehands stared at each other in astonishment until the stage manager could be found to bring the curtain down.

Georg's best review was for *The Barber of Seville*, which in the opinion of the *Sydney Morning Herald* 'included much trim and alert orchestral playing under Georg Tintner, a conductor whose wide sympathies and sensitivity have been among the few out-standing features of the current season'.[1] *Il Seraglio* and *Bohème* were broadcast by the Australian Broadcasting Commission, though Georg received no fee for it; at the time the ABC did not pay the conductor of broadcast opera on the grounds he could not actually be heard.

His debut had gone reasonably well, but he was altogether miserable and homesick, living in a seedy hotel room in a rough and grimy city of 1.8 million people. He found himself doubly a 'bloody foreigner', not only a 'German' but a New Zealander as well. He was outraged when someone told him, 'New Zealand is the only country we can afford to despise'. He also found he had to open a bank account, in spite of his belief that banks were usurers, and that earning interest was at somebody else's expense and therefore pernicious. Not to earn it was the only way to keep money in the bank with a reasonably clear conscience. As all savings accounts at the time paid interest, he found himself in some moral discomfort.

In his first week Georg came to a decision he considered one of the great milestones of his life. He realised that he could never kill another animal – something he had often done as a necessary part of farming:

> When I sat alone in that hotel room in Sydney – I learned afterwards that many people had committed suicide in that particular hotel, I didn't know that then – when I sat there I suddenly felt, I will *never* do any of the killing I had to do on the farm again, *whatever happens*. And as I didn't want to do it myself I didn't want anybody else to do it for me. I always hated it but I thought, well, that's part of life and that has to be. But after thirty-seven years I'm a living proof that it *doesn't* have to be. And may I make a prediction too – perhaps in a hundred or two hundred years people will *marvel* at the cruelty that is going on at the moment.[2]
>
> Alfred Hill invited me to come and visit him – he lived in Mosman. I had no idea about the distances of Sydney; I thought it was like in Auckland. I think I walked five hours until I got to his place, probably not the nearest way either. I arrived there pretty exhausted, and Mrs Hill, Mirrie, his second wife, she was a highly intelligent woman – a bad composer but highly intelligent – they waited with the food for me. She gave me a perfectly ordinary meal of chops, and I couldn't touch it. I will never know exactly why, but the strange thing was – as I say, she was very clever – she said, 'Are you perhaps a vegetarian?' *I said Yes!* And that's how it was.[3]

Georg wrote of his conversion to the Thompsons, who had long been vegetarians, and apologised for ridiculing them in the past. Far from being pleased, Les well knew Georg's inclination to extremism and said worriedly, 'He will go all the way.' When Annemarie heard the news she wept, convinced he was going to kill himself.

About three weeks after his conversion Sue made a brief trip to Sydney and arranged for him to live with distant relatives of hers in the prosperous seaside suburb of Dover Heights. She had no understanding of Georg's new creed. Had he been a vegetarian when they first met, or become one soon afterward, she would have embraced it wholeheartedly, but now it was just another of Georg's peculiar ideas – his dietary austerity gone to extremes.

In his first few days in Australia Georg also decided that he would give up womanising and devote all his energy, including his sexual energy, to composing. He had also begun to feel guilty about the pain he had caused Sue – and he may unconsciously have no longer felt the need to assert himself, removed as he was from the element of competition in their relationship. It was now ten years since he had begun his opera, but it was progressing only fitfully. Shortly before leaving New Zealand he sent a copy of the violin sonata to Josef Marx, who had replied:

> Dear excellent Tintner – What lovely, pleasant memories of youth your name conjures up…You are now happy in a peaceful country, endowed with nature, family, music and much positive work – that is great fortune! I congratulate you most heartily…Above all else I am delighted that the truly talented and sensitive [zart] little Tintner wields his baton on the podium, and conducts many different 'standard works' from memory. I have also looked at your Sonata with pleasure; but one thing: you must write much to loosen the wrist, and imagination will also become more 'willing'.[4]

A few years later Marx told the conductor Karl Rankl: 'The trouble with Tintner was that he was very talented but he was persecuted. He had absolute pitch, he had a beautiful voice and was shy, so as a Lutheran [sic] he was persecuted by the boys and then by the rector in the Vienna Boys Choir. Then he was in the desert of New Zealand.'[5]

At the end of July there was a week of performances in Newcastle, but the company found itself in financial trouble almost immediately. They limped on to Brisbane for a three-week season, and from there Georg wrote to Douglas Lilburn:

> I long for New Zealand (not only my own little stake in it.)
> I am not unsuccessful here…but if there were anything in
> Auckland I would race back.

> Things are still very uncertain. It would be madness to
> break up the farm before I have security in Australia. But
> even should I get this security, it will break some part of my
> heart.
>
> I think I have changed a lot. I have become a convinced
> Vegetarian. I think I am much milder and I hope a bit kinder.
> Where will life land me?[6]

When the Brisbane season finished at the end of August the
company disbanded for the rest of the year. The singers, accompanied by Georg, gave lunchtime fundraising concerts, but there
was no possibility of making a living as a singer. A few performed
at clubs, Masonic evenings and Ladies' Nights, but it would not
have occurred to them that singing was anything but a hobby, or
something one did until settling down with a family and getting
a real job. Neil Warren-Smith, whose career began in the mid-
1950s, was a butcher. Ailene Fischer was a milliner, and Raymond
McDonald was a carpenter and sometime milkman.[*]

Georg gratefully returned to Auckland early in September, 'for
how long I cannot say', he wrote to Douglas Lilburn. 'That depends
largely on the fortunes of my strange Company. Your information
about the fusion of the 2 Australian Companies [National Opera
and National Theatre Movement] is highly premature (to say the
least). The 2 ladies in charge of either do their utmost to prevent
such a reasonable solution. Mr Braithwaite allows himself to assist
Mrs L[orenz] in this nefarious activity!'[7]

By the end of the year Georg had, as Les Thompson predicted,
taken his vegetarianism to the extreme. He was now an ardent
vegan.

> I was an ordinary vegetarian for about three [months] and
> then I came back to our farm in New Zealand. I loved to
> milk the cows, and my eldest son's duty was to get the con-
> tainer of milk for me to drink. I still remember him coming
> with that container, and I said, 'I don't want it, I don't want
> it today'. What happened in the meantime was, I suddenly
> realised it all depends *why* you are a vegetarian. If you are a
> vegetarian for health reasons then I can't see any reason why

---

[*]    When McDonald stood in for an ailing Ronald Dowd as Otello in 1958, the newspapers breathlessly
       reported that a milko had come to the rescue.

you shouldn't drink milk, eat eggs, all that sort of thing, but I was becoming a vegetarian entirely for [ethical reasons]… Next to music it is the most important thing for me, to be a vegetarian.

For Georg there was no halfway position – on anything. Not only did he eliminate all animal products but he wouldn't even touch them, or eat anything that had been in contact with them. He also refused honey, because the commercial farming of bees involved killing the queen. He knew that old cows, old hens, old horses, were simply disposed of when no longer commercially viable. He used soaps made without tallow, and he wore no leather, and no wool, because the wool industry also involved killing. His view was that man did not have dominion over the animals, and had no right to exploit them, not even to keep them as pets.

He went to singers' recitals and sat in the front row, shelling and eating peas or demolishing a bag of green plums, oblivious to the stares of others. Not surprisingly, his colleagues considered him a crackpot. Although he was passionate about his views he never tried to convert anyone to vegetarianism, let alone veganism, but he was sneered at all the same. The amount of ridicule he encountered, mainly in Australia, was remarkable, given that the worst of which he could be accused was an excess of compassion.

Georg's conversion to veganism effected a profound transformation. He wrote to me that he was once 'a very "angry young man".' The description puzzles his friends of the early years, who remember him as a warm and happy person full of enthusiasms. Yet the anger and grief over being deprived of his culture and his glittering career, of always being made to feel different, of not being accepted either by Jews or non-Jews, was held deep inside, unexpressed except in his compositions. 'But all that has greatly minimised itself since I have become a vegan,' he said many years later.

It was a *burning* question before; it is not now. I still know it is there, but it is unimportant…There's no doubt that I'm physically a completely different person, I'm not saying healthier or better or anything, but completely different. But the main change is with the soul – yes, the main change is there…I have never felt that I miss something for a principle…It is the one thing in my life where I can say – only for me, not for anybody else – 'I did the right thing. And I did well'...And that of course does give one a feeling of rest, or repose, or something.[8]

In the forty-five years Georg was a vegan he did not knowingly consume even the tiniest morsel from an animal. 'One's convictions are measured by the fact there are no exceptions,' he would say. When a radio host once asked him, 'Do you ever miss anything in the dark of the night and say, "I wish I didn't believe it to be a crime against the world to have a hamburger"?' Georg replied, 'The contrary is true. If I would miss it for one second I would eat it immediately, because I would feel that I have failed. But there is not the slightest danger that I would, because the will is a very strange thing, and very powerful.'[9]

Though Georg claimed 'I don't have the religious faculty', his fanatical devotion to both music and veganism were entirely religious in nature; his conversion to veganism as much a sublimation to a higher good and ethical belief as any religious conversion. A journalist once asked him if Bruckner as 'spiritual food' was not an odd choice for a conductor who claimed not to be religious. Georg replied:

Do you think that only a religious man can conduct the *St Matthew Passion*? I disagree with you there. When I say I'm not religious, I mean that I do not believe in any creed. I do not believe in a deity, to be honest. But my other strong ethical feelings, being a vegetarian, not trying to earn a lot of money – this is also belief, in its way. And the very greatest composers are beyond such classifications. Bruckner was a deeply religious man, we all know that. But what he created speaks even to sinners like me.[10]

Cellist Paul Andreas Mahr studied conducting with Georg in the 1990s and maintains that Georg

spent his life wilfully avoiding God. For him, the God who would permit World War II and the other sufferings of this world both great and small, was abhorrent. And yet, I never saw him more alive than when he conducted the Messiah.

Within this personal turmoil he set out to balance the saint (music, diet, hypothetical pacifism) and sinner (women, reality) within him. Yet he thirsted for God, a thirst completely unquenched…It is not possible to conduct the Messiah, or Bruckner for that matter, as he did, if one doesn't believe in God. Rationally he may not have believed, but on an intrinsic human level it had to be in his heart…His attempts at a secular humanism bear great resemblance to the core teachings of the Bible. This, I believe, was no mere coincidence.[11]

Music was the supreme creation he worshipped. Veganism provided the basis of his moral code: to be kind to every living creature. The practice of veganism required rigorous discipline and, especially in the early days, considerable hardship. Georg saw it not as a burden but as a welcome adjunct to his enlightenment.* Most people thought him an ascetic, not only because of his diet but because of his devout anti-materialism. But this is not what he was. Georg never denied himself anything he wanted, except other men's wives. What others desired he simply didn't want.

Georg's moral framework created the impression that he had arrived at an understanding of Life and how it functioned, yet he was a fundamentally irrational man. And the trouble with self-disciplinary rules – especially of the strict black and white variety – is that they are incompatible with the instinctive, and in Georg's case largely subconscious, nature of artistic temperament. He never did manage to make it all work.

The trouble with becoming a vegan was that Georg had not the slightest idea how to feed himself. He bought a sack of peanuts in the belief they would provide adequate nutrition. His hair forthwith turned grey, though he was well short of forty. In due course he became very sick. He was amazed, for he was sure he could manage on conviction and willpower.

I became a vegan almost without transition, and though my mind was ready my body was not and I was very ill for about

---

\* There was even a devotional air about the way he prepared his food, though it was probably unconscious. His daily breathing exercises were in the same line: if not a spiritual, at least a meditational, act. He had learned them in the Vienna Boys' Choir and done them every day since, no matter where he was. People in airports or buses were disconcerted to see him quite unselfconsciously sitting bolt upright and holding his breath.

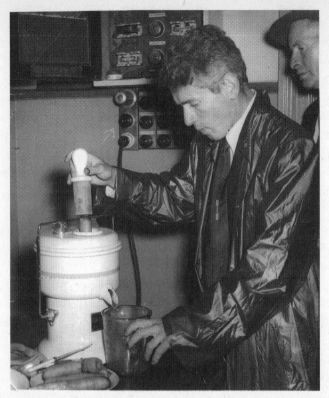

*Georg backstage with his prized juicer – a curiosity in 1950s Australia.*

three months…even the vegetarian experts said, 'Unless you eat a quart of yoghurt every day and things like that you will die but if you are lucky you may get TB instead of dying.' I said, 'I will not die and I will not get TB and I will not eat your yoghurt anyway because I know what I must do', and I think that was perhaps the one brave thing I did in my whole life…I didn't know anything about nutrition when I started it but I learned it the hard way.[12]

He bought a juicer for £25, the better part of a week's wages, and began a serious study of nutrition. It was far from easy in 1950s Australia, where rejecting meat verged on the unpatriotic. Literature on the subject was virtually non-existent, and the sort of foods he needed were difficult to find. Most importantly he learned about Vitamin B12, found almost exclusively in animal foods and isolated only in 1948, a lack of which causes pernicious anaemia and eventually death. He had to import vegetable-based tablets from England, where vegetarians were less rare. Within a few years his knowledge of nutrition was better than that of almost anyone in the country.

When Georg returned to Australia in December he took a room in a boarding house at 226 Bourke Street, Darlinghurst. It was a run-down Victorian terrace house where trucks thundered past a metre or two from the door, and the air was black with diesel. Prostitutes loitered on the footpath and the local pubs were full of men whose aim was to get as drunk as possible before closing time at six. Early in 1955 Georg wrote to Douglas Lilburn:

> I lead a strange and very strenuous existence. With last years Australian savings I aquired 2 possessions: 1.) a new upright Piano…and a bicycle (a very lovely one too with gears). I think apart from the Telegram-boys I am the only person who rides a bike in the heart of Sydney, but you know often ignorance is bliss and I enjoy it much more than driving a car. I live in most primitive circumstances with a very nice seventy year old Landlady who seems a bit too old to keep things very clean. I like her though. Unfortunately I am not the only 'guest' in the house. One of my 2 confreres is a habitual drunkard. He has reached the stage of having given up his job just getting up for the Hotel hours 'resting' the rest of the day and shouting continually at night…[13]

Georg was not entirely friendless in Sydney. The National Opera had also hired Heather Begg, and she was joined by two other New Zealand singers: Dorothy Hitch and Jean Reeve. The three took a single room in another dismal terrace house on Bourke Street, and some of the little fun Georg had was spent in their company.

Jean had first encountered Georg in the Auckland Choral Society, joined his harmony classes and fallen in love with him. Aged about thirty, she followed him to Sydney, and devoted herself single-mindedly to his care: doing his laundry, his ironing, and running his errands. She looked after him on country tours as well, while working as wardrobe mistress and singer of minor roles. But while Georg was very fond of Jean he was not in love with her. He gave her no reason to suppose he would leave Sue for her, but Jean was sure that the marriage was all but over. Others among Georg's

*Jean Reeve.*

closer acquaintances had the same impression. He spoke of Sue with appreciation, but with little affection. Nevertheless, Georg made no attempt to seduce Jean. Some singers saw her as Georg's 'puppy dog', his 'captive', and were angry with him for exploiting her good nature. The more cynical thought they should just go to bed together and get it over with. Once Jean arose in the middle of the night, penned a love letter in a script completely unlike her normal handwriting, and the next morning had no recollection of having done it.

It was five years before she finally gave up. She returned to New Zealand in the middle of 1959 and had a complete breakdown. She came to the conclusion, without any bitterness, that if she were to have any sort of life she must eliminate all trace of Georg from it. Two years passed before they were in touch again, when Georg wrote to tell her he had 'COMMITTED ADULTERY with RAELENE',* apparently without wondering how Jean might feel. She always remembered the capital letters. A few years later, after she

---

\* This name has been changed.

had made a happy marriage to someone utterly unlike him, they resumed occasional friendly contact. Whenever Georg spoke of her, he referred to her as an angel.

Though the National Opera had not solved its financial problems, it put on a seven-week season of six operas beginning in mid-February 1955. Georg was rehearsing up to three sessions per day, and reducing opera orchestrations for Braithwaite until well after midnight. He was also working for Eugene Goossens, principal conductor of the Sydney Symphony Orchestra, who 'paid me miserably', coaching singers for *Rosenkavalier* and adjusting his scores.

On 17 March, halfway through the opera season, Braithwaite abruptly resigned on 'artistic grounds'. According to répétiteur Megan Evans, he was 'a stirrer', telling singers what to do about money and to stand up for their rights. He was followed by producer Robin Lovejoy and twelve of the principal singers. The company was by then burdened with an accumulated debt of more than £30,000. The singers, supported by Braithwaite, demanded that the executive resign, including Clarice Lorenz. She declined. In a letter to Douglas Lilburn, Georg wrote:

> Things here are completely upside down. Braithwaite started strife and argument within the Company against Mrs Lorenz. He says it was for artistic reasons. It is most upsetting and is dragging everything to ruin...
>
> I am longing to be out of all this strife and in a little hut being able to think and dream. I wonder whether I could attain this modest ideal. I try to. But unfortunately I have to live.[14]

The company stopped paying the singers' salaries, and the two final performances went on only because the singers took over the box office and kept the proceeds. According to Georg, Braithwaite, 'who had a contract, demanded a year's salary and got on the next plane to England'.[15]

The National Opera was not shut down, but both the Brisbane and Newcastle seasons were cancelled. Georg's only prospect of work was the government-funded Elizabethan Theatre Trust, founded the previous year in honour of the Queen's visit to

Australia, which was in the process of forming opera, drama and ballet companies. Georg wrote to Lilburn, 'Mr B. obviously conspired with the Elizabethan Trust and I think my chances to get in there are practically nil according to the latest rather shameful developments.* Never mind I try to keep going. We shall see.' He kept himself occupied as he had done in Yugoslavia, by writing strict musical exercises. Georg's self-discipline was always at its most rigorous when trying to fend off despair.

He found some work accompanying for the singing lessons of Madame Marianne Mathy, a German Jewish refugee who arrived in Australia in 1939. She paid Georg very badly; he told a friend she tried to starve him. Eventually they fell out, although almost certainly not over money. Georg likely told her she was teaching incorrectly. He also found some work coaching *Idomeneo* for an ABC broadcast to be conducted by Joseph Post, the only conductor Georg encountered in Australia or New Zealand who was well disposed towards him. And he coached privately from a dismal room near Wynyard Station, charging hardly enough to cover the rent. Mezzo-soprano Mary Blake recalls:

> Everyone said, if you can get him to coach you, you'll never do better. You learnt your part and never forgot it. I've never known a coach like him – he was so meticulous. I remember the triplets in the Habanera in *Carmen*. Georg said, 'Miss Blake, what you must do is you must observe the three equal triplets. There is nothing more sexy or more sensual than those three equal triplets.'[16]

He became known as the best coach in Australia – a doubtful honour for someone whose sights were set so much higher.

It was the Australian Broadcasting Commission that kept him going for the rest of 1955. The ABC ran six professional Australian orchestras, one in each state capital, and was responsible for extensive orchestral and recital series countrywide, as well as all classical broadcasting. Georg had wasted no time in auditioning for them in July 1954, conducting the first movement of Bruckner's Fourth Symphony from memory and impressing many of the musicians,

---

* It has not been possible to determine what the 'shameful developments' were. However, in the time I knew Georg he remarked on just two people in Australia he found to be anti-Semitic. One of them was Warwick Braithwaite.

who had never seen such a thing before. 'Of course I was unpre-pared,' he said to Keith Jacobs afterwards, the sort of remark he made from time to time that his colleagues saw as gratingly false humility. He was approved, and they gave him some studio work – mostly half-hour broadcasts, a few with the Sydney Symphony and most with the Sydney String Orchestra. He programmed Hans Gál's Serenade on 30 April, and on 11 August the first Australian performance of the Act I Prelude from Pfitzner's opera *Palestrina* ('I was in heaven'), for which he wrote out the parts himself. He also insisted that the ABC consider Lilburn's Second Symphony,* and Georg gave its first Australian performance on 7 April, his first ABC broadcast. He wrote to Lilburn that 'the more intelligent members of the Orchestra were greatly impressed, especially by the first movement which is *most* beautiful. I still think the Finale is too long…'[17] Georg continued promoting the work, supported by the ABC's New South Wales Supervisor of Music, Werner Baer, but nothing came of it. Georg reported sadly eighteen months later:

> I tried so hard. If you were an *Australian* they might play it once a week. Strange differences! But they need local music to make up their quota. Even I here count as an outsider (New Zealander). The world is a funny place.[18]

---

\* The assessment of the Federal Music Officer, composer John Antill, was: 'In a brief look through the score it appears to be a work of merit, and is well worthy of performance. There are no new innovations apparent harmonically or melodically. In fact, the subjects are not very melodious in themselves and the structure, as a whole, gives a fragmentary impression, but the subjects are joined together fairly skillfully and could sound well. It is fairly well orchestrated, although in places it would rely on conductor's discretion, as parts could be covered. It is brassy in places and overpowering occasionally. The last movement becomes a little vague and padded. The subject matter could have been said in shorter terms with better effect.' (1 March 1955, National Archives of Australia, ABC archive, C663/T1 Box 94).

## Twelve

Georg was finding his room in Darlinghurst unbearable. He located a narrow half-acre of land at the end of Lantana Avenue on the Collaroy Plateau, twenty-four kilometres north of the city. He bought it for £725 and moved there in May. Collaroy Plateau is now a prosperous suburb overlooking the northern beaches, but in 1955 it was almost uninhabited bushland and few people, apart from Jean Reeve and an occasional intrepid piano student, trekked out to visit him. Georg travelled to the city by bicycle; only in bad weather did he take the double-decker bus, where he could be found sitting upstairs at the front, eating peanuts and scattering the shells around him.

The property boasted a shabby one-roomed fibro shack with a small verandah. The tenor Raymond McDonald, a carpenter by profession, fixed it up to a minimum habitable condition. It was unsewered and Georg dug all wastes into the ground. He washed outside under a tap, with water collected from the roof into a tank. There was no electricity and no heat; Georg wrote by candlelight until he was too cold to go on, sitting at a table that was his only furniture except for his upright piano and a mattress on the floor. He tried to grow vegetables but the soil was poor and wallabies ate whatever came up. A blue-tongued lizard lived on the verandah, and every morning the air was filled with the sounds of cockatoos, magpies and kookaburras. Georg thought it was paradise.

The isolation was good for him, and the next few years were the most productive since 1944. Now that he was both underemployed and free of the hard work of the farm, he promptly began a work entitled *Chaconne and Fugue on a Theme of J. Brewster-Jones,*\* which he dedicated to Alfred Hill. He completed it by early September and entered it in a competition for a work based on any theme by

---

\*    Hooper Josse (Josiah) Brewster-Jones (1887–1949): Adelaide pianist, composer and music critic.

the Adelaide musician. He submitted it under the name Diogenes, the alias he always used. It was an apt choice. Much of the Cynic philosopher's ideology resembled his own: to eat a vegetarian diet and to live in the most basic of conditions, free from dependence on material goods, in the pursuit of virtue. As Georg believed in meritocracies rather than aristocracies, he particularly enjoyed Diogenes's reply to Alexander the Great when he asked what he could do for him: 'Stand out of my light.'*

The work was unplaced, but at Joseph Post's suggestion he submitted it to the ABC. John Antill, the Federal Music Editor, judged it to have 'technical ingenuity more than inspiration'[1] but recommended it for performance. Georg conducted it in a studio broadcast with the Sydney Symphony Orchestra the following year.

As 1955 wore on, however, he became increasingly disheartened about his prospects. He applied for the position of director of the new conservatorium in Brisbane, which paid a respectable £2500 a year. Alfred Hill wrote in support:

> I think this musician is of such a stature that you should send for him and personally view his great possibilities. With my experience of five years at the Leipzig Conservatorium and as one of the founders of the NSW Conservatorium I should be able to know the type of musician and man who could make the Brisbane Conservatorium worthy of your great State and Australia. I have observed Mr Tintner's work here and in New Zealand and believe he is the man you are looking for. He is more than *good*. He is a genius.[2]

Two weeks later the Conservatorium appointed Dr William Lovelock,† from Trinity College in London. Georg wrote to Lilburn:

---

\*    Georg differed from Diogenes on one important point. Diogenes believed that masturbation was much better than sex with another because it saved time. Georg was of the opposite opinion, and once told the startled members of a youth orchestra that masturbation was much overrated.

†    Georg may have been fortunate to miss out. He thought nothing of the way music (especially theory) was taught in English-speaking countries and would have taught according to Continental methods. This would almost certainly have brought him into conflict with the Conservatorium board, which included a dentist and the director of a fashion store. Lovelock, with much more acceptable English training and a conservative outlook, lasted only three years before resigning over 'intolerable petty supervision'. (National Library of Australia, Hobcroft Papers, MS 8019 Box 8, folders 65–7).

Without any selfpity I must say I am passing through an
exceedingly difficult phase of my life (the most difficult I
hope it to be). However I am not all down and out. The 2
positive experiences I had lately was 1) I got to know and
admire almost without limit a great Artist and wonderful
human being Hephzibah Menuhin, she is wonderfully good
and kind to me and 2.) on her request I founded a choir with
patients of the Mental Hospital [at Callan Park] which gives
me great satisfaction and pleasure. It is wonderful to see these
people who seem so utterly sane (if there is such a thing)
taking an interest and being so kind.[3]

Hephzibah Menuhin and Georg became lifelong friends: 'She
is straight', he said, 'in difference to her brother.'[4] Hephzibah said
Georg knew more about music than anyone she had ever met.[5]
Georg was considerably less fond of Hephzibah's second husband
Richard Hauser, also a Viennese refugee, and was mystified by
her devotion to him. He once asked her why she had married
him and she replied, 'Because he's the only man I know who is
cleverer than I am.' The Hausers were social reformers, and one
of Hephzibah's projects was music therapy for the mentally ill. She,
Dorothy Hitch and Jean Reeve all sang in Georg's choir. This was
work he loved, and he spent several weeks teaching the choristers
Mozart's 'Ave verum', in English, and wrote a short piece for
them, 'Kookaburras Every Morning'. He was delighted to find
that disturbed and violent people became calm; he said singing was
just what they needed. According to Hephzibah, Georg was like
electric shock treatment.

His hospital work was interrupted by a National Opera
country tour of Madam Butterfly, funded by the state Arts Councils.
Georg conducted from the piano, performing from memory 'about
10 times weekly' until his fingers bled. He had an infection on his
hands, which he treated with indelible liniment. Audiences were
transfixed by the sight of his bright red fingers running up and
down the keyboard and jabbing cues at the singers.

It was a gruelling tour; the New South Wales portion included
twenty-two evening shows and several matinees in nineteen locations in twenty-six days, with a few lunchtime recitals thrown in
for good measure. In 'snobbish Tamworth' Georg 'blushed with
shame when I learned that some Cinemas here practise racial

*Georg rehearsing the cast of the National Opera's 1956* Madam Butterfly *tour at the Plunkett Street School in Woolloomooloo. Heather Begg is on the far left.*

segregation for the Aborigines. Good old New Zealand!' The troupe lived on a train, known as the Opera Express, which was coupled to a succession of goods trains, a few kilometres at a time. It afforded 'cramped quarters, frayed tempers, limited hot water for showers, disturbed sleep on noisy sidings, wild after-show parties and romances'.[6] In the north of the state they were delayed by severe flooding, and in rain-soaked Casino they performed with frogs hopping about in the glare of the footlights. In Lismore the love duet between Butterfly and Pinkerton was interrupted by a blood-curdling scream from Heather Begg, who went to an unlit toilet behind the hall and sat on a toad.

The company returned to Sydney for a break on 10 March to find that the Taxation Department had begun proceedings to close down the National Opera for unpaid taxes. By then it had an overdraft of £40,000 and the bank was no longer honouring its cheques. Nevertheless, the troupe set out again for Queensland at the end of May, for seven weeks. They travelled 1600 kilometres along the coast as far as Cairns and Atherton and inland to towns

such as Charters Towers and Murgon. Georg shared a cabin with
a new Pinkerton, Walter Rychtowski, who took exception to his
daily rituals. He announced to the others in his Polish accent, 'I
am *very shocked*. That Georg Tintner, he *sleep naked*. He sleep in top
bunk, he come down and stand on his head for five minutes then
jump up and down. I am *married man!*'[7]

Later that year, in Auckland on 21 November, Georg accompanied Heather Begg at her benefit concert for study in England,
his only concert appearance in the second half of 1956. It gave him
the opportunity to spend a few weeks with his family, his first since
a three-day visit a year earlier. He arrived with a large quantity of
glacé pineapple and papaya, luxury items, which he handed out
to the children as a reward for good school results. According to
Boris, 'Georg gave up on Freud and decided to try behaviourism.'

The farm, however, was struggling. That year the egg price
in New Zealand collapsed, even for Sue's beautiful prize-winning
produce. She sold property in England, the last of her inheritance,
but she made little from it because the Suez crisis caused the pound
sterling to fall. Georg urgently needed to make money. Studio
broadcasts were welcome but poorly paid, and the ABC showed
no inclination to give him a concert; they did not do so until the
end of 1958, an outdoor performance at the Moore Park Athletics
Field. Jean Reeve recalls:

> Laudable though it was that he sent home as much money
> as possible, it was regrettable that he always looked shabby,
> refusing to buy clothes. The people who mattered in the
> Sydney musical scene held this against him. We who knew
> him well were quite unconcerned (a little amused sometimes)
> by some of his more unorthodox practices such as breath-
> ing exercises on the edge of the footpath, but the starchily
> conservative in musically high places...[8]

When the ABC's Werner Baer took him to lunch with other
senior officials at one of Sydney's best restaurants, Georg offended
them by ignoring the menu and instead shelling peas from a brown
paper bag in his overcoat pocket. The ABC held a monopoly
on non-theatre professional orchestras in Australia; being on the
wrong side of it was, for a conductor, the kiss of death. Georg
could not see – or did not care – that his actions would be viewed

with hostility and derision in the conformist Australia of the 1950s. In his opinion he would stand or fall by his talent; everything else was irrelevant. 'That was the stupidity of us migrants,' says Melbourne composer and critic Felix Werder, a refugee from Berlin. 'I feel sorry for Georg, because he didn't have my cynicism. He was not a political animal.'[9]

At the end of 1956 James Robertson resigned from the National Orchestra. Georg, still longing to return to New Zealand, applied for the third time. But Robertson, who only knew Georg from an Auckland prom concert they had shared in 1955 to his own critical disadvantage, wrote to William Yates: 'I take it that no one will press Tintner – even your kindly orchestra might revolt.'[10] The job went to the Englishman John Hopkins. Georg never tried again.

Broadcasting's practice of hiring the BBC's choice, however, was at an end. Fred Turnovsky,* a member of the selection committee, relates in his memoirs:

> The usual procedure was for the job to be advertised, in Britain only…The BBC was asked to interview applicants, and submit a short list of three names, in order of merit. I was told that, on previous occasions, the BBC list was accepted without demur, and the first named candidate appointed. The whole procedure was over in an hour.

This time the selection committee decided to reject the BBC's first two choices and hire its third, John Hopkins. 'I still remember the consternation on the face of the chairman, Director of Broadcasting Bill Yates, who said in disbelief, "But gentlemen, you are voting against the recommendation of the BBC!"'[11]

Georg began 1957 conducting at the New Education Fellowship summer school in the country town of Bathurst. He coached at several schools in his early years in Australia, and at one of the earliest he met another Viennese refugee, Dr Robert King. Half-Jewish Robert König had fled to Holland, but was caught there by the Nazis. He was released only after claiming that he could not possibly be a Jew because he wasn't circumcised, and dropping

---

*    Turnovsky, an amateur pianist and music lover, was a Czech refugee who arrived in Wellington in 1940 and became a successful leather goods manufacturer. He played a leading role in the early years of the Wellington Chamber Music Society and New Zealand Opera.

*Robert King around 1991.*

his trousers to prove it. In Australia he became a teacher, claiming to have a doctorate in philosophy and psychology, and taught at private schools in Sydney. He ran salons to discuss philosophy and the arts, presiding guru-like over a circle of admirers. He took an interest in the teachings of Krishnamurti and Madame Blavatsky, often taking a sceptical Georg to Theosophical Society meetings. Though Georg always thought there was an element of the *Hochstapler** in him, Robert loved him and served him well in many ways – not least in providing frequent accommodation and housekeeping services. After he died his fourth wife went in search of his early life in Vienna, and discovered that not only had he no doctorate, but no university education at all. He had been an assistant in a bookbindery. Robert König had made his way to Australia and reinvented himself.

Early in 1957 Georg was scheduled for another National Opera tour, this one through Queensland, New South Wales and

---

*      A word of which Georg was fond: impostor, confidence trickster.

Victoria and again funded by state Arts Councils. He chose Auber's *Fra Diavolo* and selected the singers, including Rosalind Keene and the New Zealand tenor Ramon Opie whom he was keen to introduce to Australia. Another was the young tenor and motor mechanic Gino Zancanaro, who first met Georg at an audition in the National Opera's rooms in Phillip Street in Sydney. Georg's studio was in the basement and his chair and piano stood on bricks, islands in water and sewage that flowed across the floor. He asked Gino, also standing on bricks, if he could sing a high C and he replied, 'Of course!' though he had no idea what a 'high C' was. Georg liked what he heard and invited him to his Collaroy hut for further rehearsal. Armed only with Georg's poor directions Zancanaro became hopelessly lost. He stumbled across paddocks and through barbed wire fences, trekking towards a light in the distance, and fell into a moat. 'My friend', Georg said when he finally arrived with a torn shirt and covered in mud, 'you are three and half hours late.' They rehearsed late into the night, with the cobwebs that stretched from ceiling to piano glistening in the candlelight.

As the tour was about to depart the National Opera was finally closed down. Clarice Lorenz lost her company and all her money, and her husband's money as well. In just a handful of years she had put on more than 1500 fully staged performances of twenty-one operas, giving many artists employment and the opportunity to develop their singing and stagecraft. With her dream destroyed she fell into obscurity and alcoholism, and she drowned in 1981. Her brother gave her a cheap funeral in the working class suburb of Botany. Only one singer attended.

The Elizabethan Trust took over the tour but cancelled the weeks in southern New South Wales and Victoria. Georg turned forty in those empty weeks, and when Jean Reeve offered her congratulations he said it was 'a day of tragedy'. He was, at least, still composing. The opera had progressed (Zancanaro remembers it to have been 'well along' on the tour), and he was working on *The Ellipse*, a chamber work he began in 1954 or 1955. For the Elizabethan Trust's short-lived ballet company he created *Ballet Academy*, arrangements for two pianos, which was performed (with John Antill's *Wakooka*) throughout Australia the same year. Whether he was paid anything for it is unknown; he certainly received no royalties. Hoping to win some much-needed money

he entered a song and a piano piece in a 1957 competition run by
New Zealand Broadcasting. Neither won, but both were highly
commended, and were broadcast later in the year.

In the middle of 1957 the Elizabethan Theatre Trust needed
extra staff for a challenging season of four and a half months – *Tosca*,
*La Bohème*, *Tales of Hoffmann*, *Otello* and *Bartered Bride* in several
capital cities. They hired Georg as coach and associate conductor
at a weekly wage of £30, soon raised to £40. Australian sopranos
Joan Hammond and Elsie Morison were brought from Europe, and
the local talent included Joy Mammen, Wilma Whitney, Gregory
Dempsey, John Shaw, Alan Light, Neil Warren-Smith and John
Germain. In Newcastle Georg replaced an ailing Joseph Post and
conducted *La Bohème* from memory, causing a sensation. By the
end of the season he was established at the Trust, which was much
more secure than the National Opera had ever been – and it had
one invaluable asset unavailable to Clarice Lorenz: the use of the
ABC orchestras virtually cost-free. The Trust assured Georg that
annual seasons of six months would continue, and at last he felt
secure enough to bring his family to Australia.

He asked Jean Reeve to look at a house he had found in a
newspaper advertisement, giving her five or six hundred pounds
in cash and telling her to buy it if she thought it suitable. What he
failed to tell her was that he needed it to house not only himself
but his wife and four children, his mother and his aunt. Seeing
it was no worse than his hut, Jean bought it – a two-bedroom
dwelling on fifteen acres in the countryside at Rossmore, well
to the west of Sydney beyond Liverpool. By Christmas Georg
had moved there, and he began a fast to purify himself in mind
and body, and to purge his desires. He kept it up for thirty
days, consuming only water (and producing a bowel movement
around the twelfth day, to his and Jean's surprise). Of all his
many fasts over the years, this was the one of which he remained
most proud.

With the 1958 Trust season scheduled only for the second half
of the year, he survived on the slim earnings from coaching and
little casual work he could find. Every Friday he cycled fifty kilometres into Sydney to accompany singers at lunchtime recitals in
Hyde Park, on a piano deposited on the grass in the open air, and
at operatic recitals around town. One night he was accompanying
at the Hunters Hill Music Club when a very large moth landed

on the keyboard. In the middle of the aria Georg stopped and, without a word to either singers or audience, picked up the moth, said, 'You must be careful, I don't want to hurt you!' and took it outside.

On 9 May the Sydney Symphony Orchestra under Nikolai Malko played Georg's orchestration of his piano piece 'Trauermusik', a finalist in the ABC's composers' competition. He won third prize of £50 but the critics thought little of the work. Martin Long in the *Sydney Morning Herald* wrote: '*Sad Music* was more in the tradition of composers' competitions – a conventionally designed, competently scored elegy, lacking any strongly individual melodic ideas.'[12] *Canon* thought that 'all four finalists emerged as genuine craftsmen but none of them dared to depart from well-established methods.'[13] Georg was running foul of the new orthodoxy, the strict serialism dictated by the Darmstadt School (Stockhausen, Boulez and others). 'Old-fashioned' was out; one must be new at all costs. But for Georg it was important only that the music was good, regardless of the idiom. 'Composing means "putting notes together" – nothing more,' he often said. But for many others at the time, the method was the message. Georg can only have despaired in 1953 when he read an item by Ernestine Haight, the *Auckland Star*'s critic:

> A musical revolt against romanticism occurred in this century; today most composers overseas prefer music that is objective and impersonal in approach. Music which has a complex, contrapuntal texture, and which concentrates on perfection of line and beauty of proportion. Because our composers are lagging behind this world-wide movement, their music lacks the freshness and excitement, the challenging strangeness it should have. For the most part, listening to it is too easy, too pedestrian.[14]

On 6 June Sue and the children arrived in Sydney. When Sue saw what was to be her new home, her new farm – a grossly inadequate house on hardscrabble, ugly brown country – she was appalled. 'Georg never even looked at it,' she said bitterly. It was not a good beginning.

A fortnight after the family's arrival Georg left for three weeks in Brisbane, the beginning of the overly ambitious 1958 Trust season directed by Karl Rankl*: *Carmen, The Barber of Seville, Lohengrin, Fidelio* (receiving its Sydney premiere) and the Australian premiere of Britten's *Peter Grimes*. But Australia wasn't ready for such a modern opera and it was poorly attended in every city.[†] Georg was allocated a few performances of *Fidelio* and *Carmen*, which he conducted from memory. Rankl pointed out that it was a very young company where mistakes were made all the time, and told Georg the orchestra would feel much more secure if he used a score. Georg was furious. According to Rankl's wife Christine, he 'took it very personally. He was incredibly sensitive to any criticism'.[15] Rankl altogether had little time for Georg. When he wanted him at a rehearsal, he asked, 'Where is the grass-eater?'[16]

While in Melbourne, Rankl fell out of a tram when it started suddenly, and broke both wrists. He conducted the first night of *Peter Grimes* and then withdrew, leaving Georg to take over at short notice. At the end of the season he wrote to Douglas Lilburn:

> I was lucky to conduct the two operas I perhaps admire most. *Fidelio* (which I love more than anything else on the stage) and *Carmen* perhaps the most perfect Opera, greatly under-rated by the pundits because of its 'light' quality. Furthermore I conducted *Peter Grimes*. An uneven work with excellent and lesser passages. I think it suffers from an unsympathetic libretto and a certain 'slickness' but it is masterly in every note. (I had success.)[17]

When the season ended in Adelaide, in late November, the Trust announced that it had lost almost £100,000 and would cancel the 1959 season. Georg, with everyone else, was laid off until 1960. He had brought his family to Australia on the Trust's assurance of continuing employment and it had proven chimerical. And now there was no farm income to keep them going. Sue was growing potatoes and cut flowers, which Georg, when he wasn't touring, delivered to Flemington Markets in the city. But despite

---

\*    Karl Rankl (1898–1968), a Schoenberg student and conductor at Klemperer's Kroll Opera, arrived in England as a refugee from Austria in 1939. He was music director of Covent Garden from 1946 to 1951.

†    Dr William Lovelock, director of the Queensland Conservatorium, told university students that composers 'want to probe the emotions to their sub-conscious roots. Unfortunately when they go down so far, you usually find utterly sordid and depressing music – music which is not noble, and plots that are unpleasant'. He cited *Peter Grimes* (and Alban Berg's *Wozzeck*) as an example, objecting in particular to 'excruciating dissonance'.

her best efforts nothing did well because the ground was afflicted with rising salt.

It was yet another blow to their relationship, already suffering from four years' separation. Sue had never understood Georg as an artist, and he had now altered beyond her comprehension. She never came to terms with his vegetarianism, and refused to become a vegetarian herself. He complained that Sue had become fat, a failing about which Georg, despite his vow of perpetual kindness, was invariably merciless.* Unwilling to let Georg's principles interfere with the children's pleasure Sue bought them horses, which were hidden on a neighbouring property whenever Georg happened to be in Sydney. The horses always found their way home and the children had to come up with lame explanations for their presence. According to Boris, the children saw Georg's return from touring as 'a bit of a pain, because there was a list of things we had to pretend we didn't do'.[18]

Georg had long held that Sue was not bringing up the children as he thought they should. He objected to the way Sue indulged Demas, the apple of her eye, allowing him to bully his siblings with impunity. Demas had by then decided he wanted to be 'not a good boy' and was behaving accordingly. More than one person noted how little warmth and touching there was in the family and how little contact there was between Georg and Sue; a lack of small talk, a lack of love. The children had no respect for Georg, thinking him 'a wayward nut'.[19] The words of Gino Zancanaro, who observed the family at the time. Author's interview, 10 October 2001. As they weren't musical they had few points of contact with him. Especially for the twins, only two years old when he left for Australia, he was almost a stranger. Georg's children hardly knew him, and by then didn't much care to get to know him.

At the end of September Mizzi and Thilde moved to Australia and squeezed into the house in Rossmore. Mizzi had gone to stay with Annemarie in New Plymouth in 1954 when Georg left for Australia; Thilde had joined them from London in 1957. And now Sue was burdened once again with in-laws she detested. Mizzi and Thilde argued loudly and often about German poetry, but as Sue spoke no German she assumed they were fighting in earnest.

---

* Georg thought nothing of commenting loudly on overweight people in the street, and lost more than one friend by being cruel about her size. One of them never forgave him for telling her jovially she had 'the willpower of a louse'.

'I thought she was a *saint* to have Georg's mother *and* aunt staying with her', says one of Georg's friends, 'and wish I had had the courage to tell him so! Can you imagine those two old European-Jewish ladies on a farm in New South Wales?'[20] Sue treated them with disdain, driving Georg to despair. He begged her not to be nasty to them, and she would answer, 'But what do I say?' He replied that it was not what she said but how she said it. In his view Sue was treating Mizzi and Thilde with the arrogance the British reserved for 'foreigners'. Much later he said that she may have been jealous. If he were paying them attention he was no longer giving to her, it would hardly have been surprising.

## Thirteen

The Arts Council rescued Georg early in 1959 by hiring him for a four-state country tour of *The Barber of Seville*. It was the first of several they presented over the years using Trust personnel: on this tour Rosalind Keene, John Germain, Alan Light, Neil Warren-Smith and the tenor Donald Smith, all at the beginning of their careers. Georg was the sole pianist–conductor, except in Victoria where they had the luxury of an additional string quartet and flute. They travelled through Victoria to South Australia, across New South Wales and into Queensland, to the far north, and back to Sydney. Scenery, costumes, wigs and two casts were carried in a dilapidated bus known as the Monster. No matter how tightly closed the windows were, the bus sucked in so much fine dust that the singers had to wear surgical masks. If it went around a bend too fast the windows fell in, and as it clattered over rough roads the stage scenery fell around and splintered, making it hazardous to handle.

They went to a new town almost every day, some scarcely more than a name on a map, or a single street where goats stood on the cars to nibble at trees. They played in shire halls, sheds, whatever was the town's largest space, on stages that were some-times no more than three tables pushed together. The tour began in Bairnsdale, Victoria, on 9 February (where the performance was interrupted when the stage curtains caught fire) and except for a week off in Sydney in March the company was on the road for exactly three months. Audience members drove hundreds of kilometres to fill the halls, and over the years the Arts Council productions, no matter how basic, were much loved. Even decades later people sought Georg out at concerts to tell him how impor-tant the performances had been to them.

After the tour was over the ABC gave Georg a couple of broadcasts with the Sydney String Orchestra, and a televised

*The Monster, used for years to transport singers, costumes and scenery around Australia on Elizabethan Theatre Trust opera tours.*

opera. Television began in Australia in November 1956, in time for the Olympic Games in Melbourne, and only a month later the ABC began broadcasting fully costumed and staged operas in prime time under the supervision of Englishman Anthony Hughes, former manager of John Barbirolli. The scope of the series – several operas each year – and the productions themselves were remarkably ambitious, especially given the newness of the medium. In June of 1959 Georg conducted *Cavalleria Rusticana*, with Florence Taylor, Alan Ferris, Neil Easton and the Sydney Symphony. It had several complicated sets and it was also live to air, a nerve-racking experience for Georg because the orchestra was placed where he couldn't see the singers. In September he conducted Donizetti's *Rita*, and thereafter operas were pre-recorded on the new medium of videotape. Live to air was just too dangerous.

It was while rehearsing these operas that Georg met a shy young man who worked for the ABC 'putting up the chairs', and they spent many hours discussing music. His name was John Brown, and he would transform the last thirty years of Georg's life.

Sometime in 1959, after four or five years' work, Georg completed *The Ellipse*. Just sixteen minutes long,* he considered it and the violin sonata his best pieces. 'All the five movements want to describe feelings, not events. But feelings *about* events – and important events at that.'[1] He gave the work its odd title because 'it is a piece of autobiography, and what is left out is as important as what is in. So, instead of a circle, it's just an ellipse – with pieces missing.' Possibly modelled on Schoenberg's String Quartet No. 2, it is scored for string quartet and soprano, who sings in the first and third movements to German texts and in the fifth movement to an English text. He wrote the piece 'feeling very much alone', without benefit of a muse, or even sex, at least with anyone other than Sue on his occasional home visits, and even that is doubtful. Robert King claimed that Georg could not bring himself to touch her because she was handling animals. If true – and he was fanatical enough for it to be so – it can only have done yet more damage to an already ailing marriage, especially one that according to Georg was 'based on sex, in its deepest and most fundamental importance'.[2]

The three vocal movements are written in the language of fifty years earlier; the two instrumental movements contain sections of twelve-tone music and are 'bordering, without ever entering, atonality'.[3] The first movement, *Da oben auf dem Berge*, was written for the pregnant Hephzibah Menuhin and completed on 1 September 1956 (Clara was born exactly three months later). Hephzibah's name is written into the cello and second violin parts near the end: H–E–B–C–B–A (B, E, B flat, C, B flat, A in English notation). He considered the tune of this movement to be 'a "perfect melody" the best I ever invented or will ever be able to invent (probably)'.[4] At the time he wrote it he was giving much thought to what a 'perfect melody' really was, and he found at least three: the second tune of the Adagio of Bruckner's Seventh Symphony, the beginning of Schubert's Ninth, and the first tune of Mozart's Minuet and Country Dance K. 463 No. 1.

The second movement, purely instrumental,

> deals with the hardships and difficulties of my life. It is extremely complex and difficult, and when I say that, don't

---

\*    Georg was always very accurate in estimating the duration of other composers' pieces, but he told more than one person that *The Ellipse* was twenty-seven minutes long. His gross over-estimation shows how important the work was to him.

think for a moment that I'm proud of it. There was a composer between the two wars, Bernard van Dieren, who once boasted that only five people in the whole world can play his music. Well, I think there's nothing to boast about in that. It is very sad if one can't express oneself more simply than that. So, my difficulties and complexities come from a deficiency, probably, not from a particularly good brain. You will hear notes of defiance, and perhaps Kafkaesque horror too.[5]

The third movement is a setting of a short poem by Ludwig Tieck, 'Feldeinwärts flog ein Vögelein' ('Into the field flew a little bird'). The theme was inspired by sunlight playing on the golden curls of his son Boris, and is Georg's attempt to describe the 'joys of childhood' – perhaps not only that of his children but of his own, lost when he entered the Boys' Choir. The song had a remarkable effect on one of the singers in the 1956 *Butterfly* tour, Harry Quick, who was given to jealous rages over his girlfriend Ailene Fischer. 'All I know is that when on a country tour we had a rather violent Tenor in our Company; he once threatened to throw our Prima Donna out of a window (2nd floor) when he thought she had flirted with someone else...THIS SONG about the little bird was the *only* thing in the whole wide world that pacified him. The reaction was always instantaneous!! What music can do...'[6]

The fourth movement, again instrumental only,

wants to be beautiful. Beautiful in the old fashioned sense of the word, although the music is dealing with more recent language. But in the middle of it all there comes again the hard reality of life, and another of these horribly difficult fugues is coming on, and then the movement goes backwards from where it started...The only thing that interests me in music is *feeling*. I know it's a terribly old fashioned word in Art; some people think Art and feeling have nothing to do with each other. Well, I beg to differ. And if [the work] means anything to you, it doesn't matter whether you hear all the contrary motions and all these so called clever things, or the fact that in some movements the bar line is never at the same place in various instruments – it only made it harder for [the musicians], it has no significance to you. The significance *if any* is in the feeling.[7]

*The Trysting Tree*, the final movement, 'is about loneliness and disappointment'.

> Something is gone from these hillsides,
> A light, a loveliness, where we three
> Whispered alone on eventide –
> My love, and I, and the trysting-tree…
> Long we commune, but now, alas,
> Only I and the trysting-tree.[8]

Georg told the Thompsons that the poem, by Australian James Devaney, 'meant something to me at the time', and it is not difficult to see why: so much promise in his own life had turned to nothing. He was no more than a staff conductor for a shaky part-time opera company, receiving little critical notice because the music director normally took the opening nights. He struggled to support his family with interminable tours in the wilderness; the enthusiastic reviews he received there were not taken seriously, if they were seen at all, by those in charge of hiring conductors. He was living in a country where mateship, sport and beer were of mythical importance, where 'elitism' was a pejorative word, and Culture its worst manifestation. The Arts were something pinkos and poofters got up to in the dark of night.

Georg was adrift. He was now forty-two and had no idea where he was going.

John Antill recommended *The Ellipse* for ABC broadcast as 'an interesting score'. It received its first performance early in 1960, performed by Valda Bagnall and four members of the Sydney Symphony: concertmaster Ernest Llewellyn, Donald Hazelwood, Robert Pikler and Lois Simpson. The taping did not go as well as Georg had hoped: it was under-rehearsed, Valda Bagnall was ill, and Llewellyn 'never practised his part; he wanted to be a conductor and never liked me. But the other 3 practised hard and loved it.'[9] Llewellyn was given to baiting Georg; he was the only other musician in Australia Georg described as an anti-Semite.

In January 1960 Georg went to his first National Music Camp, at Geelong Grammar School near Melbourne, which marked the beginning of his enduring and mutual love affair with youth

orchestras. 'Working with young people gives me the strength
to work with others,' he said in a candid moment years later. 'I
think it is wonderful to see their enthusiasm and the wish to learn
and to improve themselves, that is very important for me.' Young
people were the future of music, and he took them very seriously.
He loved them for playing 'with shining eyes', and they loved him
in return. The composer Nigel Westlake never forgot his first
encounter with Georg, as a teenaged clarinettist:

> I was sixteen or seventeen at the time and was totally in awe
> of the musicality and compassion that informed his every
> gesture – whether he was standing in front of the orchestra
> or not. Even though he was a small-framed man, he appeared
> to tower over the orchestra, long white hair shaking, his long
> arms embracing the music and coaxing the sound to perfec-
> tion. He was the source of the music – the keeper of the flame.
> He held all the secrets and the power.[10]

Georg had an electrifying effect on the young people at
camp. They had never encountered anyone like him; a guru-like
person with his Viennese manners, his diet, his enthusiasm and
single-minded dedication to music. Some of them converted to
vegetarianism; many of the girls fell in love with him. According
to Geoffrey Michaels, then a sixteen-year-old violinist, 'The students would have followed him into a sea of writhing snakes.'

Since its inception in 1948, Music Camp had been run as
an event for 'family music-making and fun', but if anyone told
Georg he took no notice. For the First Orchestra he proposed the
Adagietto of Mahler's Fifth Symphony, Schubert's Sixth Symphony,
and Bruckner's Symphony No. 4 – the first Australian performance
of the now standard 1878/80 (Haas) version. Several players still
remember the Bruckner as one of the outstanding events of their
musical lives, even those who didn't play in it. Christine Crane, a
violinist from the Third Orchestra, remembers:

> His influence spread throughout the camp – everyone was
> swept up in his enthusiasm for the music, Bruckner in par-
> ticular. In some ways he seemed to be a direct descendant of
> Bruckner. He meditated on the oval and had a mystic quality,
> which we (or I did anyway) related to Bruckner's strong

religious faith. I had never heard of Bruckner before and I think that was the case for many music campers of the time but soon everyone was a fan.[11]

They rehearsed Bruckner in the mornings with Georg and accompanied concertos in the afternoons with conductor John Bishop, the founder of the Music Camp Association. The students enjoyed the Bruckner so much that they asked the administrator, Ruth Alexander, if the concerto sessions could be replaced with more of it. Bishop was hurt and offended, and Alexander called a meeting to lecture the students on their appalling behaviour in subverting the proper running of the camp. It turned into something of a scandal.

The Schubert and Bruckner were performed at a final concert, which took place on one of the hottest nights of the year. The temperature at start time was still over 38°C (100°F), so Georg offered to wear a thick jumper during the performance while conducting. Christine Crane recalls: 'The players would be wearing short sleeves and could look at the conductor, compare their circumstances, feel cooler and play as if heat was not important. Apparently this worked because the performance was marvellous.'[12] More than a decade later Georg still thought of this performance as his most satisfying musical experience in Australia.

In the opinion of camp officials, however, Georg had 'run away with the camp',[13] and he was not asked back for nineteen years.

The Trust resumed at the beginning of 1960 for six months, with two of Australia's leading singers returned from Europe: tenor Ken Neate and soprano Joan Hammond. Georg conducted a few performances of *The Magic Flute* and *Il Trittico*, and all *Madam Butterfly* performances. Although Hammond, stocky and almost fifty, looked unconvincing as a teenaged geisha she was successful everywhere. So, mostly, was Georg. The composer Dorian le Gallienne, writing in the Melbourne *Age*, remarked that 'Georg Tintner is an arresting conductor, in whom one sensed a conflict between a natural bent towards taut intensity and Puccini's expansively lyrical style'.[14] A less polite version of this was held by a number of singers, who thought Georg didn't understand the flexibility in the beat of Italian opera. As an ex-singer himself,

Georg knew how to breathe with the singers and accommodate their phrasing, but his insistence on preserving the structure of the opera was not compatible with their desire to linger over top notes or rush the difficult bits. Georg 'was a conductor who would rarely compromise', said Neil Warren-Smith, who took minor roles on country tours so Georg could teach him major ones on the bus.

> Tintner had set ideas and would not give them up…As a repe-
> titeur he was never bettered, but for rehearsal and coaching
> purposes, I suppose the unrelenting *as it is written* approach is
> the better one for preparing a performer. For actual perform-
> ance, however, I contend that the personal modifications
> are essential and should be arrived at, preferably in rehearsal.
> Even, when warranted, in performance…But Tintner never
> relaxed the 'authorised' version, as he saw it. Though that
> might sound like a complaint, it's not, because you always
> knew where you stood with him.[15]

*Butterfly* was not very well received in Sydney, where good reviews mattered most. The *Sun* thought 'the Sydney Symphony Orchestra played politely but unexcitingly under Georg Tintner'[16] and the *Observer* termed the playing 'most uninspired', though 'matters improved during the second act'.[17] As bad as this was, much worse was the announcement that the season had made huge losses and there would therefore be no season in 1961.

On 8 August, a week after the season finished, he began an Arts Council tour of *Rigoletto*. The singers included Rosalind Keene, Patricia Wooldridge, Donald Smith, Neil Easton, John Germain, Josef Drewniak and Neil Warren-Smith. It was the longest tour so far: 115 performances in 117 days, in 82 towns and cities over the entire eastern half of Australia. To while away the interminable travel some of the singers played cards, and Donald Smith, somehow seeing everything without lifting his eyes from his cards, would say, 'Kangaroo at nine o'clock…Emu at seven o'clock…' Somewhere on a track in western Queensland they realised they were lost; road signs were painted on bits of galva-nised iron and a local amusement was to point them the wrong way. As they pondered what to do an Aboriginal stockman on a horse appeared silently out of the bush. Georg asked very politely in his German-accented Oxford English, 'Excuse me, my friend, could you please tell us the way to Cloncurry?' There was no reaction. He asked again – still no response. Then Donald Smith, a cane-cutter from Bundaberg, said, 'Ah Christ, Gayorg, let me have a go. Hey Jackie! Which way to the 'Curry?' The stockman immediately pointed and said, 'That way, boss!'

After another delay caused by having to dig the truck out of a dry creek bed, they arrived in Cloncurry around dusk just as locals were setting out to find them. The company still performed that night, going on an hour late and with cracked lips, in a hall where the theatrical lighting was three naked bulbs hanging over the stage.

Almost everywhere the local women's committees provided post-performance receptions, which the singers called Tea and Tinies. There were cakes that sometimes contained big black ants, and lavish quantities of pavlova. Georg would pick the parsley garnish off the sandwiches and ask the singers, 'Would you mind eating a few more sandwiches so I can get at the lettuce?'

Obtaining food was difficult for the singers, but much more so for Georg. He brought non-perishable food with him, and bought what fruit and vegetables he could find on the way. He drank no tea or coffee, only water, and as they went further into Queensland the only supply came from bores. Some of it was bad, and somewhere near Mount Isa Georg became ill with diarrhoea. John Germain recalls:

> Finally he had to admit defeat and buy a bottle of lemonade, which he felt badly about. His tempi got slower, and Ros Keene and Don Smith had to take breaths where they hadn't needed to before. They mentioned to him the tempi were slower, but he said they weren't. But they were, because he was so weak. But he just kept going. We were very worried, because he was our only pianist and conductor and without him we were in trouble. Sometimes his fingers would bleed from playing so much. He had a tremendous ability to stick at something. He wouldn't give in.[18]

Georg was exhausted from the strain of playing so many performances, two and a half hours long, on almost unplayable pianos. In one town it was so cold that by the time they came to 'La donna e mobile' the piano had gone a semitone sharp; at a town hall function in Tamworth one of the city fathers asked Georg proudly how much he thought their piano was worth. 'The wood,' he said grimly. According to Josef Drewniak,

> In some place, Winton or Longreach, only half the notes played, so Georg had to play all over the keyboard in wrong octaves to get enough notes. Anyone else would have tried a few notes of these pianos and refused to play them…Georg was conductor, coach, pianist, handyman. They got a slave for nothing. They knew he had no choice.[19]

Despite the rigours of touring, he still worked on his opera, now about fifteen years old. According to John Germain, some parts were quite well worked out, and some of it Georg seemed to be improvising. He sometimes played a completed aria, 'Oh the Fair One', and become quite entranced. He had already decided that he wanted Donald Smith to sing the lead part of Giovanni.* He asked, 'Excuse me, Mr Smith, but do you think you could sing a top C while lying flat on your back?' 'Ah Christ, Gayorg,' Smith replied, 'it's right in the middle of me voice!' Georg was confident enough to mention the opera to Heather Begg: 'You might be interested to learn that I have started to write an Opera and the heroine is – you. I have your voice and personality in mind writing it. Whether I ever finish it? I hope you feel pleased. It will take me years!'[20]

---

\*     The *dramatis personae* ran to thirteen parts: light soprano, 'dramatic coloratura soprano', character mezzo, contralto, countertenor, lyric tenor, character tenor, *Heldentenor*, high baritone, low baritone, character baritone, bass baritone and basso profundo. The choice of such a large cast, and one that included several hard-to-find voice types, was odd for a man of the theatre; Georg must have known it would render the opera vocally and economically almost impossible to mount.

## Fourteen

Sometime in 1960 Georg was offered a job in Austria – now untraceable – but he turned it down. During the war he swore he would never again set foot in Austria, but by the time he received this offer he had come as far as being interested in a visit. 'It is two months less than twenty years since I saw it the last time,' he wrote to Heather Begg in 1958, 'and though I would not like to live there again (I saw too much) it would be nice to see it and hear all the delightful music.'[1] One can only wonder what could have become of his career had he accepted the job and returned to Europe.

Yet Georg never felt at home in Australia, and indeed never became a citizen. Australians thought Georg's Viennese politeness, which led him to address even quite familiar people as 'Mr This' or 'Miss That', to be pompous and standoffish. He even bowed, which they thought a little ridiculous. He never went to the pub for a beer, an all-important ritual of male bonding. He had no interest in sport in a country that worshipped it. He was incapable of small talk, and he found few people who shared his interests of music and German poetry. 'Nobody would ever dream of inviting Georg to a party,' says Clare Galambos, who knew him from the New Zealand Symphony. 'He wasn't somebody with whom you could chat. Musicians are usually quite gregarious. There are people with whom you can strike up an immediate friendship, but not with Georg. He was buttoned up.'[2]

Georg abjured flattery, thereby making many enemies. But he didn't hesitate to offer what he considered constructive criticism. According to Neil Warren-Smith:

> To be informed in Numurkah when you're tired and cranky that one of your big notes was two or three vibrations short doesn't do much to cheer you up. No good asking him how

one of your performances went in the hope of bolstering your ego. Tintner would tell you the truth. Courteously and gently, he'd inform you that 'apart from a wrong note, some wrong words and uncertainty on tempo, it was fine!' You kept your own standard up for him but he did everything in his power to help you. He gave up hours of his time to coaching us, giving us singing lessons individually and, though he might do nothing towards bolstering our egos, he certainly bolstered our techniques. There were times, however, when we could have wished he didn't have perfect pitch.[*][3]

The pianist and composer Larry Sitsky went to *The Magic Flute* at the Australian Opera in the 1970s, and sat with Georg who was then working for the company. He recalls the performance was:

under the baton of a well-known conductor…This conductor wasn't doing very well – the tempi were turgid, the beat balletic. He allowed the singers to control the flow of the music – they loved him for it, but the music suffered constant starting and stopping because of the propensity of the singers to linger when they hit a 'good' or 'top' note; and there were other purely technical disasters involving balance and so on. Georg and I compared notes and muttered about leaving after Act I…Anyway, after a few performances like this, he obviously couldn't stand it any more. I happened to be backstage when Georg appeared and confronted this conductor and then gave him chapter and verse of all the things that were wrong with his performance. It was the last performance of the season, and the conductor heard him out with increasing agitation. Finally, he said to Georg: 'Why didn't you tell me all this before?' Georg said to him: 'I kept hoping that you would hear it yourself and fix it in the next performance!'[4]

Many colleagues were irritated by what Georg called his 'absolute belief in the letter and spirit of the work of the composers'. He maintained that one must always 'try to [determine] what the composer intended'.

---

[*] Singers enjoyed teasing Georg about his perfect pitch; on tour they would ask him for the pitch of a train whistle. "Well, there's a certain amount of F sharp in it,' Georg would reply thoughtfully, not realising he was being made fun of.

A singer or player should never be allowed a single note not written by the composer. A player can interpret as long as the interpretation does not contradict the stated intentions of the composer. If it does it implies that the player knows better than the composer, which is nonsense. Most composers…are not impractical dreamers with good musical ideas, but are thoroughly experienced operators of their craft. They knew exactly what they were aiming at and performers of their work must try their best to devote all their energy and talent to the fulfilment of those ends.[5]

A score was holy writ and must be respected; he took this to be self-evident. Consequently, there is little to be learned about his interpretations from looking at his scores. Other conductors cover theirs with red and blue pencil; Georg wrote almost nothing but bar numbers.

'Like all my colleagues,' remarks baritone Alan Light,

and like most down to earth Australians, I had something of a dislike for Georg, a suspicion of someone who was such a character, but I and others also had a real wonderment and at times a great appreciation of his immense dedication to music and to his standards of life. He had at times an infuriating and illogical opinion of his abilities, and a terrible pseudo-humility, in manner but not in actuality. And yet somehow most of us could not completely dislike this overly pretentious little man. Would that we had more such characters.[6]

Cellist Paul Mahr, who played for Georg much later, observed:

The tragedy is that at heart he was discounted because he loved music as an amateur would (this is not insult, I mean this as highest, most pure innocence), and that he loved us as musicians in a way that we were incapable of reciprocating.[7]

He was consistently very disappointed in us. We would reach the end of performances and his face would sag; he paused before looking up at us, and then subsequently acknowledging the audience. He had been engaged in a life and death struggle to express the essence of the music; most of the orchestra had gone merely from point A to point B…

> Did music bring him any actual happiness? Being inspired
> and being fulfilled are two very different states. He struck
> [my wife and me] as one of the most profoundly unhappy
> people we ever met.[8]

Georg made his fourth television recording for the ABC in Sydney
in January 1961, of *Il Seraglio*, and a few weeks later began another
tour, of Mozart's *Così fan Tutte* – the longest tour of all. This time,
however, there was a second pianist–conductor, Dorothy Hobart.
They set out on 27 February to tour the length and breadth of New
South Wales and Queensland, giving about 120 performances in
115 days. As before, Georg had to play on terrible pianos, mostly
old uprights played out from community singalongs, toneless from
desiccation in the desert air, or stiff from lack of use. In Cobar, in
central New South Wales, he found the hall piano to be reasonably
in tune with itself but over a tone flat. So was every other piano
in town. As John Germain was finding the part of Don Alfonso
already rather low, Georg played the entire opera transposed up
a semitone, which he found excruciating: his mind heard the
correct pitch, his fingers played another, and his ears heard yet
something else.

The company travelled in the Monster with a driver who lived
on beer; from time to time cans whizzed over the driver's cab.
Singers sat at the front, sweating in the heat and choking on the
fine red dust that came through the floorboards and worked its way
into the costumes and sinuses. As there weren't enough seats Georg
occasionally volunteered to sit in the windowless storage area in
the back. Once, trying to prepare his food in the dark, he spilled a
bag of millet over the costumes. It was impossible to remove all the
tiny grains and the singers suffered through many performances.

Because of the limited seating the second-cast Despina took
to sitting on the floor next to Georg, gazing up at him adoringly.
Raelene was a seductive twenty-six-year-old with dyed red hair,
plenty of make-up, a dazzling smile and a magnificent figure.
She was by all accounts extremely alluring. Many thought of
her as someone who used her assets to advance her career. As
Georg himself said, tours are dangerous things. People who would
normally have little mutual interest are thrown closely together
for long periods, and loved ones are thousands of kilometres and

another world away. As one singer says darkly, 'There are people
all over Sydney who think their father is someone other than who
he really is...'

For seven years Georg had stuck to his resolve not to stray. But
Raelene was too hard to resist. Georg told me that he foolishly
allowed himself to be seduced. 'I have always done [the choosing],'
he wrote to me soon after we met, 'except perhaps once, and
allowing myself that one time to be seduced, wrecked my first
marriage, perhaps partly because it was out of style for me and I
knew it.'[9] He told me shamefacedly, 'I felt I was entitled to beauty,
and Sue wasn't beautiful anymore.'

Had he said nothing to Sue, it is unlikely he would have
been found out. But 'because it was honest' he wrote to her about
Raelene, telling her he was having an affair with a singer and that
he would give her up, but not just yet. Then at short notice he was
called to conduct the New Zealand Opera's Auckland season of
*Don Pasquale*. He left the tour in Rockhampton on 14 May, where
Dorothy Hobart took over, and returned home for a couple of days
before leaving for Auckland. When he arrived, Sue told him that
the marriage was over and she wanted him gone. For Georg it was
a catastrophe. The marriage had long been in a derelict state but it
had never occurred to him that it would ever collapse.

Twenty-six years later he said in an interview:

> I had the greatest admiration for my first wife, and still have
> as a matter of fact...I never thought, whatever I did otherwise,
> that [the marriage] would ever finally break down. I consid-
> ered this woman as a sort of anchor in my life, and when she
> finally had enough it was really a dreadful thing for me.[10]

He always believed that if he had told Sue in person instead
of writing to her, the marriage would have survived. Yet how
she found out likely made no difference. Sue hardly even needed
Georg any more. She had managed without him for four years,
and of the three years since she had arrived in Australia Georg
had been away for more than half of it. Their worlds had diverged
too much: hers as a farmer and his as an itinerant musician. Sue
had already given up thinking that Georg would ever get a secure
position; she certainly blamed him for getting himself shut out
of Broadcasting in New Zealand. She thought him immature,

and that not having a regular job allowed him to stay that way. Times were very lean between Trust seasons, and although Georg was willing to do anything musical he also did some of it unpaid, as he had in Auckland. He enraged Sue by sending what Boris remembers to have been £300 – eight weeks' pay – to a needy musician. She felt that as she had supported Georg in the past, any spare money he had should be spent on the family.

Sue had expended everything she had on Georg: her youth, her support, and her money. Relationships fail when the goodwill runs out. Sue's goodwill had finally expired.

The eight-day run of *Don Pasquale* (with Mary O'Brien, Cyril Kellaway, Noel Mangin and Donald Munro) was deemed by both Auckland newspapers to be the all-round best presentation the Opera had put on in its eight years of existence. On 4 June Georg returned to Australia and went directly to the far northwest of Queensland to resume the *Così* tour and his affair with Raelene. When the tour ended on 30 June he returned to Rossmore, still begging Sue to change her mind, but she was not to be moved. Within a few weeks she had filed for divorce on the grounds of adultery, citing Raelene as co-respondent. Georg was not only anguished but angry that Sue could not tolerate this transgression as she had the others, and he remained angry until the end of his second marriage over a decade later. In 1966 Georg told the Thompsons the story and Marjorie commented, 'Poor Sue!' Georg replied, 'Yes, poor Sue. But she was very proud, and pride is a sin, you know.'

He began searching for somewhere to live. According to Raelene, his first idea, acceptable to nobody, was for everyone to live together: Mizzi, Thilde, Sue and the children, Raelene and Georg; Sue could have separate quarters if she preferred. Georg and Raelene considered getting married, and then, as he said, 'We both thought better of it.' Already on the tour Raelene had tried to persuade Georg to toe the line. She told him to shave, and to buy new razor blades, but he said he would not take food from the mouths of his children. She told him to dress better, clean his face after eating, and to wear leather shoes because plastic ones were bad for his feet. Georg told her to leave him alone. At the same time he tried to mould Raelene into his idea of a muse. He wanted her to grow

*The Trust's publicity photo, from around 1960, over which many women swooned.*
*The unshaven look was Georg saving money on razor blades.*

her hair long. He objected to pointy high-heeled shoes, and the make-up that had attracted him in the first place, despite finding her much less attractive without it. Raelene refused to have her life controlled, and when Georg found a narrow, run-down Victorian terrace house in Paddington, an inner suburb that was then a slum, it was too much. She had grown up in squalour and had no intention of living in it again. Only a few months after the end of the tour, their relationship was finished.

At the beginning of December Georg went to Brisbane to conduct the Queensland Symphony Orchestra in some studio work and two concerts in the Botanical Gardens, replacing Rudolf Pekarek at short notice. When he returned to Sydney in the middle of December he bought the house in Paddington, at 127 Underwood Street, for which he paid £3,800; he had signed over the Rossmore property to Sue. Mizzi and Thilde moved in with him. At the same time Sue severed relations with all the friends she and Georg had shared in New Zealand, without a word, and decided to move. She spent the Christmas holidays farm-hunting, and found an isolated and hilly 1400-acre property at Watsons Creek, near Bendemeer in the New England Tablelands, 350 kilometres from Sydney. The reason she gave for moving to the country was that she wanted to get Demas out of Sydney. He had fallen in with a bad lot at school, dropped out at fourteen, and turned into a juvenile delinquent. Sue hoped to set him straight by moving him back onto a real farm. She and the children, now aged between nine and fifteen, moved there a few months later. The farm ran beef cattle, and a few friends thought she had chosen it to spite Georg. But Sue was not spiteful; she doubtless meant only to emphasise that the marriage was truly over.

The children hardly noticed the break-up of their parents' marriage. Georg was too distant a figure, literally and figuratively.

Although Georg sent Sue as much money as he could, times became hard for her. Not understanding Australian conditions, she had bought marginal land, and the farm was too small to be self-sustaining. As the years passed and the children grew up and moved away she became more and more reclusive. But her sense of pride remained undiminished. She never abandoned the martyrdom she developed in the years with Georg, what one of the children called 'her self-suffering thing'.[11] Her transformation into the opposite of a London society girl was complete. Georg blamed himself for all of it.

Early in 1962 the Trust resumed, under the direction of Australian conductor Charles Mackerras, and Georg was rehired at £40 a week. He was sent to Perth to conduct a festival season of *La Traviata* in February, with the West Australian Symphony Orchestra and the Uruguayan Ana Raquel Satre as Violetta. Mackerras had recommended the company send their very best coach because he considered Satre incapable of learning anything by herself.[12] She had been hired by the producer, Stefan Haag,[*] who was so taken by her voluptuous beauty and temperament that he disregarded the fact she was a mezzo who needed the big aria, *Sempre libera*, transposed down. She created a sensation when she slapped the Brisbane critic, William Lovelock, for daring to print that she sang flat.

---

[*]    Stefan Haag came to Australia in 1939 as a chorister in Georg Gruber's Vienna Mozart Boys Choir, stranded when war broke out. He remained in Australia and became a producer, then (from 1962) executive director of the Elizabethan Theatre Trust.

Georg rejoined the company at the Adelaide Festival, where he and Mackerras shared the *Ariadne auf Naxos* performances. The cast included Una Hale, and Trust stalwarts Rosalind Keene, John Germain, Geoffrey Chard, Neil Warren-Smith and Gregory Dempsey. He was delighted to find Hephzibah Menuhin there, whom he had not seen since she and her husband moved to England in 1957. Yehudi was also there, and he offered to help Georg start his career overseas. Despite lavish promises nothing materialised. A few years later, when Les Thompson approached Menuhin on Georg's behalf, Georg wrote to him:

> Without being asked by me *for anything* he almost forced me to accept his helping hand promising to finance my journey to America and England, some performances in Bath, even the financing of my family and inspite of being reminded of his promises by several people (Pikler inclusive) DID ABSO-LUTELY NOTHING. All that happened at a very dark moment in my not altogether rosy existence (no selfpity here!).[13]

Valerie Melrose, a mezzo in the Perth *Traviata* chorus who moved to Sydney shortly afterwards, became Georg's confidante in those bleak times. She remembers how distressed and angry he was over losing Sue, but she didn't think he would have returned to her had she asked him. She also remembers his frustration over his career. 'He still had a powerful sense of ambition and where he was going. He said, "My time will come".'[14]

In the couple of years after Raelene he took to sleeping around, and developed a reputation as a Lothario. Some of his conquests were singers looking for career advancement, but most just found him terribly attractive – an artist with striking looks, romantic notions and a refined Viennese courtliness so different from the emotional parsimony of Australian men. Women even followed him in the street. Valerie Melrose remembers all the 'disturbed young girls' throwing themselves at him: 'There was a gentle preening of his feathers that he had the "admirers".'[15] And as he told me later, none of it meant anything to him at all.

Georg offered coaching at home, but few singers were willing to go to such a blue-singlet area, 'slummy Paddington'. Those who did found a depressingly barren house with little furniture, no ornaments, no pretty curtains. Gino Zancanaro describes the front room, where Georg taught, as 'a mediaeval type of room, with books all over the place, like Vienna. Cobwebs everywhere.' Everything was black from the coke stove. 'He was the adored son in the family,' says Valerie Melrose, who studied German with Thilde. 'Everything revolved around him. Georg loved it, took it for granted. They waited on him hand and foot, they treated him with great deference. Everything was geared to when he came and went; he was the lord and master. How proud they were of Georg, how wonderful he was!'[16]

None of this, however, compensated for Georg's distress over losing Sue, which was now compounded by severe survivor guilt. The trial of leading Nazi Adolf Eichmann began in May 1961, just as Georg's marriage collapsed, transfixing the world with the horrors of the Holocaust. Valerie Melrose remembers:

> Every now and then he'd want me to go for a walk with him, and sometimes he would pour things out, and I'd just listen and I'd go home exhausted. It was a world I'd had no experience of. These things would pour out of him in a flood of sometimes great distress, about leaving Austria…He had terrible guilt about leaving Austria and surviving. He felt somehow it was all his fault, almost – he had escaped and they hadn't. It was a terrible burden; he used almost to cry. He had had this opportunity to get out, as a musician. Even ten years after the war we had no idea what those people had been through.[17]

'You once said to me when I talked to you about these things that I greatly exaggerate', Georg wrote to Douglas Lilburn in 1955. 'This statement truly amazed me, because I did not feel I did.'[18] Eventually he stopped telling people of his experiences, even his children. 'Georg didn't tell us much very personal,' says Boris. 'I was quite an age when I realised he was Jewish and why he left Austria – around high school. Very little of what Georg thought or believed was communicated to me. I don't remember talking to him about anything at all.'[19]

Georg had survived, but what had he done with his opportunity? While others equally innocent had died his life had become nothing but a series of blunders and failures. In his eyes he had squandered everything, and the burden of guilt was overwhelming.

The Opera moved to Melbourne in the middle of April, where Georg conducted more *Ariadnes*. When they were over he needed to return to Sydney quickly, and he accepted a ride from Michael Taggart, the company accountant and husband of one of the singers. They decided to drive through the night. Sometime early in the morning of 20 May, less than 150 kilometres from Sydney, a speeding Taggart missed the bend onto the one-lane bridge at Berrima and struck one of the stone pylons. The two were flung out of the car, which crashed over the railings and fell six metres to the dry creek bed. They were taken to Berrima hospital suffering from severe lacerations and shock.

Two days after the accident Georg turned forty-five, and he surely considered it the worst birthday of his life. As he lay in his hospital bed, everything must have seemed utterly hopeless. Sue had just moved to Bendemeer, ending any hope of reconciliation. He had lost his anchor through his own foolishness, but – perhaps worst of all – his composing life was in serious trouble. The singers on the *Così* tour had seen him walking the hotel corridors early in the morning singing portions of his opera, but the writing came only very slowly. 'He would say how his inspiration came in little droplets, how it was so precious,' says Raelene. 'That seemed to be his great problem: his talent came so infrequently. He had to work so hard at it.'[20] By the end of 1962 he had to write to Heather Begg: 'I had a very busy and complex period in my life. I'm afraid "your" opera I could not touch for two years.' At this point *'Tis Pity* disappears from view.

Georg was performing again by the middle of July, in Brisbane on the final leg of the Trust season: more *Ariadnes* and at least one *Falstaff*. He followed it with a three-month tour of *La Traviata* in Queensland and New South Wales, and a television recording of Menotti's *The Consul* in Melbourne. He returned to Sydney late in November in a depressed state. In what was left of 1962 he wrote two very small works: a Cantus Firmus for brass sextet, and 'Melody for Two', a one-page twelve-tone canon for the unusual combination of viola and oboe; it was a wedding present for Robert Pikler and oboist Claire Fox.

He conducted a short Trust tour of *Don Giovanni* in the Southern Highlands in February 1963 and then went to New Zealand to conduct *La Bohème* for the New Zealand Opera, with Maria di Gerlando, Ramon Opie, Ronald Maconaghie, Neil Warren-Smith and Grant Dickson. *Bohème* opened in Wellington on 6 April to full houses and excellent reviews. After six performances it went on a countrywide tour, in tandem with *The Magic Flute* conducted by James Robertson. The tour ended on 15 June in New Plymouth, where Georg stayed with Annemarie; her son Michael thought he seemed very lonely. At the performance Georg was outraged to find himself with an orchestra that was largely drunk and incapable of playing. Robertson had sabotaged him by throwing a party after the matinee, his own final performance.[21]

The costumes and scenery, borrowed from the Trust in Australia, were expeditiously packed and sent back to Brisbane for its performances to begin on 8 August, also to be conducted by Georg. To avoid carrying his heavy dress suit he put it in with the costumes, but forgot about a bag of seeds in one of the pockets. Australian quarantine inspectors, among the world's strictest, opened the costumes container, found the seeds, and impounded the entire consignment. It took intervention at the highest level to get it released in time for the premiere.

While Georg was rehearsing *Bohème* in March, the New Zealand Opera offered him the position of Music Director for 1964. To sweeten the offer they promised engagements with other orchestras, including the National Orchestra. Before deciding, he wrote to the General Manager of the ABC, Charles Moses, indicating interest in the conductorship of the West Australian Symphony Orchestra. Its music director, John Farnsworth Hall, was retiring, and the orchestra and Georg had taken a liking to each other in the previous year's *Traviata*. Moses replied that his application would be considered in due course, but in the meantime he shouldn't refuse the New Zealand position. Georg took his advice – wisely, as it turned out, for Farnsworth Hall decided to stay for another year.

When the 1963 Trust season ended Georg took a year's leave, and departed at Christmas for New Zealand.

## Fifteen

Paul Hoffmann had returned from Vienna in 1959 to become foundation professor of German at Victoria University in Wellington. Georg moved in with him and Eva and their three children, in the hilly inner suburb of Kelburn. While in Wellington Georg continued chasing women, but with greater discretion. Here he was regarded as an ascetic – 'a cross between Mozart and Saint Francis', according to Eva Hoffmann.*

A journalist who attended the first rehearsal of *The Bartered Bride* wrote:

> Georg Tintner carries a deceptive air of fragility about him. Actually he is about as fragile as a steel spring. His gentle air thinly veils complete authority and a formidable musical equipment. [His] decisive forefinger means business.[1]

It was the first printed reference to Georg's supposed frailty, a description that would dog him for the next thirty-five years. But the journalist was right: Georg was not frail then, nor was he at any time to the end of his life. Nevertheless, those who had known him in Auckland were shocked at how much he had aged; at forty-six he was now white-haired, gaunt-faced, and looked at least a decade older than he was.

The Opera was as good as its word in finding outside work for him. The National Orchestra engaged him to share two concerts with William Walton in March, part of a Walton tour that was considered New Zealand's most exciting musical event in many years. He was made music director of the NZBC Concert Orchestra, and was engaged to conduct most of the Alex Lindsay

---

* Her son Hugo, aged fifteen, once saw a bicycle chain on Georg's table and asked him if he flagellated with it.

String Orchestra's concerts while Lindsay was in London – concerts Georg later remembered as some of his most satisfying.

At the end of March, before *Bartered Bride* and *Rigoletto* opened,
the company asked Georg if he would remain as music director
in 1965. He was tempted, but he was unhappy about aspects of
the management and he hesitated. On 22 May he wrote again to
the ABC about the West Australian Symphony position, which
was vacant at last. But in the meantime John Hopkins had left the
National Orchestra to become the ABC's new Director of Music.
Years later Georg told me there had been definite talk of his getting
the WASO job, 'and then John Hopkins became Director and that
was the end of it'.

Much later he said in an interview:

> I would have stayed there, except for the stupidity of Fred
> Turnovsky...He was at that time practically in charge [as
> chairman of the board] of the New Zealand Opera Company,
> which was a thriving organisation. We had our own orches-
> tra, the New Zealand Concert Orchestra, of sixteen core
> people; it was even larger at one time. They were excellent
> musicians – most of them were not New Zealanders – but
> they were impossible people...One of their grievances was
> that they worked just as hard as the New Zealand Symphony
> Orchestra, what was called National Orchestra at that time,
> but they didn't get as much money, and so they went *on and
> on* – although they could live quite well from what they got.
> It was a question of prestige. In the end the Broadcasting
> Service was so fed up with them that they said to Turnovsky,
> 'What would you say if we disbanded that orchestra and
> had about six core players or something, and whenever we
> go to different centres they pick up some players?' I said to
> Turnovsky, '*Don't do that*. That would be the end of the New
> Zealand Opera.' And so it turned out to be [in 1971]...
>
> They had one of the best opera choruses I have ever heard.
> There was a man called Harry Brusey, he was the chorus
> master there in Wellington. It was terrific. Wherever we
> went – that was *our* opera. Even small places like Hawera, and
> bigger places like Hamilton too, it was a wonderful feeling of
> belonging. As soon as their orchestra was gone, they couldn't
> tour properly, because instead of being on the road all the

time they could only go at weekends, when the [musicians] were available from Auckland or Wellington or wherever, so the whole thing was finished...Especially as the prime minister, Holyoake, said *publicly*: the New Zealand Opera and New Zealand Ballet Company can have that orchestra as long as they want it. And in spite of that assurance from the horse's mouth, Turnovsky agreed to disband that orchestra. He was a very clever man, but that was an *idiotic* thing to do.[2]

Shortly after the government announced the abolition of the orchestra Georg declined the Opera's invitation to continue in 1965.

Until the Opera's next presentations in October, Georg conducted a number of broadcasts with the Concert Orchestra and the Alex Lindsay Orchestra. His Lindsay concert on 26 June included Mozart's Symphony No. 40 and his Piano Concerto No. 9 in E flat, with English pianist Denis Matthews. The *Listener*'s Bruce Mason thought it 'the finest Mozart playing I have heard from a New Zealand ensemble', and said he was 'bowled over'[3] by Georg. So was Denis. He considered Georg the greatest conductor he had met since Toscanini,[4] and in the ensuing few years did all he could to advance his career.

At the end of July the Auckland University Trio (Michael Wieck, Winifred Stiles and Marie Vandewart) broadcast a performance of Georg's *Fugal Moods*. The pleasure of this was cut short on hearing that Sue's divorce petition had been granted. It formalised Georg's payments of £4 per week per child until each turned sixteen, which amounted to a third of his salary. Demas had just turned eighteen, but Georg continued the payments until all the children were in their twenties.

Having decided not to continue with the New Zealand Opera, Georg wrote to Stefan Haag, who was now director of the Trust, and learned that in 1965 there would be no Trust season as such. Instead they would co-operate with conductor Richard Bonynge, who was forming his own company for a four-city season featuring his wife Joan Sutherland. Haag wrote:

> This of course, results in Bonynge's wish being our command due to the agreement Williamson's [Theatres] made with him whereby he has carte blanche on artistic say. Now when

quizzing him on the duties of our music staff as he envisages
them, he said that he is bringing, apart from himself, [New
Zealander] John Matheson as associate conductor and some
prompter from the Met whose name I have forgotten. The
idea is they will do all the premieres, but there will be a
limited number of performances available for a 'nachdirigi-
eron [sic]',* apart from all the preparatory work, of course.
However, there is one specific task that he not only made
a special enquiry about but in fact specifically asked if you
would be able and willing to undertake it. It seems he has
heard quite a bit about you in London from various people
you have taught at some stage or other and thus is somewhat
conversant with your capabilities.

The specific task in question is that of co-prompter. I told
him that as far as I knew you had no experience in prompting
and that due to the operas being performed in the original
language (except Onegin) it would be quite a formidable task
for you, but that I also had no doubt that if you said that you
would undertake it and were prepared to do so his worries are
over. It seems that short of you agreeing to do it, he would
want to bring a second prompter from overseas.[5]

Georg replied:

Thank you…for sweetening the bitter pill as much as you
could! When I received your letter last night my first impulse
was to reject this offer with indignation. But I slept over
it and though still not pleased about it (who could be?) I
searched my heart and realised I would have to learn Italian
properly which is good for me and secondly every work well
done is worth while…But one 'foreign' language is enough.
I could not undertake *Faust* in French on top of it, quite
apart from the horror of having that 'favourite' of mine again
palmed off at me…

Forgive me for making the personal observation that
I see the years slip by (I was forty-seven in May) and I am
being *de-* instead of *promoted*. Hitler cost me fifteen years of
my life and I see less talented and younger people leaving me

---

*     The verb *nachdirigieren* means to conduct subsequent, or leftover, performances.

behind. I don't think many people who have conducted seventeen different operas from memory (not to speak of many
symphonies etc) have been used as prompters. Nevertheless
the Hindus say: We are where we deserve to be – perhaps
they are right.[6]

Rossini's *La Cenerentola* opened at Victoria University on 9 October,
and before Georg returned to Sydney he conducted a number
of concerts with the Alex Lindsay orchestra, including the first
Wellington performance of Richard Strauss's *Metamorphosen*.
'Georg Tintner has given a new dimension to the orchestra's playing,' wrote Owen Jensen, now a Wellington critic. 'His passion
for detail has developed an admirable precision; his unfeigned
affection for the music has infused it with warmth and a conviction
which communicates itself to the audience. His return to Australia
is very much our loss.'[7]

In January Georg conducted a summer concert with the Sydney
Symphony: Schumann's Manfred Overture, the Adagietto from
Mahler's Fifth Symphony and Bizet's Symphony in C. The next
day the *Sydney Morning Herald* reported:

> Mr Tintner leaves one in no doubt as to where the beat
> lies, in fact, he never left a beatable moment unbeaten – a
> distinctly wearying procedure to watch. The musical results
> were, fortunately, much smoother and controlled than his
> rigid, castigating baton action would lead one to expect.[8]

It was about this time that Georg decided to stop using the
baton.

> I think one of the reasons is that I'm a left-hander, and when
> I use both hands more or less equally it is better for me. Mind
> you, there are a very few conductors who are left-handers
> who use the baton in the left hand, but I think that is wrong
> because it is all mirror fashion. I think there's a lot to be said
> for having the baton, and for *not* having it.[9]
> I thought and I still think that my hands express much
> better what I have to say than a piece of wood. It is not easier,
> I think it is harder; but [I can conduct] more expressively.[10]

Some musicians did not appreciate Georg's giving up the baton, but once he had done it he felt 'freed up' and he never returned to it.

He recorded *Cenerentola* for ABC television, with Rosalind Keene, Diane Holmes, Peter Baillie, Alan Light, Ronald Maconaghie and Neil Warren-Smith; Heather Begg, hired on Georg's recommendation, sang Rosina. The opera was broadcast in Sydney in May to an astonishingly large audience of 350,000 – 15 per cent of the population. 'Even the Sydney Symphony Orchestra, never very keen on accompanying opera, seemed to be enjoying itself under Georg Tintner's direction,' said the *Sydney Morning Herald*.[11] The ABC was so pleased with the results that it sent a tape as its cultural contribution to Expo '67 in Montreal.

Before the Sutherland season began he took *Madam Butterfly* on a two-month Arts Council tour of New South Wales and Queensland. When they reached Tamworth he went to see his family, but it was not a successful visit. Demas was no longer there; he disliked the farm Sue had bought for his benefit and had moved back to Sydney. Boris was away at boarding school, but the twins were there, and Georg went for a walk with fourteen-year-old Ariadne. She was well dressed in clothes her friends had lent her for the occasion and Georg, not knowing they were borrowed, remarked that things couldn't be too bad if she had such nice clothes. Ariadne never forgave him. He managed to offend Sue as well, by going for a walk up the hill behind the house dressed only in his underpants and a hernia belt.

Eighteen-year-old Demas had gone to live with Mizzi and Thilde. Already at the age of twelve he had been very popular with girls, and in Paddington there was a constant parade of them coming down the stairs in the mornings, to the discomfiture of everyone else. Demas had achieved his ambition to be become 'not a good boy' and to Georg's despair had taken up antisocial behaviour such as shoving elderly women off the footpath. But the more he tried to help Demas the angrier his son became, and in turn the more anguished Georg became.

A few days into the *Butterfly* tour Georg went to the post office in Yass, where a letter awaited him from South Africa:

I knew nobody in South Africa, so I opened that in great curiosity. And there is the following letter: 'You probably

won't remember me, but I remember you, because you conducted the New Zealand Symphony Orchestra in a stunning
performance of the Fourth Symphony of Bruckner and I
played the fourth horn in that orchestra.* Today when I came
to the rehearsal in Cape Town I had a lot of mail from New
Zealand and by chance in the newspapers they sent me there
were some fabulous reviews of you conducting in Wellington.
There must be a higher power in this business because while
I just read these reviews, our conductor tendered his resignation. Unless you are one hundred per cent happy in Australia,
apply for this job and I am sure you will get it.'

    I had very great doubts whether I should go to a country
whose political system I absolutely detested, but in the end my
friend Hephzibah Menuhin said to me this: 'Georg, I think
you should go, because it's all very well to detest something
but you should find out what it is *really* like.' So I took her
word for it, and I applied.[12]

    It was time for a change. After the Sutherland tour he could
at best expect more short Trust seasons at the beck and call of the
music director. Furthermore, the ABC was considering withdrawing the services of its orchestras from the Trust, as their own
concert series expanded, putting a 1966 season in doubt.† Georg
asked Hephzibah to write him a reference, but without telling him
she asked her brother to do it. In due course Georg was selected
for an audition.

In April Georg began coaching for the Sutherland–Williamson
Grand Opera Company, at a salary of £45 a week plus £10 travel
allowance. The season comprised seven operas, mostly showcases
for Sutherland including *Lucia di Lammermoor*, *La Sonnambula* and
*Semiramide*. The singers included Elizabeth Harwood, Monica
Sinclair, Margreta Elkins, Lauris Elms, Robert Allman, Alberto
Remedios, Ronald Maconaghie, Spiro Malas, Cornelis Opthof
and a young discovery, Luciano Pavarotti. The orchestra was less
illustrious, a scratch band mostly from Williamson's Tivoli pit
orchestra who had never played anything more difficult than *Hello*

---

\*    The December 1953 broadcast; the musician was Prier Wintle.
†    The Trust did lose the use of the ABC orchestras. It established its own orchestras in Sydney in 1967
and Melbourne in 1969.

*Dolly*, freshened up with a few young freelancers. 'This is a very strange Company,' Georg wrote to Heather Begg, who was now singing at Sadler's Wells in London. 'Good voices, excellent chorus, but in every other respect far inferior to the Trust (Orchestra, production, direction).'[13]

The season began in Melbourne on 10 July, with conductors Richard Bonynge, John Matheson, American William Weibel and Australian Gerald Krug. Four days later, Matheson walked out. Margreta Elkins, a mezzo Bonynge was trying to turn into a coloratura soprano as he had done with his wife, was singing Tatiana in *Eugene Onegin* and was having difficulty with the high notes. Bonynge insisted that Matheson conduct faster to make the notes easier, calling out instructions from the stalls. Matheson lost his temper and there was a showdown. He departed the next day. Georg was outraged on his behalf and unwisely went to Bonynge to defend him.

The next day, 15 July, Georg was on his way home on his bicycle when a car struck him from behind, breaking his ankle. He was taken to hospital and put in plaster, but his ankle never really healed. Eight days later he returned to conduct some of Matheson's performances, and at one of the rehearsals the orchestra applauded him, prompting a now ill-disposed Bonynge to decree there was to be no applause for conductors at rehearsals. When a singer asked a no-better-disposed Georg a question about *Lucia di Lammermoor* he replied, 'Ask Mr Bonynge. *He* is Donizetti's representative on Earth.'[14] They soon came to a dispute over *Traviata*. For the first-cast performances with Sutherland, Bonynge had exchanged the soprano and tenor parts in a duet because Pavarotti couldn't learn the lower line. Pavarotti was also singing second-cast performances, and against Bonynge's wishes Georg insisted on restoring the original. 'There is a higher authority than you, Mr Bonynge,' he said, 'and his name is Verdi.' Bonynge replied, 'There is a difference, Mr Tintner. Verdi is not here, but I am.'[15]

Surprisingly, Georg's first *Traviata* performance, a matinee for schoolchildren, was covered by the press. Linda Phillips said in the *Sun*: 'What nervous intensity, delicacy, and beauty he drew from his players, especially in accompaniment to duets and in the two orchestral preludes preceding the first and final act! He is a master of operatic score and an artist as well.'[16] In the *Age* Felix Werder wrote: 'He is one of the most prominent opera conductors in this country, certainly the best that this company has seen, and a most profoundly musical artist to boot. How strange, therefore, to find him reduced to the ranks while lesser men hog the limelight.'[17] One of the company's other conductors telephoned Werder, who found himself spending an hour defending his review.[18]

While Georg was in hospital he received a visit from a cellist in the orchestra, Cecilia Lawrence. She was twenty-one years old, tall and thin, and with a spectacular mane of frizzy long hair. She had graduated a few months earlier from the University of Melbourne in both cello and piano, and she still lived with her mother and stepfather. The Sutherland season was her first professional job. Like so many others, she had fallen in love with Georg. He wrote to his friend and fellow Viennese refugee Mizzi Bergel, with whom he would be staying when the Opera moved to Adelaide, 'There is this little girl from the orchestra bringing me fruit.'[19] When the company reached Adelaide a month later Georg and Cecilia stayed together at Mizzi's.

As he had done with Sue, Georg renamed her. Not liking her first name he decided to call her by her second, Gretel, and so she was known until the relationship was over. She converted immediately to vegetarianism and took it very seriously. When Mizzi pointed out that she was keeping the orchestra bus waiting and must leave immediately, she replied, 'Oh no. Georg told me I have to eat a pineapple every day, and I can't go until I've eaten it!'[20]

Georg already knew Cecilia's mother, the cellist Kathleen Tuohy, who had had a solo career before joining the Sydney Symphony Orchestra and then the Victorian (later Melbourne) Symphony. Her husband wanted her to have a big career, but despite their best efforts she didn't succeed, and the marriage broke down when Cecilia was very young. One parent put her into a boarding school to hide her from the other, and when the other found her she was stolen away and put into another school. She told Georg of being left alone at home, a child under ten, when her mother went to a concert; she stood in the front hall all evening, staring at the front door until her mother came home. Sometime before she became a teenager she acquired a stepfather she thoroughly disliked. She also spoke of a frightening access visit with her father, who had something else to do that day and left her with a friend who invited her to help him take a shower.

Margaret Crawford, a flute player who knew Cecilia when she was eighteen, recalls:

> She was a complicated person, complicated and uptight. We sat on a bus together on an outing at National Music Camp [in 1962]. She said, 'I will *never, ever* marry, and *never* have children' – so I was surprised when not so long after I heard they were together. She never grew up, never seemed to get past thirteen. She was frightened of men. She had a bitter mother…because the father had walked out on them. Cecilia grew up hating men. But the stress didn't show on her face, her face was relaxed, she looked dignified and simple. She looked like a wooden doll, or a Welsh doll, with old-fashioned clothes and an old-fashioned hairdo. She was like something from the Appalachians. There was something about her out of a Schubert or Mahler song, rather folksy, as if she would take up spinning and weaving. There was something inno-cent about her that would have been very attractive. She had a fairy-story side that would have attracted him.[21]

In Adelaide Georg was prompting *Eugene Onegin*, and because his leg was still in plaster from ankle to knee he had to be pushed into the tiny prompt box at the front of the stage. After the first performance on 17 August the jubilation was so great that nobody remembered he had to be lifted out again. Had the stage manager not happened to return after everyone had gone, he would have been there all night. He found Georg tugging on the curtain and plaintively calling, 'Please Mr Manager, please get me out!' This tale is famous in Australian opera history.

The season ended in Brisbane on 16 October, not a moment too soon for Georg who referred privately to 'that beastly Sutherland Company'. Georg and Cecilia returned to Sydney the next day, and on 30 October, Cecilia's twenty-second birthday, they were married at a civil ceremony in Balmain. The day was spoiled by Cecilia's stepfather, who told them on the way to the wedding that the marriage would never work.

In the two months before his Cape Town audition season Georg travelled around Australia judging the finals of the

*Eighteen-year-old Cecilia Lawrence and her mother, Kathleen Tuohy, in 1962.*

Metropolitan Opera auditions, and in December made a television recording of *Gypsy Baron*. Still uncomfortable about going to South Africa, he was looking for alternatives. He wrote to Les Thompson, still living in Oxford, with whom he had been out of touch for many years:

> A lot happened since we saw each other – good and bad. I am afraid my marriage with Sue did not stand the strain of the four years in two different countries and failed quite a few years ago to my greatest regret. – four weeks ago I married again a very young cellist. We both leave on January 1 for CapeTown where I conduct the Municipal Orchestra for two months in eighteen concerts. Then we intend to come to London and Vienna to try my luck there…I go there with a bad conscience, nevertheless felt I could not miss an opportunity I had waited for all this time in NZ and Australia.[22]

He wrote again a month later, two days before departing:

The first week of March should find us already in London. We have as yet nowhere to live and I have no work, but we are determined to stick it out for a year if necessary. I need a rest from Australasia.

*Part III*
*1966–1987*

*Sixteen*

Georg and Cecilia arrived in Cape Town on Sunday 2 January 1966, and Georg gave his first concert four days later. The *Cape Times* review next morning was unenthusiastic: 'I enjoyed his Debussy [*Nuages* and *Fêtes*] more than anything else last night...I was not so impressed by the Mozart G minor Symphony...a flat and somewhat uninspired account.'[1] The second concert three days later set the strenuous pattern for the following seven weeks: a lighter program on Sundays and a more serious one on Thursdays. As Georg put it later, he was running for his life. However well he had studied the works as a student, he was conducting the vast majority of them for the first time – his non-operatic conducting experience even with medium-sized orchestras was negligible (the Municipal Orchestra numbered forty-eight). One of the musicians overheard him mutter at a rehearsal, 'It's like a sausage machine, this.'

By the fourth week the *Times*'s Hans Kramer was writing:

> An immense feeling of security and well-being radiates from
> the rostrum, when Georg Tintner occupies it. There is no
> wavering within the orchestral forces in front of him. Tonal
> balance, secure and pleasing intonation and all the other hall-
> marks of good direction are in abundant evidence.[2]

On 17 February, in his penultimate week, Georg conducted Bruckner's Fourth, the first South African performance of the 1878/80 version. Despite the undersized orchestra, Hans Kramer wrote enthusiastically: 'Georg Tintner's conception of this tremendous work...is so sincere, so deeply felt, that it is hard to imagine a better or more eloquent advocate for its universal appeal and success.'[3] On the same day the *Cape Times* ran an article entitled 'Don't Let This Man Go', remarking that Georg had 'made a deep impression on the heart and mind of the city's music-minded public'.

His final concert on 24 February, with Alicia de Larrocha, 'gave the audience obvious pleasure and enabled them to give Mr Tintner the ovation he deserves,' wrote Noel Storr. '[The orchestra] obviously took a little time to adjust to his methods, but his mature approach, and wide experience have borne fruit, and I think that everybody will be sad at his departure. He has given us some excellent concerts during the past two months.'[4]

According to horn player Prier Wintle, 'One third of the orchestra loved him, one third tolerated him, and one third hated him, and they were the ones who wanted an easy time and didn't want to go to the end of rehearsals.'[5] Some players objected to his outspoken views on Apartheid, and some made fun of his veganism. They laughed at the canvas shoes he always wore, even with his tails, and told fantastical stories about his eating habits: one was that he threw his sprouts on the carpet in hotels and harvested them the next morning. 'When they opened the Civic Theatre in Bloemfontein there was a reception at City Hall,' says clarinettist Wolfgang Simon.

> Everyone was there, and there was anything you could wish to eat. There was salad, but there was something on it he wouldn't eat. The Afrikaners were very worried about what they could do. Georg said, 'All right, you can give me a banana.' There was everything you could want there, but no banana. The mayor sent someone all around Bloemfontein to find one, and he finally came back with a measly banana.[6]

The event, albeit somewhat transformed, went into South African musical folklore. When the pianist Michael Brimer arrived in Durban four years later, he heard that Georg had attended a big reception there and eaten the floral arrangement.

On 2 March Georg wrote to Les Thompson: 'My job is at last finished. Sixteen concerts in eight weeks, all completely different programs, everything from memory except the concertos. So I am *very* tired. At the moment we are in Johannesburg on the way to England. However we shall stop in Athens tomorrow for a few days, depending on the wheather and our finances...I have not decided yet whether to go back to Cape Town and it has not decided either (officially).'

Georg and Cecilia arrived in London on 7 March. Within a week or so they found a room in a flat in the grim-looking Prince Edward Mansions in Bayswater. They had hardly moved in when Georg heard from the Cape Town Municipal Orchestra, formally offering him the conductorship for one year from 1 September. 'I wished in a way I could refuse it, but of course I can't!' he wrote to Les on 17 March.

A few days later Georg took Cecilia to meet the Thompsons. At first they thought he had married a schoolgirl, though he seemed to dote on her. He sat brushing her hair as Cecilia beamed with delight. 'Poor kid,' Marjorie said to Les afterwards, 'she has no idea what she's taken on.'[7] Cecilia spoke only about having babies. Immediately after the wedding she had told Georg she wanted to start a family; she was 'in a terrible hurry'.[8] Because she had been very lonely as an only child, she wanted a house full of children, and for them to be 'as ordinary as possible'. At the same time she intended to have a career as a cellist. 'People in Australia said it can't be done,' she said, 'but we will show them it *can* be done.'

Georg, however, did not want children, because he 'considered the marriage wasn't in good enough shape.'[9] Already in South Africa he had found Cecilia's helplessness had worn thin. His attention strayed to a South African soprano, also in her early twenties. He didn't seduce her, but his interest did not pass unnoticed by his new wife. Georg did not love Cecilia, or so he swore after it was all over; he said he married her because 'it seemed a good idea at the time. Besides, she was very attractive.'[10] But he thought her charming and adorable, and she brought out something protective in him. He wanted to compensate for her unhappy childhood, to give her nice things, to make everything better. And he wanted to compose again. 'He told Cecilia she would have to be his muse,' says Raelene, who met them in London. 'He didn't realise how selfish he was. She wanted a conductor. Neither wanted a relationship.'[11]

Yet however much Georg was opposed to having more children he was not about to deny them to Cecilia. He had kept Sue waiting 'five years' (he said later) for hers, and he remembered only too well the damage that had caused. But he kept his reservations to himself, and to the Thompsons he seemed fully in agreement with the plan.

Still hoping to find an alternative to the Cape Town job, he consulted Sir Adrian Boult. 'He was genuinely kind and tries to help but is rather pessimistic about the whole setup,' he reported to Les. 'He advised me strongly to accept the position in Cape Town, which I have done with a heavy heart for more reasons than one.'[12] Equally dispiriting was a visit to Peter Andry of EMI Records, who told Georg on the advice of Charles Mackerras that he was best advised to work as a coach. Denis Matthews introduced him around London, with no result. In addition, Georg was unwell; he was laid up for a week or more in April with housemaid's knee, and at the beginning of June he had an operation for a hernia that had nagged him for twelve years.

In the five months the Tintners spent in England Georg found only one engagement: a concert with the Northern Sinfonia on 19 May. Although the audience was tiny the review was glowing: 'The highlight of the evening was undoubtedly a truly magnificent performance of Elgar's Introduction and Allegro for strings...they achieved a near miracle, playing with a sensitivity and a warmth and volume of tone one would have considered almost impossible... one will go far before hearing a better performance.'[13] But this was in the small Scottish town of Hawick, far from the attention of musical London.

The Tintners left on 30 July for Cape Town, and Georg went on alone to Australia mainly to visit Mizzi and Thilde. From there he spent a few days in Vienna, for the first time in twenty-eight years. 'I cried when I saw the buildings, the buildings of the Austrian Baroque,' he said, 'but the people all had the need to justify themselves. I did not go there for that.' He went to see a leading artists' agent, Alois Starka, at the urging of Eva Hoffmann who had approached him on Georg's behalf in 1964. Starka already knew of Georg from his Volksoper days. To Eva he said, '*Ich weiß, dass dieser Mann ein Genie ist*' – 'I know this man is a genius'. He added sourly, 'Should I send him a ticket?' Georg found his interview unpleasant and nothing resulted from it. If he had thought it might be possible to live and work in Vienna again, he was sadly disillusioned.

He arrived in Cape Town at the end of August and began work immediately. At an afternoon rehearsal on 6 September there

was a sudden disturbance. Malcolm Forsyth, one of the trombon-
ists, recalls:

> We were rehearsing Stravinsky's Symphonies of Wind
> Instruments in Cape Town City Hall. The strings were
> hanging about in the hall while this was going on and a
> bass player came to the stage, interrupting the rehearsal to
> tell us that the Prime Minister, Hendrik Verwoerd, had
> just been assassinated in Parliament. Georg Tintner asked
> what was the disturbance and when told, made a disdainful
> noise like *acch!* and refused to pay it any more attention,
> continuing to work on the Stravinsky. We were mightily
> excited of course, and the rehearsal was a bit disrupted as a
> result. Georg Tintner's disdain, I thought, was deliberately
> obvious and blunt.

Georg was instructed to play Nimrod from Elgar's *Enigma
Variations* at the concert as a mark of respect. 'Everyone is so sad
and upset about this,' he said cheerfully to a friend, 'but I feel like
jumping for joy!'

Georg and Cecilia rented a house in the seaside town of
Muizenberg, on the Cape. There they encountered many poverty-
stricken black children, whom they fed with sandwiches made
from bread Georg had baked; they soon had an extensive clientele.
Georg bought an ancient Ford Mercury, which he drove hanging
on for dear life. He taught Cecilia to drive and then gave it up
forever, in favour of his bicycle. Cecilia auditioned for an orchestra
position, without success, but often played as an extra. By October
she was overjoyed to find herself pregnant.

By the end of the year Georg had introduced several works
previously unknown to Cape Town audiences, including
Shostakovich's First Symphony, Bartók's Concerto for Orchestra,
and on 3 November his own first performance of Bruckner's
Seventh Symphony. By the end of the first half of the season in
February 1967 he had added the three preludes from Pfitzner's
opera *Palestrina*, Schoenberg's Chamber Symphony Op. 9b, which
the audience found too modern, Mahler's Symphony No. 4 (his
own first performance of a Mahler symphony) and Walton's
Symphony No. 1. Hans Kramer mused:

Typical of his genius for thinking up original programmes was last night's concert. Mr Tintner chose pieces that were appropriate, original and well balanced. Only in one or two instances during the season has his zest for original programme planning been too optimistic. Georg Tintner's forte, apart from his obvious gifts as a musician – and not all conductors are musicians – is the subtle way in which he has educated the musical public during his term here…In spite of what the late Noel Storr described as Mr Tintner's batonless beat, which must arouse a little confusion among the members of the orchestra, we should be most sad to lose him. In one year he has done more for the general musical education of the Thursday night audience than any conductor I can remember.[14]

Georg was indeed thinking of leaving. Everything about Apartheid appalled him, and he was frustrated by his inability to help beyond feeding children, writing protest letters to the newspapers, and attending functions at the Athenaeum Society, a liberal and illegal group of people of all colours who met for cocktail parties and lectures. Rodney Phillips, a music lover and the one good friend Georg made in South Africa, worked then as a marketer of canned fruit. One day he visited Georg in Muizenberg, leaving his black assistant in the car. Georg insisted Rodney bring him inside, despite the assistant's reluctance because such things were not done. He pointed out to Rodney that he, aged about twenty, was addressing the much older man by his Christian name while being addressed as 'Sir' in return. 'What is happening?' Georg asked, scandalised. 'What are you doing?' Rodney swore that until that minute the injustice had never occurred to him. It remained a vivid memory for them both.

Malcolm Forsyth recalls:

The fact that he had but thinly, or not at all, hidden his poor opinion of how things were done in Cape Town had certainly not helped his case politically in musical circles. As for the larger political scene, 1966 was the year, I think, when the government bumped non-conformist Cape Town into line as regards separate entrances and box-offices for all non-white concert-goers, and a new doorway had to be hacked

through the granite walls of Cape Town City Hall. Georg
Tintner saw the country at its worst in this respect.[15]

Most repellent of all to Georg was the complicity of some of
the Jews, who in his opinion should behave *better* than anyone else.

> These politically were really terrible times for me, for this
> reason, that in Austria I was the underdog, a piece of dirt.
> When I came to South Africa with my white skin, I was a
> semi-god. And I must tell you, it was harder to bear, after
> that experience, from being nobody to be undeservedly a
> semi-god. That was terrible. I couldn't stand it, so I in the
> end went back to England.[16]

Cecilia was worried about the future and begged Les
Thompson to encourage Georg to send out letters in search of
work. The possibility arose of becoming a coach at Sadler's Wells,*
where some of the many Australian singers working there had
put in a word for him. He found the prospect unenticing. At the
same time he received two bitter blows. In March he heard that
his mother had collapsed from a heart attack and died the next
day, on 6 March. He was close to his mother and he felt her loss
acutely. This news came less than two weeks after hearing that the
BBC had rejected *The Ellipse*, submitted by Les the previous year.
Les then tried to interest the Allegri Quartet but this also came to
nothing. Two years later Georg wrote to him in words that hardly
concealed his desperation:

> You know that I am not excessively arrogant about my modest
> achievements, but I must say I have the highest opinion of this
> piece as a whole and am amazed that it has so far not found
> more resonance in these parts...it has something important
> to say to those who can 'tune in' to it, and I feel dreadfully
> ashamed that because of private catastrophies and exterior
> lack of understanding the author of this Masterpiece (forgive
> me this exalted language but I do believe it; perhaps quite
> wrongly!) since then has remained practically dumb.[17]

---

* Sadler's Wells was renamed the English National Opera in 1974.

Despite his feelings about Apartheid, Georg was wavering about leaving Cape Town. At the age of almost fifty it was the first time he had a secure position, and there was a baby on the way. Cecilia, however, insisted they go to London. She detested Apartheid as much as he, and she was keen to get their careers moving. Georg therefore wrote to Sadler's Wells to inquire about the coaching position, and Les said he would ask Denis Matthews and Yehudi Menuhin for advice. Georg replied immediately, telling him of his humiliating encounter with Menuhin in 1962. 'I could not and would not approach him for anything anymore but you could make discreet use of the enclosed copy [of Menuhin's Cape Town reference] if you see fit to do it.'[18]

Les replied on 4 May:

> Menuhin rang on Tuesday. I was out, and Marjorie said he was most friendly and affable, so I rang him when I got in. Once again, most friendly and affable, and deeply concerned about the waste of your gifts. He hasn't been able to offer anything, of course – I didn't write to him for that – but I can use his name, etc., etc. He made a few suggestions of possibilities, which lead me to think that he is rather out of touch. However, both he and Denis Matthews firmly believe that it would not be a bad thing to be Senior Coach of Sadler's Wells for a while, because you would then have your foot in. They think this is important.
>
> Menuhin said that five years ago he was hoping all sorts of things would be possible, but money wasn't forthcoming. He was trying something, but the time wasn't ripe. He kept saying this – he said it to Marjorie – he seemed to have uncomfortable feelings. He hinted now at Bath, whatever that may mean, I cannot really guess. The one thing I can be sure of is his tremendous goodwill. I am sure of that if nothing else.

'I am not quite sure whether you wrote to me about Menuhin before or after my letter explaining to you his "bad conscience",' Georg replied. 'However by now you know in any case. In my opinion it is all the fault of his detestable wife Diana…'[19]

On 18 May Georg wrote again to Les: 'I am very anxious to get a reply from S. W. but they seem to have a lot of time. I must decide within a few days and to leave (voluntarily) without a job and a baby coming is a bit difficult.' Nevertheless, just before the orchestra's deadline at the end of the month he advised them he would not renew his contract. It was not until later in June that Sadler's Wells offered him 'some work depending on their budget', and on this slim offer he booked tickets to London. Cecilia, frustrated by Georg's 'absolute horror of asking for anything', asked Les to promote him. Using publicity material she sent him, he wrote to twenty-eight orchestras and organisations across Great Britain. A few showed some interest, but said that their schedules were full for at least the next eighteen months. Nothing came of the exercise.

On 9 July their first child, Chrysothemis Magdalena, was born. Cecilia had attended antenatal classes at which she was told that if she breathed correctly she would have no pain. As Georg had tried to warn her, it was not as easy as the classes had suggested, and she asked for pain relief. Georg, adamantly opposed to pharmaceutical interventions, reminded her that she had wanted a drug-free birth. She complied, but she held it against him.

The remaining six weeks of Georg's directorship began on 27 July with another first, Franz Schmidt's *Variations on a Hussar Song* (which emptied the hall), and on 24 August he conducted the Ritual Dances from Tippett's *Midsummer Marriage*. 'The orchestra detested it most heartily (a rather good sign I'm afraid) nevertheless they played it well,' he wrote to Les. These were stressful weeks, not only because of the family's uncertain future but also because Cecilia had trouble breast-feeding and a hungry Chrysothemis cried without respite.

Sadler's Wells finally told Georg he would have work until January coaching *Meistersinger*, but added that obtaining a work permit for longer than that would be a prolonged and difficult business. Still hoping to avoid the coaching position altogether, he wrote to John Hopkins at the ABC asking to be considered for the conductorship of the Queensland Symphony when Rudolf Pekarek left at the end of the year. Hopkins replied that the job had already been given to Stanford Robinson.

At his final concert on 31 August Georg presented Cape Town's first performance of Mahler's *Das Lied von der Erde*, with Sarita Stern and Gert Potgieter, and received stellar reviews. Antoinette Silvestri in the *Cape Argus* described the Mahler as 'thrilling', but reflected:

Mr Tintner's decision not to renew his contract with the Cape Town Orchestra was in part guided by the fact that there is resistance from a large part of the musical public of Cape Town who wish to listen to nothing but what is known as the basic repertoire...in the year that he has been with us, [he has] given us something that we like, and also something 'that is good for us'. Georg Tintner has in fact introduced sophistication into the choice of programme that we hear on Thursdays. There are many overtones to the term sophisti-cated, but the root of the word refers to that which is wise. Wise Mr Tintner has been to include works that are being performed in our times and not only a hundred years ago. And yet he has also been unwise, for in Cape Town we are less renowned for our crusading spirit, than for a conservative outlook. New works to be introduced on Thursday nights mean new scores and more work for the orchestra, exhaustive, sometimes exhausting rehearsals.[20]

'He was so meticulous about things,' says clarinettist Wolfgang Simon.

Among professionals he was regarded as a bit over the top, and it was a disadvantage to his 'getting on'. There was so much you can get out of such an orchestra, which was not the New York Philharmonic, and sometimes he would ride things to death. I knew what he was trying to get, but to others he was a pain in the neck. I felt that Georg was a very tragic person. He was one of the best musicians anywhere. If he hadn't had these idiosyncrasies he would have got a very good job in England, or anywhere.[21]

A week after the final concert Georg still had no British entry permit, but Les Thompson contacted his member of parliament who advised him that as a Commonwealth citizen Georg didn't need one for the first six months. Georg and Cecilia left South Africa in haste on 14 September, leaving behind his only white bow tie, jars of sprouting beans, and the Ford Mercury, which Rodney Phillips sold for them. So ended the only year of Georg's life in which he was music director of anything larger than a chamber orchestra.

## Seventeen

The Tintners found an upstairs flat at 9 West Hill in Wandsworth, in a small terrace house on a noisy main road – all Georg could afford on his weekly pay of £30. In order to save money on heating he propped a mattress against the door of the living room – the only nice room – and the three of them camped in the kitchen, with newspapers and rubbish covering the floor. Cecilia wanted very much to have a nice home, and tried hard to learn domestic arts from Marjorie Thompson. Her own mother had raised her to spend time on nothing but becoming a soloist.

Cecilia loved the warm familial atmosphere she found with Les and Marjorie and their daughters Ruth and Rachel, something she hadn't known when growing up, and the Tintners went to Oxford as often as they could. On one visit they brought Franz Röhr and his wife Esther, vacationing in England, to listen to the tape of the ABC *Cenerentola*. It was the first time Georg and Franz had seen each other since they had met at Portsmouth as Franz was on his way to America in 1939. To him it seemed that 'Cecilia was much in love with Georg and he treated her as a child, a waif. She always seemed to me to be very insecure.'[1] Marjorie, however, noticed uneasily that Cecilia was besotted with her baby and seemed to have lost some of her interest in Georg. She had seen it all before, with Sue.

Aiming to build on Les Thompson's efforts, Denis Matthews also wrote to Yehudi Menuhin on Georg's behalf:

> I spoke to Hephzibah the other day about Georg Tintner, with whom I worked in New Zealand, because I feel it such a tragedy that his exceptional musical gifts and knowledge should be so woefully underestimated and – in this country – unknown. Now I gather that you have kindly contacted some of the powers-that-be about him. The professional musical

world is tough, and Georg is too modest, but I do thank you
for your intervention as I feel he has so much to give.[2]

Menuhin arranged a meeting for Georg with William
Glock, Controller of the BBC's Radio 3, who gave Georg two
broadcasts to take place in 1969. But apart from inviting Georg
to social occasions at his house in Highgate Hill, Menuhin did
nothing more. According to Brenda Matthews, 'Yehudi had
great plans for him, but he didn't follow them up. Denis had
long talks with Yehudi. He had plans to help him, take him
under his wing, give him a career. I don't know why he didn't
continue. Denis was very upset.'[3]

Early in 1968, the conductor Harry Blech said he would find
Georg a concert opportunity with his London Mozart Players.
Sadler's Wells, meanwhile, offered Georg work until the end of
the season, and on that basis he began to look for a house to buy.
Thilde was now intending to join them; she had been lonely
since the death of her sister, and sharing the Paddington house
with eighteen-year-old Boris was a strained arrangement at best.
Georg sold the house for $12,000 in July, as the suburb was on the
point of gentrifying, and Thilde sailed for London. She spent two
weeks with Annemarie on the way, and Georg wrote to her there
that he had found the perfect house for them all, although it was
unsewered and made of wood. It had two kitchens so there would
be no clash of diets, and Thilde could smoke in peace. Its only
drawback was that it was well out of London, at Bishop's Stortford.
He also reported: 'You will be as pleased as we are to know that
Gretel expects another child (in February). I am very much against
only children. But then that will be all!'[4]

After Thilde left New Zealand she fell ill with pneumonia,
and when she arrived in London on 3 September she was taken
immediately to hospital. For the next two weeks she declined. She
begged to see Chrysothemis, but Cecilia refused on the grounds
that the hospital was no place for a fourteen-month-old child;
Chryssy must not see an old woman dying. On 20 September,
on the day of Georg's London Mozart Players concert, Thilde
died. That evening Georg conducted an unusual program: Haydn's
Overture to *L'Isola Disabitata*, Schoenberg's Chamber Symphony
No. 1, Mozart's Piano Concerto K. 449 with Denis Matthews,

and Bizet's Symphony. Heather Begg was there, and she wrote afterwards to friends in New Zealand:

> It's a long time since Georg has had the chance of doing anything in public...he's kept pretty busy as a repetiteur at Sadler's Wells, and up till now I don't think they have realised what an excellent conductor they have on their staff. I'm pretty sure his performance the other night opened a few eyes, and he must surely get more chances now... He had to return to the stage over and over again and people were cheering, the orchestra rose and applauded as well and I felt all choked up, that he was receiving recognition at last.[5]

The reviews, however, were mostly cautious. It was not until several weeks later that a truly favourable review appeared, in the magazine *Music and Musicians*:

> The Viennese-born conductor Georg Tintner made his London debut in the Elizabeth Hall on September 20, and showed those three attributes that the successful conductor must have – sound musicianship, a clear beat and a warm personality (the London Mozart Players made no secret of the fact that they liked him).

It went on to describe the Schoenberg as 'a superb performance' in which 'Tintner made the music speak as I have rarely heard it speak before. Conducting without baton or score (he used the score only for the piano concerto) Tintner proved himself to be in command of every situation.'[6] But whether the reviews were not sufficiently enthusiastic, or the people who came to inspect Georg were not impressed, no arts organisations or agents showed any interest. Glyndebourne's George Christie wrote to Les Thompson saying how much he had enjoyed the concert, but offered nothing. Sir Adrian Boult also wrote, saying, 'I am so glad he had a real success, and am very sorry that, as so often, the Press have missed the importance of things. It is a very slow business and I do hope Mr Tintner will find his niche before there are too many frustrating delays.'[7]

In November Georg went to Glasgow for four performances of *Die Fledermaus*, which Sadler's Wells had given him because they couldn't find anyone else. They were well received, and a few weeks later the managing director made him an offer. Georg wrote to Les:

> Mr Stephen Arlen phoned me up yesterday and offered me all London performances of *La Vie Parisienne* by Offenbach...I took it but had the one satisfaction that I could tell the great man that I did not think S.W. uses me to their or my best advantage! I also said that this was not exactly in my line and my specialty is rather *Fidelio* and Mozart Operas. He said slyly: 'If you can conduct Mozart well, you can also do Offenbach'. One of these half-truths!
>
> I decided that I could not afford to say no (neither financially nor otherwise). I said to him: I was in a difficult position because if I said no you would say: 'What can you do with this fellow I gave him a chance and he would not take it'. Arlen denied this strenuously, yet I know it is true...
>
> It seems INCREDIBLE with so much mediocre conducting going on of many of the masterpieces I love...I told Arlen I hope that I am not typed as an Operetten conductor. He gave me this assurance most readily *for what it is worth*![8]

On 23 February 1969 Cecilia gave birth at home to their second daughter, Esmeralda Irit Miriam. The family now urgently needed to move, not least because Chrysothemis one day managed to escape the flat and was found wandering in heavy traffic by a passing truck driver. He took her to the police station where her distraught parents located her some time later. The Bishop's Stortford house they had found turned out to be in poor condition, and so in the middle of 1969 Georg bought a house in Church Crookham, Fleet, near Aldershot. Known as The Kop, it was a timber house with a garden full of roses, and it backed onto a churchyard. They soon found that Chrysothemis cried at the sound of the church bells, and it was only with difficulty that Cecilia and her mother, then staying with them, persuaded Georg not to demand the church stop ringing them.

After conducting three performances of *Fledermaus* at the Coliseum in the first two weeks of April, Georg began the *La*

*Vie Parisienne* performances, with Iris Kells, Heather Begg, Eric Shilling, Emile Belcourt, Kevin Miller and John Fryatt. The reviews were uniformly bad. William Mann in *The Times* commented on 'a hectic reading of the score, short on precision and firm rhythmic pulse',[9] while Leslie Ayre in the *Evening News* took the contrary view that 'one feels that the singers are sometimes trying to push things along at a smarter pace than conductor Georg Tintner adopts'.[10] The *Daily Telegraph* thought the performance 'needed...much firmer and more precise direction from the conductor, Georg Tintner',[11] while the *Financial Times*'s Alan Blyth thought the third act 'too rigidly directed'.[12] Georg's tempi were slower than those of *Parisienne*'s usual conductor Alexander Faris; some of the singers thought them 'Wagnerian'. Tenor Kevin Miller says, 'I think it is true that Georg might have been considered overly cultivated for the brashness of the Sadler's Wells Offenbach revival fever.'[13]

Georg conducted only five performances before Arlen decided the reviews were so poor that he had to be removed, giving the remaining performances to Faris. It was a shattering blow, and one from which he never quite recovered. He wrote to Les:

> It seems the 'plot' was hatched by some of the singers, who were personal friends of Alexander Faris, the editor and orchestrator of the piece and also 'composer' of the previous overture (which he has of course reinstated now).
>
> The ringleader seems to have been his fellow homosexual John Fryatt and the allpowerful wife of the managing Director [Iris Kells] must have also played a rather dirty role. Even before the 1st night I had a message and hint, whether I would not reinstate Faris's overture; I politely declined. Actually my last performance was the best (a week ago it seems like years!) and everything went really as *I* felt it should go. But the big question is: can I sustain such a blow and make a go of it here?
>
> Or must I start yet another time elsewhere (for which it is mighty late anyway.)...
>
> Such a humiliation does nobody any good. It was wrong even from Arlen's point of view. He bullied me into it, therefore he was under a moral obligation to sustain me rather

than stab me in the back, after all there were only seven performances left...

I am not really despondent but the big question is whether it still makes sense to try to make a go of it here...To return to Australia or New Zealand 'empty handed' would also not be easy...

Mr Mackerras,[*] who is desperately busy, it is true, has not given me a date yet when he can receive me. But he never understood me (he knows I am a good coach) and will do so less now.[14]

Nicholas Payne, who was general manager of the English National Opera from 1998 to 2002, attended one of Georg's performances and told commentator Norman Lebrecht over thirty years later that it remained the finest *La Vie Parisienne* he had ever heard.[15]

After some *Fledermaus* performances in the regions Georg had his interview with Charles Mackerras. He reported to Les:

> Mr Mackerras was surprisingly jovial and nice, brushed my misadventure with the Offenbach aside and said that he was surprised that others far less experienced are engaged as conductors while I am not. But he has to abide by that at the moment furthermore he has to try out some other young conductors from outside.
>
> Nevertheless he offered me quite a few performances of Zauberflöte. He said, the difficulty is that he has heard I do not approve of what he does with it and nevertheless I would have to do it.
>
> I said the to me worst parts of his interpretations he had fortunately retracted and what remains is not quite as offensive to me. So we parted in good humour and I shall conduct many Zauberflötes *alla* Mackerras, both in the provinces *and* in London. Also some performances of Ariadne were offered.[†] It shows the difficulties of my

---

[*]    Charles Mackerras became Music Director of Sadler's Wells in 1970, until 1977. According to Kevin Miller, he had little time for Georg; he was 'irritated by the caraway seeds Georg had for breakfast. He was a red-meat sort of man.' (Author's interview, 5 January 2003).

[†]    It appears he did not do these.

position that I have to be glad and grateful about such breadcrumbs of mercy from the great and powerful...

Well rightly or wrongly after the interview with the great man I signed my shabby contract till June 1970.[16]

On 21 September Georg conducted a studio broadcast for the BBC, with the London Symphony Orchestra. It was arranged by the orchestra's principal oboist Anthony Camden, who had encountered Georg at the 1964 Cambridge summer school and been bowled over by his Manfred Overture. 'You will be pleased to learn that the BBC has agreed to my 4 rehearsals and pay me a phantastic fee: £100!' Georg wrote to Les. His program was Wagner's Faust Overture, the rarely performed first (1841) version of Schumann's Fourth Symphony, and Bruckner's Fifth Symphony in the original version, a first for both Georg and the orchestra. He turned up at the rehearsal on his bicycle, dressed casually in baggy shorts. One of the players told him the musicians would roast him – Georg remarked later that had he been more inexperienced the remark would have terrified him – but at the end of the sessions they gave him an ovation.

In the last week of September he conducted *The Magic Flute* in Liverpool, Bradford, Edinburgh and Sunderland ('the full orchestra under Georg Tintner was magnificent, fitting the music, from simple song to chorale, in the drama, and fusing all into an artistic entity'[17]). But the six London performances that followed, given between 12 and 30 November, were no better received than *Parisienne*. Worst of all was the *Daily Mail*'s review. Under the headline 'Georg Was a Drag', Michael Reynolds said:

> A somnolent lethargy pervaded the performance...traceable to the indecisive baton of conductor Georg Tintner. Indeed, much of the time he could be said to be following rather than directing the opera. The result was at its most noticeable in slow numbers, which dragged interminably.[18]

In November Georg conducted the London Mozart Players again, in concert and in a mostly-Schoenberg BBC broadcast. Despite the pleasure of this, he wrote glumly to Douglas Lilburn in December: 'The rat-race and our 3rd winter make me seriously

consider a return to the Antipodes. I would quite like to do something quite different, for instance being a Music-Tutor for Adult
education, preferably on the Northern tip of the North Island
[New Zealand]! We long for plenty of sun-shine!'[19]

Things were also not well at home. Cecilia was well away
from London's musical world and further from her career than
ever. The Kop was an improvement over the Wandsworth flat, but
Georg now left for work at six in the morning and returned late at
night. It was very different from the days before the children came,
when they were never seen apart. Chrysothemis was failing to
thrive, and Georg was also troubled by the fact that Cecilia seemed
not to like her second child; she said later she was very sorry about
it, but couldn't help it.

She had some Australian girlfriends who lectured her at
Georg's performances, telling her she had a career too and must
not let Georg take over her life. She began telling friends and
acquaintances that Georg didn't want her to have a career; that he
wanted her only for the purposes of bearing babies and to look after
him. One day when discussing the topic of marriage she struck fear
into Marjorie Thompson by cheerfully remarking: 'If it doesn't
work, you just try again!'

By the latter part of 1969 the relationship had deteriorated
so much that Cecilia insisted they consult a marriage guidance
counsellor. The counsellor's recommendation was to have another
baby. Georg was adamantly against this, but Cecilia thought it a
wonderful idea, in keeping with her wish for a large family – and
she prevailed. Years later Georg said, 'She couldn't cope with one,
she couldn't cope with three – what was the difference?'[20] Georg
told the Thompsons of the plan, and added with a resigned shrug,
'If that's what she wants – but she won't play the cello again.'[21]

Unexpectedly, in January 1970, the West Australian Opera
Company offered Georg its music directorship, at the instigation
of Frank Callaway, professor of music at the University of Western
Australia. Based in Perth, the company was less than three years
old and, unknown to Georg, was already riven with financial
problems and internal strife. But for him the offer had several
appealing aspects. It would be his own company, and he would
have some control over the choice of repertoire. He would be able
to train and develop the singers, unlike at Sadler's Wells where
productions and conductors turned over so fast that singers often

had no idea who the conductor would be on any given night until they sighted him across the footlights. And Perth had sunshine in abundance. Almost immediately Georg agreed to a two-year engagement to begin in May of the same year. Cecilia seemed to accept the move with equanimity. She told Marjorie Thompson after Esmeralda's birth that she had realised she couldn't have both children and a career; she said now she just wanted to go somewhere where she could bring up her children. But, sorely disappointed at Georg's lack of success, she said, 'Well, he didn't set the Thames on fire.'

About two weeks later, at Denis Matthews's insistence, the *Observer* critic Peter Heyworth attended Georg's penultimate *Magic Flute* performance at the Coliseum:

> It can take a tragically long time for a penny to drop in the mind of our vast metropolis, and in some cases I fear that it never drops at all. In recent weeks a number of acquaintances whose judgment I respect have urged me to go to hear Georg Tintner conduct *The Magic Flute* at the Coliseum. Last week I did so and was rewarded by a performance full of dramatic pace yet rich in inner life and mystery. It is (or rather was, because the revival is now, alas, over) a large-scale and many-sided reading, carried by a buoyant sense of phrase and rhythm. Mr Tintner clearly has a profound understanding of this miraculous score, knows exactly what he wants and how to get it.
>
> Such musicians are rare and would, one might suppose, be welcomed in London with open arms, particularly as we are not rich in conducting talent and Mr Tintner has for some twenty-five years had a New Zealand passport. So far is this from the case that he has felt obliged to sign a contract with a semi-professional operatic company in Perth, Western Australia – with all respect, hardly the centre of the musical universe. Mr Tintner is not, it appears, much good at fostering his own career. Nor was Reginald Goodall. Are we condemning another outstanding conductor to a lifetime of cruel neglect? If so we, as well as Mr Tintner, will be the losers.[22]

It was the break he needed. Everyone told him he couldn't leave now – Heyworth was a kingmaker. But Georg said, 'I have signed my contract, and I am going.' It was not just a matter of honour; he was only too glad to get away. After two and a half years he felt 'nothing moved', and the fiasco of *La Vie Parisienne* was fresh in his memory. He had had enough. Furthermore, Sadler's Wells had not offered him any work beyond the expiry of his contract in June. He had a wife and two children to support, a third child planned, and he was still sending money to Sue. It did not afford him the luxury of waiting to be 'made'.

Charles Mackerras says that the reason Georg was not offered more conducting at Sadler's Wells was that 'his beat was so unclear they couldn't follow it. That was said by the singers and orchestra and chorus. His vague, unclear beat was not suitable for frothy French operetta, nor would his heart have been in it. There were others with an unclear beat, like Furtwängler – but he was Furtwängler; and I'll bet he didn't conduct *La Vie Parisienne*...The English version of Georg was Reggie Goodall.'*[23]

Much later Georg said, 'It was probably a great mistake not to wait around longer,' but he meant it only as a statement of fact, not regret. Going to England had been his one attempt to get away from Australia and make a real career, and it failed. He never spoke of it, but the damage to his confidence was inestimable.

After Georg died music commentator Norman Lebrecht said:

> He came to London in the late 1960s, and that I suppose was his big chance, because London at that time was the centre of the recording world. There were four busy orchestras and they were always looking for talent. Here there clearly was talent. His misfortune was that he was working at the second opera company, at Sadler's Wells, and his face didn't fit. And that really was the tragedy of the man, because this one window of opportunity that he had to make an international career was dashed by reason of his iconoclasm.
>
> The English, as you probably know, love a good eccentric – as long as the eccentric is an eleventh earl. If he is an immigrant his eccentricity is merely dismissed as foreignness and he is shunted to one side or put in a bottom drawer, and that was really the case with Tintner. He was a vegetarian... and so he was walking around with his jar of bean sprouts

---

\*     Reginald Goodall was renowned for his very slow Wagner performances.

for lunch and he was drinking his fenugreek tea, and people looked at him and said, 'This is clearly some wacko, we don't want anything to do with him.' And he didn't get the opportunities during his three years at Sadler's Wells; he very, very rarely got to conduct. I don't think there was any tremendous hostility with his colleagues – I don't think his colleagues even noticed him, they just wrote him off as somebody who was not quite what was needed for the part.[24]

All that remained before Georg's departure was a single performance of Beethoven's *Leonore* (the first version of *Fidelio*) at the Coliseum on 15 April, and a concert at the English Bach Festival in Oxford. The latter was arranged by James Murdoch, an Australian artists' agent in London, in gratitude for free composition lessons Georg had given him in 1965. The concert took place on 19 April – Georg's first performance of Beethoven's Ninth. It was an overwhelming success that was talked about in Oxford for years.[*]

Nine days after the performance, Georg, Cecilia and the children left for Perth.

Denis Matthews said, 'What do you do for a man who won't help himself?'

---

[*] As a mark of appreciation Egon Wellesz took Georg home to show him Mahler's own score of the symphony with his retouchings marked into it; Georg found them 'excessive'.

## Eighteen

Georg soon discovered the West Australian Opera Company was not what he had been given to expect. Standards were lower, the amount of work greater. There were bitter divisions among the artists and the administration, and little co-operation between the company and the ABC, on whom it depended to supply the musicians from the West Australian Symphony. He also found that he and the company had very different ideas of suitable repertoire. At his first board meeting Georg proposed a concert performance of *Fidelio*; they wanted *Hänsel and Gretel*. He was not only the conductor and artistic director but the chorus master and the only coach as well – 'in fact the only musician',[1] he wrote glumly to Jamie Murdoch. A week after his arrival he wrote to the Thompsons:

> The Opera Company seems in an unspeakable condition artistically and 'intrigually'! But I am confident that it will change very rapidly. I had my first choral rehearsal after the chorus had 'rehearsed' for four weeks. It was truly unbelievable but the people were kind and tolerant to my unheard of demands to sing the right notes in the right places.[2]

The company provided the family with a comfortable house in Floreat Park, one of Perth's most pleasant suburbs, but neither Georg nor Cecilia liked it; Georg found the house and the neighbourhood too 'plutocratic'. Cecilia was terrified that the children might fall into the swimming pool, startling some by the extent of her panic. She was altogether unsettled in Perth, telling Les that she felt 'at limbo'. Two months after their arrival, she was interviewed by the *West Australian* on her roles as musician and mother:

> I've had to take a three-year break but, surprisingly, I think it's been good for me. I'm much more relaxed now. I used to

*Cecilia and her cello, soon after arriving in Perth in 1970.*

worry that I wasn't developing properly as a musician. Now I don't care so much. I don't want to impress people so much, I don't think about myself so much. And I know in many ways my playing is better. It will take a lot of practice to get back – eight hours a day for at least three months – but I should be able to do it.[3]

Cecilia was then two and a half months pregnant.

Before long she had found a house in Maida Vale, twenty-two level kilometres from the city, which would pose no difficulties for Georg on a bicycle. It was a ramshackle fibro house even Georg could only call 'adequate', on an acre of land where Georg could grow vegetables. They loved it; it was their romantic rustic adventure.

Before they could move there they stayed for a few weeks with Valerie Melrose, who was back in Perth and singing at the Opera. She recalls:

Cecilia was a flower-power girl. They were Nature's children, that was her philosophy. It was some sort of fantasy – a few people thought that. She had an immature view of life with Georg, an unreal view of how life was lived, rather like how she wanted things to be rather than how they really were. Georg needed someone who could really look after his career and interests and that wasn't Cecilia. She didn't like playing second fiddle...There was a sense of hysteria about her. I guess she was too young for him. By the time he'd reached that age I just think he would have been better with somebody who was much calmer and happier...She wasn't a really good companion for him. *He* wasn't a companion – I can't imagine anyone being comfortable with him.

Cecilia couldn't cope; she was hopeless at housework. She was a bit slapdash about the care of the children...but she was very caring about them. I thought it was hard for her having to bring the children up as vegetarians – there was always something that had to be boiled up.

I did feel concerned for her. It was all just wrong for Perth. The kind of people they were just didn't fit into the narrow suburban life that most of the people in the musical world and the upper artistic levels in Perth probably led: neat homes, neat gardens, neat lifestyles...Just as Georg hadn't really fitted in in Sydney, he certainly didn't in Perth.[4]

Just before Georg left England he had unexpectedly met up with someone from his television opera days in the 1950s – John Brown, the Sydney Symphony's chair-stacker, now bearded and ponytailed. 'I was very fond of this young man. We talked about music and he was very knowledgeable and he loved it...I hadn't seen him then for years and years, and he had in the meantime [gone to] Canada and headed the National Youth Orchestra.' Brown had seen Heyworth's review, and he asked Georg if he would be interested to conduct the orchestra. Georg had responded with enthusiasm, and on 10 November a telegram arrived from Brown inviting him to conduct the National Youth Orchestra's 1971 summer season. The scheduled conductor, Walter Susskind, could not attend, and Georg had to decide by noon the following day. But the Opera's chairman, Vince Warrener, said it was impossible: *The Masked Ball*

*john brown, without capitals as he preferred, at the time of Georg's first National Youth Orchestra visit.*

was to start just days after Georg's proposed return in September and he was needed to do all the rehearsing and coaching. A desperate Georg appealed to Frank Callaway, who told the Opera what an enormous honour it was for their music director to receive such an invitation. Without his intercession Georg would not have gone, and his life would have been immeasurably different.

On New Year's Day 1971 Cecilia gave birth to their third daughter Hephzibah Wanda, who was named in honour of Hephzibah Menuhin. Almost immediately Georg began preparing *Die Fledermaus* and *The Masked Ball*, with the help of the pianist David Helfgott. David, whom Georg considered 'brilliantly gifted', had returned to Perth after a breakdown in London the previous year. After his release from hospital Georg hired him as a rehearsal pianist. He knew that playing was David's lifeline, and he made sure the opera company employed him whenever possible. When Georg collected some interested singers to work on the first act of Wagner's *Die Walküre*, just for the love of it, David accompanied. He played the music perfectly on sight, and with such beauty that the singers stopped singing and listened in awe. They worked on it for months at a church in the city, but because there was nobody to sing Sieglinde or Hunding it was never performed.*

*Die Fledermaus*, the 1971 season opener, was performed in June. Vince Warrener had insisted they do an operetta to make money, and after strenuous objections Georg chose *Fledermaus* as the least objectionable to him. It was a great success; all the critics marvelled at the progress the company had made.

Early in July, just before leaving for Canada, Georg had his remaining few teeth extracted. He had never looked after his teeth, and years of eating dried fruit after the damage inflicted by rhubarb had left them too loose to be saved. He insisted the dentist pull them all without anaesthetic. He was enormously proud of this, and he often told the story as an example of what willpower could achieve. When it was over he got on his bicycle and went directly to an orchestra rehearsal, still bleeding freely. The dentist never recovered from the experience.

Georg arrived in Toronto in the middle of July, beginning an association with the National Youth Orchestra that brought him some of his greatest joy. The orchestra was founded by Walter Susskind in 1960, and by 1971 it offered an entire summer of music-making to students from across the country. They paid only a fifty-dollar registration fee to attend; even their fares were provided. They trained with some of the world's finest pedagogues, including violinists Lorand Fenyves and Maurice Clare, bassist David Walter, hornist Eugene Rittich, trumpeter Fred Mills, trombonist Richard Erb, flautist Ørnulf Gulbransen, violist Steven Kondaks, cellist Ede Banda and percussionist Alex Lepak. Yet the organisation was plagued by management and financial troubles, and for John Brown to hire Georg, an unknown from the other side of the world, was a dangerous gamble.

Georg's choice of repertoire was eclectic and demanding: *La Mer*, Bruckner's Symphony No. 4, Schubert's Symphony No. 6, Vaughan Williams's *Tallis Fantasy*, and the first two preludes from Pfitzner's opera *Palestrina*. There was also *Nekuia* by Canadian Robert Aitken, and in honour of Aaron Copland's visit to the

---

\*      Georg knew every note of Wagner's operas except *Rienzi*. When any of them was broadcast, he would place his chair in front of the radio and sit without a score, deeply immersed, giving cues to the invisible participants. With the exception of one concert performance of *Dutchman* he was never given an opportunity to conduct any of them.

orchestra, his *Billy the Kid* Suite. (Copland told Georg he liked his performance very much but it was 'too beautiful'.) Georg also scheduled extra events: a lecture-demonstration on *La Bohème* and *Madam Butterfly*, conducting the youth orchestra and singers from the University of Toronto, and another on Schoenberg that included the Chamber Symphony No. 1 conducted from memory. 'He offered himself completely,' says Joel Quarrington, who attended as a sixteen-year-old bass player.[5]

After four weeks of rehearsals the orchestra toured several Ontario locations and two in America. The morning after the final concert he flew to England; he stayed less than twenty-four hours, just long enough to see Denis Matthews and the Thompsons, who took him to visit The Kop, occupied at the time by Kathleen Tuohy. She lectured Georg on the things her daughter could not be expected to do without. That evening he departed for Perth and arrived only days before the first performance of *The Masked Ball*. The tenor Lloyd Masel met him at the airport just hours before his first rehearsal. Masel recalls:

> Georg was tired – he looked worn out. On hearing the first few bars of the overture he nearly passed out. The sound was atrocious. 'I knew this would happen', he said to me. 'In my absence the company has let me down badly.'

This was the company's first co-production with the Trust, which was supplying some of Australia's finest singers for the occasion, and Georg worked frantically to rescue it. After the second performance Georg wrote to John Brown, reporting that he 'was lucky enough to achieve a good performance inspite of frightful orchestra handicaps'. He went on:

> I am still amazed that you had the enormous courage to engage a completely unknown person after all these illustrious names…I am so glad for my own but also your sake that your faith did not let you down. Because I am quite aware of the fact that had I failed you could not have lived that down… By showing this courage you have given me one of the great joys of my life!!
>     In love and gratitude, Georg[6]

Georg's relationship with John Brown was one of the most important in his life. What made it so, at least for the first two decades,
was John's admiration and devotion. It was pure and unlimited,
and Georg returned that love to someone who gave him a rare
sense of security. Signing his letters 'Love, Georg' was something
he seldom did even to his family. Devotion was the sine qua non
to be counted among his close friends, who in fact numbered very
few. He wrote to them rarely, and saw them less often, but he was
always sure of their loyalty – a loyalty he returned. Some, such as
Franz, were blind to Georg's failings; they were offended by any
suggestion that he may even have had any. If some, such as the
Thompsons, nevertheless had doubts about some of Georg's actions
(and everyone's sympathy was with Sue in the break-up), or about
the development of his *Weltanschauung*, they kept it to themselves.
Yet Georg's need for *unqualified* esteem – and it was no accident that
he referred to his girlfriends as 'my admirers' – had nothing to do
with arrogance, or an excess of artist's ego; it came from a deep
insecurity he kept carefully concealed.

Just once in his thirty-year friendship with John Brown did
that insecurity appear, lurking in the lines of a letter he wrote in
1975:

> My dear friend John
>     I feel the need *just once* to write to you *without wanting
> anything*, except to tell you, that I value your friendship and
> kindness towards me very much indeed.
>     It is not only that you have greatly contributed to my
> exterior progress, even more important, I can feel your sym-
> pathy and liking for the *person* Georg, apart from the fact that
> he has some musical gifts.
>     I shall always be grateful to you

Georg's frantic work to rescue *The Masked Ball* showed him
that his company could not continue without a dedicated opera
orchestra. Hiring West Australian Symphony players, busy with
ABC concerts, was difficult and they disliked playing in the pit. At
his insistence an orchestra of twenty-nine musicians was formed,
the West Australian Arts Orchestra. (It lasted about two decades, until the state government diverted its funding to the West
Australian Symphony Orchestra.)

At the end of September John Brown sent Georg a cheque
for $1000, the equivalent of almost two months' Opera salary, as a
bonus. 'Your kind letter and gracious gift moved me very much!'
Georg replied.

> I am at present nurse, nursemaid laundryman cook etc. My
> wife, who is never very strong is ill and not able to do much
> for the children and all the help we engage is getting sick or
> otherwise occupied. – All the more joy gave me your totally
> unexpected *gift*...– I have asked for time to the end of this
> month to decide whether to renew my contract. On the same
> day as your letter came a not uninteresting offer of [Edward]
> Downes from the Trust Opera. I am not very keen. – Why
> should I get an extra $1000 when I ADORED EVERY MINUTE?
> I should PAY!

Cecilia was against Georg's returning to the Trust. The
thought of moving again made her feel anxious and insecure, and
she did not want to do so unless it was back to England and The
Kop, both of which she sorely missed. She was now very unhappy.
She had missed Georg while he was in Canada; he had never been
away for more than a few days, and this time he was gone for
almost eight weeks. During his absence she called David Helfgott
to say she needed Georg back as soon as possible because she
couldn't cope. 'She was very nervous and emotionally very fragile.'
he remembers. 'She was not well – like me.'[7] She came down with
pleurisy, and by October she was in hospital with pneumonia. She
felt Georg had neglected her, and for many years remained angry
that a sexist man had abandoned her with three small children.

On 27 October Georg heard again from John Brown, who
told him they had made an accounting error and if he had not
already spent the money he should return $682.

> My dear friend John, you can not seriously believe, whether
> I spent the money or not, that I would not hasten to return
> what was never meant to be mine...As a matter of fact when I
> heard 2 days ago that my first wife (a very wonderful person)
> was in great financial difficulties through *no* fault of her own I
> sent her (with the full agreement of my second wife) your gift
> of $1000. This was the first time in all these years I could do

*Cecilia with (left to right) Chrysothemis, Hephzibah and Esmeralda in 1971.*

more than what I had to. I am glad your letter did not come 2 days earlier; but we shall manage and soon I get paid again.[8]

Cecilia may have agreed to Georg's sending the money to Sue but she was anything but pleased. She said nothing to Georg – he told me that Cecilia never complained about payments he sent to Sue – but she complained bitterly to at least one of her children after the marriage was over that Georg had sent all his money to his first wife and kept them in poverty.

Six years into the marriage and Cecilia's dreams were in ruins. She became angry that Georg had left England, and asked the Thompsons with some desperation if there were not some job for him there. She lived in a primitive, isolated house she had come to hate, and had few friends. Georg begged her to practise, for he considered her very talented and wanted her to have a career. When she didn't he thought her lazy; he couldn't understand why she did not make the most of her gifts. But he also did not understand that concentrated practice was next to impossible while supervising three small children.

By the end of 1970 Cecilia was looking after few of the children's physical needs. She was often ill in bed, which some ascribed to her being so 'fraught'. Georg saw it as feeling sorry for herself. He considered her indisposition psychosomatic and, given his overwork, selfish to the point of sabotage. He did the laundry before leaving in the morning, made the bread when he returned at midnight and tended to the children during the night. As instructed by Kathleen, he bought Cecilia a car. He hired a housekeeper, and asked his friends to help. One babysitter spent an evening with her feet on the sofa, terrified of the rats and mice scurrying about, and never went back. (Georg said, 'But I *like* rats!') Another who came was Maria Vandamme, to whom Georg taught piano in exchange for home help.

> My impression was that she just could not cope with the demands of being a mother – the practical tasks of feeding, clothing, stimulating and keeping clean a family, much less a house...Cecilia needed as much care as the children did, and cheerfully blamed Georg for her plight. She was more concerned about being a cellist than in her role as a parent.[9]

Georg objected to her buying women's magazines, accusing her of 'getting ideas' from them. These were the heady early days of feminism, when women believed they could have and do it all; *The Female Eunuch* had only recently been published. Cecilia felt Georg did not take her seriously as a person and didn't understand her need to perform. She thought he was a sexist pig, and told distant relatives of his in London that he had forced her to have the first two children to keep her at home under his thumb in the kitchen, and that the third was an accident for which he was responsible.

Yet she didn't challenge him about things she didn't like, from sending money to Sue to Georg's insistence that detergent was bad and dishes should be washed only with scalding water. Georg believed that a good diet obviated the need to vaccinate the children, but when someone persuaded Cecilia this was wrong she waited until he was out of town to have them vaccinated. He never forgave her. Her only protest was to cut her hair short, which Georg saw as 'an act of defiance'.

Cecilia became frightened of living in the country, and at night she would sit on the windowsill, looking out fearfully, waiting for Georg to come home. When they went to bed she was terrified by the sound of possums on the roof, thinking someone was breaking in, and to Georg's intense frustration she insisted every night that he get up to check. There were now terrible scenes where she screamed hysterically at him, and sometime in those months he suggested that she see a psychiatrist; she refused on the grounds she was cleverer than they were. Georg thought this was probably true and didn't press the point. To some it seemed, at least in retrospect, that Cecilia was having a nervous breakdown.

Cecilia later told her children that one of the reasons the marriage failed was Georg's temper. She felt she had no choice but to leave, and that it would be terrible for the girls if she didn't. Valerie Melrose recalls:

> There was probably that element of being slightly afraid, because he could be so stern and his standards so high – remembering the sort of person he could be when he withdrew, the sort of silence that conveyed a certain disapproval or disappointment. We were all females who came up against him, wanted to please him and didn't...
>
> Georg wasn't the sort of person who could really give you support. My feeling is that the ones who got on with him best were the women who had a secure partnership with someone else. They could worship at his feet and feel quite secure in themselves.

## Nineteen

In February 1972 Georg went to Sydney for a concert with the Elizabethan Trust Orchestra. He wrote to Sue, hoping to visit her while he was in eastern Australia, and mentioned that he had heard that she was getting married again. It was a false rumour. She replied:

> Never again, I assure you, after those stupid and frustrating twenty years with you. After the fuss you made when I asked you to look after the children for one night while I took Mizzi to see Sir Lawrence Olivier, I would have thought you realised that to look after four children is a full time occupation for one person.[1]

Her words stung Georg bitterly. Yet he still thought of her as his anchor, and now he needed her more than ever. 'Frankly, without wishing to be cruel I don't see any point in meeting again,' she wrote, clearly unnerved by the idea. 'I have tried to build up a civilised front by letter and the children, but your views infuriate me as much as they always did…'[2]

Georg stayed with Robert King, who decided to introduce him to a friend, a former student of Abbotsleigh School where he was teaching. I was that friend, but I declined Robert's dinner invitation; my summer job was finished and I was returning the next day to Canberra for my second year of university. Georg and I didn't meet for more than four years.

After the financial success of *Fledermaus*, Vince Warrener insisted on presenting another operetta, *The Gypsy Baron*. There were seventeen performances in sixteen days, beginning on 10 May; Cecilia played as an extra. All performances were sold out and enthusiastically received, but Georg was only willing to concede 'there are a lot of people coming'. His fifty-fifth birthday occurred near the end of the run and he marked the occasion by attending a recital by David Helfgott, who gave what Georg considered the greatest performance of Beethoven's 'Tempest' Sonata he ever heard. Yet within eighteen months David was in such a dire mental state that he was admitted to Graylands Hospital. Georg visited him there as often as he could, and gave him money. He was appalled to discover that David was prohibited from practising on the grounds it would disturb the other patients, and insisted he be allowed a piano.

Also on Georg's birthday a letter arrived from England, which Cecilia opened and did not show him. It said the tenants of The Kop had left and the house was now vacant. On 30 May Georg returned home from rehearsals to find the house in darkness. There was no sign of Cecilia or the children; there was no car, and no note. He searched for them frantically, calling the police and friends to help. Two days later he came home to find the car at the house again, but it had only been returned by the people to whom Cecilia had fled, Lloyd and Shoshana Masel. There was also a telegram from Cecilia. She had gone to her mother in Melbourne, who received her with open arms.

A few days later he wrote in an exercise book:

> Today I am on the 7th day of a fast. The total nourishment is this awful Allopurinol and water. The motives for my fast are mixed. If Gretel were still here I would certainly have wanted to bring moral pressure on her (the only kind that isn't completely bad *alla* Gandhi). But also this need to purify, to think. Despite a tremendous effort I am not pleased with my musical achievement. I *must* accomplish something creative. Whether I will really die? Life at home was dreadful already for a long time, but I am insofar 'lucky' that so many people value and admire me and we all need that. So it was not completely so unbearable.[3]

Losing Cecilia did not upset Georg much; he was 'fed up and glad to see the last of her'.[4] But the loss of the children was a disaster. Fifteen years later he said in an interview:

I wasn't sorry to lose the relationship to my second wife who seemed not to attach very great importance to that relationship and who finally left me. But it was a matter of profound grief and despair that I thereby lost three very young children. You know how an aging father is sort of doting – especially they were all three daughters – and there were moments when I really felt quite genuinely I might not survive this dreadful thing that happened to me. But time is a great healer, and I would like to say that it was music that pulled me over this crisis.[5]

Two years after Cecilia left, he said to Keith Jacobs, 'She didn't like playing second fiddle – but she had to.'[6] And he added resignedly, 'It was a fairy tale.' Marjorie Thompson believes that had he succeeded in England and made a good income the marriage might have survived. Georg himself was acutely aware that one of his main deficiencies in Cecilia's eyes was failing to become famous, and it rankled with him for the rest of his life.

If Georg wrote at all about major personal events such as his divorces, marriages, and deaths of relatives, it was only in one or two laconic sentences with no mention of his feelings. But the letters he wrote to the Thompsons in the next few months overflow with grief and bewilderment.

I am utterly heartbroken because I love these children beyond measure and can't imagine life without them. But quite apart from these selfish reasons I am utterly convinced that the children need their father. When Chrysothemis heard that she was leaving she cried desperately but not even that helped. I don't exactly know why she went but I would endure even greater humiliations (I was banned from the marriage bed for months and slept outside for instance...) if I could have them back!!![7]

When the Thompsons told Egon Wellesz, he said: 'One should never marry Mélisande.' Les replied, 'Unless one is Pelléas.' Marjorie thought, '*Especially* if one is Pelléas.'

The devastation wrought by the loss of the children was so great that Georg, at least for a short time, lost his reason. Sometime in the two weeks after Cecilia left he asked Melodie Meyer, a member of the opera chorus and sometime singing student of his, to marry him. Melodie was a fourteen-year-old convent schoolgirl, half Chinese, with long hair. Georg told her he wanted to marry her in order to have mixed-race children, his favoured solution for so much of the world's disharmony. He also needed a muse to aid his increasingly frantic need to resume composing. Melodie was terrified by Georg's offer – although not threatened; he never touched her. She didn't even know what a muse was, but she knew that at the institution where she was studying music the seven muses sat on an arch, and she wondered if it meant she would have to sit on one too. She refused him, and transferred shortly afterwards to another singing teacher. Georg told her he would contact her every six months until she turned eighteen, hoping she would change her mind.

Georg sent Cecilia some money, then sold the car and sent her the proceeds. He heard only from her mother, who reprimanded him for selling it too cheaply. Shortly afterwards, at Kathleen's behest, Cecilia retained a lawyer. Two weeks later he was served with a summons,

> stating that I had left Gretel on May 30 without cause and had failed to support her in any way. This summons was UNDER OATH and signed in 2 places by Gretel. As I learned only afterwards there is something called 'Constructive desertion' which means that the remaining party was so beastly that he is really the deserter. After many troubles I managed to phone Gretel but instead of asking how my beloved children are I had to ask her whether she had gone mad. She was very superior and explained constructive desertion and said she did not read the part about the money: she had received my money alright. So she committed perjury. But her attitude was worse than the deed.[8]

Cecilia told him she hadn't read it because the lawyer told her it was 'the standard form'.

During those terrible weeks Georg wrote a small canon and sent it to the children. There was a second piece, a lullaby, for voice and two bass-clef instruments, almost certainly cellos; perhaps he hoped that Cecilia and her mother could find it in their hearts to play it to the children. Whether he actually sent it to them is unknown; Maria Vandamme found a copy on the floor in Georg's house apparently ready to be thrown out. She played it on the piano and he became very agitated. 'When he was left alone, he was completely distraught, demented with grief,' she recalls. 'Georg, I must stress, really adored his children and the devastation of having them removed was very intense. I shall never forget his grief. It was a tragedy.'⁹

Early in July Georg wrote to Cecilia asking if he might visit the children for Chrysothemis's fifth birthday. Almost immediately he received a two-page letter from Cecilia's lawyers, which in shock and despair he copied out in its entirety and sent to the Thompsons. Cecilia said that it was not convenient for him to visit this weekend, though she did not wish to deny him reasonable access to the children and that almost any other time but this would be convenient. All such arrangements must be made through her lawyers, and he was instructed neither to upset the children nor to remove them from Kathleen's home. The letter said that Cecilia could not return to Georg because while she believes he genuinely wants the children back, he is not sincere in wanting her to return. Further, he had subjected her to 'severe mental cruelty' to the point where 'she feared for her mental and physical health as long as she continued to live with him', and she believed his behaviour would not change. She rejected his maintenance offer as inadequate and insisted, though she was on her way to live at The Kop, that it be raised to include rent.

'My friends, I feel like in a made [*sic*] house,' Georg wrote at the end.

> This [lawyer's] letter was written on July 5 while 2 days later I wrote to Gretel taking largely the blame: because it suddenly occurred to me that she might have really been all the time utterly exhausted and not being able to help doing practically nothing but the children which I hitherto considered rather selfishness and self pity. I suggested she and I should live one year apart and I try my best...I of course don't want to see the children under these offensive and impossible conditions, and dread already the week I shall conduct in M[elbourne] in October. How can Gretel allow all this to GEORG???¹⁰

Georg may briefly have considered killing himself. The day after this letter he wrote to Heather Begg, 'I can't say that I miss her all that much as the last few months were difficult, but I don't know yet whether I like to live [i.e., keep living] without those lovely children.'[11]

The maintenance amount Cecilia stipulated was about a third of Georg's gross salary and, in addition to his mortgage, proved a considerable burden. As he lived very frugally he had only one way of reducing his costs, and so he very reluctantly wrote to Sue to explain he could no longer afford to send her money. All their children were now in their twenties, although the twins were still at university. She replied:

> I am very sorry, honestly, to hear of your troubles. I can only say, thank you for the money you have sent. I will manage…I have paid off part of the overdraft, and if [the twins] get jobs in the long holiday as they intend, that will save me a lot of money. And now it's raining, so let us hope that is the end of drought. Hope your troubles resolve themselves.[12]

Late in July Cecilia's lawyers advised him that the maintenance amount must be apportioned two-fifths to Cecilia and one-fifth to each child. The object was to ensure Georg would support Cecilia in perpetuity, after the children had grown up. If he did not agree to this he would be required to appear in court in August. Georg did not dispute the total but insisted it be apportioned one-third for each child, and so on 18 August he went to Melbourne. When he arrived at the court Cecilia's lawyers told him they had agreed to his wishes, and that his appearance was no longer necessary. Foolishly, he said he wanted to go to court anyway, because he still had no idea why Cecilia had left him and he wanted to find out. Even more foolishly, he represented himself because he couldn't afford a barrister. It was a disastrous experience, and he would not talk about it except to say that his words were twisted by Cecilia's lawyers, and the more he tried to extricate himself the worse it became. He said he was painted as a domineering older man and a sadist, and he felt all the sympathy of the magistrate drifting towards 'this little girl sobbing at the side of the court'. Georg did write at the time to the Thompsons:

[Gretel's] evidence was absolutely terrifying, but she believed it I think. I read to them about 20 passionate and loving passages she wrote to me to Canada only 9 months before she fled; she simply said she felt it her duty to back me up but did not mean any, in fact she never loved me at all. She also cried (quite genuinely) and my refusal to kill rats and mice who were only there because Gretel did never clean food from table or floor tipped the scale. Nevertheless I am glad I went and heard Gretel say these horrifying things because it showed me 'in the flesh' that she really meant what she said these last few weeks that it is hopeless and she would never come back. This whole action actually gave me a new strength, so it served some good. I am sad about my adored children. But under the circumstances I want to stay away until they can think for themselves.[13]

Georg never really recovered. His closer friends noted that he became withdrawn and shut in. He was a changed man. His attempt to create a career in England had come to nothing; two marriages had failed, he had lost his children, and his sexual confidence had been undermined. He coped with his grief the only way he knew: by burying himself in music, and working even harder. Intensive rehearsals followed his return from Melbourne, for an opera season that opened on 14 September: a double bill of *The Barber of Seville* and *Madam Butterfly*, both enthusiastically received.

Around this time he invited two music-loving artists he had met at *Gypsy Baron* rehearsals, Simon and Genette Kay, to live with him. Those who knew of Cecilia's departure – and by no means everyone did – were relieved Georg would be looked after. The Kays did much of the housework, and mostly kept out of the way. But despite living at close quarters for two years, they learned little about him. He did not mention Cecilia once, nor did they know Sue's name. They knew nothing about any of his children, not even their names; there were no photos to be seen.

In the middle of October Georg went to Melbourne to conduct a concert and was able to see his children. A few days later Cecilia wrote to him setting out some financial requests; she added that she hoped he felt seeing the children was worthwhile, and asked him not to cut off Hephzibah at any future visit because he didn't know her, or because she had changed too much. Two days after this she asked him for his written approval for her to take the children to England. Georg was strongly opposed to their leaving Australia, but he decided it was the lesser of two evils. If Cecilia were prevented from returning to her beloved Kop 'she would take it out on the children'. Worse, he knew that if she stayed in Melbourne she would continue living with her mother. He was convinced that Kathleen would turn the children against him, and this he wanted to avoid at any cost. She had aided in the break-up of the marriage, because, he said, she was jealous: 'She was interested in me long before I knew she had a daughter.'[14] Marjorie Thompson was also convinced of it, and it was said as far away as Sydney that 'Kathleen had pushed her daughter toward him but then got jealous'.[15]

Georg complied, and on 13 November Cecilia and the children departed for England.

Georg spent the final weeks of 1972 rehearsing two operas for the Festival of Perth in February: Britten's *Albert Herring* and Kurt Weill's *Threepenny Opera*. He was wretchedly miserable, unwell, and in financial trouble. He had unexpectedly received a hefty tax bill at the end of August and was still struggling with both his mortgage and payments to Cecilia. He wrote to John Hopkins seeking an ABC job from June 1973, when his contract expired, but Hopkins replied there was nothing available. Georg then wrote to the ABC's State Manager in Perth, asking for the first time in his life for a raise. The letter was forwarded to head office in Sydney. Anthony Hughes, who had hired Georg for the television operas, sent a memo to Harold Hort, Acting Director of Music:

> I was astonished to read on your card system that Georg received £45 for a concert in 1962 and is still listed as *$90* today* – Which means he is getting *much less* today than in 1962! This is absurd…I would say, over the last years, a 75 per cent increase should apply for cost of living PLUS some acknowledgement of Tintner's great improvement as a conductor. That makes, shall we say a 125 per cent increase

---

\*    Australia decimalised its currency in 1966 at the rate of two dollars to the pound.

i.e. $202.50 (say $200 for concert fee). What do you think? I
*cannot* be party to these unacceptable payments.[16]

Hort concurred, and the ABC settled on a fee of $120 per
concert.

*Albert Herring* opened on 1 February to mixed reviews. Three
weeks later Georg conducted the opening night of *Threepenny
Opera* with the Playhouse Group, who put it on because Georg
wanted to do it so badly – 'I take Weill very seriously (perhaps
my generation and background!)'[17] After the first performance he
disappeared, and a chorus member eventually found him sitting
at the bottom of some steps at the back of the theatre, crying.
He asked worriedly, 'Was it so bad?' Georg replied, 'I'm crying
because I'm so happy!'[18]

John Brown's response to the news of Cecilia's departure was to
offer Georg the 1974 National Youth Orchestra season. He also put
Georg's name forward for the Edmonton Symphony conductorship,
strongly supported by the departing incumbent Lawrence Leonard,
who had also seen Peter Heyworth's *Magic Flute* review. John
wrote to twelve British organisations, including Sadler's Wells, but
all replied in the negative.

Georg was finding the opera company increasingly disagreeable. He didn't get on with Vince Warrener, who had previously
been a mining company executive. Warrener wanted to make
casting decisions; Georg was adamant that artistic matters should
be left to him. He found Warrener interfering, and Warrener
thought Georg difficult. 'He had very little flexibility,' he said.
'Musically you have to get the best you can from the capabilities
you are working with. Georg felt that if it couldn't be done as
Beethoven said, then it couldn't be done at all.'[19] Georg wrote
again to John Hopkins, who replied that no conducting position
was available in 1973 or 1974. Swallowing his pride, he even visited
Yehudi Menuhin when he gave a concert in Perth on 14 April.
If he could get back to England he could again be close to the
children. But Menuhin only said, 'Nice to meet you again', and
brushed him off.

In the middle of 1973 Georg reluctantly renewed his contract for one more year, just as things began to improve for him
artistically. On 24 May he conducted Beethoven's Mass in C and

*Christus am Ölberg* at the Intervarsity Choral Festival in Perth; on 2 and 3 June he conducted a concert performance of part of *Fidelio* for the opening of the new Festival Theatre in Adelaide. '*Fidelio* stands or falls principally by its music,' said the *Advertiser*, 'and in Georg Tintner as conductor, the performers had a spiritual guide as well as a time-keeper, for in his field he is one of the most inspiring and best-loved conductors we've seen.'[20] He returned to Perth for a season of *The Merry Widow* beginning on 14 June – yet another operetta chosen against his wishes. 'Lehár is not a composer,' he told Vince Warrener. 'At first I thought I would hate it throughout,' he wrote to Les Thompson, 'but I see some MUSICAL merit in it *apart* from the five or six magnificent tunes.'[21]

This was followed by three Sydney engagements. He conducted *Albert Herring* for Young Opera from 13 to 15 July with Paul Terracini, Patricia Whitbread and an orchestra of mostly Sydney Symphony players; Maria Prerauer said in the *Sunday Telegraph* that Georg 'directed one of the most musically accurate and spirited performances ever heard in the short history of local opera.'[22] On 22 July he conducted a Mozart program with the Royal Philharmonic Society Chamber Orchestra. 'Closely to watch Georg Tintner conduct…was to run the risk of being mesmerised by the visible vitality of his batonless style,' wrote the *Sydney Morning Herald*'s Fred Blanks, who never wasted an opportunity to wax eloquent on Georg's appearance. 'In turn, he drew on the pliability of a willow, the curtness of a traffic policeman, the short jerky gestures of a dynamic marionette with a new battery; but what he used most of all was the arm-and-finger outstretched command of a faith-healer intent on exorcising musical spirits.'[23]

His final Sydney concert, on 28 July, was Handel's *Samson*, with Maureen Forrester, Gerald English and the Sydney Symphony, which David Ahern of the *Daily Telegraph* thought 'magnificent… The clarity, incisiveness and vitality of his baton technique is a pleasure to watch.'[24] At the end of 1973 Ahern voted Georg Conductor of the Year for this performance. 'His virile, curly-cued interpretation of Handel's [*Samson*] was a five star winner. Tintner is a conductor of world class – why doesn't the ABC (and the Australian Opera) use him more?'[25]

Surprised and cheered by the abundance of good reviews, Georg wrote to Heather Begg on 17 August: 'You will doubtless rejoice: I have absolutely tremendous successes quite unexpectedly;

so everybody is very polite to me now...' To the Thompsons he wrote:

> Today I feel extravagant and send you some copies of reviews of my Sydney and Melbourne activities by AIR. I know you will be glad that they suddenly have discovered that I have some talent...I am very tired and still have trouble with my never resting hand.
>
> I think of becoming a freelance conductor as the doors begin to open.

Tapes of Georg's concerts around this time show an impassioned vibrancy radiating from them: *Samson*; *Transfigured Night* at the 1974 National Youth Orchestra; and in 1975, Tchaikovsky's Sixth with the National Youth Orchestra and *Fidelio* for the Australian Opera. 'Somebody who deals with art,' Georg said much later, 'who dares to call himself an artist, sometimes needs the darker side of life, the crisis. I think it helps him to get under the surface of the things that matter.'[26]

A couple of weeks after the *Samson* performance Georg realised the ABC had not sent him his fee, travel allowance and airfare. The ABC was startled to discover that they had not issued a contract and there was no documentation at all. John Hopkins notified Georg that as he had been in Sydney anyway he would get his fee but no allowances or airfare unless he could demonstrate it would leave him out of pocket. A contract was sent separately, which Georg refused to sign. He wrote to Hopkins:

> I had (until a few minutes ago when I read your letter) no *idea* that your offer was made to me *because you knew* I would be [in Sydney anyway]. As you seem to think that the princely sum of $120 is an adequate fee for my humble efforts let us leave it at that...But I can't help thinking that it is not right that the ABC lets the desperatly poor Young Opera and the (perhaps not so poor) Royal Philharmonic Society shoulder the cost of my coming here (to Sydney I mean) and going back and thereby SUBSIDISING the allpowerful ABC![27]

Hopkins backed down and authorised the travel allowance, which had not been paid 'due to an oversight'. He also sent Georg's fee to Vince Warrener with a note: 'We would like to be assured that future negotiations for Mr Tintner's services will continue to be handled through your organisation, to avoid further confusion.' Notwithstanding this tart request, the ABC recognised they had created an almighty mess.[28] As it turned out, Georg would be made to pay for it. But in the meantime he acquired John Duff as his agent, which pleased and relieved the ABC until it occurred to them that Duff would likely ask for higher fees. This he did, getting Georg's concert fee raised to $344.

In September Georg conducted three performances of *Albert Herring* in Adelaide with New Opera although he was ill with double pneumonia. For a while he was plagued with hyper-acute hearing, and his right hand and wrist were so painful that for half a year he wrote with his left hand, sometimes in mirror-image.[*] He realised that overwork was seriously affecting his health, and he decided not to renew his Opera contract. 'After three and a half years…I am pretty fed up with their lack of appreciation of my gigantic efforts,' he wrote to John Brown on 27 October, 'and look for a change though I love PERTH.'

Georg must have realised that freelancing was too risky, and when John Hopkins left the ABC at the end of 1973 he wrote to the Acting Director of Music, Harold Hort:

> I take the liberty to offer my services as resident conductor of the W.A.S.O. I think I can claim to have made some small contribution to the operatic, orchestral and choral endeavours in Perth. I am equally interested in purely orchestral conduct-ing as in opera…I can claim to have some following in the musical public of Perth. Another point in my favour might be that in thirty-five years of conducting I have never been rude or 'nasty' to a player or singer, and I am not going to start now.[29]

Anthony Hughes sent a memo to Werner Baer noting that arrangements had already been made for the orchestra with the British conductor David Measham, but that he wanted details of Georg's forthcoming ABC engagements before replying. Michael

---

[*]    Georg was left-handed but had been made to write with his right hand at school.

Corban from Programming reported: 'Tintner was offered no interstate engagements in '74, mainly because of the difficulties [over the *Samson* payment] he caused this year (probably inadvertent)...In Perth he will conduct Jan 27 Free and Feb 27 Special with [Geoffrey] Tozer.'[30]

Hughes replied:

> I do not consider, having studied the file, that we should have any implied 'black mark' against such an excellent musician – the point that matters is the standard of musical performance which can be achieved for us – and, is he paid properly for his services? Although tending to be something of the 'school-master', which can aggravate professional orchestras, there can be no doubt Mr Tintner merits appreciably more work than listed above even if only 'casual'. As he now has an agent the 'Admin' side should be easier. I suggest we have a discussion between all concerned on [Hort's] return on Monday re Georg's future value to us in all areas.[31]

Werner Baer added to the same memo: 'Too good a man – right under our very nose! To ignore and overlook for two essentially obscure men...! Criticism about non appointment of Australians (born or naturalised) would be *well warranted*.' In the end the matter was settled by the manager for Western Australia, who said he had no interest in offering Georg the position. Shortly thereafter, Georg signed a three-year contract as Senior Resident Conductor with the Trust, now renamed the Australian Opera.

On 25 April he began his final West Australian Opera season. *Il Trovatore* and *Die Fledermaus* ran concurrently, seventeen performances in the same number of days. The season ended on 11 May and the next day Georg left Perth for good. 'He has transformed the opera company in the last four years,' said the *Record*:

> I believe he has expressed disappointment in what he has been able to achieve; nobody else has reservations. The amateurishness of the early years has almost disappeared. While we have a long way to go, neither of the current productions would disgrace some of the minor European opera houses.
>
> Musically, Perth owes Georg Tintner a great debt.[32]

## Twenty

In June Georg went to Vancouver for his second National Youth Orchestra summer. He began with a lecture demonstration on Verdi's *Il Trovatore*, in which he conducted the orchestra and sang all the parts himself, and then gave several lectures on composers, including Wagner, Weill, Beethoven, Tchaikovsky, Schoenberg and Bruckner. Although the lectures were over ninety minutes long they were entirely extemporaneous. Georg didn't even have notes, let alone a script. In his Bruckner lecture he gave a detailed harmonic analysis at the piano of the Andante of the Seventh Symphony, though he had not looked at the score for eight years. The audiences were spellbound. The Canadian Broadcasting Corporation taped the lectures and edited them into ten half-hour talks, which were broadcast worldwide; they still receive occasional airplay over three decades later. The CBC paid Georg $2500 for the rights, the equivalent of almost four months' pay in Perth. He gave it all to the youth orchestra.

His two-month residency gave him enough time to prepare three difficult programs, one of which he called 'Symphonies No. 5 in B flat' – those by Schubert and Bruckner. Another included Weill's *Threepenny Opera* Suite, Passacaglia and Fugue by the Canadian composer Harry Somers, Schumann's Symphony No. 4 (the 1841 version), and Schoenberg's *Transfigured Night*. Georg had argued with John Brown for months over the Schoenberg: 'Don't let the experts persuade you that it cannot be done! I know it can and would do them a tremendous lot of good…I have no doubt that we would succeed and my young friends would find the emotionally laden atmosphere very congenial as I do.'[1] Including the sectionals, the work was given thirty rehearsals, and in the end he was vindicated: the Vancouver *Courier* said the orchestra 'was nothing short of awesome in its responses to conductor Georg

Tintner'.[2] The musicians never forgot it, and twelve years later one of the viola players would change the direction of Georg's life.

In a final questionnaire one of the students wrote:

> Our musical director this year, to me, was a study of a man totally into music…I had never really seen or met a person like this before, and no description could have such a profound effect on me as Mr Tintner in person, really did. His total dedication to the art and humanizing of that same thing set a great example to me. He is a great conductor, and I love NYO for bringing him to conduct us. It is certainly worth being here, just if all we did was listen to his lectures, for the man is a goldmine of descriptive experiences. I don't think it will be easy for me to forget my summer spent with NYO in 1974.[3]

There were many similar assessments. But Georg had not recovered from the events of the previous two years and he was completely exhausted. As he left Canada he wrote to John Brown: 'The collaboration between you and me is one of the joys of my profession and I am again glad that I have not let you down. I gave every ounce of my strength and ability (such as it is).'[4] A week later he wrote: 'I was sad that you thought that you had failed me – is that perhaps a polite way of saying that I did not do quite as well as expected? Perhaps I did not; yet I never *conducted* better (or even as well perhaps.) Yet also I feel I could have done better…'[5]

From Canada he went to England for a few days to visit the children. He had not seen them for almost two years. The later recollection of Hephzibah, then three and a half, was of someone called a 'father' pushing her on a swing, having no concept of what a father was. To Georg's surprise Cecilia told him she was considering returning to him. She was finding life difficult; the help she had expected from their Oxford and London friends had not materialised. She was ignored by almost everyone except distant relatives of Georg's in London, the doctors Henry and Gerda Tintner. Georg told the Thompsons that it just might work 'with a great deal of goodwill on both sides. But she must not think I will wait around forever with cap in hand.'[6]

He spent most of the rest of 1974 in Adelaide, conducting a short season of *Idomeneo* with the University of Adelaide, and *The Tales of Hoffmann* in November with the Australian Opera. His final appearances for the year were ABC concerts in Sydney, including the *Messiah* at the Opera House. Under the title 'Hallelujah! A Good Messiah', Maria Prerauer said in the *Sunday Telegraph*:

> This year there was a minor miracle. At the Opera House the ABC put on the kind of Messiah that Handel must have intended. Along with most of the listeners I sat there thrilled to bits. The orchestra was the same (the SSO), the choir was the same (the Philharmonia), so what was new? The conductor, Georg Tintner. He both resurrected and revitalised the true essence. No false Messiahs for him. More than anything else it was the restoration of the right speeds that made the difference. Fast was fast and slow was slow…But Georg Tintner's miracle-working went even further than mere technicalities. He was able to inject life and spirit into every last performer…The performance sent me home elated, my faith in the Messiah fully restored – for this year, anyway.[7]

Georg now had time to collect his household goods from Perth – some old beds and mattresses, his mother's eiderdowns and table linen, and his books and scores, almost nothing else. The Kays, still living in the house, made him take a large Royal Doulton vase he loathed, a gift of some value, by filling it with mung beans. His upright piano he gave to a tenor who had long admired it. And he heard again from Cecilia who said she would not, after all, return to him. 'Perhaps she is right,' he wrote to Les Thompson, 'but it is sad for the children.'

He found a white stuccoed 1940s house for rent in the leafy suburb of Waverton. It was unfurnished and unrenovated, but it had the virtues of being opposite a park and within cycling distance of the Opera House across the Harbour Bridge. Robert King's wife Ilse fixed him up with an old lounge suite, and he bought a small Zimmerman grand piano, the first grand he had owned. On 25 January 1975, now aged fifty-seven, he wrote to John Brown: 'I live in a beautiful big house, alone. I used to like to live in solitude but I find it hard now. (perhaps a sign of my age…) Hoping for a

MUSE.' In this lonely state he wrote to Heather Begg asking her to send a copy of his song 'Frühling' they had recorded for the ABC in 1956. Heather returned the song, and Georg replied sadly:

> A few minutes ago your beautiful parcel with three copies of *Frühling* arrived! I played through it after all those years and felt ashamed for my present state of creative impotence because I thought that song most beautiful. As it is *thirty-eight* years old, it is really by another person, so I can praise it.[8]

In January he conducted Sydney performances of Kurt Weill's *Rise and Fall of the City of Mahagonny*, with Ronald Dowd, Rosina Raisbeck, Grant Dickson, Robert Allman and Lone Koppel Winther. His conducting was judged 'classy work' and 'an auspicious conducting debut with the Australian Opera'. But Georg was already unhappy. Some of the artistic decisions, including casting, were not to his liking, and he was frustrated by producers, the new stars of the opera world, who, in his opinion, had little idea of what the operas were actually about. According to artistic administrator Moffatt Oxenbould, Georg 'seemed much more isolated than he had been in the Trust'.[9] He was considered aloof because of his continued refusal to use first names, and altogether simply strange. Rae Cocking recalls 'he rode a bike and was vegetarian. It wasn't the right image.' Indeed, the *Australian* reported:

> Between the clatter of glasses and the sniping of critics [at an Opera party] Georg Tintner, the tiny white-haired vegetarian conductor of *Mahagonny*, nibbled at his carroway [*sic*] seeds and mourned the passing of passionate music and the bicycle…'My bicycle is a symbol of what I believe in. I am a pacifist and, if you like, the bicycle is the ultimate in harmlessness', he said. 'I am also a vegetarian, I do not eat any animal products whatsoever…I would die before I ate them…I hope.' In fact the fifty-seven-year-old conductor almost did die two years ago when he collapsed from malnutrition two days before a concert in Melbourne. Now his diet of seeds, grain and fruit is more carefully balanced…[10]

Outraged, Georg wrote to the newspaper:

*Georg pausing in a rehearsal for* Mahagonny *in 1975.*

Five years ago I worked in London. One day a phone call came from Melbourne and a sympathetic voice inquired what I had died from as there had just appeared my death notice. In your paper I had to read that two years ago I collapsed from malnutrition and nearly died two days before a concert in Melbourne. For the sake of truth and veganism, may I state that the one story is as untrue as the other. I never collapsed in my life and did and do not suffer from malnutrition. I have never tried to prevent others from eating corpses and therefore have the right to be spared untrue stories about my more humane diet.[11]

'The thing with people with extreme views,' says Sam Atlas, a West Australian Opera singer, 'is that it prompts people who probably haven't thought about the issue before to bait one – rather like baiting a performing monkey.' In relentlessly conformist Australia it was all too tempting to ridicule those who were different. Georg, always happy to discuss his beliefs, made it all too easy.

Only weeks after starting at the Opera, Georg heard that Richard Bonynge was to join the company as music director. For him this was a disaster, not least because he thought Bonynge would change the Opera's repertoire to a diet of second-rate *bel canto* operas to suit himself and his wife. And general manager John Winther had broken his word that Georg would have no musical director above him.[12] He wrote to John Brown on 25 January: 'I was *shattered* to hear of the appointment of Mr Richard Bonynge to be Musical Director of the Australian Opera from June 1976. I consider this appointment a MUSICAL disaster and betrayal. Though I have a three year contract, I want to leave the AO by that date.' Winther admits, 'I appointed Bonynge and Sutherland as a political move. Everyone wanted Joan, and he came with the package. Also to get rid of [Edward] Downes, and Georg's leaving was an unintended by-product.'[13]

The question for Georg was how he could leave. He had by then parted company with John Duff, who in two years had not found him a single engagement. A possible escape route presented itself with the foundation of the Australian Chamber Orchestra, an ensemble of twenty string players. An initiative of the players themselves, but set up under the aegis of the Elizabethan Theatre Trust, it was to be directed jointly by Georg and Robert Pikler. Georg's first concert was scheduled for 16 May, and the program was already at the printer when the performance was called off. He never heard from the orchestra again. For a while Christopher Kimber was advertised as artistic director and conductor of the inaugural concert rescheduled for November, but by the time it took place Kimber had departed and it was conducted by Robert Pikler.[14] When Pikler heard afterward what had happened to Georg, he resigned in protest.

In the middle of July Georg went to Halifax, on the Canadian east coast, for his third National Youth Orchestra summer. On the way he spent two weeks at the Banff School of Arts, arranged by John Brown, giving lectures and conducting the Canadian Chamber Orchestra. Early in June, while still in Melbourne with *Mahagonny*, he wrote an unaccompanied song for Melodie Meyer. She was turning eighteen on 15 June, and he wrote her a final letter.

Allow me to present you with this little gift for your birthday next Sunday. You may not like it at all. It is not meant for public performance. The poet [D. M. Dolben] must have written the words, when he was about your age; If you do not care for it as music, perhaps it would be of some use in reading and pitching...

If you prefer that our contact shall not be resumed, please simply do not reply. I shall understand and not try again...I want to assure you, that I did not teach you singing in order to put you under an obligation towards me. My mind does not work that way...

It is difficult to write into a void and I close with my best wishes. I hope also the rest of the family is well.

yours very sincerely, Georg T.[15]

Georg was already in Banff by the time he received Melodie's reply saying that she was happy to be his friend but didn't wish for marriage. As he had promised, he did not try again.

A few days later he met a young woman working in a summer job for the Banff administration. Erica Munn was twenty-two years old and an 'anorexic poetess', as Georg described her, with a complicated and difficult family life. She was, in her own words, 'very mixed up, very naïve, very green', and felt she was somehow 'different'. But she was a vegetarian, and her mother encouraged her to meet Georg because she thought they had much in common and would be just right for each other. Lonely and still looking for a muse, Georg turned up one day at Erica's door and invited her to have lunch with him. He made crushed nuts with grapes, which she thought delicious. They went for a few walks together, and on his last day he attempted to throw her onto the bed. She reacted with horror. Nevertheless, she agreed to let him write to her.

His youth orchestra visit was brief, allowing only one program: Mozart's Symphony No. 34 in C, Beethoven's *Leonore* No. 3 Overture and Tchaikovsky's Symphony No. 6.[*] He had at first proposed the Ritual Dances from Tippett's *Midsummer Marriage*,

---

[*] Georg had at last come to love Tchaikovsky. 'As a teenager I felt quite superior to Tchaikovsky because I could not then understand that the private hell contained in his writing was so sincerely felt. I felt it was "put on" and that there was simply too much of everything. The Sixth Symphony is one of the very greatest treasures in the symphonic repertoire and can only be truthfully realised if one takes his agonies seriously.' (Interview with Roger Woodward, 16 February 1992, unpublished).

explaining that they 'mean a great deal to me and as I have been born too late for my tastes and passions I have a *duty* to pass on especially to young people the *few* contemporary delights I *can* experience.'[16] Georg always said he was born fifty years too late; 'If I had heard no music written after 1920 or thereabouts, I would have lost very little.'[17] In his opinion the last great pieces of music written were Alban Berg's *Wozzeck* (1922) and Hindemith's *Mathis der Maler* (1934). Expecting an argument from John Brown, Georg added, 'I insist on NOTHING but I remember the Transfigured Night [in 1974]...You may think now, what a *difficult* friend is that Georg!!'

John vetoed the Tippett, but Georg did manage one peda-gogical innovation: daily madrigal sessions. He considered singing to be of the highest educational value and an important part of becoming a musician. Scheduled immediately after breakfast, they remained in the program for many years. At the final concerts the musicians, instead of playing an encore, gathered in the centre of the stage and sang a madrigal. It never failed to reduce the audience to tears.

Georg's 1975 visit was more positive than that of the previous year. In an end-of-session assessment the horn teacher Eugene Rittich wrote:

> When Georg Tintner arrived the whole session took on an aspect of seriousness that left no doubt that music is an art of the greatest significance to man. I was greatly pleased at my own reaction because I found in him qualities I had not appreciated or observed in previous years. His conducting technique is not much better than it ever was, but I am now much more convinced of the quality of his interpretive sense. The students, not too knowledgeable in these matters, reacted intuitively to the qualities of greatness in the man and their respect for him was rather awesome. His acuity of hearing, his profound grasp of the structure of the music, the knowledge and understanding he displayed of the social, artistic, and particularly the literary forces that influenced the composers at the time these works (of the romantic period in particular) were written, gave a richness and relevancy to his interpretations that is indeed rare.[18]

In September and back in Sydney Georg conducted four Australian Opera performances of *Fidelio*, with Nance Grant, Eilene Hannan, Ronald Dowd, Raymond Myers, Robert Allman and Donald Shanks. Some people consider these performances to be the Australian Opera's greatest conducting success. Over twenty-six years later the critic John Carmody wrote: 'My gold standard for the conducting in *Fidelio* (and I have heard Karl Böhm* do it) is Georg Tintner's white hot performance in Sydney.'[19] Roger Covell wrote in the *Sydney Morning Herald*:

> Tintner could be seen to be strongly, even violently, in the service of Beethoven. The conductor's saintly white mop of hair tossed like a dandelion puffball in the powerful breeze of his extraordinarily energetic movements in the pit…The audience recognised the fervent impetuosity of the conductor's intentions and, rightly I think, applauded it warmly. It presumably accepted without hard feelings the many fluffs and imprecisions in the orchestral playing.[20]

And in the *Australian Financial Review*, under the heading 'Tintner's Conducting Skill Thrills Sydney':

> Sydney will never be the same again musically. We have a new Toscanini in our midst.
>     Conductor Georg Tintner is creating a sensation in Sydney with his thrilling performances of Beethoven's opera *Fidelio*. His passion and urgency reminds one immediately of the great Italian master. Such vivid and exhilarating Beethoven has rarely been heard in this country. Audiences, too, are aware of the extraordinary significance and have been wildly enthusiastic.[21]

His run of good reviews, however, ended abruptly with *Così fan Tutte*. The opera began on 15 January 1976, with Joan Carden, Isobel Buchanan, John Pringle and Anson Austin. The *Sunday Telegraph*'s David Ahern wrote: 'Speaking of hatchets, quite a few

---

\*    The comparison would not have pleased Georg. According to John Matheson, 'He said that Böhm was a good musician, but he didn't admire him very much. He said, "He wanted to make an impression, so he conducted slow music slower than anyone else and fast music faster than anyone else". Then he swivelled around to look at me, and his eyes blazed. "Besides, he was such a fanatical Nazi".'

people would probably have liked to have murdered conductor
Georg Tintner. A highly seasoned and very capable conductor
(remember his volcanic *Fidelio* last year, please), Tintner slowed
everything to a snail's pace…a dull, heavy *Così*.'[22] And in a review
that stung Georg and which he never forgot, Roger Covell said:

> Such musical leadership was not forthcoming on Thursday
> from Georg Tintner, whose conducting failed to keep orches-
> tra and singers in step or to secure a well-tended orchestral
> ensemble. Whenever the singers achieved a finely turned
> phrase on stage their work was undermined by sloppy attack
> and timing in the pit.
>
> Mr Tintner's experience and musicianship are not in
> doubt. I learn that some of his well-wishers have even hailed
> him as the Toscanini of the southern hemisphere.
>
> If he is such a remarkable conductor, however, how
> is it that the orchestra and the total ensemble makes such
> a ragged sound under his hands? Bonynge, Mackerras,
> Cillario, Pritchard, among others, have shown us what can
> be done in that pit with that orchestra in music of comparable
> transparency.[23]

*Così* went to Melbourne in March, and the reviews there were
better. Felix Werder in the *Age* thought it 'a relaxed and exemplary
piece of Mozart conducting'.[24]

Since his return to Australia Georg had written to Erica Munn
weekly, trying to persuade her to join him. Erica kept telling him
she had no interest in him. 'But things might change,' he replied,
begging her to give him and Australia a try. Finally Erica's mother
persuaded her it was the chance of a lifetime, and she joined Georg
in Melbourne. Despite his enthusiastic pursuit he mentioned neither love nor marriage, but told her only that she was his muse. He
wrote two compositions for her, now lost: she remembers them
as a piano piece of a few pages and a song entitled 'Akire' (*Erika*
reversed). Maria Vandamme, his Perth piano student who was now
a music producer for the ABC in Melbourne, found Erica 'very
young, very *lost, fragile*, likeable but definitely totally unsuitable for
Georg…I do remember Georg's voice, that melodic gentle voice
intoning her name, but it was more a fatherly concern for someone
who needed his care.'[25]

When *Così* finished Georg returned to Sydney with Erica. 'I didn't understand why Georg liked me romantically,' she says. 'I didn't love him, but I liked him. I was bemused by his attentions. He was so kind, so sweet to me.' She found him closed in, unwilling to talk about his previous life except to say he missed his children. 'He'd come home and wouldn't know what to do – he knew I was unhappy. He said, "Let me take you shopping"…but it was very strained because he wanted to get home to his scores.' There was little physical contact between them – some hugging, mostly when they met in the street, very little kissing, and no sex. 'He had no sense of romance whatsoever, except in music…I knew nothing about sex, but I didn't want it. Every night he would ask but I would refuse. He was very patient.'[26]

In May Georg conducted six concerts with the Sydney Symphony and pianist Rudolf Buchbinder – the first main-series subscription concerts the ABC had given him in his twenty-two years in Australia. The program of the first group included two preludes from Pfitzner's *Palestrina* and Schumann's First Symphony. And though he rarely found an opportunity to conduct Schumann, it was among the music he conducted best. He solved many of the orchestration problems of which Schumann is usually accused,[*] most notably by means of his customary arrangement of violins split left and right. He understood Schumann's Romanticism, the quality of longing in the music – what he called its *schwärmerisch* quality: 'sort of star gazing, that exuberant adoration of something; this is in a nutshell what Romantic music is about'.

'Bravo Georg Tintner,' said Roger Covell in the *Sydney Morning Herald*:

> [Tintner's] fervour, like his musicianship and his thorough knowledge of scores, has always been unquestioned. But there have been occasions in the opera pit recently when the musical results of his direction have been less than tidy. Not so on Wednesday. Mr Tintner has an awkward, jerking-from-the-waist manner of feeling the basic pulse of the music he conducts; but the SSO betrayed no serious difficulty in following his signals. Gesture is less important in conducting than a number of other factors. Yet Mr Tintner's small

---

[*]    Georg disagreed with this opinion. He considered the Manfred Overture in particular 'a masterpiece of orchestration'.

repertory of hand and body signals does impose limitations on the variety of phrasing and emphasis that comes back to him (and the rest of us) from the orchestra.[27]

And in the *Sun-Herald* Lindsey Browne mused:

> Tintner, a Viennese long resident in this part of the world and known to all his acquaintances for his quite unassailable personal and musical integrity and for the eternal youth of his enthusiasms, gave us a concert on Wednesday which not only routed all who might have doubted his eligibility to maestrise at this caste level but also thundered his claims to future preferment when first-rate duty-doing is imperatively needed.[28]

He received similar accolades for the second group of concerts, which included his first performance of Bruckner's Ninth Symphony. 'Georg Tintner…was a giant in his conducting of Bruckner,' proclaimed the *Daily Mirror*. 'He conducted with a passion that fired the orchestra…the performance swept one along with an enveloping sense of majesty.'[29]

Georg was to begin a tour with the Queensland Symphony just a few days later. He asked Erica to accompany him but she declined. They both knew the relationship was over. She remained in Sydney one more week and then returned to Canada. They had been together a little more than two months.

It was many years before Erica realised that the reason she felt 'different' was because she was a lesbian, but by then she was long out of touch with Georg. If he was dejected over his failed attempt at a new relationship, he didn't show it. So private was he that barely a handful of people knew Erica had ever been there.

Early in April Georg had received a telegram from the chairman of the West Australian Opera, John Breese, telling him that Vince Warrener was now 'a paid servant of the company'[30] and they would very much like Georg to return. He had replied he was very interested, but he heard no more until being advised several weeks later that Vince Warrener had been appointed general manager and Alan Abbott was now the music director. 'I feel I have been taken for a ride…' Georg wrote angrily to Perth soprano Ruth Atkinson.

'The other day I was fifty-nine. I feel very young and conduct better than earlier but I can't risk another mistake. I am too old for that. I feel I was treated as a convenience with contempt. O.K. with me!'[31]

Another possibility arose, this time with the Queensland Theatre Orchestra in Brisbane. An ensemble of twenty-eight players, it was formed in 1975 to play for the state opera and ballet, and to give concerts when required by neither. It was funded by the state government, but after little more than a year it was struggling, financially and especially artistically. Although Georg's salary would be paid by an ultra-conservative National Party government he detested, and it was the city's second-ranking orchestra, he did love Queensland, he would have his own orchestra, and he would not be deprived of opera because Queensland Opera had assured him of work. He would also be allowed twenty weeks free in the year for other engagements. 'I don't quite know how it will work out,' he wrote to John Brown on 29 June, 'but they told me quite frankly that if I don't accept the position that orchestra will fold up.'[32]

Nevertheless, he was uncertain enough to write to Harold Hort asking to be considered for the Queensland Symphony. A few weeks later the conductorship became vacant, but the manager vetoed Georg in favour of Vanco Cavdarski. Hort suggested Georg for the Tasmanian Symphony in Hobart instead, and Anthony Hughes canvassed his thoughts. 'Georg said he would very much like to take a position as conductor with the ABC and he would not turn down any offer (including TAS). His only reservation was a health one. i.e. he is better in hotter climate…He welcomed our interest after twenty years.'[33]

In July Georg began rehearsing two Janáček operas, and on a free night he went with Robert King to a Sydney Symphony concert. This was the night I met him, and made my unpromising comment about Bruckner. We enjoyed the concert all the same, and the three of us parted in good humour.

## Twenty-one

It was late August, after one of the *Jenůfa* performances, when Georg wheeled his bicycle out of the Opera House loading bay to find me standing at the stage door. Would I have heard from him again had I not waited for him that evening? Georg would say there are no 'ifs' in history, but years later I found my Bayreuth postcard among the few letters he had kept. The next day when we went for a walk in the city, and the following day as well, I told him I was twenty-three years old and studying music for a second degree. I was also a freelance reviewer of concerts and records, which made me one of his least favourite people: a critic. Even that didn't deter him, for it was on that second day he asked me to marry him. His proposal was the last thing I expected and I had no idea what to do. When we met again that evening at the Opera House to attend a performance of *Carmen* I was acutely embarrassed and Georg, wearing a hangdog expression, was overly polite and attentive. Neither of us knew what to say, so we confined ourselves to occasional brittle trivia.

Late one night, after a few days of silence, I went to see him at home. I knew that by doing so I was linking my life to his, though just how, I wasn't sure. Georg had only just returned from judging a singing competition. He opened the door, huddled into a disintegrating dressing gown, holding a large plastic bowl full of salad. He was startled and happy to see me; he wanted to kiss me but remembered his salad was full of raw onion. He apologised abjectly and offered to rinse his mouth.

He took me to his living room, which contained nothing but a squat old lounge suite covered in brown hessian. The floorboards were bare and there were no ornaments or pictures but for a single photograph in an empty bookshelf, a slightly faded portrait of three little girls. Georg knelt on the floor before me. Gazing at me with ardour, he told me a little about his life. He told me he was fifty-nine, much younger than I had supposed, and he said he had no right to ask someone as young as I to marry an 'old codger' like him. He said he needed a muse, and my long hair would be a key ingredient in his inspiration. He must write the music he felt was still in him: an opera, *'Tis Pity She's a Whore* and, if he could finish that, another based on Dostoevsky's *The Brothers Karamazov*. Only for this could he justify his proposal; the opera would be the only reasonable compensation for all his handicaps, which he went on to detail: his dentures; his unrepaired second hernia; the chronic pain in his wrist, feet and knees; the fact that his second wife had destroyed his sexual confidence and that, with one brief exception, he had not had a physical relationship since his second wife had left four years earlier. Apart from his music, Georg offered only his handicaps. He hoped that, like George Bernard Shaw's Candida, I would choose the man who offered his weaknesses.

I stayed with him that night. I had recently read the memoirs of Alma Mahler and been envious of the passions she aroused and the great works of art she had inspired. This was my opportunity to emulate her, I thought with supreme conceit.* At the same time I felt cornered. I had been asked to make one of the most important decisions of my life before I even knew my suitor. As for Georg, he told me a few days later that when he had seen me standing at his front door he knew at that instant he loved me. Only much later did I ask him why he had asked me to marry him at the bus stop when he wasn't then in love. His reply was: 'It just seemed possible.'

Love letters began arriving almost daily, some hopeful, some disconsolate. One came with a potted dahlia, another with a small, leather-bound volume of Heinrich Heine's poetry, probably his mother's. From Auckland at the end of September, on his way to Wellington to rehearse *Jenůfa*, he wrote:

> When I rattled off all my weaknesses and ailments I was for the first time aware of the ENORMITY of my request…And it became quite clear to me that I can only expect the ultimate 'sacrifice' of you, if you can truly LOVE (then it would not really be a sacrifice.)…PERHAPS EVEN FOR YOU, THERE MAY

---

* Georg, it should be said, had met Alma Mahler 'holding court' at the Vienna State Opera and thought her detestable.

BE TOO MUCH TO COPE. Even up till now, you have greatly enriched my life. Don't allow me to empoverish yours.[1]

Shortly after he arrived in Wellington he wrote to me about 'Dämmerstunde'. He had played the song to me before leaving and I told him I thought it beautiful. He found even this simple remark so encouraging that his first action on arriving was to write the song out and send it to me.

> I spent last night reconstructing the song you like: without the music and without a Piano. It is almost note-perfect. While I drew the lines the bath was running over and flooded a carpet, but fortunately I could repair the damage with a heater. All was well by 2 am. I feel a pauper sending you a song 40 years old, instead of writing one now FOR YOU. I hope I shall be able to soon.[2]

On 4 October he sent me 'my first poem since I was nine years old. So please treat it indulgently'. Its final lines were: Domina NON SUM DIGNUS/What is not mine I yet dread to lose/DOMINA MISERERE MIHI (?) or ME?

*Domina non sum dignus* – Lady, I am not worthy. He meant only that he had yet to compose something to justify his 'acquisition' of me as wife and muse. But the line took hold in his imagination. He wrote later the same day:

> I found the beginning of a melody which wants to express *what I felt* seeing you laying there with your lovely hair on the floor…Perhaps the tune will never get off the ground, but I want you to have my music which is written for and because of *YOU*.

Georg went to Brisbane on 8 October to sign a one-year contract as music director of the Queensland Theatre Orchestra. He gave up his Waverton house the next day, and returned to New Zealand for *Jenůfa*, his final Australian Opera performances. I joined him in Wellington a few days later, and when I arrived at the hotel I found a single red rose and a note: '*Domina non sum dignus ut intres sub tectum meum*. (Lady (= *Herrin*) I am not worthy that you enter under my roof!)' After I returned, he wrote from Auckland:

> I want to write a vocal fugue on the theme: *Domina non sum dignus ut intres sub tectum meum*. Perhaps you can use it one day. So far I have not even sorted the theme out. Dearest Tanya: never did I want to be more 'whole' and healthy than just now.[3]

Several months later he completed *Tanya's Fugue*, a short but difficult four-part choral work on the Latin text. He also wrote a canon in four voices, a consolatory piece about someone in the record industry who was causing me trouble: 'Don't Be Scared of That Nasty Stan, Lovely Tanya'. When I ran late with my university composition exercise, he wrote it for me and I submitted it as my own. My tutor wrote: 'Ends too abruptly', and graded it C-minus.

Georg had a difficult time in New Zealand. He found the New Zealand Symphony uncooperative, and his hernia had become very painful. According to the conductor Gary Brain, then a seventeen-year-old timpanist:

> Georg outdid himself. It was a riveting production and Georg made the orchestra sound like it should not have. It was also my first experience of indifferent orchestral musicians. I was often seconded into the NZ Symphony Orchestra and they treated him awfully. What they really needed was a boot in the pants but of course he would never do that and as a consequence I believe they understood this to be a weakness and used it for their stupid amusement.[4]

As the critic Roger Covell puts it, 'Georg's almost ostentatious non-aggression invited aggressive behaviour.'[5] 'I am of course a pacifist and all that goes with it,' Georg said much later, 'and some people mistake my intended gentleness for weakness. I have no defence against that. They are very welcome to interpret it like that. They are wrong of course. That is the little cross that any pacifist has to bear.'[6]

He finished with the Australian Opera on 30 October '(which happens to be Gretels birthday and our wedding anniversary so a triple festivity)'.[7] The company gave him a silver pocket watch, which he gave to me, and told him they would bring him back to Sydney often to guest conduct. They never asked him there again.

In the six weeks before moving to Brisbane Georg stayed with Robert King. One day he received a letter from Cecilia reporting that she was in Sydney on vacation. He had not heard from her for several months, since she had sent him a telegram from Tel Aviv. Gerda Tintner had told him she was thinking of going there, apparently to study with a cello teacher in whom she had taken a personal interest, but he had not taken the news seriously. He was dismayed, afraid for the safety of the children. Cecilia had said in the telegram that she could get support money in Israel if he could prove his racial background, and asked him to send his birth and racial details immediately. Georg had never hidden his Jewishness to save his skin, but nor had he ever used it for gain, and he refused.

In the letter Cecilia advised him that if he wanted to see the children they would be available the next afternoon at a friend's house in a nearby suburb. It was sixteen months since Georg had last seen them. He returned a few hours later, distressed and agitated. A child had come out to greet him, and thinking only that it was a rather nice-looking little boy, he kept on walking. It was Esmeralda with her hair cut very short, and he hadn't recognised her.

As Georg's departure date grew nearer, he stepped up his persuasive efforts. He claimed, a little defensively, that men marry women for their beauty but women marry men for their achievements. He said that Oona O'Neill, the much younger wife of Charlie Chaplin, had wished her hair were grey, the better to blend with her husband, which I thought rather silly. He was unnerved when I met with friends:

> I *must not* resent that you look for fun and amusement else-
> where, when I can't supply them (this has nothing to do
> with my age, I was even more serious with twenty-three!). I
> must not get worked up about roasts and birthday parties of
> rather remote persons, and certainly stop interpreting these
> non-events as lack of interest in me…I MUST NOT rub that in,
> but rather beat *my* breast and say: Georg, if you could keep
> her amused she would not crave for that sort of thing!!![8]

Georg did not expect me to become a vegetarian, although he said he would find it difficult if I didn't. But I had been a sympathiser from the age of six when I had been made to go fishing, and within weeks I had converted. There was no compromise with alcohol, however, and Georg insisted that if I were to marry him I would have to give it up. This I found unacceptably dictatorial and we argued about it for months, eventually arriving at a compromise agreeable to neither: I would not keep alcohol at home, and he would say nothing if I drank at receptions. As a youth Georg had enjoyed beer with his friends in Vienna, and when Sue arrived in Auckland he had been amused by her stories of how she had drunk the ship's crew under the table. But his hatred of alcohol had grown over the years, and bordered on the hysterical. He had seen many musicians ruin their lives with drink, especially in Australia, but his view had most to do with his romantic picture of women:

> I find it worse in women than *even* in men. I consider the consuming of (especially hard) liquor A DEFILEMENT of something so supremely lovely as a female body and personality. NOT because they are 'frailer' than men not because they are 'purer' (which they are NOT) but because they are *lovelier.* This has nothing to do with putting you and your sisters on a piedestal [*sic*], this is an opinion arrived at through lifelong admiration and gratitude.[9]

We never agreed on this, and there were several public scenes over the years. At a reception in Brisbane Georg broke into my conversation with a friend, demanding to know what I was drinking. I said it was soda water. He turned on his heel and strode away, scowling. Half an hour later I realised he had disappeared, and I found him sitting in the car boiling with rage: 'You were drinking *whisky!*' I said I had told the truth and that his behaviour was outrageous. He apologised and sat contritely silent all the way home. When, many years later, unwitting friends brought us bottles of wine as a gift, I promised him I would give them away as soon as I could. After a few weeks he couldn't stand the sight of them any longer. He took them to the park across the road and left them on a bench for the local winos.

One of the benefits of marrying him, Georg told me, was that he could teach me harmony and counterpoint. He said, rightly, that I would learn far more from him than at the university: 'If you come to live with me in Brisbane and elsewhere I PROMISE to spend each day at least one hour in teaching you music (IN A TOTALLY UNPATRONISING WAY).'[10]

He sent letters once or twice daily, and in several he begged me to give up my studies for a year to join him in Brisbane to see if our relationship would work: 'I want you to devote this year to musical studies including reviews with me and to OUR RELATIONSHIP (I am not allowed to say Union) This frail and vulnerable plant needs more than the mere breadcrumbs you allot to it. What is one year for a twenty-three year old? nothing but for a fifty-nine and a half year old (tomorrow) it may be everything!'[11] A few days later: 'You once "accused" me of trying to make you stop everything you are doing now, in order to be my MUSE. That is an exaggeration, but there is some truth in it. Don't *only* count the losses!!'[12] Georg had already told me that in order to create he only needed to love, he did not need to *be* loved. 'My *need* to love and adore is supreme.' He was facing permanent creative impotence and was grasping at his last chance for deliverance.

I took no notice of his admission to frailty and vulnerability; he seemed so much 'of himself', so self-possessed. It was an astonishing admission for him to make – and how true it was. But I didn't realise. And I turned his theory lessons down. The difference in our ages made our relationship already too much like teacher and pupil, and I knew he was fond of this model of marriage – he loved the story of Abelard and Heloise, except for the castration. So I threw away the opportunity of a lifetime, and that is how long I shall regret it.

## Twenty-two

Georg took only a day or two to find a rental property, at 37 Marine Parade in Redcliffe, a seaside settlement forty kilometres north of Brisbane. It was, as usual, hopelessly impractical. He had to cycle fifteen kilometres to the train, two of which were a bone-shaking ride over a single-lane wooden plank bridge; the train took another hour to the city, ambling between station platforms littered in summer with fallen mangoes. But the house was opposite the beach, and Georg swam every morning at first light, splashing happily among the stinging jellyfish.

With 1000 kilometres between us he became more imploring. He wrote on his first day in Brisbane:

> What you need to do is to sum up all my disadvantages *which I cannot change*, with the best will in the world, and find out how you feel about them; whether they are 'fatal' or only grave handicaps. And then you should make a list of all the things I do which I can change, like forgetting to close my 'fly' or having the back of my shirt hanging out.*

Georg was in an unaccustomed role; he was petitioning a woman, possibly for the first time. I wavered between visions of a happy future and doubts about how it would work. I applied for jobs in Brisbane – but also in Sydney. Georg was alternately elated at my expressions of affection and downcast by my changeable behaviour. What was certainly true was his comment to me on New Year's Eve: 'I think one thing Tanya and Georg have in common: their absorbsion in their *own* problems.'[1]

Trying to warn me, a friend pointed out in a visual handwriting

---

* Georg's standard response when caught with his fly open was to quote Otto Klemperer's reply to a musician who pointed out he was rehearsing with his fly undone: 'And what has that to do with Beethoven?'

joke how easily 'muse' could turn into 'nurse'. This prospect didn't trouble me at all. I was certain Georg would die as he wanted: suddenly, while conducting the 'Hallelujah Chorus', or perhaps the final chorale of Bruckner's Fifth Symphony. I was also sure that with his vegan diet and superior fitness he would live to be 100. Even Georg said, although with less than complete conviction, that conductors live a long time because conducting enables them to get rid of their frustrations. But the witticism plunged Georg into despair:

> I was deadly serious…that the fears of your friend MUST NEVER COME TO PASS. I don't want to be a burden to anyone LEAST OF ALL to my beloved Tanya. Your generosity would then be abused. I don't ever want you [to] be my permanent nurse except in the sense that every wife often is the soul nurse of a 'normal' husband and vice versa.[2]

He was deadly serious. Twenty-three years later he would prove it.

At the end of January he went to Melbourne for five weeks of work with the Melbourne Symphony. He began with some studio recordings, and an Australia Day concert. He also conducted all four of the annual Sidney Myer Music Bowl summer concerts, with substantial programs including the Seventh Symphony of Bruckner. They were enthusiastically received, despite poor amplification and a breeze that blew the musicians' parts off their stands. The studio recordings had not gone nearly as well; the Supervisor of Music reported crossly to Harold Hort that Georg had turned over some of the recording time to the concerts, and as a result none of the recordings, in his opinion, was usable.[3]

I found a job in Sydney, and although Georg was very disappointed he found me a flat and came to visit between concerts in Brisbane. The Theatre Orchestra job was not turning out as well as he had hoped. The orchestra was, as he had expected, rudimentary, and there was a shortage of strings because the pay was less than that of ABC orchestras and the musicians considered pit work beneath them. The manager tried gimmicks such as offering free cases of mud crabs, a local delicacy, without success.

Then Georg received a letter from an Adelaide violinist, Carmel Hakendorf, who had a stellar career in England in the 1940s as a soloist and protégée of John Barbirolli; she later joined the South Australian Symphony Orchestra. In 1958 she complained to the musicians' union that the concertmaster, her stand partner, was regularly drunk, but the union took his side and ultimately Carmel's life was ruined. She told Georg she wanted to leave Adelaide and make a new start, and he hired her at once. But when she arrived at Brisbane airport she was so high on drugs that she was unable to recognise her suitcase; she was clearly in no state to play. She and her husband and six-year-old daughter moved in with Georg, who was at a loss as to how to help.

In the middle of March he came to Sydney to record Ravel's L'Heure Espagnole for television, and he asked the ABC's Acting Supervisor of Music, John Harper, once again for a permanent position. He also mentioned that they had neglected to pay his fees for the five weeks in Melbourne. Harper wrote to Harold Hort:

> Georg Tintner came to see me on March 3rd to discuss what may or may not happen in relation to his further career with the A.B.C. with particular reference to Queensland and Tasmania. He wishes to let it be known confidentially that he really doesn't feel that his health would allow him to accept an offer of an engagement as a Chief Conductor in Tasmania because of the climate…
>
> I commented that our fear would be, as with any other musician of his calibre, that his interest in remaining in the country could not be sustained without the possibility of permanent engagement. However, he seems to be of the feeling that he would appreciate whatever the A.B.C. can give him even if it means that he hasn't got a permanent position…
>
> My own feeling about it is, that Georg will be a terrible loss if he doesn't receive encouragement to stay in Australia and if Cavdarski is going to be recommended and appointed to Queensland, we would still have Georg's use. It would allow us also the chance to appoint somebody in addition in Tasmania. It would seem that whatever decision is made regarding Queensland, Georg's talents would still be available to us for some time yet.[4]

Hort replied: 'My own feeling is that as Georg is becoming rather erratic we might be safer *not* to appoint him to one of our orchestras. See folio 92 [about the Melbourne recordings] – there was also a lot of trouble over his payment from Melbourne...I think – don't give Georg an orchestra, but continue with major engagements with all orchestras (except perhaps in Melb. where there seems to be friction with the supervisor).'[5]

Not long afterwards the ABC formally offered him the co-directorship (with John Lanchbery) of the Tasmanian Symphony Orchestra, but the weeks they offered were in winter. He surmised, correctly, that these were Lanchbery's leftovers – an offer he thought 'borders on the offensive'.[6] 'I have to consider this very carefully,' he said to me. 'The ABC will never forgive me if I turn this down. They never forget. They will make me pay – they will give me even less than they do now.' Shortly afterwards he turned it down. So did Lanchbery. Despite Hort's recommendation to 'continue' with major engagements, it was almost three years before the ABC gave Georg a major concert anywhere. At Maria Vandamme's instigation, however, they started recording for radio his lecturettes on music, and introductions to other conductors' concerts.

Early in July 1977 we went to Canada, first to the Banff School of Arts and then the National Youth Orchestra. After a few days in Banff I went to Toronto to work as the youth orchestra's librarian, in exchange for my ticket to Canada. Georg was struggling financially once again. He had voluntarily increased Cecilia's payments by one third to compensate her for a rising pound, just as he took a substantial drop in salary on joining the Theatre Orchestra; he was now sending her almost half his take-home pay. What upset him, however, was that he almost never heard from her or the children, and deeply resented being treated as 'a cash cow, only good enough to send money'.

A few days after I arrived in Toronto, while Georg was still in Banff, I realised quite definitely that I loved him and wanted to marry him. He was one of the most principled, interesting and original people I had ever met, and we had much in common beyond our love of music and belief in the importance of creativity. We were both pacifists, we voted left, and shared a socialist view of 'service' personnel such as hotel porters and taxi drivers, who we went to great lengths to avoid. We were non-believers,

non-conformists, and atrocious dressers. We had Continental ante-
cedents, and we knew what being a refugee and a foreigner was
about, albeit at different removes: my father, Hans Buchdahl, was a
German Jewish refugee who was deported to Australia in 1940 on
the infamous British ship *Dunera*, and I grew up feeling 'different'.
Neither of us had ever fitted in, and neither of us felt there was
anywhere we truly belonged. I once asked Georg where he felt
at home, and he answered as I expected: 'Like all Jews, nowhere.'
He reflected for a moment and added, 'But if it were anywhere, it
would be New Zealand.'

For the first time Georg would be marrying a Jew, or more
exactly, a half-Jew. In the 1950s he said to Jean Reeve that he was
still enough of a Jew not to want to marry a Gentile – a curious
remark from someone who had already been married to one for
fifteen years or so. Yet when he married a second time, it was
again to a Gentile. His statement is the more surprising given his
views on miscegenation. Many post-war Jews feared the demise
of Jewry by attrition and intermarriage. Georg took the opposite
view, and believed the only solution to racial disharmony was for
all racial groups, especially persecuted ones, to interbreed so that
differences would disappear and there would be nothing left to
hate. He hoped that his children would marry people from other
racial groups, and was pleased when one of his daughters found
a Chinese husband. Nevertheless, something in him must have
gravitated towards something familiar, and someone who might
have more understanding of him.

I bought two wedding rings with which to surprise him. The
orchestra was now in residence at Queens University in Kingston,
and he arrived in the evening of 30 July. I presented him with the
rings and told him of my decision. He seemed pleased. I said I had
told everyone he was arriving late the next day, a free Sunday, so
that we might have time to celebrate by ourselves. 'Impossible!' he
exclaimed. 'I'm here to *work*! I have to see John Brown and I have
to talk to the faculty, and check the parts to see that everything
is in order!' I was very disappointed. We did, however, have time
to call my parents, whom Georg had met when conducting in
Canberra in June. From the tone of their voices I knew they were
appalled, but they didn't try to talk me out of it. Nothing would
have changed my mind anyway. Georg then wrote to them:

My dear friends, my handicaps are obvious and I am only too
aware of them! Nevertheless I want you to believe me, that
I am not seeking a housekeeper (I could do better elsewhere,
if I wanted that) or a nurse to look after my old age, but that
I love her very sincerely and want to make her as happy as I
can. I want to emphasize that I did not put any pressure on
Tanya; you know very well it would not have worked, had
I tried…I hope your friendship towards me will endure past
reading this letter.

Georg's main concert was his 110-minute 'Unfinished' program: Mahler's Tenth Symphony ('not the outrageous Dereck
Cooke concoction but the Original'),[7] Schubert's Eighth and
Bruckner's Ninth. As in 1975 he also led daily madrigal sessions
after breakfast, not only with the standard fare of Morley and
Gibbons but with a six-part madrigal he had written for me in the
preceding few months: 'Under the Greenwood Tree'. The students
found it very difficult, but for me it was an immense pleasure.
Georg was composing again; everything was unfolding as it should.

Yet I had hardly seen Georg alone after that first evening –
only before breakfast and late at night. It was as if he had decided
no further effort was required as soon as I said I would marry
him, and he was now free to get back to what was really important: music. The ardent attention and imploring gaze vanished
overnight. One evening I went for a walk along the edge of Lake
Ontario, where the Thousand Islands cruise boats departed, and
pondered whether I had made the right decision. Would it be like
this in future, seeing almost nothing of Georg, being told that to
want his attention was being selfish? I decided, after several hours,
that the National Youth Orchestra was something different, these
summer sessions something special, and that ordinary life would
be less concentrated. And once I took over the management side
of his career I would be more important to his life – although he
had said, 'That isn't what I want you for'; it was as a muse that I
was to be useful. I concluded that I had made the right decision. I
never regretted it.

This summer was the beginning of the end for Georg and
John Brown, though it took several years to play itself out. It had
only been a few months since Georg wrote to John: 'I'm absolutely

sure that you are the best friend I have in the musical world (and one of the best out of it too)', and so he was shocked when John's first words to him were 'I will never employ Tanya again!' He may have thought Georg was not paying his usual undivided attention to the orchestra. It is also possible that John felt I had come between him and the object of his worship.

After a short tour of the 'Unfinished' program Georg returned directly to Brisbane to conduct *Il Trovatore* for the Queensland Opera in October, with the Theatre Orchestra, and we met up again in Wellington. On 27 and 28 October he conducted concert performances of Wagner's *Flying Dutchman*, with the New Zealand Symphony and singers mostly from the Australian Opera (Lone Koppel, Anthea Moller, Tony Benfell, Neil Warren-Smith and Robert Allman) – 'as stirring a concert performance as one could expect to hear'.[8] He also recorded for radio Douglas Lilburn's *Diversions* and the 1961 Third Symphony ('What a joyless piece that is; I much prefer his early works!').[9] We visited Douglas in his simple house on Ascot Terrace, a steep and quiet laneway in the picturesque inner suburb of Thorndon. He rarely went out and did not welcome visitors, especially (as Georg warned me) women, but he greeted us warmly. 'Hullooo Georg! Come in! Have some vino!' he said jovially, though it was the middle of the morning. They discussed the parlous state of contemporary composing, and scoffed at composers who couldn't write a note without a grant. To me he was gracious and affable.

On a free weekend Georg took me to New Plymouth to meet Annemarie, who was now chronically ill and mostly housebound. He had warned me I wouldn't like her. She was uncultured and a bit rough, he said, and hardly had two thoughts to put together because she wasted her time reading penny-dreadfuls. He was surprised to find we liked each other immediately, and we remained close until her death nine years later. Down-to-earth Annemarie had little time for Georg's being 'artistic', and was given to snapping, 'Don't be so bloody silly, Georg!' At the age of sixty-one she had not yet gone grey but she had the familial bad feet, and severe arthritis, which the doctors had treated with cortisone before anyone knew of its side effects. Her spine was disintegrating, and she walked, shrunken and stooped, with a stick. She was in constant pain, but never complained, at least about her health. She complained loud and long about the large table taking up much of the living room on which her husband kept the model train set she scornfully called 'Frank's choo-choos'. Frank took no notice and sat peacefully in his recliner chair reading the newspaper, cigarette pinched between thumb and forefinger.

After the Wellington visit I moved into Georg's house in Redcliffe, which he had to himself again now that Carmel Hakendorf and her family had gone. On his return from Canada he had found her lying on the floor in a drugged stupor with her hair dangerously close to a burning radiator. He told her he had had enough and she must get help immediately. She complied, and within a few months she was well enough for Georg to employ her as his concertmaster at last.

The house had once been a beautiful traditional wooden Queenslander with deep verandahs on three sides. It was raised on stumps to let the air circulate in the hot, sticky summers. Decades of holiday lets had turned it into a scrappy sort of place. The verandahs had been walled up and stuccoed in the 1940s, the beautiful red-cedar floorboards covered with grey linoleum, and the walls painted rental cream. The central room contained an abandoned red sofa and the telephone; the living room only Georg's brown hessian-covered sofa, and the walls were decorated with trucking stickers: 'You are passing another Fox'. In the bed-room, part of the old verandah, Georg had put two mattresses, but there were no pillows because they were too comfortable. Until he was instructed to use one by a chiropractor trying to fix his neck problems, he slept on his folded hands. When I bought two overstuffed armchairs from a junk shop he refused to sit in them for the same reason. More than once at the homes of friends I saw him move from a sofa to a hard upright chair. Comfort actually made him uncomfortable.

The only pleasant room was the front verandah, where Georg put his piano so he could look out at Moreton Bay as he played. There was a bookcase for his German poetry and a cardboard box on the floor containing a very small pile of his manuscripts. There was also his antiquated all-in-one Bush portable gramophone. Georg never listened to recordings recreationally, and only rarely when he had to learn something difficult at short notice. He didn't care what the sound was like; his ideal was already in his head. I brought better equipment with me, but he preferred his own machine because it had only a power switch and a volume control. Anything even slightly technical confused him; he had never progressed beyond the technology of the 1930s. All his life he shaved with a brush and blade, refusing to use an electric shaver because he was sure he couldn't make it work. 'You can't teach an old dog new tricks,' he insisted.

His was a curiously functioning brain; his sense of spatial relationships was virtually non-existent. If I pointed at an object he was unable to extrapolate where he should look. He might be out by as much as ninety degrees. The only way he could work out where I was pointing was to stand behind me and look along the length of my arm. He also had a poor sense of smell and taste, and often mis-described colours, though he was not colour-blind like his father. It was as if one part of his brain, the part where music and musical ability were stored, had developed extremely at the expense of all the rest.

Georg was firmly mired in the romantic notions of the beginning of the century: only matters of the mind were important. How he dressed was irrelevant, and had nothing to do with his ability as a musician. '*Kleider machen Leute*', he said disdainfully: clothes maketh the man. Nobody could convince him that others saw it differently. It was common for him to go out in a combination of clashing colours with his trouser legs caught in his socks, his sweater bunched over his shoulders, and with his mis-buttoned shirt hanging out. His scruffy clothes once almost had him arrested. He was late for a rehearsal, and when a policeman saw him running with a new briefcase I had given him he stopped him on the assumption he had stolen it. It is also said that Georg was denied entry to Brisbane City Hall, the old concert hall, because the guard refused to believe he was the conductor. What is certainly true is that he came home one day very indignant that he had been prevented from paying his Amnesty International dues because the ladies in the office had taken him for a hobo (or as he said, a vagabound) and locked him out.

Curiously, he was particular about his hair, but in an odd way. I cut it quite long, because it suited him and because I couldn't manage short back and sides. Georg hated haircuts and it took a week of persuasion before he capitulated. Once it was done he would exclaim in horror that I had shorn him like Samson. Yet unless I adjusted his daily combing ('Leave me alone!') he would leave his hair plastered down with bits sticking out at all angles. He refused to comb it in front of a mirror because to do so was vain.

I was miserable in Redcliffe. Fashionable before the war, it was now a faded suburb of retired bank managers, teenage single mothers and louts in noisy vans. The smell of stale beer and cigarettes spilled out of the esplanade pubs, and pensioners sold raffle tickets on the footpaths. Our neighbour, a pensioner with a dog that never stopped barking, spied on us from behind his kitchen curtains, mowed his lawn daily, and reported us periodically to the local council for failing to mow ours. Few people came to visit, and when they did Georg sat them down on the filthy red sofa in the corner by the telephone and discussed work, not bothering to introduce me. When I protested he said it was my fault for not joining in. 'If you want to have a friend,' he said irritably, 'go into town and make one.' Instead I sat on the front steps in the blistering heat waiting for the seabreeze, and felt very sorry for myself.

I had thought that Georg's change of attitude once I agreed to marry him was only temporary, but I was mistaken. The adoring looks and the ardour were gone, and he began to grow rather distant and silent. He left early in the morning and returned tired after six hours of rehearsal and over four hours of commuting. As soon as he arrived home he turned on Thilde's old valve radio for the news and commentary. He sat on a high stool with his big plastic bowl of food on his knees, bending over to read a score on the kitchen table in front of him – he had no trouble listening to spoken word while reading music. One night, after several weeks of this, I set a table in the dining room with tablecloth and candles. 'What's this?' he asked me when he arrived home. 'I thought we might eat together and talk.' 'I have to work!' he said. 'I don't have time for such things.' Georg had lived alone for so long that he had fallen into bachelor habits, and he saw no reason to change them. On free days he would rush to the kitchen every hour from six in the morning until late at night to listen to the news, even if one of us were in the middle of a sentence. 'You heard it only an hour ago!' I would say, exasperated. 'But something might have changed!' he replied excitedly.

He was now strenuously pursuing a divorce from Cecilia, but his Sydney lawyer was apparently having a nervous breakdown. Cecilia was also missing. 'I haven't heard from G. and the children for nearly a year,' he wrote to Les Thompson on 6 October. 'The only thing I was told was to transfer their lavish "allowance" to Tel Aviv for 6 months since March or so I send the money again to Fleet, but have no idea where they are. She must be terribly bitter (what about she has what she wanted even the house!) It is bad for the children unfortunately.' They were no closer to a settlement than they had been five years earlier. When Cecilia eventually reappeared in England, they agreed that Georg would take the Perth house, and she would keep The Kop and the increased alimony until each child turned eighteen. She then claimed through a Legal Aid lawyer that, according to the 1975 valuations, her house was worth less than Georg's, and to even things up he should buy her a car. When both properties were sold two years later Georg's house fetched a price only two-thirds of Cecilia's, but he had neither the money nor the will to fight.

He soon discovered that he would not be paid for the *Trovatore* he had done for the Queensland Opera in October. The Opera had assumed he came with the orchestra; the orchestra assumed Georg would negotiate for himself. Ex post facto, nothing could be done. The tax department then decreed that child support payments to non-residents were no longer tax deductible, and he learned that John Brown could not afford to bring him to Canada in 1978 because Banff had decided against hiring him as musician in residence. It was financially very fortunate that he had three ABC *Messiahs* in Sydney in December and an Australian Opera tour of *Don Pasquale* in northern New South Wales early in 1978. Georg just managed from one payday to the next, but not once in twenty years did he fail to meet his obligations.

The decree nisi was granted on 23 March and as soon as the tour was over we applied for a marriage licence. The decree absolute was granted on 14 April, although the financial settlement was still incomplete, and we set the wedding date for the Saturday after Georg's sixty-first birthday.

Georg wrote asking John Brown to be one of our witnesses, but there was no reply. He wrote to the Thompsons introducing 'Tanya, whom I am going to marry on May 27 THIS IS TOP SECRET, if Cecilia hears about it prematurely she will squeeze me even MORE.'[10] He was terrified Cecilia would find out, and when a journalist asked me for an interview in Armidale, a country town on the *Don Pasquale* tour, Georg turned pale. 'You can't do it, you

*Georg and Tanya, just married, in 1978.*

must cancel it!' he said. So frightened was he of finding himself in court again that he agreed to anything. When Cecilia's English lawyers told him it was too much effort to recover their costs from Legal Aid in Australia and he could save them the trouble by paying the few hundred pounds owing, he sent it without demur.

Our wedding day did not work out as planned; we only just managed to get married at all. We were to be married secretly at the Redcliffe registry office at one o'clock, accompanied by my parents, sister and two witnesses. My relatives were to fly from Canberra, but when I arrived at the airport to collect them I discovered they were still there, trapped in fog. Nobody knew when flights would recommence. I rushed back to the registry office in Redcliffe to beg for a little more time. 'No worries,' said the official, 'I'll go up the RSL and bend the elbow.' My family finally arrived well after three, and we sped out of the airport into a traffic jam. The Saturday afternoon races had just finished, and the only way out of the racecourse was along the two-lane airport road. At 4.15 I left them at the courthouse and rushed home to change into our best clothes – Georg into his conducting dinner suit and I into a blue dress with matching jacket originally my mother's. Georg had given me a bicycle as a wedding present and, because he wanted it so much, we cycled to the registry office. We pedalled frantically along the main street and arrived at five minutes to five. The official, who hadn't counted on spending the entire afternoon at the pub, scowled and said darkly, 'Another five minutes and you wouldn't of got married today!' At exactly five o'clock Georg and I were pronounced husband and wife.

We returned to the house for a few refreshments. My parents gave us a wedding present of $1500 and I cried with relief. After everyone had left I propped up a time-delay camera and took some pictures of us to commemorate the occasion. Georg looks pleased in some, philosophical in others; I look happy in all of them.

## Twenty-three

Our first year was difficult. All his life Georg's women had worshipped him without reservation, at least in the beginning, and for the first time he had one who didn't. It confused him and he resented it. My admiration for his musicianship and integrity was unlimited, but it did not extend to idolatry. He told me meaningfully that when he and Karl Wolfskehl had sat in the kitchen in Herne Bay discussing German poetry, Sue sat gazing at Georg in admiration. He couldn't understand why I didn't do the same. He didn't see that Sue and I came from different generations and our expectations were very different. Women of my generation expected many sorts of equality. I did not see a man as the 'head of the household', whose wishes ranked first. Cecilia, twenty-five years younger than Sue, was caught up in the first heady waves of feminism when she was already feeling a victim of circumstance. Georg blamed feminism for many of their difficulties, and became virulently opposed to it, claiming against all evidence to the contrary that there was absolutely no sexism to be found in Australia.

As he saw it, admiring him and looking after his every need was serving not the man but the artist. It was less sexism than his old-fashioned view of the importance of the artist, who is in turn the servant of music. He had no difficulty accepting women musicians, nor even women conductors, almost unknown at the time (although he said it wouldn't work if he were married to one), and in his view women *who had something creative to do* should have as many opportunities as a creative man. His view was that 'either you let women out in the world and compete with them equally, or you keep them at home and put them on a pedestal and adore them. I prefer the latter.'[1] He did, however, tell his friend Margaret Hoyle not long after we were married: 'Thank God she is not a musician!' Cecilia's wish to become a successful cellist could not help but create conflict; as genuinely as Georg wanted her to succeed, and respected her desire to do so, he would always have needed a devoted, self-sacrificial wife, and she could not have been both.

Almost as soon as I arrived in Redcliffe Georg said he wanted to have children. This seemed financially foolhardy in our current circumstances, but I was also suspicious of his motives. I knew he had not wanted to have children either with Sue or Cecilia; and then a friend of his told me it was such a terrible pity he had lost his daughters, should I not think about replacing them?

Georg maintained a comprehensive dogma on the proper conduct of pregnancy and labour. Women who put on weight after their first baby had no willpower. Morning sickness happened only to women who had too much time to feel sorry for themselves. His proof was that Sue had worked so hard that she had not had time for morning sickness. Nor had Cecilia suffered from it, he said, 'but then she was happy to be pregnant'. He also did not believe in pain relief in childbirth, and cited the extraction of his teeth as a comparison. Cecilia had done without, as had Sue, 'the bravest woman I ever met.' Just think, he said: Mahler read Kant to Alma to distract her from her labour pains. His point was not that Mahler's idea was bad in principle; he meant only that at such a time Kant may have been a little hard to follow. He sighed and said, 'There are some people who can withstand pain, and there are some people who can't.' I wasn't sure if I could live up to Georg's gestational and parturitional standards, and I was too intimidated to find out. In the end it was left an unresolved, festering issue.

Georg had now been directing the Queensland Theatre Orchestra for eighteen months and was finding raising the standard more of a struggle than he had anticipated. Feeling dispirited, he tried the ABC again, but there is no record of a reply. There was a pressing need for me to get a job, as I had lost most of my well-paid reviewing on marrying. Georg believed that a man should support his wife, but money was short and he also thought a job would 'put some regularity into your life'. Arguments over my lack of employment went on for months, Georg maintaining that I was too choosy, and I feeling ever more a failure. He couldn't understand how anyone might not want to occupy every minute with doing something constructive. He felt only too keenly how little time there was, while I, at my age, thought there was plenty. Sometimes when I read a book he would say irritably, 'What are you doing? You should be doing something useful. You could do some housework, for example.' He himself had long since given up reading; in the twenty-three years I knew him he did not read a single book. His knowledge of literature and the Classics came from decades earlier. Now there was time only for scores, which he read in cars, trains and buses, when visiting friends, in doctors' waiting rooms – he was hardly to be found without one.

Unnerved by my turning out to be a poor artist's wife, Georg began citing Sue as a model of wifely perfection. Indeed, all his theories on the way women functioned were based on Sue – or more exactly, his idealised re-creation of her. Georg believed that married women should not have the vote, on the grounds that if they were getting on with their husbands they would vote as he did to please him, and if they were not, they would vote the opposite; his proof was that in the 1949 New Zealand election he had instructed Sue to vote for the Communist Party and she did. He believed that all women should be sexually satisfied in five minutes and, in a breathtaking extrapolation from the particular to the general, his proof for this is that Sue was. Anything else was 'deviant'. Later, when we had a very private garden, he asked why did I not agree to sex outdoors whenever he wanted it? Sue did. Why did I not get out of bed at five in the morning? Why did I not wear my hair loose at all times to please him? Sue did. ('It is truly incredible to me, how you ration me *also* with that *favour* (such a comparatively small inconvenience…) Is that a bit of a powergame or feeling it as infringement on your "equality"?')[2]

Already two years after Cecilia left the anger he felt about Sue's presumed lack of understanding had dissipated, the resentment was gone. In the light of what he saw as Cecilia's laziness and her personal and financial vindictiveness he recognised the value of Sue's hard work and support, her long-suffering dignity and her refusal to settle any scores. He was overcome with remorse for what he had done, and came to the conclusion he had ruined her life. For the rest of his life he was tormented by guilt, even for Sue's later difficulties and misfortunes that had nothing to do with him. When Georg met Keith Jacobs in Vancouver after the 1974 National Youth Orchestra session, he told him, 'Sue – that was really the one.' The process of sanctifying her had begun. She was always thereafter 'the one'.

From the first time I went to his house Georg had not hidden his admiration for Sue. With a sense of resigned disappointment

I began to see I could never live up to his picture of her; I could never be 'the one'. It was a bitter pill to swallow. Yet the truth was that Sue gave Georg a level of devotion to which nobody else came close. No wonder he was nostalgic.

In the weeks following our wedding Georg composed two more difficult six-voice madrigals for me: 'Up, Up! Ye Dames and Lasses Gay', and 'Spring'. They were the last substantial pieces he wrote. After completing them he also, to my great regret, gave up playing the piano at home. His right hand had never recovered from overwork in Perth, and an operation in Sydney to cure his tendonitis had had no effect. Thereafter he played only when absolutely necessary.

He asked me to write a libretto for his opera, 'Tis Pity, and I refused. He was offended at what he took to be lack of interest in his composing, but this was not so – I just knew I had no ability either in scriptwriting or adaptations. At the time I did not know how strange a request it was. I discovered much later that he had already completed a libretto, written in green ink into three exercise books. Perhaps he meant I should help him with it, but that is not what he said. It never occurred to me to ask if he had written any of the music, because he spoke of it in the future tense and there was nothing operatic among his manuscripts. Not with one word did he say he had been occupied with it for over thirty years, or that much had already been written. What happened to it will remain a mystery. All one can say for certain is that in 1962 he had completed a substantial amount of the opera, and in 1977 not a note of it remained. The only clue comes from Boris, who remembers Sue telling him probably in the early 1960s that Georg had realised he didn't have what it took to be a composer and had destroyed his work. If that is what happened, it must have been an act of monumental despair.

When, after Georg's death, I told Marjorie Thompson and Keith Jacobs, they were incredulous that Georg might have destroyed something so fundamental to his being. 'But these were his children!' Marjorie said. But everything he needed as a composer had been lost: his creativity had been assaulted on all fronts, not only personal but practical. The very language of music was in upheaval and, like so many mid-century composers, he found himself with nowhere to go. When Berthold Goldschmidt, a German refugee who arrived in England in 1935, found himself at odds with the serialist orthodoxy of the times, especially at the BBC, he gave up composing in 1958 and remained silent for a quarter of a century. The Polish composer and conductor Paul Kletzki, another refugee, gave up composing in 1941 after hearing that his family had been exterminated in a concentration camp. He left his earlier manuscripts in a trunk in the basement of his Milan apartment building before escaping from there in 1936, and when the building was destroyed he assumed the music had gone with it. When the trunk was discovered intact after the war and returned to him he refused to open it, and it remained untouched at his death in 1973. It may well be that he could not face the evidence that once he had something to say, and had known how to say it. 'I think all creative people in our dreadful age are in a sort of no man's land, in limbo,' Georg said in 1987, 'because nobody really knows what to do any more. That sounds a terrible admission, but it is true.'[3]

What, then, was the answer? For Georg, there never was one. It was not looking backwards, now that he had come so far. The old ways held no appeal, as they did for his friend Hans Gál. While occupied with *The Ellipse* in the 1950s Georg wrote to Douglas Lilburn:

> I think it speaks for him to remain eclectic and 'old fashioned' because he feels it that way than try his hand at some of the things he can't believe in. His music is probably not important but *he* is[4]...It is completely mad that politics spit out a man who is (both for good and ill) so utterly one with the Viennese traditions in[to] Edinburgh. And yet I think he likes it very much, but I am sure he was much too old to create a synthesis, if that is possible even for a younger man I wonder?[5]

First-generation immigrants may be too steeped in the culture they have left to be able to adapt fully to the new one. In Georg's opinion, Weill and Korngold wrote nothing in America as good as their European work. It is the immigrants' children who absorb characteristics of those in the new culture, and become just like them. Only more so. The essence of America is both summed up and created in the music of Aaron Copland, George Gershwin,

Leonard Bernstein and Irving Berlin, and all were the children of Jewish immigrants.

Whether Georg tried to make a synthesis – or even wanted to – is unknown. A synthesis of Viennese and Antipodean traditions was impossible because he did not feel himself a New Zealander, and still less an Australian. Australasian music was in any case firmly rooted in British traditions, which had little to say to him. Within a year of leaving Vienna he tried full atonalism, beginning with 'Trauermusik'. He experimented with serialism, although there is only one full piece (of twenty-seven bars) in the style extant. 'The twelve-tone composers reminded him of the early Christians, embracing the faith,' said Keith Jacobs. 'In the Forties Georg had had cogent arguments against it, saying it blocks certain aspects of music. It was something that was a blind alley. He said, "Twelve-tone makes it easy to write a melody – it makes a lot of things easy."[6] He came to the conclusion that serialism was not the answer. So did other composers. Even Schoenberg departed from strict serialism after the war, but Georg, isolated in New Zealand, didn't find out until later.

In a lecture Georg gave at National Youth Orchestra in 1974 he said:

> I consider that Schoenberg was a very great man. The composer of the Chamber Symphony [No. 1] and *Pierrot Lunaire* was a great composer, there's no doubt in my mind. Nevertheless, I think that these composers wrote good music in this system *in spite* of this system, not because of it. And I think the final question, the reason why all these things were brought about, has not been solved by it. These rules did not do much, if *anything*, of what they were supposed to do, to bring a new order into the self-created chaos [of the demise of sonata form]. They didn't do that, whatever they may have thought…Even [so], the serial system will contribute to the musical Messiah, if he comes. He will take something of this and something of that and will make it into his own, and it will be great because of that. Therefore nothing that happens in music is wasted, I'm sure.[7]

Melody and feeling, so important to Georg, were left out in the cold. 'I am really only interested in EXPRESSION, in feeling,' he said, 'naturally enshrined in form and all other essentials of art, but it is the *feeling* that makes me "tick", a highly unfashionable and "romantic" attitude to art.' Electronic music, the antithesis of affective music, became the latest and best from the late 1940s, and when Douglas Lilburn took it up Georg was mystified and disappointed. After hearing a performance of some of it in London in 1969 he said unhappily, 'Can Douglas *really* believe in it?'*

He wrote to Lilburn in 1955:

> Our position is so different. It is not only the temperamental and national difference but the fact that practically all music written in the 'progressive' style during the last 40–50 years means actually nothing to me: so you see it is true I was born too late. I have seen signs not only in your 12 tone piece but also elsewhere that Frederick Page was not so wrong after all – I think you move into those directions. But it is quite possible and fervently to be hoped that your so very different personality will make a different impact on it than those overintellectuals† from Vienna etc. And the [Berg] Violinconcerto and slow movement of Lulu–Suite has shown me that it is not the method that is all important but the man who employs and uses it. May I respectfully suggest if you have the chance that you listen also to the best works of Pfitzner *Von Deutscher Seele* and *Palestrina*,‡ the last 3 Symphonies of Bruckner (don't sneer mentally they are very different from No. 4) even *Ich bin der Welt abhanden gekommen* by Mahler and the *first* movement of his 9th Symphony not to convert you but if for no other reason to see what latecomers like me adore in newer music.[8]

Georg's difficulties were also practical. He worried that being a conductor – especially one who conducted from memory – would keep his mind filled with other people's music, and the risk was that it would find its way into his own. To be a conductor who composes, he said, one has to have a bad memory. 'Not everybody is as supremely great as Gustav Mahler was who could compose

---

\*   He said to me that Lilburn's electronic music was still better than anyone else's, and that showed that a good composer was always a good composer irrespective of his means of expression.

†   A mistranslation of *über*; he meant super-intellectuals.

‡   Georg considered *Palestrina* the greatest opera of the twentieth century, in company with Debussy's *Pelléas et Mélisande* and Alban Berg's *Wozzeck*.

for two months in the year and conduct for ten months…and keep that more or less apart; and even he in his works shows sometimes traces of the music he conducted…' Once Georg began to work as a conductor and coach he found himself with less and less time, and as much as he wanted to retire to a hut and compose he was trapped by the need to earn money for himself and his family. How he admired Mahler who had both the wherewithal and the strength of will to disappear into his hut in Toblach every summer and compose single-mindedly!

The final straw came when Sue ended their marriage. Georg strenuously denied that losing Sue had stopped him composing, but it dealt a grievous blow to his confidence. She had not understood him as a musician, but that was unimportant to him. She had taken an interest in his compositional activities and done everything she could to support them. It was not losing Sue as a muse that did the damage, for her usefulness for that purpose had faded after the first few years. She was his anchor in uncertain times, and when she went, the compositional game was over.

## Twenty-four

In January 1979 Georg conducted at the National Music Camp in Geelong for the first time since 1960. He was allotted the first orchestra, and he programmed Mozart's *Don Giovanni* Overture, Richard Strauss's *Don Juan* and Bruckner's Fifth Symphony. He stipulated that he would conduct only the original version of the Bruckner, but when he arrived at camp he discovered the ABC had supplied the parts of the long-discredited Schalk edition. He took a train back to Brisbane, 1800 kilometres away and a round trip of four days, and returned with his parts of Bruckner's Fourth Symphony. At the concert, attended by many important people including ABC officials, Georg made a speech about the Schalk Fifth, saying it should be burned, and condemning its provision by people who should know better – people who didn't know the difference between the versions and, worse, didn't care. He offended and embarrassed everyone. The camp administration concluded that Georg was more trouble than he was worth and never invited him again. He did, however, conduct the Fifth with the Australian Youth Orchestra (an adjunct of music camp) in May, at the Sydney Opera House. But the AYO tour of China Georg was to conduct later in the year was transferred without notice to John Hopkins.

A few days after returning from camp we received a letter from our landlords, advising us they had sold the house and we must be out in four weeks. We decided to buy a house in the Samford Valley, just outside the city limits. It was uninviting and in poor repair, but the situation was enchanting. It was on a little more than an acre, a very small allotment by local standards, on the lower slopes of Camp Mountain and at the end of a road that was no more than tyre tracks. Just days from being evicted we managed to arrange a loan, and we moved to Banana Bend (so called by previous tenants) early in March.

*Georg and Tanya in Christchurch in 1979. Georg in that year was much too thin.*

*Georg with his first home-grown pineapple.*

We soon found that we were sharing the house with other creatures great and small. Carpet snakes, with skins like an Oriental carpet, hibernated in the roof in winter. They grew as long as four metres but were quite harmless except to rodents, birds and possums, which they swallowed whole. To us they were gentle, benign creatures and we loved them. There were many types of spiders, one of which could build a sticky web across the back door in only a few minutes. Hand-sized Huntsman spiders came out of hiding when rain was approaching. Wasps built nests of mud on the kitchen walls, but left us alone. When thunderstorms hurtled over the mountains bringing hissing, spattering rain, bullfrogs croaked in the downpipes and tiny green tree frogs set up a chorus so loud and shrill that we had to close the windows, no matter how hot and humid it was. Warty, plate-sized cane toads hid under logs and waited for nightfall. When we returned from concerts we would catch them in the car headlights, sitting impassively on the lawn like garden ornaments.

It took somewhat longer to realise that with our almost non-existent knowledge of subtropical farming we had taken on more than we could manage. Georg had farmed only in a temperate climate, and had no experience of the exuberant growth of the subtropics. Yet he didn't see heavy garden work as a burden; on the contrary, a connection with the land was very important to him. He put in an hour or two every morning as soon as it grew light, before cycling into town for rehearsals. He struggled with Panic Grass, named for the speed of its growth, which stood two metres high in clumps so tenacious they could be dug out only when the ground was sodden with rain. After several months he won the battle, and planted pineapples the length of the driveway. He tended them lovingly, and when he picked his first pineapple he was enormously proud. When we cut down our first bunch of bananas Georg could only marvel. When he had been a good boy at the dentist his mother had rewarded him with a banana, a luxury of surpassing rarity in 1920s Vienna. That he could ever grow his own!

We decided to turn the top half of the allotment into an orchard, and over the years we planted fruit trees both conventional and exotic. Georg dug the holes for them, magnificent excavations by the dozen. 'You are the brains, I am the brawn,' he said. They were among our happiest times. In the garden there was no question of competitiveness, or who was the more important.

Within a few years we were picking papayas, mangoes, soursops, custard apples, litchis and citrus. For Georg it was deeply satisfying to wander up the hill to gaze over the valley to Mount Glorious – 'one of the most beautiful views I know' – and return with fruit from his own trees.

In July 1979 Georg went to his fifth National Youth Orchestra to conduct two small-orchestra programs: Mozart's last three symphonies; and Beethoven's Second and Seventh symphonies with his own arrangement of Beethoven's song *Die Himmel Rühmen* as the choral encore. He shared the season with Marius Constant, and John Brown warned us belligerently to stay away from him, as 'he is quite a reasonable man, unlike Georg'. At very short notice John cancelled a planned fourth week, and then sent a telegram that read in part:

> Have allocated maximum total seventeen [rehearsals] for complete program...If these conditions unacceptable please cable answer so I may engage alternative conductor...Your stay with us may extend to include night Monday August six but no later. Regret departure mandatory Tuesday August seven yourself and Tanya.[1]

Georg replied:

> If I would not love the Canadian Youth Orchestra and if I did not need the money I *would* ask you to take another conductor, because I am amazed and saddened by your bullying tactics. It is not the number of rehearsals I question (they are adequate) but the way you carry on! Is that really the John Brown I have known for so long and have always admired?... When you sent me this silly form about the rehearsals and my right to cancel the concerts but not to get more rehearsals I thought you were joking and I was *mildly* amused; but it was serious Well well well Georg[2]

A little contritely John sent us to Quebec City for a vacation to fill the cancelled week but the atmosphere remained strained. On

15 December Georg wrote to him trying, somewhat clumsily, to make peace.

> It is close to 1980 and I want to wish you all the best. I must say that I was very unhappy about our slight friction; the other day I was sixty-two and a half (though I don't feel it) and it is too late in the day to lose one's friends (especially when it is for a trifling reason). This was the second time you obviously intended to hurt me (I don't know why)…but however I might have exasperated you…to threaten ME of all people to replace me unless I sign the dotted line was a bit 'strong'. May I beg you to bury the 'weapons' and let us be friends again.[3]

John left the letter unanswered for two years.

On his way home Georg stopped in Auckland to conduct two concerts with the New Zealand Youth Orchestra. From there he wrote to me:

> When I turned on the Radio on this morning (I have no other means of knowing the time) they just started: [Delius's] *The Walk to the Paradise Garden*. It was beautiful. The balance and intonation perfect, the pacing exquisite. I thought: *Why can't I do things like that?* I listened enthralled. My first surprise was when they said it was the NZSO (I quickly thought, that wretched Mr Hopkins must be better than I thought after all) then I heard MY NAME and I CRIED.* I never thought I could shape something so perfectly. I tell you this story *NOT* to proclaim how great I am; on the contrary to show you that you are not the only insecure person in this world!!![4]

Georg expressed doubt about his conducting to me only once again, two decades later. As we walked to the first rehearsal of a Bruckner concert with the National Symphony Orchestra of Ireland he simply said, 'I'm frightened.' To have actually admitted it he must have been much more than frightened. About his conducting he presented an air of serene confidence – yet, though he claimed never to dream, he occasionally woke in a panic from

---

\*    It was a studio recording he made in October 1977.

nightmares that expressed classic performance anxiety: he would arrive at the concert hall and realise he had learned the wrong piece, or brought the wrong score. All the same, he knew what he was worth. In 1964 Georg told Hugo Hoffmann that, in comparison with Beethoven, Toscanini and Furtwängler, 'Ich bin ein Wurm. Aber die anderen sind Halbwürmer'. I am a worm – but the others are half-worms.

In September, a quarter of a century after arriving in Australia, he conducted his first main series concert with the Melbourne Symphony Orchestra: Mozart's Symphony No. 34 in C, some Mahler and Brahms with Australian mezzo Yvonne Minton and Schumann's 'Spring' Symphony. 'I was very lucky with both concerts,' Georg wrote to me. 'Both were amazingly good and the reactions and reviews marvellous. One fool in Melb. wrote G.T. is a *wonderful* (?) conductor but why on earth did they play Schumann's First Symphony?' Georg was unforgiving if someone insulted music he loved. When Peter Dart, a clarinettist in the Queensland Theatre Orchestra, remarked flippantly on a country tour that Bruckner wrote the same symphony seven times before he got it right, Georg ignored him for two days. Finally as they were getting off the bus he stopped at Dart's seat and said, 'I'm so surprised at you. Bruckner is a god to me.' Some time afterwards Dart commented to Georg that he didn't like Beethoven's Fourth Symphony. Georg said nothing, but when they did Beethoven's Sixth two years later he encountered Dart in an elevator and said, 'Tell me, Mr Dart, do you approve of this one?' He replied, 'Oh yes! It's one of my favourite symphonies.' Georg said, 'How good of you.'[5]

On 2 October he went with some trepidation to see his doctor, who removed a growth. 'For the last weeks in Canada a little swelling on my stomach, which I had for about 10 years started to hurt rather badly,' he wrote to me a few days later. 'A few minutes ago I heard the verdict: It was fatty tissue and *completely* harmless.'[6]

At the time I was in London. I went there on the way back from Canada to find a temporary job to prove to both of us I was employable. We were not doing well. I felt I was a disappointment to Georg, not only in this respect but in failing to live up to his principles. My daily cup of coffee proved to him that I was addicted, as Sue had been 'addicted' to tea, and he couldn't understand how

I could have so little self-control. He considered medicines an abomination and the taking of them a weakness. When I pointed out that when he felt an attack of gout coming on he wasted no time in taking pills, he said, 'But I couldn't work!' For Georg there were two types of illness: those that might prevent his working, which must be treated immediately, and those suffered by people who were doing nothing creative and were therefore unimportant. Illnesses caused by the pursuit of one's creative life, such as repetition strain to the wrist or painful feet from constant standing, had a legitimacy that illnesses that 'just happened' did not. Thus, when he became ill at the end of his life with a disease that had nothing to do with conducting, he didn't know how to cope with it.

One of Georg's central tenets was that anything not creative had little or no value. When I wrote magazine articles Georg read them carefully and made useful suggestions, but when I did graphic design for a city guide he said, 'You make advertisements. Anybody can do that.' When I replied that my work was important to me and he should respect it, he asked how I could possibly compare what I did with what he did. Making judgements about the relative value of a partner's activities had to my mind no place in a relationship. Georg persisted in doing just this, and thereby caused extensive damage to all three of his marriages.

He was given to referring to 'your blasted competitiveness', which made no sense to me until long after he died. As I researched this book, it became clear that he thought Cecilia had competed with him, and he had no wish to revisit it. I realised that several things I had done may well have reminded him of their life together. Though he often promised to brush my hair, he could never bring himself to do it. He would take the brush, contemplate it at length, and put it down again wordlessly. When we visited Muizenberg years later he claimed to have no idea where his and Cecilia's house was, and when I suggested we look for it he refused sharply, suddenly anxious and frightened. Strangest of all was an afternoon, just after we were married. The orchestra manager telephoned Georg about a minor matter and he offered to go into town to discuss it. I drove him to the train, but I suddenly fell ill on the way with vomiting, diarrhoea and crippling cramps. He angrily demanded that I take him to the train, until finally he walked away – a long way from the station – shouting, 'You are trying to sabotage me!'

At the time I thought him slightly insane, but I didn't know about Cecilia's illness in their last year together, and that Georg had considered it hypochondria and a deliberate drain on his emotional and physical resources – in other words, sabotage. While I knew he wanted a wife like Sue, it never occurred to me that he wanted one not like Cecilia. Only once did he say anything like it, when one night he begged me agitatedly not to read in bed because Cecilia had done it to show him she wasn't interested in his attentions and he couldn't bear to be reminded of it. I didn't realise how much damage his divorces had caused him, in their different ways – permanent, insurmountable damage.

Georg showed much concern for the downtrodden and the politically oppressed, but showing concern for strangers was easier than for those who were closer, where emotional investment was required. When Georg chatted with acquaintances I had an uneasy feeling that he had not really connected with them. But they hardly noticed; they were happy to be talking to someone they admired, and assumed his was the manner of the naturally superior. And as conductors are generally held to be self-absorbed and arrogant, Georg was thought kind and considerate when simply behaving in a civilised manner.

As happens with those who speak in absolutes, Georg appeared to have worked out life's questions and answers and achieved a certain serenity some saw as his 'aura'. Some who searched for a model of the meaning of life turned him into a saint and worshipped him. Others were not fooled; Valerie Melrose thought Georg the most neurotic man she had ever met. By the time I knew him he was in such distress that he had no internal resources to deal with the difficulties of others, especially of those closest to him. They were feeling sorry for themselves, taking themselves too seriously, or as he would say in eloquently resigned tones, 'We are all in love with our neuroses.' Coping with the miseries of others was beyond him. He could hardly cope with his own.

On a day on which he was particularly withdrawn I asked him if he were depressed. The idea outraged him. Depression was nothing more than feeling sorry for oneself, a weakness, a complaint of people without self-control. He was so insistent this was nonsense that I believed him. After all, he didn't appear morose or moody – on the contrary, he prided himself on never having moods. In hindsight it is clear Georg was severely depressed, and all the denials in the world did not make it otherwise. But he was not even willing to admit it to himself, let alone give in to it. Instead, he propped himself up with a scaffolding of principles, chief among them willpower. He was determined never to be a *Vey ist mir* Jew.

On my way to England I went to Vienna to see Alois Starka, the agent Georg had visited in 1964. I gave his materials to two employees, who, assuming I spoke no German, amused themselves by making cheap jokes about the difference in our ages before showing me the door. It was often said that Georg refused to have an agent because he didn't believe in them. He certainly disliked them, but the fact was that, with a few exceptions of brief duration, nobody would take him on.

I had better luck with finding a job. I was offered two positions on my first day in London, and took one of them for a few weeks. While I was away we wrote each other sometimes angry, sometimes pleading, sometimes conciliatory letters trying to solve our difficulties. And letters were the only chance we had to solve our problems. In all the time we were together we had barely two or three serious arguments, because if I so much as raised my voice Georg would run to the bedroom, slam the door and sit on the bed with his fingers stuck demonstratively in his ears. Never again was he going to participate in screaming matches.

Insecurities on both sides were confessed, and disregarded. Georg begged me 'to be more understanding when I'm up against it and to realise that I'm short of time and courage' – another startling admission. I bewailed the constant comparisons to Sue, and asked him, quite seriously, if he would like to get divorced and marry her again, as he seemed to be still in love with her. He thought my suggestion was insane; he said he rarely thought of her but when he did he felt only guilt and great respect. In the end, after many letters, we reached some sort of understanding. On my way home I reported that I was homesick, and Georg replied immediately from the Cambridge Music School in New Zealand: 'I write mainly to tell you *again* that your letter…*warmed* my *heart*…I send you a LOT OF LOVE. May we do well.' At the time he was pursuing a twenty-year-old student at the school, but he assuredly meant his words. Things were never as bad again as they were in those months. Yet at the same time something was lost, perhaps something I had squandered, and I realised it only long after Georg died and I re-read his letters. I think he saw that in trying to find a muse he had failed once again. As he realised his opera may never come forth, disillusionment set in.

Late in 1979 the divorce settlement was at last completed. Georg sold the Perth house for well under the valuation and less than even our worst expectations, but it was enough to pay off Banana Bend. Cecilia sold The Kop and moved to Melbourne, although it was a year before Georg found out. Because she did not feel up to working he paid the full maintenance amount until the children were in their twenties, and gave them small legacies as well. It was not enough. Not long before he died one of his daughters wrote to me that he had been grossly deficient in his support in every way, financial and fatherly, and if he wasn't able to support children he shouldn't have had them in the first place. I kept the letter from him. It would have broken his heart.

By the time Georg discovered Cecilia was back in Australia, late in 1980, it was too late for him to re-establish a relationship with the children. 'I doubt whether I shall see them that much oftener,' he wrote to me. 'I am not sure whether I should see them at all…'[7] He gave no reason; but he was certain the children had all but forgotten him. He visited them every couple of years or so when a concert took him to Melbourne, but each time he came back very disturbed at what he had seen. When sixteen-year-old Esmeralda wrote to ask his permission to get married, he replied sadly that he didn't know why she was asking, given that in the previous thirteen years nobody had bothered to consult him about her and her sisters' education, activities, whereabouts or anything else.

Georg was close to none of his seven children, and long separations were only partly to blame. But as much as he loved his children – and there is no doubt that he did – he didn't seem to understand he had to show it, and that loving gestures were necessary. He rarely even wrote to them on their birthdays, except for Hephzibah whose birthday on New Year's Day he could remember. I once asked him why he signed his letters to the older children 'Regards' instead of 'Love'. He looked puzzled and said, 'But they're adults!' It was part of his remoteness, and all of his children suffered from it. So did his wives, but it was harder for the children, who had not chosen their relatives. 'Georg seemed kind and interested, but when you got closer you saw he was really into his own music,' says Valerie Melrose. 'He could talk to people he was not so close to, but for people he had to be closer to, he kept something back for himself. There was a part of him that couldn't be shared with other people. His life was too important – the purpose that he felt he had in life with his music. It just took over from everything else.'[8]

By late 1979 Georg was becoming a victim of his own success, and he wrote to me: 'Actually it seems I did too well with the QTO. It is now in such demand [from opera and ballet] that it seems I am squeezed out of a job.' So when the Sydney *Sunday Telegraph*'s gossip column reported that he was a front-runner for the South Australian Opera's music director position, he wrote immediately to express his interest. He received a non-committal reply. The rumour circulated for months, until the company hired Denis Vaughan. Then the tenor Gregory Dempsey, recently returned to Australia after an international career, asked Georg if he would return to the Australian Opera if Bonynge were gone. He was interested. Peter Hemmings had become general manager in 1977 and he knew Georg from his *Fledermaus* performances in Glasgow; he would be happy to have him. Dempsey told him a fight was breaking out between Bonynge and Hemmings, and Georg had only to wait. Dempsey miscalculated. Georg wrote to me in October:

> Peter Hemmings has left the country. The person who finally ruined him was John Hopkins, the 'expert' on the Board, who turned round in a disgusting manner after saying they make a poor exchange between a top administrator and a third rate conductor and a declining diva. He must have been bribed.[9]

Georg saw Harold Hort at the ABC and expressed interest in becoming resident conductor of any ABC orchestra except Tasmania from 1981, but said he would also be glad to guest-conduct any of the orchestras. Hort confidentially canvassed the state managers' opinions. The most favourable reply came from the Concerts Manager in Sydney, Ian Peter, who wrote:

I personally regard Georg Tintner as one of the finest conductors resident in Australia. He possesses a great deal of
public credibility as an interpreter of fine music. However,
his talents are limited in some areas. His quiet and withdrawn
personality makes him quite unsuitable for Schools, Family
and Youth Concerts, unless this deficiency can be overcome
by the employment of a narrator. Ideally, these concerts
should be left to those better endowed to communicate with
an audience. I don't think it is valuable to expose any conductor annually to the same audience, with the exception of
the Chief Conductor. Therefore, if we were to give Georg
Tintner a set of Red, White and Blue subscriptions one year
– and I think he would be well received – I would hope
that his employment in the following year would be more
limited, or at least restricted to other concert areas, say the
Town Hall and Saturday Afternoon Series, a special concert, a
mini-festival, Messiahs etc. In short, I feel that Georg Tintner
is quite suitable to conduct major concerts in Sydney, but only
for as long as we avoid over-exposing him.[10]

Victoria and Queensland had limited interest in him as a guest
only. The Concerts Manager in Victoria was unimpressed by his
recent concerts with Yvonne Minton and thought little of him as
either conductor or public personality.[11] The Queensland manager
thought that his abilities as musician and conductor did not out-
weigh a disagreeable attitude towards the orchestra; in any case
he would not be suitable as music director because he 'refused' to
conduct light music.[12] Perth was also willing to accept him only for
limited free concerts and studio work because the orchestra found
his rehearsals tiresome;[13] the Concerts Manager added that in his
opinion Georg had had little appeal for ABC audiences when he
lived there.[14] Adelaide's Concert Manager said he would be very
suitable for choral or vocal performances; the Supervisor of Music,
James Christiansen, added:

Mr Tintner is the kind of Conductor needed in South
Australia as a foil for the more flamboyant Mr Serebrier. We
would have to caution you however that Mr Tintner does
not go down particularly well with the Adelaide Symphony

*Georg conducting the Christchurch Symphony Orchestra in May 1980.*

Orchestra…we think it would be fair to say it is partly due to his iron will and high expectations from whatever Orchestra he controls.[15]

Noel Clark, the acting assistant director of music (General), who had worked with Georg on two young-performer Beethoven concerto evenings for the Sydney Festival in January 1980, reported irritably that Georg had become obdurate and excessively demanding and he had found dealing with him for five days exhausting. He allowed, however, that he was one of Australia's better Mozart conductors.[16] In short, said Michael Corban, Acting Director of Music (Programming):

all States would accept (if not welcome) Mr Tintner for restricted periods, with the type of work to which he is assigned carefully planned. It is evident that he is not suited for Youth/Family-type concerts or others where verbal communication with the audience is essential...Tintner is suitable for major concerts, as long as he is not over-exposed in any particular series. We feel that, as long as there are sufficient overseas names in the various series, Tintner could be scheduled in subscription series in all States...[17]

Thereafter the ABC gave him fewer subscription concerts, just three in the next five years, but they did raise his fee to $515.

On 21 August 1980 Georg conducted two of Douglas Lilburn's works in a studio broadcast with the Queensland Symphony Orchestra: the Third Symphony, and *Diversions*. I suggested we invite Douglas to stay with us and attend the performance, but Georg said there was no point – he was now so reclusive that he scarcely left his house. To his surprise, Douglas accepted. The day after he arrived the grease trap under the kitchen window blocked up, filling the air with the stink of rancid fat. We apologised and promised to fix it as soon as we had run an errand. When we returned we found that Douglas, aged almost sixty-five, had crawled into the narrow space behind a large fern and cleaned it out. 'Think nothing of it!' he beamed. 'I'm a farmer's son.' In spite of the drain he thought it 'one of the best ever holidays I've had'. Georg had 'honour[ed] my music with a couple of understanding and exhilarating performances which seemed to convince the orchestra and the audience (those rows of dear old mums nodding and smiling at me in the interval!)'.[18]

In September Georg conducted *Don Pasquale* for the Queensland Opera Company, and in October *Samson and Delilah* (an opera he disliked) with Margreta Elkins and Donald Smith for the Queensland Light Opera Company. Just before *Don Pasquale* began, Carmel Hakendorf resigned to take a job in England, apparently offered on two days' notice. 'I give you some cudgel to chastise me with,' Georg scribbled in a note to me. 'I lent Carmel and Brit $2700 [for the airfares]. Nobody else would, and she would have missed out on a job with the ENO. I am aware that I might never see it again, though I think I shall...' We heard from her a few days later, announcing her arrival at a luxury hotel in London, and never again. Once more we were in financial difficulties; the money Georg gave Carmel was almost every penny he had.

Throughout 1980 the state government considered amalgamating the state-funded Queensland Opera and the privately

*Georg and Tanya visiting Douglas Lilburn in his Thorndon house in 1982.*

funded Queensland Light Opera, and installing Georg as music director. Abruptly the government withdrew funding from the Queensland Opera in December, and it promptly collapsed. The decision was made on the recommendation of the Light Opera's general manager and occasional conductor, David Macfarlane. A year later the Lyric Opera of Queensland was formed, subsuming the Light Opera, and David Macfarlane was installed as its artistic director. This was for Georg a serious misfortune. Macfarlane was, as répétiteur Megan Evans puts it, 'hideously jealous of Georg', and went out of his way to shut him out. The major attraction of Brisbane – the deciding factor in moving there – had been the prospect of conducting both symphonic concerts and opera, and that was about to be snatched away.

In February 1982, after a long programming dispute with the ABC, Georg conducted Beethoven's *Christus am Ölberg* with the Melbourne Symphony, but his crusade on behalf of a 'neglected masterpiece' went for nothing. The critics objected to its inclusion in the Moomba Festival where 'everyone is expected to get together and have fun', calling it 'a wooden oratorio'[19] and 'a barren and dull work'.[20] Georg gave two more Beethoven concerts at the festival, in which Roger Woodward played all five piano concerti just three days apart. It was the beginning of a long and mutually admiring artistic partnership.

After the festival Georg began rehearsing *Albert Herring* at the Conservatorium in Brisbane, and then went to Christchurch for a concert. I had been working at the Conservatorium for almost a year, and while Georg was in New Zealand I resigned, unwilling to work any longer with the director, Dr Roy Wales. Georg, ever loyal, wrote immediately to Wales, with a copy to at least one board member, telling him that he was 'a bully and a muddler'. Incensed, Wales wrote back, firing him from *Albert Herring*, but the letter missed him. Georg had barely begun his rehearsal at the Conservatorium a few days later when Dr Wales stormed in and, in front of startled students, ordered him out of the building. The Theatre Orchestra and Conservatorium boards did their best to resolve the mess, but without success. Georg remained banned until Wales departed, several years later.

The day before his sixty-fifth birthday Georg conducted Beethoven's *Missa Solemnis* at the Intervarsity Choral Festival in Sydney. Shortly before the festival began there was a strange phone call from the ABC. 'When I walked into our office,' Georg wrote to John Brown, 'I was told that the ABC in Sydney tried to verify for you that I had died in a car accident. This is the second time I was reported dead (the first while I was in England twelve years ago with obituary etc). Perhaps the third time I shall oblige, but not yet.'[21] Ten days later Annemarie's eighty-year-old husband Frank died of a heart attack. Such reminders made Georg only too aware that his time was running short and he was still not composing. So that he could have a quiet place in which to do so, I had the large packing shed behind the house rebuilt as two enormous studios. It took several years, but the results were worth it. Georg's room was sunny and restful. It was furnished with a table and chair, his books and scores, and the piano standing in the centre from which he could look out over the garden. But for one or two trifles, not a note was composed in it.

## Twenty-five

Georg returned to the National Youth Orchestra in August 1982 to conduct, inter alia, Bruckner's monumental Eighth Symphony. There were to be two performances, and he proposed that, as an exercise of the highest educational value, one should be of the original 1887 version and the other that edited by Robert Haas, a hybrid of the original and Bruckner's extensively revised and shortened 1890 version. The 1887 version had been published only in 1972 and had never been performed in North America. John Brown had written to Georg in September 1981, ending a two-year silence:

> I was encouraged by your friendly letter to me and your evi-
> dent intent to be agreeable to me personally...The success of
> the NYO has always depended very much on the good will
> and involvement of the staff in the whole enterprise, so please
> pay attention to their needs and try and curb your irascibility.
> They have not known you as long as I have.[1]

Georg replied in part:

> Funny indeed that I, whose politeness and gentleness toward
> his fellow musicians is known and acknowledged wherever
> I go, am accused of rudeness (or whatever the word was) BY
> YOU of all people!!! I hope you see some merit in my idea of
> a juxtaposition of both versions of No. 8. It would only need
> 4 more [rehearsals]![2]

John did not reply, but Paul Hawkshaw, the coordinator of artistic affairs, wrote to say they would do only the 1887 version.

Georg's first concert included Beethoven's Fifth Symphony, Chausson's *Poème** with Myriam Pellerin, a student and John Brown's fiancée, and Vaughan Williams's *Five Variants of Dives and Lazarus* for strings (he had ninety-one players) and harp. The *Whig-Standard*'s Richard Perry gave it one of Georg's finest reviews:

> Kingston music lovers who may be staying away from the National Youth Orchestra concerts because they presume that there's just a bunch of kids up there are wrong, wrong, oh so wrong. Last night's concert in Grant Hall…under the baton of one of the great 'unknown' conductors of the world, Georg Tintner, offered the kind of exhilarating and satisfying musical experience which we seek in the concert hall but so seldom find…What the ecstatic audience heard last night was that rare thing: a performance of Beethoven's Fifth which sounded as if the players had just discovered it…the greatest praise must be reserved for the conductor, who not only conjured up the Promethean vision but also communicated it to his youthful players. Quite honestly, I have not been so stirred up by a Beethoven symphony reading since I ran across Horenstein's old performance of the Ninth on Vox. Tintner's reading had that same exciting power and the NYO responded marvelously.[3]

The first North American performance of the 1887 Bruckner Eighth, taking eighty-five minutes, was given in Kingston on 30 August and repeated the following night at Massey Hall in Toronto. 'The musicians, under Viennese-born conductor Georg Tintner, were thrusting and inspired from first to last,' wrote Arthur Kaptainis in the *Globe and Mail*:

> Tintner, who looked like a Leopold Stokowski with shaggier and longer white hair, was an intelligible and unlanguorous Bruckner leader, inclined to steady, fast tempos and neatly (but richly) shaped melodies. His beat was a little unyielding in the middle parts of the opening movement, and his quick

---

\* Georg was disappointed to find that the originally scheduled Violin Concerto of Alban Berg ('one of the greatest works of this century') had been cancelled. 'You know that the first performance (in Barcelona) was entrusted to his friend Anton Webern who took several days over the first few bars – so it had to be taken away from him and entrusted to a mediocricy [Hermann Scherchen, on 19 April 1936].'

tempo for the Scherzo, while innovative, seemed to rob the
movement of some of its demonic, piston-like thrust. But
the slow movement unfolded gloriously, and the crescendo
Tintner fashioned in the opening bars of the final movement
was overwhelmingly powerful.[4]

Given the importance of such a premiere I tried to interest
record companies. George Mendelssohn of Vox-Turnabout regret-
fully rejected it as too expensive. Fred Maroth of Music and Arts
was interested, but the musicians' union vetoed him because his
company was not Canadian. Nevertheless, the orchestra liked the
idea, and the performance was issued two years later by James
Creighton's Jubal Records. 'Usually I dread to listen to my own
efforts,' Georg wrote to Paul Hawkshaw, 'but this time it gave me
real pleasure.'[5] John Brown sent a brief, acid note reading: 'I am
glad you enjoyed the Bruckner. The total budget was quite large
and we lost about $20,000 for sure.'[6]

Almost as soon as Georg returned to Brisbane there was a series
of misfortunes. His new bicycle was stolen, and soon after that he
was leaving the Conservatorium on my bicycle when he crashed
into a boom-gate he hadn't seen and fell to the ground, injuring
his face. He was also sent to a dermatologist for the removal of
lesions caused by sun damage. He announced to the doctor that he
wanted it done without anaesthetic, citing his dental extractions
in Perth. 'I did not flinch,' he said. The doctor was unmoved. 'I
said, "Then you've come to the wrong person", because diathermy
without anaesthesia would be torture. I could see what sort of
person Georg was from that. A zealot.'[7] Then, on a visit to my
parents, Georg picked some plums at dusk and didn't see a bee
on one of them, which stung him on the tongue. He was upset
only that the bee would die, and he ignored all entreaties to go
to hospital. Against expectations he didn't choke to death, but he
wasn't himself for days.

Given his refusal to kill any creature, living in the subtropical
countryside was sometimes a challenge. Every May rodents moved
into the house when it turned cold outside. One year there was a
plague of them, and no amount of cleaning and rodent-proofing
made any difference. They nested in the sofa, shredded the curtains, chewed the bedding and ran across our pillows in the middle

*Georg doing his early-morning breathing exercises atop Mount Ainslie, early 1980s, ignoring the impressive view of Canberra.*

of the night. After weeks of ever-increasing damage I convinced Georg they had to go. With a heavy heart he agreed, and after two or three nights of suffering through the sound of snapping traps we knew they were gone.

Georg's love for all creatures extended even to cockroaches, one or two of which appeared in the house whenever rain approached. The flute player David Cubbin, who came to stay for a while, went to the bathroom one morning and found a six-centimetre cockroach in the shower, waving its feelers menacingly. 'Perhaps I'll come back later,' he thought, and returned to his room. After a few minutes he heard Georg go to the bathroom. 'Hul-*lo!*' Georg said in very friendly tones. David heard footsteps, the sound of the back door opening, and Georg saying affectionately, 'Good bye!'

'The other day I had a phone call from no less than Mr Hort himself!' a surprised Georg wrote to me early in October. 'He said that he is very conscious of the fact that the ABC has neglected me rather badly and he wants to talk to me either on my way to

Hobart or on the way back.'[8] He suspected there was rather more to it, and he soon discovered that the ABC had been given an ultimatum by Bill Hennessy, the concertmaster of the Tasmanian Symphony Orchestra, who told them that if they did not give Georg more work, preferably in Hobart, he would refuse to renew his contract. As a result they gave him two weeks there at the end of 1982 and seven weeks in 1983. Georg wrote Hort a bitter letter about the way the ABC was treating him. He mentioned the 1976 subscription concerts in Sydney and said, 'That was the end of it.' Hort sent a friendly reply saying that they were keeping Georg's interests in mind while providing variety for their audiences. Georg was not mollified. He knew he was getting slim pickings from an organisation that presented over 600 orchestral concerts a year.

In May 1983 he conducted *Fidelio* for the Lyric Opera. The company's general manager, Neil Duncan, backed by David Macfarlane, had tried to avoid engaging Georg by changing the dates to a time he knew he was unavailable. Prevented from doing this by the Theatre Orchestra, they tried to take over the orchestra and appoint Brian Stacey, a local ballet and light music conductor, as the new music director. As Macfarlane had cronies (or as Georg called them, croonies) in the government there was a good chance he might succeed. He was stopped only just in time by a number of equally well-connected concertgoers.

That year Georg was to give a number of concerts with the Auckland Regional Orchestra, an ensemble that had developed from his String Players, and of which he was Artistic Advisor. But in February he received a letter from the manager, Michael Maxwell, informing him that John Hopkins had been appointed Principal Conductor. Georg felt he had been ambushed, and by his 'own' orchestra at that. Twenty years of frustration over being thwarted by John Hopkins, at the ABC and elsewhere, boiled over.

> I am looking forward to my association and concert with the ARO in May and June, especially as they will *have to be my last.*
>
> I herewith resign my honorary title of musical advisor. I never quite knew what I was expected to do in that capacity and lately I was forced to realise that it means mighty little... And to engage a principal conductor without seeking the

advice of the advisor but to advise the advisor of the accomplished fact makes a mockery of the whole business.[9]

All the musicians signed a letter regretting his decision, and the concertmaster Brecon Carter sent a long plea of his own, to no avail. Georg did conduct them again, but not until after Hopkins departed when the orchestra collapsed in 1991, to be resurrected some time later as the Auckland Philharmonia.

In August Georg toured country New South Wales with the Sydney Symphony Orchestra. When we reached Tamworth it was plain that he wanted very much to visit Sue, still living nearby, and I drove him to the farm. She appeared at the top of the driveway, a crone-like figure with a walking stick. She waved us to come in and took us to the small cement-block house the children had built for her. To Georg's surprise she was pleasant to me; he said afterwards (not quite accurately) that I was the only woman she had ever liked. It was almost twenty years since he had seen her and he was visibly moved. He was also shocked at how much she had aged, at the loss of her teeth, her stooped and haggard appearance. Sue must have thought much the same about Georg, for the children said later they had been amused to hear from both parents how dreadful the other had looked.

The one happy event of 1983 was a performance on 29 July of *The Ellipse* at the Brisbane Conservatorium.* 'In all modesty I still consider it a MASTERPIECE (how modest)', he wrote to me – perhaps pointedly, perhaps not – 'and it is a pity that I haven't had the strength (apart from lack of time) to go on creating in a void…'[10]

Because of the tribute to Hephzibah Menuhin written into the first movement, and because she had died not so long before (on 22 April 1981), Georg sent a tape of the performance to her brother. Yehudi replied from Baden-Baden:

> Your wonderful and touching gift reached me here…in this supreme Kurort where I could listen to *The Ellipse* in repose and total amazement. Your revealing and witty introductory remarks to what seemed a most sympathetic audience must have contributed to my receptiveness – but the feeling

---

* It was given by soprano Janet Delpratt and a sympathetic student group (John Rodgers, Warwick Adeney, Brett Dean and John Napier).

did come through – as well as the immense and so well-coordinated performance of the brilliant young players and the soprano. I even recognized your tribute to our darling Hephzibah in the very last phrase on the second violin of the first movement.

I so wish we could be connected musically – for I have continued my sister Hephzibah's great respect for your knowledge, integrity and talent…[11]

Although Georg didn't think the letter particularly sincere, he sent a copy to his youngest daughter, Hephzibah Menuhin's namesake, now twelve. In return he received a distressing letter from Cecilia, saying that Hephzibah was in hospital with anorexia, but she was making a good recovery and would reply to his letter shortly. She asked if he would come to see the children, and he made a brief visit on his way to Hobart early in November. His worry lessened only when he heard a few months later that Hephzibah had taken up ballet dancing and intended to make it her career.

Less than a year before Georg died Hephzibah asked him bitterly why he had not come to visit her when she was ill. Georg, confused because he was sure that he had, said, 'I would have had to cancel a concert and one just couldn't do that with the ABC.' Hephzibah said, 'So you chose a concert over me,' and Georg, even more puzzled and not understanding quite how he had failed her, replied that he supposed he had. It was not until long after his death that I learned Hephzibah had been anorexic not for a matter of weeks but for at least two years. Georg had not been told. And that, in turn, was something that Hephzibah would never know, because by then she was also dead.

The events of 1983 left Georg quite dispirited. In need of some support he wrote in September to John Brown, trying to repair their friendship.

I still remember the interesting and enthusiastic conversations we had in the Kings Cross Studio…Since then *you* have gone on in the world, while I stayed pretty stationary…Perhaps that is the reason why you hardly ever reply to my letters and surround yourself with an aura of mystery. But why? I still remember when I was told a little over a year ago

what a privilege it was that I finally saw you at all, because
the conductor before me was not accorded this honour!
What NONSENSE!...I would like to renew our friendship
whether I come to conduct for you or not![12]

It took John two and a half years to reply.

In November and December Georg spent six weeks with the
Tasmanian Symphony, the engagement for which Bill Hennessy
was responsible, and enjoyed himself. He did some studio recordings and lunchtime concerts, the *Messiah*, and the Three Composer
series: Tchaikovsky, Beethoven and Dvořák. But Georg's arms
were very painful, and several weeks' rest in summer made little
difference. He was still in pain the following February when
he conducted the Sydney Symphony Orchestra's 1984 Three
Composer Festival: Beethoven, Tchaikovsky and Mendelssohn.
Nevertheless, his conducting was energetic and it was commented
on by several of the critics. Fred Blanks wrote of the first concert:

> The impression of a slightly underfed Old Testament prophet
> castigating the doubters of his congregation, which Georg
> Tintner gives on the conducting platform, seemed particularly
> apt for the heroics of Beethoven on Saturday evening. Not
> that doubters in the Sydney Symphony Orchestra were often
> prominent. But they might have been less so still had Georg
> Tintner used a baton to add extra length to his vigorous and
> comprehensive signals.
>
> As things turned out, the performances may not always
> have been the last word in tidiness, but even the second
> last word became more acceptable when combined with the
> dramatic sweep, attention to detail, and obvious affinity for
> Beethoven...What we heard this time was a strongly outlined,
> dynamic performance [of the Fifth Symphony], which stayed
> a marathon course not because the conductor dawdled – far
> from it – but because he liked to observe repeats to the extent
> that he seems to re-repeat repeats already repeated.[13]

Unless forestalled by the likelihood of running into overtime
Georg always observed repeats (and conducted them a little differently the second time). He maintained they were not mere
convention but part of the structure. He pointed out that Mozart

omitted the first movement exposition repeat in a few of his symphonies, which proved to him that Mozart intended the ones he
did write to be played. This, however, did not endear him to
orchestral musicians.

On 28 and 30 May Georg conducted a program of operatic
arias for the Lyric Opera in Brisbane. The singers included the
young Lisa Gasteen, and he brought soprano Wendy Dixon and
tenor Tony Benfell from New Zealand. After the first performance
David Macfarlane said, to the surprise of everyone in the Green
Room, 'Of course, Georg is good at this sort of concert, but in full
operas he's no good at all.' As 1984 went on members of Georg's
orchestra began turning against him, though he did not at first
realise it. When the acting Concertmaster, Tony Bonetti, resigned
at the end of October because the musicians no longer supported
him (Bonetti),[14] he wrote to the general manager, Denise Wadley,
detailing his dissatisfaction with Georg as music director, objecting
in particular to his poor beat, his failure to discipline the orchestra,
his being out of touch with playing in the pit and encouraging the
attitude that it was beneath the players' dignity.[15] Mrs Wadley then
wrote to the board detailing her own dissatisfaction with Georg:

> ...he is 'pure music' to the exclusion of almost everything else.
> This can be dynamite in an administrative sense!...He has no
> PRESENCE here, he takes no initiatives, makes no suggestions,
> does not keep abreast of what else is on the QTO programme
> and keeps no 'fatherly' eye on things...The Music Director
> gives *no* direction...[16]

Her solution was to propose appointing the Principal Viola and
novice conductor, Robert Harris, as Georg's assistant. With little
enthusiasm, Georg agreed.

In March 1985 he conducted eight performances of Richard
Strauss's opera *Capriccio** for the State Opera of South Australia.
The *Adelaide Review* critic complained about the choice of such
a 'trivial piece' but went on to mention Georg 'glistening in the
pit' with 'conducting scarcely heard in this theatre for a decade'.[17]
When it was over the company offered him *Flying Dutchman* in
1986. He was delighted; it was his first opportunity to conduct

---

\*   In Georg's opinion, 'It is remarkable enough for a composer aged seventy-nine but of course it is no
    *Falstaff* or *Parsifal*...It has very good things in it, but most of it he has said (better) before.'

staged Wagner. He asked the Theatre Orchestra for leave, but the dates conflicted with concerts the orchestra could or would not reschedule. Georg became so angry that he threatened to resign. After several anxious weeks the Opera offered him *Macbeth* instead, at a different time. But a few weeks later Ian Johnston, the company's manager, wrote to say that he had not first consulted the incoming music director, Andrew Greene, who had most specific views about the conducting of *Macbeth* and in fact wanted to conduct it himself. He was therefore obliged to withdraw the offer, though he hoped Georg would return in 1987. Georg replied that he would never conduct for them again.

At a few days' notice the ABC asked him if he would replace an indisposed Charles Mackerras in subscription concerts in mid-July. The program was Schumann's piano concerto with Jorge Bolet, and Mahler's Ninth Symphony. Although he had never conducted the symphony before, and had only three rehearsals, several ABC officials enthusiastically congratulated him after the concert and promised him more work in future. He returned to Sydney a few weeks later to substitute again for Mackerras in another subscription program that by chance contained one of his greatest loves: Bruckner's *Te Deum*, in which he 'called up its big choral climaxes as if he were willing the world into existence'.[18]

Despite the ABC's promises Georg heard nothing further. Several months later he wrote to them with a number of program suggestions. They were not interested. In the following year he had less work from them than in any year since 1955: one studio broadcast in November. Deeply disheartened, the idea of disappearing for the rest of his life into a hut in the rainforest to compose had never seemed more appealing. When the dairy farmer next door cleared a strip of public land between us by mistake, we created our own rainforest there. I searched out rare and endangered plants and Georg dug several hundred splendid holes for them. It took only two or three years for the pioneer trees to grow to fifteen metres and, as the canopy filled out, uncommon native birds arrived. Scrub turkeys built huge mounds of leaf litter in which they incubated their eggs; they would fly clumsily into the banana stands to eat the still-green fruit, and wait under the litchi trees for Georg to finish digging in vegetable scraps so they could scratch them up again. Despite such quibbles with the wildlife, we were building our little piece of paradise.

## Twenty-six

Early in 1986 Georg received an invitation to conduct Symphony Nova Scotia, based in Halifax, Canada. It was an ensemble of thirty-seven musicians, formed in 1983 after the collapse of the much larger Atlantic Symphony Orchestra. Georg had never heard of them and it made no sense: why would a small and presumably poor orchestra bring him from the other side of the world for just one concert? We guessed they might be looking for a music director – a surmise made more plausible on hearing that the invitation originated with the Assistant Principal Viola, Burt Wathen, who had played in *Transfigured Night* in the National Youth Orchestra in 1974 and never forgotten it. His one stipulation for the concert, scheduled for October, was that Georg should include the same work.

Early in May he conducted the Hong Kong Philharmonic in a program that included Beethoven's Symphony No. 6 – a performance that was 'positively majestic. The Philharmonic players, under Tintner's authoritative and insightful direction, achieved a unanimity that, in my hearing, they have never surpassed.'[1] The night after the concert the phone rang close to midnight. Georg answered, said almost nothing, but looked increasingly uncomfortable. When I asked who it was he blurted out that it was a woman he had visited that afternoon, whom I shall call Eunice. He had met her at the 1984 Hong Kong Youth Music Camp, where she had been a staff musician. She had fallen in love with him, apparently one of several musicians with whom she was in love. She was Chinese, married, and a little younger than I. That afternoon they had intended to go to bed together but decided against it because she was six months pregnant with her second child. She had called Georg in a state of hysteria, insisting she must see him one more time before he left Hong Kong.

In the interests of honesty he went on to tell me that for the previous few months he had been having an affair with a woman in Brisbane. Mercia Morton was an amateur artist in her late twenties who lived at home with her devoutly Catholic mother, and who had met Georg by asking to draw his beautiful profile. Their arrangement was that Mercia would pick him up from Central Station on Thursdays and they would drive to McAfee's Lookout, the national park on the hill behind our house, and make love in the rainforest. To be as honourable as possible under the circumstances, Georg had refused my offer to drive him to the station on days when he was meeting Mercia. It was rather touching, in retrospect.

It was a shock to discover that Georg was involved with not one woman but two, and it did not help that he said he was astonished to discover he could love two women at once. I counted three, and it seemed to me I was the odd woman out. He said much later that he hadn't meant that, but it was very painful at the time. It was not our best evening – indeed, I cried bitter tears. But I realised even then that it was the first time in almost ten years that I had Georg's undivided attention.

He said I should accompany him to his meeting with Eunice the next day so I could see for myself what a nice person she really was. I had no wish to see her, but because we had to go to a luncheon immediately afterwards I agreed. We waited in the appointed place for half an hour but Eunice didn't come. I went around the corner to post a letter, and when I returned a minute later there was no sign of Georg, and he didn't reappear until half way through the luncheon. Eunice had been hiding behind a tree, hoping I would go away. Georg told her she was 'completely stupid' to have telephoned, not caring whom she hurt by doing so. He told me that because Eunice was pregnant she was hormonal and couldn't help her actions; she had 'pregnancy-induced madness'. It was the only time Georg ever allowed hormones as an excuse for anything.

They never did sleep together, though they met on all Georg's subsequent visits to Hong Kong. He told me with what seemed a mixture of regret and faint contempt that she had 'decided to be a good wife and mother'. Because she had acted so ruthlessly, his interest in her as anything but a musician quickly faded. But she stayed in touch by sending messages via Franz Röhr, who thought she 'did not seem to mean a great deal to Georg'.

As for Mercia, Georg informed me that he would continue to see her. Accordingly, on the first Thursday after we returned to Brisbane he left for his weekly assignation while I remained at home in a jealous rage. But in the two weeks he had been away Mercia had found another boyfriend and moved away. Georg arrived home very unhappy, with the news that she had dumped him. He told Mercia I knew about the affair, and she took him aback by confining her response to 'I hope she doesn't tell my mother – it would kill her!'

One morning about a month later, a very strained month later, Georg left home for the city on his bicycle. Half an hour later a strange car pulled into the driveway and Georg stumbled out – a shocking sight, saturated in blood. He had a gash in his forehead, bruises and grazing, and flesh gouged from his left forearm. I tried to clean the gravel out of his wounds but the damage was too great and I told him we must go to hospital. 'You are going to hate me,' he said, 'but I have first to make a phone call.' He left a message with Mercia's mother that he couldn't meet with her daughter that afternoon. Mercia was visiting Brisbane, and Georg thought – or hoped desperately – that she had disposed of the new boyfriend and was returning to him. He had been in such a hurry to see her that he took a corner too fast, skidded in the gravel and smashed into the side of a cutting, knocking himself out.

At the hospital he was X-rayed for fractures and given a tetanus injection despite his objections. Before he was wheeled away I offered to call Mercia to let her know what had happened, and he accepted, relieved. Mercia wasn't interested. She had merely been visiting Brisbane and thought of saying hello to her old friend. We had an amiable chat for an hour or so, until Georg reappeared on a trolley, cleaned, stitched, bandaged, and very crestfallen. As far as I know he never saw Mercia again. Shortly afterwards she moved to Melbourne and took a media job requiring her to perm her hair and wear make-up and high heels, which Georg called 'selling out'. She wrote to him occasionally via Franz, but within a few years she had become a proselytising religious fanatic, and Franz and Georg ended contact with her.

These women, and the women he slept with in Sue's time, were only of fleeting importance to him. For Georg there were two very different classes of women: wives and lovers. Wives, and only wives, he worshipped according to the Romantic ideals of artists of the past. However unsuitable we were, wives captured his imagination, and that was never true of lovers. Wives were muses and a means to an end. The attentions of his 'admirers' allayed his insecurities and boosted his confidence, but no more. Whatever his claims, they seem not to have had anything to do with his needs as an artist; they were not muses, nor did he want them to be. And because they were transient, they were held to no particular standards. Some of them wore make-up, which he detested, and as far as I can determine, none had long hair. Not a note was written for any of them.

'He had a plaster-cast idol of what a woman should be,' says Valerie Melrose. 'Let them grow their hair and worship at his gate.'[2] The place of an artist's wife was to enable her man to create; it was a higher calling. This for Georg was a given. If, at an award ceremony, he heard a man thank his wife for her support, he was both baffled and embarrassed. He had what I called a Leonora Complex – the need to find a noble and perfect wife whose devotion and service to her husband were boundless, as Beethoven portrayed his archetypal heroine in *Fidelio* (tellingly, his favourite opera). The trouble was that such a paragon couldn't, and never did, exist, and he knew it. But he never stopped hoping. In the opinion of Marjorie Thompson, 'Georg understood *Don Giovanni* so well because Don Giovanni was a frustrated idealist. He was not a lecherous viper. He was looking for an ideal he never found.'[3]

Georg was more or less mended by the time he went to the National Youth Orchestra at the end of July. There was time for only one program – Schumann's Manfred Overture, Sibelius's *Rakastava*, Hindemith's *Mathis der Maler*, and Strauss's *Till Eulenspiegel* – in two concerts. Both nights were a triumph, but the visit came to a sad end. A few months before, Georg had sent his program suggestions to the artistic coordinator and received a surprise response from John Brown, answering his letter of two and a half years earlier.

> You are mistaken about our talks in the Kings Cross Studios; most of our conversations occurred in Studio 226, at the TV Studios, but principally at the Elizabethan Theatre Trust. They were rarely about music and in later years in England you did not recall ever meeting me. Let me say that none of this detracts from the value of the experience to me or

diminishes the memory of the adoration I felt for you at that time. I think we should both agree to laugh at our youthful follies. However, if it gives you any satisfaction you should know that I still consider you to be one of the greatest conductors and musicians living in this century, even though personally I would not trust you as far as I could kick you down the stairs (as I have often felt like doing).[4]

Georg was, and remained, profoundly shocked and offended. After the final concert he disappeared, summoned to see John for the first time. A short time later he came rushing down the footpath, more distraught than I had ever seen him. John had said something terrible to him, something to do with kicking him down the stairs; he was 'totally abusive and mad'. Georg swore he would never return to the National Youth Orchestra, and never again did he see or hear from John Brown. It was a tragedy. Georg had lost another of the very few anchors in his life. John had loved him unreservedly, and Georg had desperately needed it. He never understood how John could have turned on him, never understood what he might have done to cause it, and never recovered from the loss.

Georg returned to Brisbane and I followed three weeks later, visiting Annemarie on the way. I arrived in the evening of 5 September, and found her in bed in extreme pain. I called an ambulance and her son Peter, and we went to the hospital. She said how sorry she was to be causing trouble; within an hour she was dead. We heard only much later that she had died of peritonitis caused by metastasised cancer nobody had known she had. I called Georg to give him the bad news and said I was coming home immediately, but he insisted I did not as he was leaving in a few days' time on a country tour. He wrote to me:

I am sorry that you had to endure the final agony, but I am sure it was good for Annemarie to see you before the end. She liked you much better than me...

My time here was in every (or in most) way(s) rather nasty. I felt constantly tired; when on my way to last Monday night's rehearsal I felt suddenly terribly weak in the head (I imagined one must feel like that before fainting) and I had to

294 TANYA BUCHDAHL TINTNER

hold myself against the Piano...I felt I must find out. In order to prove to myself that I was quite well I cycled there and back to [the doctor in] Redcliffe on my free day. She found out that my bloodpressure was this time too low. In the end she thought it had to do with the fact that I had three bites by Ticks twenty minutes [after] I arrived here from Canada! In any case the marathon did not do me any harm and I am much better. She only prescribed rest...[5]

The round trip to Redcliffe is ninety kilometres, half of which is hilly.

The Lyric Opera of Queensland offered Georg *Don Pasquale* in the coming year and the ABC gave him some concerts around Australia also in 1987, in honour of his seventieth birthday. There would soon be trouble over these engagements. At the beginning of October he conducted two concerts with the Theatre Orchestra while he was preparing a concert performance of *Carmen* for the Lyric Opera, to take place on 7 October in the Albert Park sound shell. Georg wrote to me:

[General manager] Mr Weston and Mr Macfarlane accused ME of deviousness by doing the Choral concert while under contract to them for Carmen. I tried to explain that I did not put these concerts on...[and] that I do what am told. I spoke to Macfarlane who was very nasty...

They have still not given me permission to do the Sydney Concert [in 1987]. But I told them that the ABC had put on these 5 concerts for my birthday and I'm going to do them in any case...[6]

The *Carmen* performance, with Margaret Russell and Alberto Remedios, was a popular success. Val Vallis wrote in the *Australian*:

Georg Tintner...conducting without a score, presented a *Carmen* equally notable for its vigour and its sensuousness...It is amazing that although he is the resident conductor of the Queensland Theatre Orchestra, the one the Lyric Opera is accustomed to using, Tintner is rarely given an opportunity to display his obvious mastery in this art.[7]

This was too much for David Macfarlane who, a day or two later, fired Georg from *Don Pasquale*. Georg had asked for two days off in the first week of a seven-week contract to do one of the ABC concerts in Sydney, and Macfarlane called this his 'inability' to accept the engagement. The Theatre Orchestra board resolved to protest, but in the same meeting they approved a concert for 1987 with an ambitious program Georg had long wanted to do – and gave it to Richard Mills, a local timpanist, composer, and beginning conductor. For months Georg had thought he was expendable – and now he was certain.

In a June concert he had conducted a concertino by Philip Bracanin, a local composer and member of the Theatre Orchestra board. Something in the work had not made sense to him and he politely asked the composer if it was what he had really meant. Bracanin took offence, and began to undermine him. Richard Mills told an orchestra associate that Georg was 'one of these Central European parasites' keeping perfectly good Australians out of a job. Robert Harris, Georg's assistant, had turned against him, and so had the wind principals. The concertmaster he had just hired, Deborah Fox, said she was 'embarrassed to get on the same stage as Georg'. He didn't stand a chance. He resigned.

Everything looked very bleak. Georg had no chance of getting another conducting job in Australia, he was too old for a university job, and his income from guest concerts covered only his payments to Cecilia and little more. What I earned from freelance journalism was nowhere near enough to live on. We could only hope fervently that Georg would win the job with Symphony Nova Scotia. A week after his resignation we left for Canada, relieved to get away.

Georg had chosen a program of favourite works that were anything but 'party pieces' to impress a selection committee: Mozart's *Impresario* Overture, Beethoven's Second Symphony, Schubert's Third Symphony, and (as Burt Wathen had insisted) Schoenberg's *Transfigured Night*. Georg and the orchestra liked each other immediately, and more so as the rehearsals continued. The curious thing was that nobody said a word about the music director position. Finally, when Burt came to take us to the dress rehearsal, Georg said, 'Isn't someone going to talk to me about this job?' Burt's eyes opened wide: 'You mean you'd be *interested*?' We had been mistaken. It was simply a guest concert, nothing more.

The orchestra had already reduced 240 applications to a short-list of seven and was on the point of making its decision. Burt hastily called as many members of the board and selection panel as he could find and insisted they come to the concert that evening, 29 October.

The following day critic Stephen Pedersen wrote:

> The orchestra has never sounded more beautiful...the person most responsible for the limpid clarity and dolcissimo radiance of the music, was diminutive Austrian-born conductor Georg Tintner, who conducts without a baton, his eloquent fingers and hands sculpting music from the air with elfin magic.
>
> Musicians will not often admit that a conductor has all that much to do with the quality of sound they make. But in this case, with a leader like Tintner whose every motion has a clear musical meaning, and who is himself so immersed in the heart of the mystery that there is no trace of ego in the air, the players give first their respect, and then their love. And if there is one single word which describes Wednesday night's music, it is just that. Love.[7]

The chairman of the board, Norman Newman, spoke with Georg at the end of the concert, and the next morning we were interviewed by the selection committee. The atmosphere was friendly, and we felt it went well. We left the next day feeling hopeful.

On Christmas Eve Norman Newman called to offer Georg the position of music director and principal conductor of Symphony Nova Scotia, a three-year contract beginning with the 1987–88 season. He was the unanimous choice of the orchestra, the board and the selection committee. Obviously expecting Georg to make a counter-offer, Newman offered $45,000 for a thirty-week season, a low amount for such an orchestra. He must have been very surprised when Georg merely said, 'Very nice. Thank you.' We discovered later it was only half the previous incumbent's salary, but it was more than double Georg's Theatre Orchestra salary and it seemed a fortune.

Over the next few months we arranged our residence permits and I found an apartment to rent, which generous board members furnished with the basics for us. Georg hated the idea of living eleven storeys up in the centre of town, but I relished the idea of having everything we needed within a few blocks.

On 11 April 1987 Georg conducted one of his birthday concerts with the Sydney Symphony – as it turned out, his last with this orchestra. The program included Bruckner's Fourth Symphony, for which he received a review that enraged him:

> The work itself I find patchy – no doubt a subjective opinion. The andante meanders by like a dull landscape seen from a slow train. Anti-climaxes become an art form. There is poverty of plausible connecting passages. Some climaxes are exciting, but their shape is repeated too often. A few interesting thematic ideas, such as the opening four-note theme, are done to death. But you have to respect its sincerity, its persistence.[8]

One of Georg's burning ambitions was to promote Bruckner wherever he went. He had made little headway in Australia.

In Sydney he stayed with his son Paul, whose wife Margaret Cooke interviewed him for a study on the problems of aging:

> Have I any fears?…I think the only fear I really have is to be incapacitated. I can honestly say I am not at all frightened of death – but of a quick death. My body is very used to pain; pain itself doesn't frighten me either. But what does frighten me is the possibility of helplessness or paralysis or being in a wheelchair. And then I will do my utmost to do away with me if I possibly can. But that is the one fear I have, and that is a very big fear.[9]

On 28 November, two days before departing, he conducted a special Mahler concert with the combined Brisbane orchestras and choirs: the Adagio of Symphony No. 10 and the Second Symphony, with Judith Henley and Elizabeth Campbell. Patricia Kelly in the *Australian* wrote of it as 'a triumph for all concerned, a sincere, urgent performance that developed soundly from the quality of sectional ensemble. But it was a major triumph for Tintner, who well deserved the prolonged standing ovation his mammoth undertaking received, a fitting and grateful farewell.'[10]

*Part IV*
*1987–1999*

## Twenty-seven

'Georg Tintner opened last night's Symphony Nova Scotia concert at the Cohn with a cautionary curtain speech,' wrote Stephen Pedersen.

> 'Who deals with eternal things has plenty of time,' he said, warning the audience about the length of Bruckner's Fourth Symphony, which he was on the point of conducting. 'You need to adapt to its time scale,' he added. It was a gracious gesture. But an hour and ten minutes later, when the final chord of Bruckner's organ-like apotheosis had ceased ringing in the packed hall, no one seemed to care what time it was. Few thought, in that moment of release, to look at their watches. We had been totally absorbed in listening to a new orchestra. It was not just that extra strings, horns, and trombones had been added. Tintner transformed the sound itself into something finer than we have yet heard from SNS... there is no doubt that the concert was a triumphal beginning for SNS under its new conductor. It was the first time in years that a Halifax symphony audience was moved to a standing ovation.[1]

Less than a week later he conducted the *Messiah* in the original Dublin version and the Mozart version the following evening. Stephen Pedersen thought it 'a corker!' Life had not seemed so promising, nor been as happy, for a long time.

Although a relatively small city of 350,000, Halifax had six universities, a large teaching hospital and a leading art school, and its well-educated residents took Georg to their hearts. When he was seen at virtually every musical event in the city, including student recitals and amateur choral concerts, he was admired all the more. Everyone recognised him when he went out on his bicycle in warmer weather, and regarded with gentle amusement the big rubber wellingtons he wore all winter. People greeted him as he picked out produce in the supermarket, a little surprised that he did such mundane things. Nobody thought ill of his 'eccentricities' – on the contrary, he was regarded the more fondly for them. They didn't mind that he detested post-concert receptions and would escape as soon as he could: 'What people don't realise is that I am the only person who has been standing all evening, and all I want to do now is sit down!'

His only real failing – at least in the view of the Canada Council, a major source of orchestra funding – was that he conducted almost no Canadian compositions. Georg was determined to perform music based on its quality, not the composer's nationality, and he found little that pleased him. Works he did like he prepared meticulously; composers (among them Oskar Morawetz and Bruce Mather) were gratefully surprised at the time and attention he gave to them. About works he didn't like, he could be brutally frank. After perusing one of Jordan Grigg's early works he told the young composer that the best thing he could say about it was that he got it down on paper.[2]

Georg's second season in 1988–89 was much busier than the first, and he began to suffer an assortment of ailments. He needed a rest, and I persuaded him to use a free week in February to visit the Thompsons for the first time in almost twenty years. We went on to Vienna, staying as guests of Dr Walter Tautschnig, Georg's contemporary in the Sängerknaben who later became the choir's director. Georg took me to the places where he had lived: in the Stubenring, the grand apartment now subdivided and converted into offices, and in the Schellinggasse. The Wildpretmarkt slum was gone, bombed in 1945. We walked along the Himmelpfortgasse, his favourite street, and tears came to his eyes at the beauty of it. He loved revisiting the streetscapes and the churches; his favourite was Maria am Gestade. We searched for the Café am Stadtpark, where his father had played chess with Josef von Manowarda, but it was gone, replaced by, of all things, a bank.

Georg was uncomfortable in Vienna: he felt 'a complete and utter stranger'. He knew that anti-Semitism had not been expunged by the de-Nazification trials and remained an integral part of Austrian life. Tautschnig, no anti-Semite, suggested that Georg send him his publicity materials and he would try to help him. It was a valuable offer, because connections and titles are everything in Austria and Tautschnig, as a *Wirkliche Hofrat*,* was a very important person. I sent a publicity package as soon as we returned home, but we heard no more. When we saw him again, two and a half years later, Georg asked if he had received it. Tautschnig replied cheerfully, 'Oh yes. I gave it to a Jewish agent in town.' Georg looked as if he had been struck.

On 30 April he conducted the Canadian Brass and the principal brass players of the New York Philharmonic and Boston Symphony in New York's cavernous Cathedral of St John the Divine. They went on tour in June, to Tanglewood, Wolf Trap and several Canadian cities, and then, in July, made a recording for Philips in the acoustically magnificent Manhattan Center on West 34th Street. It was an all-Beethoven disc with masterly arrangements of *Wellington's Victory*, the Egmont Overture and the Fifth Symphony. James Mallinson, a leading producer, was brought in from London. They played through the first movement of the symphony, and at the end Mallinson said on the intercom that it was going very well but needed to be faster. Georg inspected the back of his hand and conducted the movement again at exactly the same tempo. Everyone then went into the studio to listen. Mallinson said again that it just needed to be faster, and Georg lost his temper. 'Excuse me,' he said, pounding the table with his forefinger, '*you* go out there and conduct Beethoven's Fifth!' There was a long, embarrassed silence. At the break Phil Myers, the principal horn player of the New York Philharmonic, beckoned to Georg confidentially. 'Maestro, I must tell you something. In New York, the producer is king. He tells Lenny to do something, Lenny does it. He tells Zubin to do something, Zubin does it.' Myers grinned and added, 'I'm *so* glad you said that!' Mallinson said nothing more about tempi, and at the end he graciously told Georg he had enjoyed working with him. The recording was released late in the following year, and was warmly received by Ivan March in *Gramophone*, who thought Georg's reading of the Fifth was 'impressive'.

---

* Literally, actual or substantial court councillor, though Austria has not had a court since 1918.

From New York we went to the National Youth Orchestra, which Georg had agreed to do because John Brown was no longer there. His program included his first performance of Mahler's Symphony No. 1. Mahler was for him something of a special case. He did not love his music as he loved that of Bruckner, Beethoven, Mozart and Schubert; he had, in fact, 'a love–hate relationship' with him. In his opinion many of Mahler's symphonies were flawed: his 'striving for the monumental was in my opinion not good for him'. It was his songs, 'among the greatest things of the century', that would live the longest.

> I don't love many of his symphonies, not because they are noisy but because he could not always fill the 'vast canvas' with worthwhile ideas. I think his popularity (often with fairly unmusical people) has to do with his state of general 'Angst' and terror…Yet there are wonderful movements in his symphonies. For instance the FIRST movement of his 9th symphony is WONDERFUL, while the rest of the symphony does not say anything to me.* The two *Nachtstücke* in his 7th are lovely, while the last movement is AWFUL. I think the most moving aspect of his songs is his frantic effort to be '*Volkstümlich*' [popular] and naive. It is an artificial naivety…I find the 'bellringing'† Mahler hardest to take (like at the end of No. 2 and even more the final *Alles vergängliche* in No. 8, where he completely misunderstood the gently ironical words of the old Goethe!)[3]

Georg understood Mahler very well, as the persecuted Jews from the Austro-Hungarian Empire they both were. Although he conducted Mahler even more rarely, Georg lectured on him almost as often as he did on Bruckner, and his remarks were sometimes revealing:

---

\* 'The first movement of the Ninth Symphony…is not only the greatest piece of music Mahler wrote but is one of the great pieces of music of this century. (Alban Berg [found] it *the* greatest piece of music of the century from his point of view.)…But one has to know that Mahler always made a lot of corrections and changes after he had heard his works. He never heard his *Song of the Earth*, which didn't seem to hurt it, but he also never heard the Ninth Symphony and many people, not only I, are convinced that he would have done a lot to the other three movements had he heard them. These movements are very long even for Mahler, very long indeed, and he seems to say the same thing he had perhaps said better in earlier works.' (Lecture on Mahler, Banff Centre, July 1975).
† Georg means 'bell-ringing' metaphorically and is not referring to instruments.

Mahler says to us through his music, 'Look at me – I want to help you, I want to do good, I'm not [so] terrible, I'm not [so] awful, not at all, look at me!' I come back to another such case in music, Tchaikovsky. Tchaikovsky's music says the same thing of self-pity, 'I am a homosexual and what is worse, I have to hide it. I have to play a role...' Is it surprising then that these composers wallow in what can only be called self-pity? They absolutely *ooze* self-pity in their works. I'm not saying this as a criticism, I'm just saying it is a different thing, and it would be very sad if that were not in their works, as it belongs. They have a reason, and it is perhaps that which gives them their relevance. This is something new and it is something slightly shameless, something like laying yourself bare before the listener who may not be very sympathetic, but there it is, and we have to take them or leave them as they are.

There is another element in his music, which is so familiar to us, that had never happened before. That is what the Germans call *Angst*. Anxiety is not the same, *Angst* is much more. It is not just fear, it is unreasonable, unreasoned, unmotivated fear. *Seemingly* unmotivated fear that is in [Kafka's] books, and that is in Mahler.

There is yet something else. And to me that is the most moving of all. I come back again to that infernal Jewish question, because I have to. There is a tremendous desire in Mahler and therefore in Mahler's music to be just like anybody else...Therefore all his life he tried to write folk music, popular music, and the *Songs of a Wayfarer* is an admirable example. It is seemingly music of the people, just as they would sing in the street, something like that, *but!* it never rings completely true. The music rings true, utterly true, but that effort to be just like anybody else, just like one of the people, that does *not* ring true. Perhaps only to a Jew like me...perhaps that means nothing to you, but to me that is perhaps in a nutshell what the tragedy of Jewry is altogether: that they are so clever, and so sincere too, in taking on what is given to them from their surroundings and perhaps make something new and worthwhile of it, yet they are always strangers. When I say they are always strangers I know how *I* felt in Vienna, and I wasn't the only one. And there you have it. It is not one and it is not the other. And perhaps this *Zwiespalt* – this inner contradiction – is what also creates something valuable. Perhaps.

There is something else that is also a rather touchy subject, but dependent on everything else. This is the famous 'banality' in Mahler, intentional and hurtful banality…There is something unique in the Jews, which I can only call as self-hatred. And I think the reason is not far to seek. The Jewish self-hate may well have to do with the fact that he has been thought for so long to be inferior in intellect and all the rest of it that however much we want to deny it, something remains. Perhaps he needed it occasionally, and here I speak for myself. I want to quote a famous political writer of the nineteenth century called Ferdinand Lasalle, who said, 'There are only two things in this world I absolutely *loathe*: journalists and Jews – and I am both.' [*Audience laughter*]

Now, may I respectfully say, this is not funny to us. This is the opposite of funny, and in Mahler you find a lot of that intentional cheapening, of that self-hatred…I want to remind you of the movement [in the First Symphony] which has the canon with the double bass solo…in the middle of this movement the oboes, and then helped by the trumpets, start a tune of such *disastrous* cheapness that one winces hearing it – and Mahler knew just as well as you or I that it was disgusting. It is a sort of self-loathing, I can't describe it in any other way, but it is a very important ingredient of his music… Perhaps people like me are more sensitive to its awfulness, and I want to point this out as it is no use glossing over this sort of thing, as it is terribly important. It may *well be* that that part of Mahler is one of the most valuable. Because he was the first who *dared* to be vulgar when he felt he was vulgar, and in fact these negative sides may be more important than the 'bell-ringing' Mahler in the Finale of the Second Symphony, and most of the Eighth Symphony.[4]

Georg once said, 'I think there is one thing I haven't got, that is self-pity, and that is rare with Jews. Because Jews have plenty of reason to be sorry for themselves. But I have seen that, and I reject it *utterly*. I think I am too proud to be sorry for myself.'[5] If Georg ever desired to be 'one of them' – and it could only have been in

Vienna, his home in a cultural sense only – he did nothing to gain acceptance. For that also, he was too proud.

More than once Georg answered when asked if he was a Jew: 'Yes, but I'm not proud of it.' The reply invariably offended other Jews, but he did not mean he was ashamed of it, only that he found no reason to take pride in it.

> A Jew is really – it's perhaps a race, but it is a *fate*. It is something that is standing apart from any other community, because of what has been done to them and also the exceptional position in many ways they hold. I think one of the worst things that has befallen the Jews is the feeling that they think they are the salt of the earth. I don't feel any of that. But I do feel that they are an exceptional case, insofar as there is not a Jew in the world, especially in European circumstances, who hasn't got a persecution mania. But you must never forget that in 95 per cent of all the cases it is justified.[6]

It was important for Georg to perform Mahler's music because he understood it so well; he could recognise himself. It is no surprise that his favourite Mahler work was the song 'Ich bin der Welt abhanden gekommen' – 'I am lost to the world'. But he rejected Mahler's *Weltanschauung*.[*] He preferred what Bruckner gave him: what he called his 'assurance', 'that sort of cosmic feeling that, in spite of every horrible thing, the world can be a good place'. It was not an exploration of Mahler's and his own psyche that he needed, but consolation, and that he found in Bruckner.

The youth orchestra gave eight performances in a tour that began in Kingston on 3 August and finished in Halifax eleven days later. On 5 August they gave a hastily arranged sold-out performance at Pollack Hall in Montreal; people sat in the aisles, and 200 more were turned away. The students played as never before and the concert was a sensational success. 'Georg Tintner is an absolutely fascinating person,' wrote the famously hard-to-please critic Claude Gingras in *La Presse*. 'He conducts with energy and lucidity that are obviously a source of inspiration to all those young musicians

---

*    In a 1977 interview for Television New Zealand Georg said that he preferred conducting Bruckner to Mahler because 'Mahler's neuroses overwhelm me'. (Ian Fraser [the program presenter], letter to author, 12 January 2011).

who could be his grandchildren, even his great-grandchildren…
Here we had a conductor who clearly had something to say…'[7]

Although Georg now lived in Canada, and soon became
a Canadian citizen, he never conducted the National Youth
Orchestra again. I tried for several years to interest the new administration, but gave up after I was told that the orchestra was to
tour Europe and they had to have 'a Canadian conductor – a *real*
Canadian'. The loss for everyone was inestimable. An alumnus
from the 1970s was moved to remark three decades later that
Georg 'single-handedly was the best thing that ever happened to
Canadian orchestral training, by far'.[8] For Georg it was the loss of
perhaps the most rewarding activity of his life. He never stopped
missing those summers and their joyous idealism.

At the end of summer he went to Toronto to rehearse *The
Marriage of Figaro* for a tour with the Canadian Opera's training
division. While he was there I called for the results of his sperm
test. Since moving to Halifax we had been trying for a baby,
without success. He had said that if he turned out to be 'at fault'
he had no objection to my having someone else's baby. It was an
astonishingly generous offer, even more than I realised because I
didn't then know the story of Sue and Demas. But it wasn't what
I wanted. In a disapproving tone untempered by any compassion
the matron announced that the sperm was no good. I never told
Georg, and he never asked. The subject of babies simply vanished.
Five years after he died the conductor Paul Mahr told me that
Georg had always known the result of the test. He must have done
as I had: called the hospital when home alone.

In the first week of December Georg conducted a concert
with the Winnipeg Symphony. At the administration's request
we visited Dr Ferdinand Eckhardt, a leading arts patron and the
widower of the composer, violinist, pianist and self-described
genius Sophie-Carmen (Sonia) Eckhardt-Gramatté. Eckhardt,
eighty-seven years old and still sprightly, told us the story of Sonia's
life, insisting that his latest research showed almost certainly that
she was the illegitimate daughter of Tolstoy. Eckhardt told us
that he and Sonia had lived during the war in Vienna, his home
city, and that his wife's career was disrupted by the fact that she
was erroneously included in the *Juden ABC*.* I first heard about

---

*     *Judentum und Musik, mit dem ABC jüdischer und nichtarischer Musikbeflissener (Jewry and Music, with an
ABC of Jewish and Non-Aryan Music Practitioners)*, Hans Brückner and Christa Maria Rock, Hans-
Brückner Verlag, Munich.

it in 1938, he said, by which time she had been in three editions since 1932. He produced a copy of the book, a listing of Jews in music to be avoided. Well, he said, I was outraged, and I went immediately to the authorities to have my wife's name removed. 'But Dr Eckhardt, we thought that as your wife's maiden name was de Fridman...'

'No, no, no, that was not her real father, how dare you say my wife is a Jew? How *dare* you say my wife is a Jew?'

Georg jiggled his knees and inspected the back of his hand. He quietly told a story from his own days in Vienna and added pointedly, 'Yes, immoral laws make immoral people.' I riffled through the book and remarked that two Tintners were listed in it, but it was all lost on Eckhardt. He told the story again in case we hadn't understood it the first time. Georg brusquely refused to eat any of the fruit and nuts offered to him, and insisted we leave immediately. I asked him afterwards how it was he had not lost his temper, and he replied grimly, 'I decided he was senile.' Eckhardt sent us some of his wife's recordings and a very friendly letter, but Georg ignored them, saying he had better things to do.

He gave his debut concert with the Montreal Symphony on 17 December, with Mozart's Symphony No. 41 and the Haydn Violin Concerto with Scott St John. Two days later on a bitterly cold night he conducted the Messiah at the 3000-seat Basilique Notre-Dame. The choir had threatened to go on strike, and agreed to sing less than three hours before the performance. 'An uninspired *Messiah*,' announced Claude Gingras the next day. 'This Messiah, rather romantic in approach, was always beautiful and musical, in the choir as well as the orchestra, but it was rarely moving and rarely exhilarating. It was actually at times very boring...'[9] And the *Gazette*'s Arthur Kaptainis said: 'Union war whoops notwithstanding, Handel's *Messiah* arrived on schedule last night at Notre Dame Basilica, though not in complete or conventional form. A few arias and choruses from the perennial choral masterpiece appeared to have gone on strike, and several tempos were embroiled in a militant slow-down campaign. Even some woodwind parts called in sick. But this is what must be expected when Georg Tintner assumes the Montreal Symphony podium. The seventy-two-year-old Austrian-born maestro hails from an era and environment in which authenticity was a word used mainly in connection with cake at the Sacher Hotel...'[10]

Georg, who argued with critics rarely, and only on factual matters, wrote to Kaptainis to point out that the woodwind players were absent because he was doing the original – authentic – Dublin version. He was very upset by the reviews, and was not consoled by standing ovations at all three performances. But this Messiah was also a warning to him. 'Authentic' or 'historically informed' performances of Baroque music were now the norm and old-fashioned ones like his were unacceptable, at least to critics. Georg had no time for the new movement; he said it was a fashion that would fade, although not in his lifetime. He rejected double-dotting and abhorred the ornamentation and cadenzas singers added to their arias.* Most intolerable was the revised tuning, a semitone or so below the customary A = 440. His sense of pitch was so powerful that if one played in the wrong key the main tune of a work he conducted often and from memory, it was only with great difficulty that he could identify it. As he grew older his sense of pitch drifted downwards by a semitone (an almost universal occurrence for people with absolute pitch): a piece he knew to be in C would sound to him in C sharp. As absolute pitch is a matter of recognition, the pitches used by the period instrument practitioners confused him, in a way he found frightening.

He wrote scathingly in a program note for a Mozart concert he conducted two years later:

> Over 60 years ago Willem Mengelberg came to Vienna to conduct Bach's St Matthew Passion. I sang the Cantus Firmus with the Vienna Boys' Choir. The success with the public, the press *and* the performers was overwhelming. When we hear this interpretation nowadays we positively squirm hearing all these rubatos and romantic indulgences. A reaction to this approach had to come and it came with a vengeance; the aim with many clever people is to make these masterpieces sound exactly as they did when they were written. Even if that were possible it would be quite undesirable. We are neither eighteenth century Burghers of Leipzig nor Rococo citizens of Salzburg and each age must find its own way to love, understand and interpret these manifestations

---

* When the Australian soprano Marilyn Richardson demonstrated to Georg her cadenza for a *Messiah* aria, for the ABC's 1975 Adelaide performance, he said resignedly, 'I will do it. But I will not enjoy it.'

of human spirit (without doing violence to the composer's intentions).

These great works have a universal significance and each generation must find new meaning in them suitable for *its* state of the soul.

Maybe in another sixty years people may marvel at the futile efforts to play Beethoven strictly according to the very dubious metronome markings*...instead of how we (after a lifelong study of his works and style) feel the music speaks *to us.*[11]

But he saw the writing on the wall. To avoid antagonising critics he gave up programming Bach and Handel in guest concerts, and hesitated even to include Haydn and Mozart.

Georg spent most of the spring of 1990 at home with Symphony Nova Scotia. He conducted Bruckner's Fifth Symphony with far too few strings, and Brahms's Third Symphony – his first and only performance of it. He gave a semi-staged performance of *The Gypsy Baron*, and a light Viennese program. Though he was usually thought of as a 'Germanic' conductor specialising in slow and weighty music, he loved the masterpieces of lighter Viennese music, especially those of the Strauss family. He considered the Emperor Waltz a work of genius. He used far less rubato than is traditional, and there was none of the stretched-out notes one usually hears in works such as 'The Blue Danube'. He didn't try to replicate the slight hesitation between second and third beats that Viennese orchestral musicians employ, because 'if it isn't in the blood you can't teach it'. Yet the authentic Viennese flavour was always there, the gentle lilt, the spirit of the city at its genial best. Georg knew well enough what lurked under the surface of Viennese gaiety and charm, but it was his world and he loved it. Like him, Johann Strauss Snr was the grandson of an immigrant Jew from the Second District, who portrayed Viennese culture and its defining attributes in his music.

Jews wandered to the far corners of the world, unwanted everywhere, yet those who became artists often became more native than the natives. Adapting like chameleons was a survival technique of

---

* Georg had no time for metronomes and did not own one. He could, however, accurately beat any metronome marking.

the underdog. With an element of longing, the Jewish operetta composers of the Austrian monarchy (Oscar Straus, Emmerich Kálmán and Leo Fall among others), like the Jewish composers of Broadway, absorbed the characteristics of their surroundings and created a fantasy world where happiness reigned and everything turned out right. Yet no matter how hard they tried, they were never really 'one of them'.

In March and April the orchestra toured eastern Canada, giving concerts in Nova Scotia, New Brunswick, Ottawa and Montreal. The morale of the orchestra was never higher than on this tour and in the season's final concert in May, a few days before Georg's seventy-third birthday. The program comprised two works, Beethoven's Ninth Symphony and the moving elegy *From the Diary of Anne Frank* for mezzo-soprano and orchestra by Oskar Morawetz, sung by Jean Stilwell. The orchestra, according to Stephen Pedersen, 'gave the mighty Ninth that level of perform-ance under the sure hand of Georg Tintner, one of the great Beethoven interpreters of our time'.[12]

Georg was by now the most admired man in Halifax. The symphony board was therefore very relieved when he renewed his contract for another two years. Given his popularity, and the increase in ticket sales, I thought it time to request a modest pay increase, and the board readily agreed. When I told Georg, he rushed to the symphony office to tell them he didn't want it. It was sometimes difficult to be Georg's agent.

In April he went to Banff, in the beautiful Rocky Mountains, for the Festival of Canadian Youth Orchestras. He called me one day to tell me that he was feeling 'weak in the head'. I pointed out that Banff was about 1400 metres above sea level and he may be suffering from altitude sickness, but it became a recurring problem. A few times a month he would have days of 'weakness in the head', and though many tests were done, nobody could explain it. It was years later that Georg happened to say, 'I'm hungry', and all was revealed. He always claimed his ideal weight was between 59 and 63 kilos and stubbornly insisted he knew exactly how much he needed to eat for optimum health and weight, even when he looked emaciated as he did in 1979. I pointed out that hunger was telling him his body needed more fuel. He pondered this for a few minutes, and agreed I might have a point. He added a slice or two

*Georg conducting a rehearsal of Symphony Nova Scotia around 1989.*

of bread to his lunch, with the result that he never felt weak in the head again.

We were in Australia for the summer of 1990 when the CBC released *Down Under*, a recording Georg and Symphony Nova Scotia had made in 1988 of mostly Australasian music. He persuaded the CBC to include Douglas Lilburn's *Diversions* and George Dreyfus's Serenade for Small Orchestra (originally titled 'Music for Music Camp'), but was unable to eliminate several items by Percy Grainger, whose music he did not admire. 'I managed to avoid conducting Grainger in Australia for thirty years', he grumbled, 'and I had to come to *Canada* to be made to do it.'

Richard Perry, who had been so enraptured by Georg's National Youth Orchestra performances a decade earlier, wrote in the *Whig-Standard* that:

> The search will now begin for a music director to replace
> Gunther Herbig [at the Toronto Symphony] at the end of

the 1991–92 season. I would like to make a suggestion to the search committee that most certainly will not be heeded because my nominee is seventy-two years old, has a very small if devoted following, has committed to vinyl very few performances, has remained on the periphery of the classical music show-biz world, is eccentric, and worst of all, is already working on Canadian soil. I have in mind Georg Tintner, a conductor whose work I have heard only a few times but which has left an indelible impression for the high level of inspiration he was able to instil in his players, and for an attention to balance, dynamics and phrasing that always kept the composer's expressive purpose in mind…

Although the program is hardly one to reveal what Mr Tintner might be able to do with a superior orchestra and meaty repertoire, the results the conductor obtains on this disc certainly suggest that he deserves the opportunity. No, that is not quite the point. It is the Toronto Symphony which deserves the opportunity to work with Mr Tintner, who himself seems to have a well-entrenched, Taoist lack of false ambition…[13]

His article had no effect, and Jukka-Pekka Saraste took over the orchestra in 1994.

On 20 November Georg conducted Symphony Nova Scotia combined with the Kitchener–Waterloo Symphony Orchestra in his first and only performance of the *Symphonie Fantastique*. Stephen Pedersen reported the next day:

The audience, temporarily stunned by the intensity of the performance, finally rose as one and called Tintner back to the podium a half-dozen times. Tintner's treatment of one of the richest orchestral scores in the repertoire was typical of the iron will to display every gleaming detail of a score that makes so many of his performances of works you have heard many times before sound as though you were hearing them now for the first time.[14]

Georg was in fact not particularly fond of the piece, but he preferred it to most of Berlioz's other works, which 'didn't follow the rules'.

I must confess that I have a very odd relationship to Berlioz's music. I know that he was in many ways (not only in orchestration by any means) a very great composer. But his 'waywardness' makes me extremely nervous; I know it is my fault not his. So I avoid him most of the time.[15]

We spent the summer of 1991 in Australia. I visited my sister Kate, a violinist, who was suffering from Hodgkin's Disease and was in hospital in Sydney undergoing a bone-marrow transplant. Georg and I went to Chrysothemis's wedding in Canberra, then spent three weeks at Banana Bend. But Georg seemed restless, and in need of seeing Sue again. I bought him a bus ticket and he went for the weekend, staying in Tamworth with Ariadne. Sue found him just as impossible to talk to as she always had, but he returned somewhat calmer. It was good that he went, for he never saw her again. Less than a year later, she died of a ruptured stomach ulcer. He wrote to a few old friends about it: to Paul Hoffmann who eulogised her youthful beauty, and to Reg, who sent his sympathy and the remark that Sue had died for him a long time ago. Georg refused all comfort and said not a word. His silence spoke of his grief and his overwhelming sense of guilt.

## Twenty-eight

For the first time in his life Georg was persuaded to teach conducting – something he had hitherto refused to do because he thought conducting could not be taught. At the end of July we went to Czechoslovakia for a three-week conductors' workshop, the project of a retired psychology professor in Toronto. Dr Harry Hurwitz fled from Berlin to Cape Town in 1933 and grew up wanting to become a conductor, but it was not possible in South Africa at the time. He decided to spend his retirement giving young conductors the training opportunities with professional orchestras he had been denied. Western orchestras were unaffordable, but he found what he wanted in Czechoslovakia: the Bohuslav Martinů Philharmonic Orchestra in Zlín.

Georg was unsure if he could find the food he needed – mung beans, sesame and sunflower seeds, soya flour, almonds, and an arsenal of vitamins – in a country only recently emerged from behind the Iron Curtain. He usually brought his food even to familiar locations, together with the big plastic bowl, a saucepan, a grater, a sieve and a nut grinder and, when necessary, an electric hotplate. It took a day or more to weigh and pack it all, and it was at times like this that hotel restaurants assumed a certain allure.

When we arrived near midnight at Břeclav on the Czech border, on the Chopin Express from Vienna, the border guard told us we did not have the necessary visa. He was polite until Georg lost his temper. He ordered us off the train, marched us with our thirty kilos of food and scores to an overheated waiting room and told us to stay there. The room was supervised by a uniformed, pistol-toting guard who was determined that none should sleep on her watch, and to ensure this she kept a television set suspended from the ceiling playing at maximum volume. As each channel closed down for the night she climbed on a chair, unpadlocked the controls, changed the channel and refastened the lock. Anyone caught dozing off she whacked on the shoulder. Five hours later sentries marched us onto the Vienna-bound Chopin Express and stood guard until it departed. Only with difficulty did I persuade Georg not to take the next plane back to Canada.

The major work Georg taught was Bruckner's Fourth Symphony. Many of the forty-eight conductors had come specifically to study it, but few could conduct it. The orchestra scratched away politely but resignedly. One morning a student was having so much trouble with flute entries that Georg went to the podium to demonstrate. He bowed to the musicians, said, 'Guten Morgen', stated a bar number and began conducting. The orchestra was transformed. The entries were perfect, the sound was blended and beautiful. The conductors scattered around the hall looked astonished. Afterwards they said, 'Did you see that? Did you hear that?' It brought to mind the comment of the clarinettist Jack Brymer: 'I think maybe conducting is the only evidence I've ever had that telepathy does exist.'[1] Paul Mahr, who was there, said:

> It was one of my life's great musical experiences. It was the greatest musical climax I ever heard, and this accomplished with a third or fourth rate orchestra. I have heard many concerts live by Philadelphia, New York, Boston, Berlin, Vienna, etc. so you would think that this moment would have occurred with them, but not so. I thought the roof was going to lift, and this not through volume, but rather intent.
>
> Bruckner 4 first movement is done generally in two, as an *alla breve*. Leading into the climactic point Mr Tintner began to conduct the 2/2 bars as 4/4, eight bars before the climax. This gave it incredible drive, especially since I believe it is the only place in the movement he did in four. Let me also state that this was unusual for him from a musical standpoint. I don't recall him otherwise using this sort of rhythmic intensity condensation on any other occasions, in other repertoire...It is something however that should be used sparingly; otherwise it can turn into musical cliché. It certainly worked that day.
>
> Mahler always conducted his climax points upward, not down as is usual. This is also what Mr Tintner did during the Zlín Bruckner. I spoke to him about this method...and while he admitted the Mahler connection, he said that that was

merely how he felt it. I remember him using this only very
rarely. If one does it right, it is like a cloudburst.[2]

Georg found the workshop uncongenial. He thought it bad
for the students to hear conflicting advice and opinions from
several teachers, and thought there was too much emphasis on
baton technique at the expense of rehearsal technique, let alone
understanding of the music. He despaired at the sight of young
conductors practising gestures in front of the mirrors in the concert
hall lobby. What one needed to know about baton technique, he
said, could be learned in an hour.

> It doesn't matter what you do. What matters is that you can
> convey what you feel. I always say: *Stand on your head* if you
> want to, it doesn't matter. What matters is what comes out.[3]
>
> I think one can only learn conducting by doing it. And
> if you *then* have somebody with more experience to tell you,
> 'Now, that was very nice but perhaps it would have been
> easier if you had done this or this or this', that can be helpful,
> but to sit down in cold blood and say, 'You put your left hand
> there', and so on, that's all nonsense.[4]

The final straw was when Jiří Bělohlávek arrived to give a
demonstration of 'the correct conducting method', in which he
asked conductors to do exercises such as raising their right arm
and letting it fall. The next day, in protest, Georg gave a lecture
entitled 'Conducting TechniqueS [*sic*] I have known', in which he
demonstrated the widely differing styles of Toscanini, Furtwängler,
Klemperer and others.

> I haven't forgiven Adrian Boult one thing: he said that
> Toscanini was a wonderful conductor with a very mediocre
> technique. I completely disagree with that. That shows that
> no two people are in agreement on what technique really is.
> I thought that the perhaps ten times I saw Toscanini conduct
> in the flesh, it was the most perfect conducting technique
> I've ever seen. Because it was not only to the point, it was
> most *beautiful*, and you somehow felt that the movements
> perfectly conveyed the spirit and meaning of the music. And
> that is what I call great technique. But Sir Adrian is not in

agreement with me, although he admired Toscanini tremendously, so it shows what an odd profession we've got that we can't agree on anything.[5]

Georg could not be persuaded to do the workshop again. 'What I have cannot be taught', he said, 'and the rest can be taught by people who do it much better than I.'[6] He conveyed the pulse of the music with body language. His beat was not elegant and many professional musicians found him difficult to follow, though youth orchestras never had trouble with it, no matter how inexperienced they were. He knew when to subdivide the beat for extra precision, and could manage feats of multiple beating, such as in Bar 73 of the first movement of Bruckner's Ninth, where he could simultaneously beat four in the left hand and six in the right while executing a *ritardando*. Rolf Gjelsten, a cellist at the 1974 National Youth Orchestra, recalls the students amusing themselves by asking Georg to beat eleven against seven, or nine against eight, and he had no trouble doing so.

According to Paul Mahr,

> I found Mr Tintner to be incredibly clear in the music that needed it, i.e. 20th century repertoire, some thorny concertos such as the Szymanowski Violin Concerto No. 2, a monstrously difficult piece. He did it so beautifully, it was impeccable, even with the soloist taking a lot of liberties. He got the nuances, knowing what Szymanowski was about; he had passionate and committed ideas about the piece. He loved these exotic hothouse-type pieces, very chromatic. In the music we were expected to know, Mozart and Schubert, his shaping of the music as opposed to Conducting-101 beats that most musicians seem to want, was enlightening to some of us, perplexing to the rigid or lazy...Mr Tintner conducted the music, not the orchestra. I found it incredibly inspiring. However, I can see that over the course of an entire season that level of expectation may [ask] more than some are willing to give.[7]

'I would say,' Georg said, 'that my skill – if it is a skill – is the power of communication of the intense feeling and love I have for the music, that I can impart that on *willing* players...I have known *very* great musicians who failed as conductors, because though they felt *everything in the world* they didn't have that certain quality that *communicates* their feeling to the players, and indirectly thereby to the audience.[8] His principal example was Pablo Casals, one of whose recitals Georg heard as a child and which remained among his greatest musical experiences. Another was Richard Strauss:

> whom I saw conducting many times. He was actually an excellent conductor, in difference to Hans Pfitzner, who was clumsy and awkward. Richard Strauss was a very professional conductor who was in opera houses for many years, and also as a symphony conductor he used to conduct all the great orchestras…But when you saw him conduct, as I did only in the latter part of his life, you couldn't really work it out what he did, whether he had done it all at rehearsal – which I doubt because he was rather lazy for things like that. But he said the famous pronouncement that 'the left hand of a conductor should be in his pocket'. And with the right hand, the smallest beat I ever saw. He never did anything except just beat very…And yet they played like angels. That is only a proof of what I always think, that the movements and all that is not what really matters in a conductor, what matters is the power of communication. First of all he has to feel a lot, but he has also to transmit that feeling, and not all great musicians have that particular gift, and some people have the gift who are not great musicians. It is the art of communication.[9]
>
> Reginald Goodall has lately been considered the greatest Wagner conductor alive, and he was a *very bad conductor* – an *extremely* bad conductor. There is for example that famous chord at the end of the first act of *Meistersinger* where the orchestra plays *dum* – and so on – and he *could not* get it together. He couldn't give a proper downbeat to get it together. *Yet* – what does that matter?…The most important is that that man understood and knew more about Wagner's music than anybody else…
>
> The world is full of highly efficient conductors, but what they have to say is – limited.[10]

Georg's kind of conducting has become increasingly uncommon. Especially in the music of Mozart, Haydn and Schubert he brought out the charm and tenderness, not often heard in this technological age. He had the courage to play slowly to let the music breathe. His tempi were often slower than those of many conductors – although by no means all were; his final movement of Schumann's First Symphony was faster than almost anyone else's. But his fast tempi never sounded hasty or frenetic. There was a gentleness underlying everything he conducted. There was no bombast, and not a shred of aggressiveness. As he aged his tempi remained fairly constant, with the exception of Beethoven's Seventh and Ninth and Bruckner's Fourth, which became slower. His sense of pulse and rhythm was flawless – a rarer attribute than one might think – so that a piece so dependent on it, such as the final movement of Beethoven's Seventh, was overwhelming in its sense of inevitability. The tempo modifications he did make were not so much a new tempo as a deviation from the basic, unifying pulse – the structural pulse; each modification had a meaning in relation to the whole.

What made Georg's performances so satisfying was not speed and volume – features of many modern performances where the conductor electrifies by skirting the limits of the orchestra's capabilities – but rather his sense of structure,* both architectural and harmonic (the importance of key relationships, as one might expect of a composer with absolute pitch). It gave his performances an intellectual satisfaction more subtle than the visceral thrill of loud and fast. He put much thought not only into tempo relations within individual movements but between all movements of a work, which added to the sense of unity. He knew where he was heading from the first note. You set out on an adventure, discovered much, and returned home safely. His *Messiah* was the supreme example: it was not a collection of arias and choruses but a drama, a story that unfolded in the manner of an opera. His performances had a sense of gravitas, perhaps because every note and every marking in the score had its important place. Many listeners heard things in Georg's performances of standard works they had never noticed before, especially inner voices. As Keith Jacobs put it: 'Georg had an ability in conducting based on profound knowledge of composing.'[11] He knew exactly where the climax was and never let a false climax take its place. You knew it was

---

* A few reviews of his late Bruckner recordings commented that his conducting of the finales seemed to make less of an impact than earlier movements. Perhaps Georg's sense of structure revealed the weaknesses in their construction – the 'finale problem' of Romantic composers.

approaching, and when it finally came, exactly in the right place, it was overwhelming.

To all appearances Georg was happy in Halifax, but without warning in November 1991 he notified the orchestra board that he would not renew his contract when it expired in mid-1993. He had two reasons for this, neither expressed publicly: he thought he felt the first stirrings of discontent in the orchestra and, more immediately, he felt he could no longer work with the general manager, Michael LaLeune, who had joined the symphony in the middle of 1990. LaLeune had a friend in Toronto, the son of a famous conductor, who was beginning his own conducting career, and to us it was plain that LaLeune wanted his friend to have Georg's job. When the musicians heard the news they were 'very emotional – there was shock, there were tears, and expressions of anger and fear for the future',[12] and they begged Georg to reconsider. The public's reaction was similar. The outpouring of affection surprised and moved Georg, and as he departed for a concert in Auckland a few days later he announced he would reconsider.

On 4 January 1992, still undecided, he gave a concert in the Sydney Opera House's Mostly Mozart festival, arranged by his Cape Town friend Rodney Phillips, who was now the building's deputy general manager. By the time he returned to Halifax he had decided to renew his contract after all – although he advised the symphony board privately that he would not continue if more than 10 per cent of the players were against him. He also declined his salary increase for the coming season, in sympathy with the musicians who had lost theirs due to hard financial times. It was only later that it became clear just how rash his resignation had been.

In the following few weeks he crossed the country several times in a gruelling schedule of concerts, and overwork finally caught up with him. Aching all over, especially in his shoulders and his damaged right wrist, and hardly able to turn his head more than a few degrees, he went to a specialist who found he had degenerative spine disease and sent him for a long course of physiotherapy. It gave only limited relief. His mood was low, and sometime in those months he began an affair with at least one woman – a country music singer with a specialty in line-dancing in cowboy hat and boots – and possibly others, although I didn't find out until after he died.

He was in no better frame of mind in November when he conducted two concerts with the McGill University Orchestra in Montreal. Three students sang Shostakovich's *From Jewish Folk Poetry*, to which Georg added Bruckner's Eighth Symphony in the Haas version and the overture to Hans Pfitzner's *Das Kätchen von Heilbronn*. Paul Mahr was at the first performance:

> He came out in his usual shuffling fashion. When he launched into the Pfitzner, it was really exciting. The strings were a bit sloppy, some winds had some problems, but all in all it was really exciting. Then the Shostakovich. The singers sounded, well, young; not much there. But oh that duet with the chromatic strings, with tympani in the background (Mother's lament or something). You had to be there. It made the little hairs on the neck stand up. I have never actually heard anyone else portray the pain in Shostakovich's music so well. I almost couldn't breathe.
>
> The Bruckner began well for about two minutes, and midway through the first climax lost steam, never to recover. After the show, we went to retrieve him backstage…We drove him to his hotel and spent some time with him in the coffee shop. He seemed very sad.[13]

*La Presse*'s Claude Gingras attended the following night's performance, and wrote:

> Georg Tintner is definitely a phenomenon! At seventy-five, the small, nervous man with a totally white mane seemed tired when, at 22.40, he mounted the podium for a fourth or fifth time to acknowledge the public, the orchestra, and again the public after having directed the Eighth Symphony of Bruckner, which took eighty-two minutes of almost uninterrupted concentration and the deployment of both arms – and this after a substantial first part to the program… Georg Tintner, who grew up in the environment of this music, transmitted the spaciousness, the emotion and the nobility to his hundred young musicians, boys and girls, who were hanging on his glance. A few little mishaps, inevitable in the circumstances, did not harm the unfolding which was always enthralling to follow.[14]

A matter of days before these concerts I heard that my sister was now mortally ill. None of the treatments had worked. I flew to Canberra to wait with my parents and brother for the end. Kate's world, once the concert halls of Europe, had shrunk to nothing more than her bedroom. We found her a companion dog, a golden retriever, but the dog knew something was very wrong and avoided her, to her despair. My clearest memory of those days is of feeding Kate strawberries from a neighbour's garden when she was too weak to do it herself. Her skeletal little figure began to drift away from us, and on 10 December she fell into a torpor. Grasping at some sort of normality I went out to buy dog food. When I returned my father met me at the door with the words, 'You're too late. She died a few minutes ago.' Little Kate, twenty-eight years old, clever, funny, scatter-brained, and who had never expressed a mean thought about anyone, just stopped breathing.

Four days later, and the night before Kate's funeral, Georg called me to say that he had made up his mind, and that he would leave the symphony when his contract expired in 1994; it was better to go before they wanted him to. Publicly, he cited the case of his teacher Weingartner, who had stayed with the Vienna Philharmonic for twenty-three years: 'He stayed too long and they behaved like naughty schoolchildren. They were bored.' Privately, he had still not recovered from the humiliation of his departure from the Theatre Orchestra and was determined it would never happen again. He told me that ticket sales had fallen, which proved he was no longer the draw he once was. He refused to accept that the explanation might be that the Canadian economy was in deep recession, and that the symphony board had eliminated cheap seating and was trying to sell the entire house at A-reserve prices. That he had no new job hardly mattered, he said, he would not be living much longer anyway. Nothing I said could persuade him to change his mind, especially when the protest mounted by the orchestra and public was more muted than it had been in 1991. The general opinion was that Georg had done this before and must therefore really mean it this time. Frustrated, I asked him just how much admiration he needed.

The question is an interesting one. Some performers are driven by a sometimes insatiable need for the love of the public, perhaps as a replacement for love that was absent in their childhoods, but that did not apply to Georg. He certainly liked public adulation, but he knew perfectly well when he had given a good performance and didn't need the audience to tell him. What was important was the respect and co-operation of the musicians. Many conductors regard the dislike, even hatred, of their players with supreme indifference, but not Georg. It was a professional character flaw, given that sooner or later musicians always turn against their conductor. Where another conductor may have shrugged off the events surrounding his departure from the Queensland Theatre Orchestra, Georg never recovered from the enmity and ingratitude he encountered. Perhaps it reminded him of the petty and incomprehensible victimisation of the Vienna Boys' Choir days. And perhaps it was there that he learned his 'terrific resignation', which later transformed itself into pacifism. 'Georg had passivity,' says Margaret Crawford. 'Things just happened to him; he accepted it. [But] he was stubborn. There are people who are passive-aggressive. He wasn't passive-aggressive, but passive-stubborn.'[15]

Though he claimed he did not need to be loved, he certainly needed to be unconditionally admired, which is something very different. It was not conceit but the reverse. His self-image was of Georg the musician, not Georg the man. Georg the musician was everything, and his insecurity – well hidden though it was – was mitigated only by unqualified admiration.

## Twenty-nine

Early in 1993 Georg became a Canadian citizen, whereupon the
government immediately awarded him the Commemorative
Medal for the 125th Anniversary of Canadian Confederation.
What Georg wanted much more, however, was reinstatement of
his Austrian citizenship. Despite what the country had done to
him, he never considered himself anything but an Austrian, and
when Austria at last made it possible in 1992 he applied. He was
told it would take years, and would cost as much as $1,000; he was
also obliged to furnish a police statement from every jurisdiction in
which he had lived for the previous twenty years to prove he was
of good character.

He therefore found it a little ironic that in November 1992
Austria awarded him one of its highest honours, the *Grosses
Ehrenzeichen* (Officer's Cross of the Austrian Order of Merit) for
his services to Austrian music. Halifax's Honorary Austrian Consul
Michael Novac presented the medal on stage at a symphony concert on 10 March 1993. After Novac had read the citation, Georg
stepped to the front of the stage and made a speech. He made a
point of 'not falsifying history', noting that most Austrians welcomed Hitler when he annexed the country in 1938 and that he, as
a Jew, had been 'spat out like a piece of pussy phlegm'. He pointed
out that the Nazis who rounded up his father and others and made
them scrub the streets with toothbrushes were not German but
Austrian. But, he said, we have to forgive because we have to live
with each other:

> I'm not pointing an accusing finger. One thing I have learned
> in the fifty-five years since is that there is evil in all of us; no
> group is especially evil. Austria is for me like a mistress, with
> whom one has a love–hate relationship. My personal relation

to Austria has been one of unrequited love. I do love Austria
with every fibre of my being – the landscape, the meadows,
the buildings of the Baroque. Most of all I love the music
from and for which I really live.

He said he appreciated the recognition as a sign that the
country had come around from its darker past, and it had rekindled
and reinforced his love for the good part of Austria. 'Austria has
certainly showed me that my love is not all in vain. I am happy
about the honour – I don't deserve it – it's the feeling that at last
I am accepted as one of them.'[1] The final sentence was his only
concession to politeness. Not for a second did he believe he was
accepted as one of them.

He told me afterwards that had he not made the speech he
could not have accepted the honour.

The next day we went to the Czech spa town of Mariánské Lázně,
better known as Marienbad, for another of Harry Hurwitz's workshops; Georg had grudgingly agreed to do this one because he was
the sole teacher and could design the course himself. Nestled into
the West Bohemian hills, Marienbad was faded but still enchanting, filled with the ghosts of the famous, the fashionable, and the
wealthy Jews from the east who brought their daughters to find
German husbands.

Overlooking the central park was the graceful cast-iron
*Kolonáda*, where healing waters were dispensed morning and afternoon. It was the only thing in Marienbad Georg really enjoyed. As
soon as the workshop sessions were finished he rushed there with a
plastic cup – no fashionable porcelain spa-mug for him – to drink
as much as he could of the metallic orange water. Almost everyone
else at the workshop discovered it had unexpected laxative properties, but not Georg, who drank several gallons daily without the
slightest effect.

Georg lectured on what he thought was important in the
profession of conducting. Stick technique was ignored, except
for correcting students when they were unclear or imprecise.
Observing that some of the participants had inflated opinions of
their worth, he gave a talk about the value of conductors. They are
a necessary evil, he said; they are glorified traffic policemen.

A conductor needs to know his place. He is by no means as important as some people think. He *is* important, but he is only the second in command. What is important is the one who wrote the piece. The conductor, if he is worth his salt, is important insofar as he must convey the spirit and meaning of what the composer intended to his players, and thereby indirectly also to the audience. That is his only function. It is a very noble function, but it is not the most important thing in the world. The most important thing in the world is the person who is able to write the first three bars of the Eroica. *That* is important.[2]

He maintained that talent was more important than experience. Conducting was '*ein Schwindel*' (a swindle), he said, and he told a story about a grand deception:

Conducting is a *suspicious* profession, I really mean that...I know one bass player of the Concertgebouw orchestra. He was no fool – far from, he was very clever...He and I think eighteen of his friends from the orchestra formed a chamber orchestra. They looked for a conductor, and they thought they had found one, and that was a man who came with the highest credentials: he was a pupil of Bartók and Ravel in composition, and equally eminent people in conducting. They gave very successful concerts for a whole year. And after a year they found out that this man had practically no musical training whatsoever – had never been *near* these giants in music. He must have been a tremendously gifted person, but the fact remains he could fool eighteen or twenty eminent players of the Concertgebouw Orchestra. (They fired him, but of course they should have doubled his salary *immediately*!)

Now which other profession, I ask you, could do that? A player would immediately show whether he could play or not, I mean, it's *obvious*. But there, this funny profession of ours, you get away with murder. Therefore, I think there is a special obligation on us to practise this profession *not* to get away with murder, but to take it seriously, and *never, never* to think what so many of these dictators of the baton think: 'Isn't it *marvellous!* There are a hundred people and they have to do what I want!' Ladies and gentlemen, the first time I would think that, that would be the last time I conducted. And that is a promise. Because it shows such an immaturity of outlook. The conductor, if he is anything at all, is not just doing what he wants, he is doing something exceedingly ·responsible, he is standing there as the representative of the person who is really the person who matters, the person who was clever enough to think of the great music he conducts. Therefore I always compare the conductor with the priest in the Catholic Church – I'm an outsider, I'm not a Catholic and so I'm not trying to hurt anybody – but I want to say this. Let us presume one among a million priests is perhaps not as marvellous a person as he might be. While he stands there and fulfils what is to him a holy office, he is the representative of something much greater than himself, and scoundrel though he may be, he represents something that is sacred, and unique. And to me, I feel that is the same.[3]

Conductors, he said, should never be rude to a musician: 'Never forget that musicians know infinitely more about their instruments than you do.' Singers must be treated with special consideration because 'there is not even a piece of wood between the singer and what comes out'. He cited the behaviour of Erich Kleiber, when a flute player couldn't get something right:

Kleiber said, 'Again', and it didn't work. He very kindly said, 'Again – try hard', but it still didn't work. The flute player said in utter desperation, 'I just don't know what to do. I'm so upset, and I'm very sorry.' Kleiber said, 'Do you know what this is?' and he had his baton in his hand. He said, 'Yes, it's a baton.' Kleiber said, 'If there were bells on it, you would know how many mistakes *I* make.' Now that of course was an exaggeration; he was a brilliant conductor and probably made very few mistakes. But he wanted to make this fellow feel at ease.[4]

He warned the conductors not to repeat something without telling the orchestra – and especially individual musicians – why. He told a cautionary tale of the personnel manager of one of British orchestras, whom he had met in the 1960s. Surprised at how much the man knew about orchestral playing, Georg asked if he was a musician himself, and he replied that he had once been a horn player. A conductor had demanded he repeat a passage over and over, without telling him either what he wanted or what was wrong. The man's nerve was destroyed and he never played again. To Georg this was an inexcusable abuse of power.

On the other hand they should not talk too much, a common mistake especially of inexperienced conductors, because it bores musicians. He warned the conductors not to over-rehearse (something of which Georg was sometimes accused), or to under-rehearse, however much musicians like being sent home early. He mentioned a performance he had heard of Beethoven's Fifth Symphony conducted by Hans Knappertsbusch, who was famous for his dislike of rehearsing. He had rehearsed so little that when they came to the first movement exposition repeat in the concert, half the orchestra went back and half the orchestra went on.

He said that a conductor should always admit his mistakes, though he should make as few as possible. Not to do so results in a loss of respect. He spoke about the great conductor Victor de Sabata:

> an Italian of the utmost brilliance. I attended a rehearsal of *Don Quichotte* by Strauss. I don't know if many of you know this piece, it is a very complicated and involved piece with a solo cello and solo viola and an enormous orchestral apparatus. He rehearsed from memory, and he knew everything – he knew *absolutely everything*. He suddenly stopped and said to the Eighth Horn player in the Vienna Philharmonic Orchestra, 'You held that note an eighth note too long.' He said, 'Yes, maestro!' The whole Vienna Philharmonic Orchestra gaped in amazement that a man could know his score to that extent that in the enormous sound there was, he could spot that the Eighth Horn played just a shade too long. Now that was not silly, that was clever. It was brilliant.
>
> After that he rehearsed the *Bolero* by Ravel. Suddenly he stopped again and said to the little trumpet, 'Why didn't you come in when I gave you the sign to come in?' in very broken German. And that man said, not a little embarrassed, 'I still had two bars' rest' – which should have prompted Victor de Sabata to say, 'I'm sorry, I made a mistake.' But you may have noticed that conductors never make mistakes.

Instead he said, 'But *yesterday* when we rehearsed that, you came in at this place.' Now, the whole Vienna Philharmonic Orchestra roared with laughter – and the spell was broken. And I dare say, though they still admired him as a supremely great artist, something had happened – because they realised he was a great artist but he was a very small man. He *could not bring himself* to say: I made a mistake. This is something every conductor ought to learn to say. Very few say it.[5]

His final words of advice were to conduct as much as possible:

Collect a few musicians and ask them to play for you. Prepare one or two works so well that you think you know all you can know [about them]. You should know what each instrument can do and what is written, precisely, for each instrument. Then say to them: 'Please, play exactly as I conduct. Don't help me, and on the other hand don't make it hard for me. Just follow the beat.' Preferably while you do that, have an experienced conductor sitting in. Then you will learn infinitely more than if you sit in a classroom for *twenty years*.[6] If you find that a few details don't work, then don't be too proud to have another look at the score. My experience is that when something doesn't work two or three times with an experienced orchestra, then it is usually the conductor's fault and not that of the players.[7]

It doesn't matter whether there are ten or fifty players, or if they are choristers. It is an old fable that some people can handle choruses well but not orchestras. If they know something about the orchestra, even if they never stand in front of one, they should be able to do just as well as in front of choirs…[However,] orchestras are usually professional, and choirs are amateur. Amateur singers don't mind to spend a lot of time on anything because they are there to enjoy themselves, where professionals want to get away as quickly as possible. So there is a *psychological* difference, which is terribly important to think of.[8]

After the workshop Georg conducted the only two concerts he ever did in Continental Europe: with Marienbad's West Bohemian

Symphony Orchestra, and the Slovak State Orchestra in Košice. When we returned to Halifax I set about finding him a new job, because I was sure he would be lost if he could not make music. There was also the matter of paying our rent, because we had none coming in from Banana Bend; Georg had lent it to our neighbour's children because 'my socialist principles do not allow me to be a landlord'. I wrote applications – Georg was impractical in these matters – to many American orchestras, without success. In retrospect it was a poor choice; Georg's conducting was much more suited to European tastes. He had no better luck with Canadian orchestras and music schools. At the same time guest-conducting invitations disappeared, immediately after the announcement of Georg's resignation. Neither of us had realised the importance of the podium exchange system. We were accustomed to Australia, where concerts were dispensed by the ABC. With no podium to trade, Georg found himself ignored. Apart from two concerts a year with Symphony Nova Scotia, he had no concerts with any professional Canadian orchestra in the last five years of his life.

Orchestra administrators may well have assumed that Georg, aged seventy-six, had retired, as indeed the national newspaper reported. Nobody could believe that anyone would quit a secure job without another in prospect. As for Symphony Nova Scotia, it took them three years to find a new music director, and as the increasingly cheerless search went on Georg said to me, a little contritely, 'I might have been a bit hasty'. It was the only time I heard him admit to a professional mistake.

On 6 April 1993 he cycled across Halifax to see the city's leading dental pathologist. He had a growth in his mouth, on his hard palate, which was troubling him. The pathologist asked him if he drank or smoked, and when Georg replied he did neither he told him he had nothing to worry about. Nevertheless, he excised the lesion, and a few days later reported that it was harmless. But Georg had come home uneasy; he thought the dentist had been much more interested in impressing a female student than in making a thorough examination.

We were soon leaving for Australia, and as it had been six years since Georg's last ABC concert, I wrote to Nathan Waks, the new Director of Music. He was a cellist Georg had known for decades, and he immediately offered a concert with the Melbourne Symphony and a studio recording of Australian repertoire in

Adelaide. The concert took place on 2 July, and Waks came to Melbourne to check that Georg was still up to the ABC's standards. The program was all Beethoven: *Wellington's Victory*, the Triple Concerto and the Seventh Symphony. The audience was enthusiastic, and so were the reviews: the *Age* commented on 'the intense conviction and dedication of...one of the finest resident conductors ever to work in Australia',[9] and the *Sun-Herald* referred to 'a radiant performance...Georg Tintner, developed extraordinary passion, drive and power. His encyclopedic musical memory, intuition and keen hearing, selfless dedication and lifelong study have made him a much-loved and respected custodian of Viennese traditions.'[10]

Three weeks later I visited Nathan Waks in Sydney, confident that Melbourne's positive response would result in more concerts. I was bitterly disappointed. I should already have suspected what was coming when Waks had taken us to supper after the concert. As we entered the restaurant he said, 'Such a pity, Georg, that you had to follow right after Skrowaczewski.' In the interview he told me that the Melbourne Symphony had not liked Georg, and nor had the Adelaide Symphony in the recording that followed. The MSO considered him 'too old, and past it'. He had 'failed to establish authority' and he 'couldn't beat time' – probably, Waks added uncomfortably, because he didn't use a baton. He said he had personally enjoyed the Seventh Symphony, but 'anybody can conduct that'. The orchestra's evaluation was now the ABC's Current Assessment, superseding all others, and they had nothing for Georg in the foreseeable future. 'No-one is gunning for Georg in the ABC,' he added.

I couldn't hide this terrible interview from Georg, who was already back in Halifax. He wrote sadly to Waks:

> Tanya phoned to report on your 'abortive' meeting. She was very angry. I am *not at all*...But one or two things did surprise me. Not only in the press but also by many listeners the *unusually* great *precision* was praised. How then that they could not follow the beat? (a *new* accusation in nearly 60 years of conducting. I am often praised for the 'clarity' of my gestures!)...and yet your 'experts' within the MSO seem to consider me a geriatric fool. I might add in passing that three keyplayers congratulated me after the concert and said how much they enjoyed it!; two of them went even as far

as: approving Beethoven's (NOT MINE) repeats! Some of the players might have also resented my telling them frankly that their lack of discipline was most unprofessional…

No, you did not hurt me this time. But once earlier on, you did! Years ago (at the time of your friendship with Eilene Hannan who then had a most beautiful light Soprano voice) I submitted to you my 'masterpiece': *The ellipse* for Soprano and Stringquartet…My score and parts were returned WITH-OUT A WORD. That *did* hurt. It has been played a few times in Vienna, Vancouver and Brisbane, but it would have been important for me…[11]

The letter missed Waks, who had gone on leave, and it was the end of September before he replied. By that time a much greater misfortune had befallen Georg. The lesion the pathologist had excised from his mouth in April had grown back, and by June he was so worried that he called the pathologist from Brisbane, who agreed irritably to see him again when he returned. As soon as Georg arrived he called, only to be told the pathologist was on holiday. By now truly frightened, he went to another dentist, who biopsied the lesion.

On 12 August I was leaving to help at a conductors' workshop in the Czech Republic, and as I walked out the door the telephone rang. It was the dentist's office, asking Georg to come in that afternoon. We thought nothing of it, and I flew to Toronto. From there I telephoned Georg and found him distraught. The dentist had told him the lump was cancerous and must be removed immediately. He was to go into hospital that evening. I said I was coming home but he refused; he did not want me to be there and insisted I go to the workshop as planned. All I could think was – Georg was fit; he ate only healthy food, not a morsel of rubbish crossed his lips. All the statistics said he was the person least likely to get cancer. How could this be?

Years later I came to the conclusion that Georg's cancer probably had little to do with his physical life and everything to do with his state of mind. Georg's disappointments remained trapped inside. He had been struggling to express himself for over forty years and nothing had come out. He felt strangled – impotent. He had felt an *obligation* to compose, because he had survived, and he had not fulfilled it. Conducting didn't count: that was recreative, expressing the feelings of others. His cancer may well have come, in W. H. Auden's words, from 'foiled creative fire'. And if depression is anger turned inwards, as is often posited, it was a toxic mixture. Attributing psychological causes to illness is dangerous, for it seems to blame the victim. Yet the frustration Georg suffered put unbearable stress on both his mind and his body. His failure to compose ate him up, and in the end it literally ate him up.

Long after he died I found out what happened between his visit to the dentist and my call a few hours later. He rushed to see Walter Kemp, the professor of music at Dalhousie University and the one person to whom he felt close enough to visit occasionally for conversation:

> He sat down opposite me and told me he had just been diagnosed with cancer and not to plan anything because he might be dead in a month. I said, 'Now if you would really be dead in a month they would have told you.' He was clearly devastated. And then suddenly he collapsed, he began to cry, just began to weep, and he fell onto my chest and cried, and I put my arms around him and let him cry. He said, 'I am not crying for myself but for Tany. I do not want her to be alone. I am not afraid of death, I have faced death many times, but I am afraid for Tany that she will be alone. She seems so strong but she will be lost without me. She seems so resilient but she is such a little girl, she depends on me so much.' He said he would feel he had failed you. I said that you gave him a reason to live.[12]

Georg had amelanotic mucosal melanoma, which despite its name was not skin cancer. In the original biopsy in April the pathologist had missed it. Nobody will ever know if the delay of four months meant the difference between life and death. But with a disease that kills 50 per cent of its victims in two years, and 90 per cent in five, four months is a long time.

On Friday 13 August Georg was given extensive tests and scans, and he told the doctors that if the disease had metastasised he would refuse surgery. None was found, and on Sunday evening Dr Elhamy Attia removed the lesion, carving away part of the hard palate towards the nasal cavity. Georg presented a brave front to the nurses, and he was discharged five days later, still with a swollen face, 'pleasant and cheerful mood noted'. But on the day before he had written (in German) a disaster-diary page:

> I shall consider every day from now on as a gift and get as much as I can out of it. *But* I am so tired, and was already for months before the operation…
>
> If things turn out badly which is to be expected, I hope for Tanya that it comes to an end quickly. I have thought of suicide, but so long as I am not a permanent burden for others that would be an act of cowardice. Especially as Tanya isn't here she would (*completely without justification*) feel guilty and responsible. I am not afraid of death not even of the pain (providing it is *bearable* for me). So far I have refused all 'painkillers'. Hopefully it will continue that way. I have written to two of my admirers, who think a lot of me, that being old is bad enough for young ladies but to be old and mortally ill is an impossible combination and I want (and insist on it) to break *all* my connections to them.
>
> Whether I can still write music now? I try it rather weakly. – The people in this hospital are charming (not only to the big fish in a *little* pond) but to everyone. Despite that it is completely hateful to me. Because I can't eat anything solid (not because of the wound but because (temporarily, I hope) the upper denture has absolutely no grip.) they have no clue how to feed me; but perhaps the 90 per cent fast does me real good in the circumstances!…Unfortunately I am worse than yesterday. If I have to die how would it be to breathe the air of the Austrian Alps? Hinterbichl? or Townsville??? Or here? (That would be the cheapest and simplest.) My life after the Ellipse was bungled. I have achieved nothing after that (except that I could give joy to many people, which is not to be undervalued.) Because I can't believe in Providence I must *myself*

Here he reached the end of the page. If he wrote more, it is lost.

Over the next few weeks he had to learn how to eat again; it was very difficult. But he was fortunate that the symphony season was over, and almost nobody saw him with his swollen face. Georg, never social, could hide at home and recover in secret. By the time he conducted the opening concert of his final season six weeks later, on 28 September, he was to all appearances completely normal.

Two weeks later we went to Australia, where at Rodney Phillips's invitation Georg was to conduct the twentieth anniversary concert of the opening of the Sydney Opera House, on 22 October 1993. The program was the same as that conducted by Willem van Otterloo in the opening concert: John Antill's fanfare *Jubugalee* and Beethoven's Ninth Symphony. At the end of the concert Nathan Waks paid Georg a visit, evidently attempting to limit damage from the Melbourne Symphony business in July. After my meeting with Waks I had sent a report to Maria Vandamme, with whom we had stayed in Melbourne. Unknown to me she forwarded the letter to Tony Fogg, Head of Concert Music (Programming). The ABC had been in trouble earlier in the year when Roger Woodward publicly accused it of failing to appreciate and utilise Australian artists, which resulted in an official inquiry into the hiring practices of the Concert Music department. Worried that more trouble might be stirred up, Fogg suggested to Waks he see Georg at the anniversary concert.

Georg wasn't fooled. As soon as he returned to Halifax, he wrote to Waks:

> I was utterly STARTLED that you suggested my orchestral seating [Second Violins on the right] has such merit that you want others to consider it! I – the Ninkompoop (?) who is not worthy of conducting the MSO…should have something positiv to offer – fancy that!
>
> By the way in Melbourne the performance of Beethoven's 7th was the first one I felt I had at last conquered it and however often the orchestra had played it, it is with No. 6 perhaps the hardest to bring off…
>
> Let bygones be bygones.[13]

Autumn was quiet. Georg had several check-ups and tests and the doctors declared themselves very pleased with his progress. We returned to Australia for Christmas and on 31 December he conducted another Rodney Phillips concert, a New Year's Eve celebration with the Sydney Opera House Orchestra in a program of Viennese operetta. It was choreographed exactly to finish in time for Sydney's famous fireworks. As I stood on a terrace at the front of the Opera House in the balmy summer air, watching the display over Sydney Harbour, things at that moment seemed hopeful. Perhaps Georg had been lucky. Perhaps his cancer had been caught in time, and he would still live to be 100.

## Thirty

Late in 1993, as a parting gift for Symphony Nova Scotia, Georg orchestrated his song cycle *Young Love*. That he brought the songs out now was surprising; perhaps he felt he was running out of time. It was years since he had made a real effort to have his music performed.* In his 1987 interview with Margaret Cooke he said, 'I have already written a few works, but works which in my opinion are of great importance. I don't propagate them or anything, I don't try to tell anybody about them, but they are there and I think that they made some mark, I don't claim more.'[1] Few in Australia and almost nobody in Canada knew he composed at all. In the early years in New Zealand Georg had not disabused people of the idea that he was a genius, and irritated some by claiming it himself. But that was a long time ago. A genius has to have something to show for himself, and to his mind he had very little.

When Margaret asked him if he felt satisfied with life, he replied, 'Very *un*satisfied. I feel that for the gift I have, I have achieved very little, and when I say "achieve" you must never think I mean material progress or fame or anything like that. No – achieved in myself. Very little…'

He orchestrated only four of the five original songs in *Young Love*, and the mezzo song *Frühling* as an extra. Why he didn't orchestrate *Mondnacht* is unclear. It is possible he just forgot about the song, which is not as unlikely as it may seem. When he introduced the cycle both on radio and in his podium introduction he said that with the exception of *Dämmerstunde*, sung by Joan Hammond, none of the songs had been performed before in public.

---

* 'Weingartner is one of the reasons I am very reluctant to do anything about my compositions. Because Weingartner was a dreadful composer, yet he wrote seven operas, ten symphonies, or something…The whole world wanted him to conduct Beethoven but he would only conduct if he could also include one of his own works, and in the end he had the delusion that they wanted to hear his music instead of what they really wanted to hear. And that is the danger, you know, with conductors – that they peddle their own wares. I'm quite free of that danger.' (Interview with Edward Benyas, 18 July 1996, private tape).

He had evidently forgotten the Leslie Daykin performances in 1949 and 1951, and Heather Begg's 1956 broadcast and recording of *Frühling*, all of which he himself had accompanied. Given that his compositions were more important to him than anything else, and that his memory for musical events was prodigious, how he could have forgotten these performances is a complete mystery. It is just as mysterious as his carelessness over the whereabouts of his manuscripts.*

Despite scoring the songs for chamber orchestra the sound (but little else) is reminiscent of Richard Strauss. He said to the near-capacity audience at the performance on 18 January 1994 (with soprano Sue Ferraioli Doran):

> When you listen to these songs you may consider them extremely old fashioned. As a matter of fact, fifty-seven years ago even *then* they may have been old-fashioned. But composing means putting notes together – nothing else. It doesn't mean 'do something nobody else has ever done before whether it is beautiful or ugly'. And therefore I have written these songs with the utmost feeling I was capable of.

The audience gave them a standing ovation. 'To my surprise these "oldfashioned" songs were a sensational success,' Georg wrote to Les Thompson, 'also with the players who love them… The success of my 4 lovesongs and *Frühling* have persuaded me to dig out my feeble beginnings of: "It's a T'is pity she is a whore". Whether I can find the inner strength to pursue her?'[2]

Over the next few years Georg occasionally sat at the piano trying things out – a few notes, a few chords. When I asked as gently as possible what he was doing he just shouted, '*Nothing!*' Once he just said sadly, '*Blicke mir nicht in die Lieder*'.† One day he came to me and said, with a despairing expression, 'I don't know how to do it.' It was a terrible admission, and it showed the extent of his desperation. He had been in this quandary for fifty years. 'I want to write the music that is still within me,' he had told Margaret Cooke, 'but whether I ever shall I don't know.' And

---

\* Georg lent many of his originals to singers and musicians in the hope they would perform them, and for that reason was unwilling to retrieve them. In the end he forgot who had them.

† A reference to the title of one of Mahler's *Rückert Lieder*, which means both 'Look not into my songs' and, as Georg meant it, 'Look not into me through my songs'.

because he never lied to anyone, including himself, he added, 'And it may well be that I use all this overwork I have as an excuse for something missing.'[3]

Do creative people really know where to find the wellspring of inspiration, or know how to recognise it if they find it? Mozart liked his wife to read him fairy stories as he composed. Schiller wrote poetry to the smell of rotten apples. Schubert slept with his glasses on because, he said, he could lose the beautiful melodies he had just dreamed in the time it took him to put them on. Georg was certain he needed to love and adore, to worship his Eternal Feminine. And then, he may have been altogether mistaken. Perhaps it had nothing to do with women at all.

Georg probably came closest to finding the distant sound when he wrote *The Ellipse*, all alone.* Tellingly, it was his most important work, and autobiographical at that. He never did sort his way through searching for the ideal muse and finding what he needed in himself.

The concert with *Young Love* was one of his last as music director of Symphony Nova Scotia. On 1 March he conducted the Brahms German Requiem, from memory, and on 26 and 28 April he gave his final concert, with Beethoven's Second and Ninth Symphonies. The audience was rapturous, but for me there was only a deep feeling of loss, and sadness that this period of security and content-ment had ended. Georg still had no new job, and with his pride wounded he insisted I stop trying to find him one. He wanted to go back to Banana Bend. He wanted to get away from apartment living, the cold, his chilblains; he longed for our farm where he could dig and weed and be warm in the sunshine.

Returning to Banana Bend seemed to me the worst of all options. He would get no work in Australia, and almost no Canadian orchestras could afford to bring him so far for guest appearances. Georg was unmoved. He would write his music, and if nobody ever gave him another concert it wouldn't matter at all. But after so many years of travelling to Georg's concerts in interesting places, and of making friends in many of them, I dreaded the isolation and loneliness of Banana Bend. Georg was much more withdrawn now than in the early days, silent

---

* 'Frühling,' one of his two finest songs, was also written without female association.

and almost reclusive. I once accused him of putting music before everything else including his wife, but his answer was that I should be *glad* he spent so much time with his scores, and that I should *encourage* him in his work. But it was not easy, when what I craved was his attention – to be let in. You can't compare music and wives, he said, but the comparison made itself in the amount of time he allotted to each. Such compulsive devotion to serving one's art was not compatible with what most would call a functional marriage. Romantic gestures never crossed Georg's mind. Dining out was a waste of time and money; anniversaries and birthdays passed uncelebrated. Walking arm in arm was an unacceptable display of public affection, and should I throw my arm around his shoulders in public he would elbow me away saying, 'Don't do that! I am a figure of respect!'

Sometimes I wondered if Georg cared if I were there at all. Yet, from time to time when I went out Georg said sadly – and incorrectly – 'You do everything you can to get away from me.' If I didn't sit next to him on an airport bus because we had too many bags, he looked hurt and made comments about the *cordon sanitaire*, assuming I was embarrassed to sit with my ancient husband.* I suspect Georg did know how terribly lonely I was, but had no idea what to do about it. I felt like the cartoon coyote who keeps running in air after he runs off the edge of the cliff, and only plunges to the bottom of the canyon when he looks down. The trick was never to look down.

Georg gave in and we remained in Halifax, but he was very unhappy. He must have thought – though he never mentioned his composing – that I was depriving him of his last chance to write in peace. Had we returned, would he really have written anything? I doubt it; but this is not the point. I denied him the opportunity – because it never occurred to me. Lack of understanding by almost everyone, including me, caused him to withdraw into himself, and as time went on he drifted away into a great solitude.

Unexpectedly, Georg came up with the idea of living in Vienna for a year.† He had finally re-acquired his Austrian citizenship – not as a result of the cumbersome application he had already made but

---

*    If someone referred to Georg as my father, he would raise an admonitory forefinger, smile brightly and say, 'Grandfather! Grandfather!'

†    Even more surprisingly, a few years later Georg wanted to move back to Vienna permanently.

through the intercession of Canada's new Austrian Ambassador, Dr Walther Lichem. At a reception in the autumn of 1993 Dr Lichem began a speech with the comment that he was pleased to see so many Austrians in Halifax and he hoped they would all retain their citizenship. Georg interrupted him angrily: 'Excuse me! Excuse me! I've been trying to get my passport back for *fifty years!*' Embarrassed, Dr Lichem promised him he would come to his final Symphony performance in April 1994 and bring an Austrian passport with him. He kept his word.

Georg now had all he wanted from Austria. When in 1996 the country finally offered *Wiedergutmachung*, reparations, of a few thousand dollars, he refused to apply. Long before I met him he had also refused reparations payments from Germany, though short of money at the time. Dr Lichem tried to persuade him to change his mind, suggesting as a compromise he take the money and give it away, but Georg was adamant. 'I will not accept their dirty money. No amount of money can make up for what they did to me. If I needed it I would take it, but I don't, and I won't.' Curious, I asked him why he felt he could not accept money when the Nazis, Austrian as much as German, had deprived him of his career. 'Oh, I don't know,' he replied resignedly. 'There was so much anti-Semitism, who knows how far I could have gone?'

In the middle of 1994 Georg's recording of Bruckner's Sixth Symphony, made in 1992 with the Bohuslav Martinů Philharmonic, was released on the Deutsche Schallplatten label. At the same time the CBC released his 1991 Symphony Nova Scotia recording of Delius, including the Violin Concerto played by Philippe Djokic. It became surprisingly successful, selling thousands of copies despite having little distribution outside Canada.

In July Georg directed another of Harry Hurwitz's workshops, this time for opera singers and conductors, in Opava in the Czech Republic. On the way back to Canada he collected another award for his services to Austrian music, the *Silbernes Ehrenzeichen* (Silver Cross of Honour) of the City and Province of Vienna. The presentation took place at City Hall on 25 July, attended by Georg's cousins Liesl and Rosl. He made a speech similar to the one he gave when he received the *Grosses Ehrenzeichen*, about how he had been spat out of the country, about how there is evil in all of us.

The officials, none of whom were old enough to remember the war, smiled politely and were very gracious.

As summer turned into autumn there was more bad employment news. Georg had applied for the directorship of the Bohuslav Martinů Philharmonic in Zlín, but only after inquiring discreetly if the orchestra had any interest in him. The reply had been strongly in the affirmative, but although most of the principal players wanted him the job went instead to Kirk Trevor. He found this so humiliating that when an acquaintance in Halifax told him of an orchestra in South America that was looking for a volunteer conductor through an international aid agency, Georg applied. He was quite serious. Had we not met Klaus Heymann, the owner of Naxos Records, we might well have gone to Ecuador.

In October we went to Hong Kong at the invitation of Anthony Camden, who was now dean of the Academy for Performing Arts. I intended to visit Klaus Heymann to ask if he might consider Georg for a recording, preferably Bruckner. In his extensive catalogue Bruckner was the only major composer still missing, and he had been trying for some time to find the right conductor. Before calling him I consulted Anthony, who recorded for Naxos. He had already spoken to Heymann about Georg, saying he was the finest Bruckner conductor alive, but Heymann had someone else in mind and had not reacted.[4] Anthony was not very hopeful. Heymann did not view recordings made for other companies favourably, and not only did Georg have three for the CBC but he had already recorded Bruckner for another label. Nevertheless, and in spite of Georg's trying to talk me out of it, I made an appointment.

As I was about to set out on the agreed morning Georg said he wanted to come – a surprise, given his aversion to self-promotion. Heymann received us genially and I explained my mission. He knew there were many different versions of the symphonies and he began to muse on how they might best be recorded and sold. He and Georg chatted for a while and discovered they both loved Pfitzner and Franz Schmidt. Then he said, 'But I hear you are under contract to another label.' The agent for Deutsche Schallplatten had told him so earlier in the year. When I said this was untrue, Heymann asked, 'Then in a year or so Mr Tintner could record for us?' I replied that Georg could record for him tomorrow. 'In that case', Heymann said, 'you can record all the symphonies, in all the versions, and all the choral music with orchestra as well.' This amounted to something like twenty-five discs. It was such an astonishing change of fortune that neither of us told anyone for six months in case it was too good to be true.

Why did Heymann do it? I think he took a liking to Georg, an old-school European musician that he, as a well-educated German, understood and respected. Perhaps he just had an instinct. For the rest of Georg's life Heymann accommodated his every wish, and showed us considerable personal kindness. Georg, in turn, took a liking to Heymann, something of a surprise given his low opinion of commerce. Perhaps the fact that Heymann loved Pfitzner and Schmidt outweighed his being a 'captain of industry'.

On 20 November Georg conducted the first of two audition concerts with the Niagara Symphony, in southern Ontario – Mozart's Symphony No. 34, Copland's *Appalachian Spring*, Schumann's Third Symphony – which was a great success, and the following February he conducted a light Viennese program. A few weeks later the orchestra appointed a young Pops conductor, Michael Reason. It was a considerable shock for Georg – not only had the board led him to believe the job was his but it was the first time in his life he had not won a position for which he had actually auditioned.

In summer 1994 he taught his second opera workshop in Opava. A few days after we arrived he noticed a lump under his jawbone. He knew immediately what it was. Don't make any plans, he said, this may be the end. Nothing could be done until we returned to Halifax, after Georg made his first Naxos recordings. After considering Riga and being turned down by the Toronto Symphony, Heymann decided to record the symphonies with the New Zealand Symphony Orchestra. They would begin with the Ninth and the Sixth, with six sessions each, at the end of July.

The sessions went wrong from the start. The producer fell ill the day before, and was replaced only just in time by Tim Handley, brought in from Australia. The musicians were not feeling co-operative; Heymann had cancelled their appearance at his festival in Hong Kong because of a dispute over instruments and the recordings had been scheduled instead. Adding to their displeasure was the use of Lower Hutt Town Hall, which had extremely loud and live acoustics; one of the bass players registered his protest by wearing airport-grade earmuffs. Wellington was in the middle of its coldest winter in many years, rendering the hall all but unheatable. The heating system, labouring valiantly, could be heard on tape and had to be replaced by industrial kerosene heaters run at full power at every break. But as soon as the temperature fell below 19°C the union representative called a stop-work. Many musicians had influenza and one after another went home sick, including almost all the front desk string players. Some weeks after the sessions, and despite Tim Handley's best efforts, the recording of the Ninth Symphony had to be abandoned. In a symphony with eight horns, twelve first violins were just not enough.

After returning to Halifax, early in August, Georg's lump was removed. It contained melanoma, and a scan showed that there was melanoma also in his parotid gland, below his ear. On 24 August part of the gland was removed, but the nerve to the right side of his lower lip was unavoidably severed, causing his mouth to appear much more lop-sided than it already was. Those who didn't look too closely thought he had had a stroke. Georg fortunately had very few concerts that autumn, and he was able to hide at home and recover.

On 17 October he conducted Symphony Nova Scotia with Menahem Pressler as soloist, and then went to Hong Kong for a concert with the Academy orchestra. He returned to Halifax with two scarves as a gift. As he handed them to me he said, scowling, 'You wouldn't have these if it weren't for Margaret [Crawford]. She asked me what I was bringing back for you and I said "nothing". She said, "You can't do that", and she took me to a shop and made me get something.' I still find the story, and the thought of Georg trying to flee the Wing On department store, very funny, but at the same time heartbreaking. For him the only worthwhile present was a new composition – and that he could not provide.

Because it hadn't been possible to remove all the melanoma he was persuaded to see a radiation oncologist in January 1996. A clever young doctor lectured Georg sternly about the severity of the radiation that was required, and listed every side effect that would or even might result: brittle bones, deafness, brain damage and more. Georg turned whiter than the doctor's coat and when he could stand it no longer he fled. He was no coward – he was *anything* but a coward – but hospitals frightened him because he didn't understand them. Doctors confused him; he didn't know what they were doing to him, or why. It was essential that I attended every consultation because he misheard everything. Unsurprisingly, he rejected the radiation therapy.

A few weeks later I happened upon a long review of the Zlín Bruckner Sixth in *Fanfare* magazine, by Michael Jameson:

> I've not been overly impressed by examples of [Tintner's] work on disc...and on present evidence, he is scarcely a Brucknerian to be reckoned with...he has failed to evince the architectural majesty of the work, and has, I think, neglected to ascribe sufficient thought to his preparation of the great Adagio, among Bruckner's finest...Tintner is utterly uninspired...intonation is dire, and neither is Georg Tintner wholly guiltless in this hapless, and fraudulently wayward, account of this great work...(with Tintner, who apparently strives toward a diametrically opposing goal, any focus or clarity is only detectable by its almost total absence!)... Emphatically a Bruckner release to avoid.[5]

This was a catastrophe. It was only six months since Georg had recorded the same symphony for Naxos. Would Heymann conclude that the unhappy recording sessions had been his fault? Would he think he had hired a no-hoper and drop him before any more symphonies were recorded? I was careful to keep the review away from Georg, for had he seen it there is no question he would have stopped recording immediately, and possibly stopped conducting altogether. I showed it to a lawyer friend, whose opinion was that it was defamatory in several places. I wrote accordingly to the editor and asked that, in view of this, he give Jameson no more of Georg's records to review. He did not reply, but he complied with my request. Georg never knew any of this, and as for Heymann, he brushed it off, saying he took no notice of reviews. His belief in Georg never wavered.

Heymann decided not to continue recording Bruckner with the New Zealand Symphony, but many precious months went by before he found a replacement. He tried several British orchestras, but they refused to risk a conductor they had never heard of. He finally persuaded the Royal Scottish National Orchestra to take a chance on him, and they scheduled the Fifth Symphony for four sessions on 19 and 20 April 1996. Georg said it wasn't enough time for such a difficult work, but he was assured the symphony was already in the orchestra's repertoire. When he arrived at the first session he discovered not only that the symphony had not been played in living memory, which went back to 1951, but due to a postal delay the parts had arrived only the night before and the musicians hadn't even seen them. Eventually someone persuaded Georg to stay by telling him the musicians were wonderful sight-readers. Still unconvinced, he was about to start rehearsing when the producer said he couldn't record the orchestra as Georg had arranged it – second violins on the right, and the cellos next to the first violins with the double basses behind them. Georg said he would not change the seating under any circumstances. Half an hour was lost while the producer referred the dispute to a Naxos official in England, who told him Georg's seating would remain. When the session finally started Georg discovered that the musicians were indeed remarkable sight-readers and, in just ten and a half hours, they did an outstanding job.

Before returning to Canada we had hoped to visit Les and Marjorie Thompson in Oxford, but it wasn't possible. Georg was uneasy in Glasgow, saying several times, 'I have a bad feeling about Les!' He was right. When we arrived in Halifax we found a phone message saying he was in hospital and not expected to live. Georg managed to get a message to him just before he died on 26 April. He was very shaken. Les had been his devoted friend from his second day in New Zealand; someone on whom he could always rely, a musical kindred spirit.

On 24 May Georg conducted Beethoven's Ninth and his first piano concerto with Roger Woodward in the twentieth anniversary concert of the Queensland Theatre Orchestra (now Philharmonic): 'a triumphant return'. He had an uneventful medical check in the middle of June and a few days later we went to Opava for the annual opera workshop. Georg must have discussed his composing, or lack of it, with one of the conducting students, Jeanine Trent, for she insisted that one of his songs should be performed at the workshop. He set about writing out *Dämmerstunde* from memory, and one of the student sopranos, Ani Imastounian, volunteered to sing it. They performed the song, Georg hunched low over the piano and in another world, in a final recital in the

Minorite Church in Krnov. One of the opera directors, Michael Lochar, loved the song and he said he would try to get Georg's music published. As he was the Czech representative for Ricordi it was no idle promise. When we returned to Halifax Georg put together a modest package of his compositions: the Violin Sonata, 'The Ellipse', four of the 'Young Love' songs, 'Frühling,' and the short piano prelude 'Sehnsucht.' The score of the latter had been missing for many years so he spent a few days reconstructing it from memory, sixty years after its composition. In the end Ricordi was not interested, or perhaps they didn't even look at the music, and the idea just faded away. Once again Georg's music could not speak, and the boost to his confidence provided by Jeanine's and Lochar's interest ebbed away to a quiet misery.

I still ask myself why I left it to a stranger to encourage Georg the composer. Every so often Georg would say, 'You do nothing for me.' When I pointed out that I did everything for which other conductors employed a secretary and an agent, he replied, 'I pay you for that.' Another time he said, 'You pack a few suitcases and do my tax return – what is that?' But after he died I realised that he was not thinking of matters quotidian, or even of his conducting career, but of what he had wanted me for in the first place. I did not provide him with the support he needed to compose, and this was what he really meant by 'doing nothing'. Not long after we first met he wrote accusingly, 'Perhaps I was a little spoiled by my first wife, who always tried to take these sorts of burden [packing suitcases] off my "slender" shoulders, in order to leave room and time for things I considered more important.'[6] What I didn't see was that his idealised version of Sue related in no small way to the fact that she provided that support and he had composed without difficulty, in the days when there was still time for a future. By comparison with what came afterwards, he had been living in Arcadia.

In Vienna on the way home we had just enough time to visit the new Jewish Museum in the centre of the city. On the second floor is an exhibition hall, in the centre of which is a square painted on the floor with quotations from Jewish writers inscribed around its edges. Though standing caused him considerable pain, Georg contemplated each one silently for an uncommonly long time. 'Yes, because I was born into no Fatherland, this is why I desire a

Fatherland more than you do' (Ludwig Börne). 'When will it seem that my efforts on this earth have been successful? When poor Jewboys turn into proud young Jews' (Theodor Herzl). 'Nowadays, when they demand that we don't forget "the past", they mean only the concentration camps – and under no circumstances should we recall the celebrated scholars, writers, priests and statesmen who created the climate in which the builders of the gas chambers were able to flourish' (Ludwig Marcuse). 'We respect and love the German loves and the German heart as these are our loves and our heart' (Berthold Auerbach). 'How much home does a man need? – A fair bit of home' (Jean Améry). They found in him a deep resonance.

*Thirty-one*

The next two Bruckner recordings were made in early September 1996, with the National Symphony Orchestra of Ireland in Dublin. This time Georg had the opportunity of conducting the works in two concerts first, which he considered extremely beneficial for the recordings. He began with the Second Symphony in the original (1872) version edited by William Carragan, which had been recorded only once before. It was the first time he had conducted the work, in any version. Rehearsals progressed well enough on the first day. But at lunchtime the next day, as soon as we left the concert hall, Georg said, 'Something terrible has happened!' The orchestra manager told him at the break that the orchestra thought he was incompetent and did not want him to continue. At the beginning of the afternoon session he made a speech to the orchestra. I was too far away to hear much of it, but the last sentence was: 'Don't count the old codger out yet!' At the afternoon break several musicians told Georg that the manager's statement was not the opinion of the whole orchestra, and they were sorry. The rehearsals continued without incident, but for Georg all the pleasure had gone out of it.

The recording followed the concert, with Chris Craker from London as the producer. On 20 September Georg conducted the second concert, which was to be followed by the second recording; the 1887 original version of the Eighth Symphony. Most of Bruckner's symphonies exist in more than one version: some are his originals, some were heavily edited by his well-meaning friends and students such as Ferdinand Löwe and brothers Josef and Franz Schalk, and some are with alterations Bruckner made, willingly or otherwise, according to their suggestions. Scholars continue to argue over what Bruckner really wanted, and the solutions may never be found.

The first editor of his *oeuvre* for the International Bruckner
Society was Robert Haas, who worked before and during World
War II. He was removed in the postwar de-Nazification proceedings and replaced by another Austrian, Leopold Nowak. Georg
said:

> Robert Haas, a little, half-blind, brilliant scholar had Nazi
> sympathies. I attended his totally unpolitical lectures in the
> mid-1930s. Politically he was just as misguided as the English
> conductor Reginald Goodall, who was also a small, half-blind
> man. Goodall had to be interned for his Nazi sympathies in
> the War; but afterwards the British had the good sense to let
> him pursue his calling...Postwar Austria was not as forgiving.
> It removed Haas from his life-work – replacing him *not for
> artistic or scholarly reasons!* Yet his fellow-Austrian Karajan, for
> example, was one of the earliest members of the Nazi Party,
> but he sailed on to fame and riches unhindered...
>
> Are we not allowed to read the novels of Knut Hamsun
> or the poetry of Ezra Pound just because these great artists
> were politically crazy?
>
> The greater shame is that his successor was in my opinion
> probably more politically acceptable than scholarly accept-
> able. I have known all three people: Alfred Orel [editor of
> the original version of Bruckner's Ninth Symphony, 1932],
> Robert Haas and Leopold Nowak. I didn't like any of them.
> But I think the first two were first rate scholars and I think
> the last one is not.[1]

The case of Haas was examined at a conference at Connecticut
College in New London, in February 1994. Attention was drawn
to the fact that Bruckner's music was a particular favourite of
Hitler. Haas was therefore accused of editing Bruckner's scores
according to 'Nazi principles' and blamed for the 'Nazification' of
tempi in Bruckner performances. The conference concluded that
the slow tempi of wartime conductors were the express wish of
Hitler and his henchmen. Furthermore, the idea that the 'original'
editions edited and published by Haas should be preferred over
later editions is only the result of Nazi funding and Nazi ideology –
an attempt to strip the influence of Bruckner's Jewish colleagues

and students from the revisions. When Georg heard four years later that Leon Botstein (who had attended the conference) was to conduct the generally discredited revision of the Fifth Symphony by Franz Schalk, assisted by William Carragan, he wrote in frustration to the latter:

> It is a tragedy that Bruckner, who was probably the least political of all creative artists, is dragged not only by the Nazis but unfortunately also by the anti-Nazis into the quagmire of politics. As far as metronome marks are concerned, I have very little faith in them even with an intellectual artist like Beethoven, and none with the naive inspired Bruckner. We all know what Brahms said about metronome marks, who tried it for a year or so and then gave it away, but I question altogether whether a composer has the necessary cerebral equipment to recapture what he had in mind sometimes years before. You probably know the story of Kubelik and Stravinsky: Kubelik inquired of the composer whether he should observe his metronome marks or the tempi he did in his own recording. Stravinsky said, 'I must listen to both tempi' and then he wrote to Kubelik, 'Do what I did, not what I wrote'. The difference between the metronome marks and his performance was enormous.
>
> The idea that the Nazis were responsible for different tempi is totally absurd. Do you really believe that a supremely great conductor like Furtwängler would have taken the slightest notice of what these mostly illiterate fools would have liked? And I heard in Vienna in the early 1930s very slow Bruckner performances under the Jews Bruno Walter and Otto Klemperer. Altogether I feel that according to this theory I would have to be a super-Nazi.
>
> In my opinion the totally *political* dismissal of Robert Haas was an utter tragedy for the whole development of Bruckner research. I know that he is being blamed for the amalgamation of two versions [temporally] so far apart as the versions of the Second Symphony, and he was probably wrong there; but I'm certain that of all the three existing versions of the Eighth Symphony, his is the best. The Nowak edition (1890) has totally illogical and absurd cuts. Please

don't tell me that Bruckner sanctioned them – I'm sure he did, but it means nothing except that a pretty desperate composer, after having been rejected by his most ardent supporter Levi, would have agreed to almost anything.

So you see, dear Dr Carragan, that we have a fundamental disagreement about the composer we both love. The difference between us rests mainly on the fact that I (with Haas) believe it is our duty to eliminate as far as possible the influence of lesser men, irrespective of whether our master – because he was a master – agreed to and even collaborated with those interferences. The fact that even Bruckner objected to some of the most terrible suggestions does not mean to me that in his heart he agreed with those he accepted.

I am so sad that the recent development of rehabilitating what can only be regarded as makeshift arrangements for an un-understanding public is doing a lot of harm to the purity and uniqueness of this wonderful music. And I want to close by saying that I am probably the only musician alive who was conducted by Franz Schalk many times. And I am second to none in my admiration for that remarkable conductor – but that does not mean that I can possibly agree to what he and his friends did to Bruckner's scores.[2]

Following the success of the premiere of his Seventh Symphony conducted by Artur Nikisch, Bruckner sent the score of his Eighth Symphony to the conductor Hermann Levi in 1887. Levi, however, did not understand it, and Bruckner was driven to despair. He sent Levi a letter that 'reads as if a naughty boy has been caught stealing apples'.[3] He set about revising it, making many improvements but also, under the influence of others, doing what Georg considered to be unforgivable damage to the work. This was the 1890 version (published in 1955, edited by Nowak). When Haas came to edit the work in the 1930s he made an amalgamation of the two versions according to what he thought Bruckner would have come up with had he been left to his own devices. His edition, though used by many leading conductors, is now regarded with such disfavour by Bruckner scholars that it no longer appears in the standard English-language reference book of orchestrations.[*] In Georg's

---
[*]    David Daniels, *Orchestral Music: A Handbook*, Fourth edition. Scarecrow Press, Lanham, USA, 2005.

opinion Nowak was a scientist, a literalist who printed Bruckner's alterations because they were there, whether they made musical sense or not. To William Carragan, who considers the scholarship of Robert Haas to be in many instances (including the Eighth Symphony) suspect to the point of worthlessness, he wrote:

> Anybody who knows about the inner proportions of a work of art cannot possibly believe that Bruckner intended these barbaric cuts and reorchestrations to be anything else but temporary expedients. It is quite true that even Bruckner, with all his humility, occasionally stood up against the worst ministrations of his friends. So for me, who has been fortunate enough to conduct the 1887 and the Haas versions of Bruckner 8, it is absolutely clear that Professor Haas tried to distinguish between the things that Bruckner changed out of his own creative will and those changes that were forced upon him. I believe that Haas had the understanding and soul of an artist, while to me Nowak was a very conscientious bureaucrat. And I must confess to you that I shall conduct the Nowak [1890] version of No. 8 most reluctantly if I am forced to do so.
>
> I personally love the 1887 version, but I would be the last to deny that Bruckner made some substantial improvements, like the clarinet fifth at the beginning of the symphony, or the Trio. I recommend all who doubt that Bruckner's confidence and belief in himself was shattered after the rejection of the first version to read his letters, where he writes as though he would be a completely useless amateur who committed the crime of writing his symphony the way he did.[4]

Georg subsequently decided that the 1890 version was such a travesty that he would refuse to record it at all. Nor was he entirely happy with Haas's version, and he told me that if he had time he would make an edition himself. He never did.

On Monday morning, 23 September 1996, the first recording session for the Eighth was scheduled for ten o'clock. The time came and went with no sign of the producer, and after several hours of frantic phone calls he was found in America. He had been given incorrect dates. All that could be done until Chris

Craker could return from London was for an Irish Radio (RTE) producer to roll tape while Georg conducted long stretches of the symphony and the orchestra grew increasingly frustrated. Craker arrived just in time for the morning session on the third and final day. This monumental work with a duration of an hour and a half was recorded in just five and a half hours. Georg left Dublin unsatisfied with the Adagio, which he thought was lacking the necessary feeling. As he considered it one of the two greatest slow movements ever written (the other is in Beethoven's Ninth) he was very disappointed.

After the recording was released many expressed puzzlement that he should have done the 1887 version, and inferred that he preferred it to the others. It was never meant to be his only recording of the Eighth; he merely wanted to start with this version because he thought a lot of it and it was almost never recorded. He was keen to do the Haas version as soon as possible, not least to improve on the Adagio. I suggested to the Scottish National that Georg perform it in concert, after which Naxos could record it, thereby sharing the cost of bringing four Wagner tubas from London. They were very interested, but they never found a date.

The Fourth Symphony was recorded with the Scottish National the following month. The two days, 16 and 17 October, went perfectly, the first recording to pass without disruption. When much of the work had been taped Georg made a request to the musicians: they had played very beautifully but the first movement didn't have the necessary cosmic feeling; would they humour him by playing it one more time? They did, and at the end there was a long, moved silence. Georg had the performance he wanted. The Assistant Concertmaster, Bill Chandler, recalls,

> he would give us so much space and time that it would almost seem like he wasn't actually really in control of what was going on with the orchestra...But I think really what his intention was, was to let the music breathe and to give it lots of space. I think in Bruckner that was just vital to make the music come alive, and that space and that sense of freedom gave the orchestra a certain amount of relaxation. Because he's not over-beating and because he's not dictating anything with his conducting, his hands are up in the air – open palms – and it's almost as if he's cradling something and just caressing

it gently. What happens is that the concentration level rises
in the orchestra and because everything's not being given
to them the listening is increased and the whole dynamic of
everybody working together really comes to the fore. And I
think that's where his strength was as a conductor. He knew
how an orchestra breathed, he knew how an orchestra needed
to listen, and to play together, and he just gave this certain
amount of pacing that allowed all of that to happen.[5]

Georg spent the last weeks of 1996 writing liner notes for the
Bruckner recordings. As he was never entirely comfortable with
English he found the process something of a trial, and he was
annoyed that I had suggested it to Naxos. In the middle of January
he recorded the filler for the Eighth Symphony recording, the
Symphony in D minor, 'Die Nullte' or No. 0, with the National
Symphony Orchestra of Ireland. 'The orchestra was generally co-
operative and helpful', he reported to Klaus Heymann, 'though
I thought they were not terribly enthusiastic; perhaps they were
tired. There was not the same spirit that I have found both times
in Glasgow, but then the Scottish National is exceptional in both
ability and interest.' Although Heymann's intention had been to
record the early symphonies in Dublin, he replied that all five
remaining recordings would be made with the Scottish National.
Perhaps he had heard about Georg's earlier difficulties in Dublin,
or perhaps he had superior intuition. Whatever the reason, Georg
was pleased and relieved.

Late in February 1997 Georg spent four weeks conducting *The
Magic Flute* at the Academy. Hong Kong was one of his favourite
places, and the only place he visited professionally where he willingly went sightseeing. He loved the pressing crowds, the vegetable
markets, the noise, the energy. He loved going to the Peak on
the no. 15 bus, full of young people shouting excitedly. We went
there often to take the path around the top of the mountain, an
hour-long walk in the forest, high above the skyscrapers and dirty
air. On free days we went to Lamma Island, where there were no
cars, and it offered relief from the city's relentless jackhammers
and pile drivers. The ferry pulled in to a fishing village, and at the
end of the jetty we climbed steep stairs to a hilltop pathway. On
both sides was small cemetery, where the cremated were buried

with the best possible view of the South China Sea. In a small pagoda-like shelter almost hidden in long grass we sat looking over to Lantau Island, shrouded in haze, and did something rare: we conversed, quietly. Then we went down to the narrow lanes of the village, past outdoor fish restaurants to a vegetarian café run by expatriate hippies. Georg protested only mildly when I ate there, and was grateful that the owners gave him no trouble when he shyly produced his lunchbox.

We both liked Hong Kong so much that already in 1995 I had asked Anthony Camden if he might be able to find Georg a job. He was very interested, because he was trying to establish a new position, Head of Orchestra Studies. We waited hopefully for a couple of years but the position was never funded, and when Hong Kong was returned to China in 1997 any possibility of a Western-music position disappeared.

In Glasgow in May Georg recorded Bruckner's Seventh Symphony (the Haas edition, without percussion), and then the Ninth Symphony, to replace the New Zealand recording. He used the standard three-movement version of the Ninth Symphony, refusing to consider either of the Finale completions made by others then available. To second-guess the thoughts and intentions of a great composer he thought a first-class effrontery. Heymann had sent Georg a concert tape of the Samale–Phillips–Mazzuca–Cohrs completion, hoping he would approve of it and record it. He refused even to listen to it.

> The already ailing Bruckner spent the last two years of his life trying frantically to complete the Finale of his Ninth. It is not meant cruelly when I say that I for one am glad that Fate did not grant him his wish, because the material intended for the Finale is just as unworthy of what is perhaps Bruckner's great-est music, just as was the case with Schubert's Eighth. The various efforts of the brilliant scholars who have recently made performing versions are of entirely historical interest. Similarly brilliant people (among them the great Felix Weingartner) completed Schubert's Eighth. Who plays that now?

Describing the final Adagio movement as 'a heartrending farewell to this world', he said, 'I for one do not want to hear anything after this most moving of all farewells...'[6]

Two days after returning from the summer workshop in Opava Dr Attia found yet another lump on Georg's neck, which was immediately removed. More worrisome was the scar tissue where the major surgery had been done, which was a hard mass of tangled nerves – if I touched his upper arm he would ask me not to touch his ear – that contained a scattering of cancer cells. Because surgery was pointless radiation was suggested again. Georg was against it, but I pleaded with him. After being assured by the oncologist that it would almost certainly not result either in deafness or brain damage he agreed, to please me. At the beginning of September, with many misgivings, Georg began four weeks of high-dose radiation to his neck.

The day before it ended he began rehearsing for the opening concert of the Symphony Nova Scotia season. Leslie Dunner, the music director, had a burst appendix and the orchestra, not even knowing Georg was ill, asked him to step in. The concert took place on 30 September, after an afternoon checkup in which the oncologist noted Georg's severe sore throat and 'bad dysphoria'. The program included Beethoven's Seventh Symphony (with all repeats); critic Stephen Pedersen thought the concert 'stunning' and the musicians remember the Beethoven to have been a wonderful, monumental performance, but a recording tells a different tale. The first two movements are filled with a dreadful tiredness; it was only in the last two movements that Georg rises above it – a triumph of spirit and determination. Five weeks later he conducted Schubert's 'Unfinished' symphony, a performance utterly unlike any other I have ever heard. This was Schubert, and Georg, confronting Death – staring into the void. In this interpretation there was no need for a third and fourth movement. There was nothing more to say.

In September Naxos released the first of his Bruckner recordings, the Fifth Symphony. Critical opinion was much more cordial than Georg expected. Anthony Hodgson, in the British magazine *Hi-Fi News & Record Review*, elected it Record of the Month: 'I found myself making comparisons with Karajan, Jochum, Wand and Furtwängler, finding that Tintner was bringing insights to the music worthy of any of those great names.'[7] *Gramophone* listed it as its top recommendation for a budget-priced Fifth, the French magazine *Répértoire* thought 'the internal logic of this interpretation is truly remarkable', and Michael Dervan in the *Irish Times* said: 'Octogenarian Georg Tintner, who impressed in Bruckner in Dublin last year, triumphs over glitches and adversities with a visionary clear-sightedness that's heart-warming.'[8] Georg was very relieved.

At the end of 1997 he made a two-week visit to Yale University, organised by Paul Hawkshaw, the Associate Dean of Music. Until he played in the Fifth Symphony at Georg's National Youth Orchestra in 1974, Hawkshaw had never heard a note of Bruckner; the impact on him was so enormous that in time he became a leading Bruckner scholar. He brought Georg to Yale to conduct the program that had started it all: the 'No. 5 in B flat' symphonies of Schubert and Bruckner (a total of 105 minutes of music). The day before the concert I asked Georg idly if he were intending to conduct from memory. 'Acch – don't be ridiculous!' he replied. Yet the next morning, to the admiration of all, he conducted the dress rehearsal from memory, and the concert that evening. When I commented on it afterwards he said accusingly, 'I wasn't going to. But *you* made me do it!' Memorising the last movement of Bruckner's Fifth, he said, was more difficult than memorising the whole of *La Bohème*.

Unlike most conductors who memorise, Georg did not 'read' the score as he conducted, eyes closed. His memory was not photographic but harmonic and structural.

> I have not a visual memory at all. But what I *do* have is far more important. That is an intuition *why* the music goes the way it does go. And I can only have this intuition with great pieces of music that I can love, and understand. So, music I don't like I find extremely difficult to retain in my memory, because I don't know *why* it goes where it does go – because to me it could go somewhere else. A masterpiece never could do that, it *must* go *just there*, and I know that before it happens.[9]

A piece such as Mozart's 'Linz' Symphony, No. 36, he conducted relatively rarely because he found it very difficult to memorise. He said one could see it had been written in a hurry, because the construction was not quite perfect.

He studied in meticulous detail. He would notice there was a certain staccato mark in the exposition that was not there in the recapitulation, and he would spend days pondering its possible significance. He sometimes found wrong notes even in standard items of the repertoire (among them Donizetti's *Don Pasquale*, Strauss's *Metamorphosen* and the Brahms *Haydn Variations*). So intently did he study scores that he sometimes fell into a type of trance; to all appearances he had fallen asleep. Observers found it unnerving; but he would jerk back to life as if nothing had happened. He also claimed that he had only so much room in his brain, and therefore to memorise a new piece of music he had to put another one out. So he said, but one day in 1996 he sang to me the tune of the Hungarian national anthem which he had not heard since he sang it with the Vienna Boys' Choir in Budapest in 1928.

Georg thought his memory for non-musical things was not particularly good, but it was not so. He remembered what interested him, and nothing more. He could remember the phone numbers of his girlfriends, but not his own, certainly not in Halifax. He was never quite sure of the address either. But he could remember the location of every greengrocer in any town even thirty years after he had last been there.

Early in 1998 we went to Australia for Esmeralda's wedding in Sydney, and for a February concert with David Helfgott at the sold-out Cultural Centre in Brisbane. Much had changed for David since Georg had seen him the last time, playing in a Brisbane restaurant with a cigarette drooping from his mouth. His life story had been turned into the enormously successful movie *Shine* and he was touring the world, surrounded by groupies, performing to rapturous adulation. Everywhere he played the Rachmaninov Third Concerto, the putative cause of his London breakdown, to show his triumph over adversity. The rehearsals went well; he kept his eyes fixed on Georg and was note perfect. But at the concert he ran in front of the beat in the first minute, and although it came together again the performance never settled.

Five weeks at the Academy in Hong Kong followed, where Georg conducted Puccini's *Suor Angelica* and *Gianni Schicchi*. In the middle of rehearsals we learned that his recording of Bruckner's Second Symphony was to be an Editor's Choice in the May issue of *Gramophone* magazine: 'It is a beautifully shaped performance, characterfully played and vividly recorded...shrewd and affectionate, tellingly phrased and beautifully paced...an exceptional record.'[10] The American magazine *Fanfare* concurred: 'The Irish band plays for him as if divinely inspired; this immediately takes its place in the first rank of Bruckner Second recordings, regardless of price or edition.'[11] The recording was released at the same time as the Sixth Symphony, which received similar reviews; the leading Swedish magazine *Musik och Ljudteknik* went as far as to nominate it 'the most satisfactory version on record ever'.[12]

Early in May Georg went to Prince George, a mill town in central British Columbia, to make a fund-raising recording for Paul Mahr, who was now the music director of the Prince George Symphony. On a free day they went for a walk in the woods:

> Georg remarked that he didn't know if he was any good as a conductor, something he had said to me once or twice in the past, but this time was different. Normally he would respond in a sort of stage persona voice with this type of statement, but on this occasion it was just the man. He talked about the importance of his composition and then dismissed that too. He said he just wanted to sit in his garden in Australia, because it was hot, there were birds, and because it brought him so much pleasure to just pick a piece of fruit off of a tree when he was hungry. It is a lovely picture.
>
> What was clear was that he didn't really care about conducting anymore, and also had given up on composition. He just wanted peace.[13]

I think it more likely that by that time Georg was trying to reconcile himself to the likelihood that he would do neither again. He was now conducting a mere four or five concerts a year; nobody seemed to want him anymore.

While he was in Prince George I was in Australia, and I made sure to return on 27 May, to be with Georg on our twentieth wedding anniversary. I asked him cheerfully if he knew what day it was. As I expected, he looked puzzled. When I told him he grimaced dismissively, shrugged, and said nothing. The subject was not mentioned again. I suppose he felt he had nothing to celebrate. It was not long afterwards that he said, and I no longer remember the context, '*You* are not important. *I* am the important person in this marriage.' At the time I considered walking out and staying away for a week, but decided against it; he was too sick. In retrospect his statement seems only very sad. Only a man desperate to reassert himself as artist and superman could have said such a thing.

The annual summer opera workshop was this time in the Slovak city of Košice. We had only one night in Vienna on the way home, and the next morning at breakfast I remarked that it was a pity we were leaving so soon. There was a special exhibition of Egon Schiele's paintings showing in nearby Tulln. It also seemed a shame that Georg had never been to St Florian, the monastery near Linz where Bruckner had been the organist for seven years, and where he is buried. When we arrived at the airport we discovered our flights had been mixed up and we had two more days in Vienna.

Those two days turned out to be among the happiest of our years together. Georg must have decided to make the best of it and make it special for me, for as soon as we returned to the hotel he said, 'We are going to a restaurant for lunch.' He even knew the location of a vegetarian establishment, close to the Volksoper in the Währingerstrasse. He did his best not to look unhappy, eating food he didn't like and struggling with a fork. It was so long since he had used one he hardly remembered what to do with it. After lunch we took a train to Tulln and walked along the Danube to the Minorite monastery where the Schiele paintings were on show. One of them showed a nun and a priest kneeling on the floor, facing each other closely with their robes wrapped around them and their knickers around their ankles. Georg cackled with delight. Seeing such a blasphemous painting hanging in a monastery had made his day.

The next day, hot and sunny again, we went to Linz and took a bus several kilometres out of town to the monastery of St Florian, peaceful and free of tourists that day. Strangely, Georg was uncomfortable in this musically hallowed site. We noticed there was to be a recital on Bruckner's own organ at one o'clock, which would give us an opportunity to hear the sound (and its decay) that Bruckner wrote into his symphonies. We waited in the coolness of the church, alone but for the organist practising. As I stood in the nave looking at the organ in the loft at the back, Georg came up to me and said, quite seriously, the most surprising statement I ever heard him make: 'You must never turn your back on the altar.'

When the poorly played recital was over I asked him if he wanted to take the earlier or later bus back to Linz. 'I want to go now,' he replied, 'I want to get out of here. It's too Catholic.' We waited hours in the blistering sun, for what nobody told us was that the bus deposited passengers at the monastery but didn't pick up there. The sun was setting by the time we took the train back to Vienna. As we went through the stations Georg declaimed their names, delighting in the sounds. 'Purkersdorf!' he exclaimed. 'Rekawinkel!' In those two days he didn't once look at a score. He had made them everything I could want.

## Thirty-two

Georg recorded the remaining three Bruckner symphonies in Glasgow at the end of August 1998, which were the Third, the First, and the early Study Symphony in F minor sometimes known as No. 00. He had never performed any of them – the Study Symphony he had never even heard. He chose the 1873 original edition of the Third Symphony, the longest and 'much the best of the three versions'. Of the other two, 1877 and 1889, Georg considered the latter almost as much a travesty as the 1890 version of the Eighth Symphony.

For most of the symphonies of Bruckner (indeed, of most composers) he favoured the composer's first thoughts, with the exception of the Fourth. In the case of Bruckner's First Symphony, he was recording an 1866 version even earlier than the so-called first ('Linz') version. I had suggested it to him because it would be of considerable musicological value, and in keeping with his preference for 'first thoughts'. When the recording sessions were first arranged a performable edition did not even exist, but I knew that William Carragan would be able to assemble one from Robert Haas's critical notes. Georg didn't want to do it, and would not explain why. I suspect he thought the material couldn't be prepared in time, and he couldn't risk postponing the recording. I persuaded him to do it by promising to look after all the correspondence.

Just three weeks before the recording date, a question arose as to the pitch of some trumpet notes in the Finale. Bill Carragan noted that in Bar 216 the trumpets played E flat in the 1877 'Linz' version but D in Haas's critical notes for the 1866 version. He also noted that in the second half of Bar 376 Haas said that 'all parts' that play C in the 1877 version should play B in the early version, yet when he then listed the individual instruments to which it applied he didn't mention the trumpets. Georg wrote to Bill:

In both Trumpet cases it is clear to me that Haas was right. In 216 the E-flat in Flute and Oboe is a suspension resolved to D in the middle of the bar (such cases are not rare, and [in 376] it is obvious to me that the trumpets STAY on the C (pedal point) that is also quite frequent!...[1]

I am still of the opinion that Haas omitted to mention the trumpets [in 376] intentionally, because I would be very surprised if it was Bruckner's intention to let the trumpets play in octaves the leading note going to the tonic, which is a very different thing from the single instruments that he did stipulate. It wouldn't be the only case that Bruckner stayed on a pedal point while the rest of the harmony changes. In any case I promise (though time will be very short) to try the octave doubling of the leading note if I am not as convinced as I am now that the trumpets, especially as they have played the Cs for quite a while, shouldn't stay there during the diminished seventh chord, thereby anticipating the following tonic. I think it is a good sign that we can worry about things like this, and it certainly is a case where opinions can differ.[2]

The questions troubled Bill so much that, five days before we left for Glasgow, he drove over 500 kilometres to consult Paul Hawkshaw's microfilm of the original parts. Bill remarked to Paul in passing that the point was so minuscule and so much else was going on in the orchestra at that moment that Georg would likely not notice the difference if the trumpet part weren't corrected. Paul told him he wouldn't want to bet his house on it. In the event, Georg was right on both counts. Bill wrote, 'You can imagine my feeling yesterday when I saw the *real notes* in the copyist Schimatschek's beautiful hand looking up at me. Theophany! Truth! It didn't matter a bit who had said what – now we knew. I wouldn't have missed this experience for anything.'[3] When I told Georg what Bill had found, his eyes flooded with tears of relief. 'What's all this about?' I asked him, surprised. 'You know everything about Bruckner.'

'I *don't* know everything about Bruckner,' he said. 'But I know something about music!'

While we were in Glasgow Georg's recording of Symphonies Nos. 8 and 0 was released. *The Times* praised Georg's 'majestic, surely-paced conducting', and added that he was becoming talked about in Great Britain, 'deservedly so, for his Bruckner series is interpretatively in the first league'. I took Georg to a large record retailer in Sauchiehall Street where, to our astonishment, two dozen copies were displayed on the 'Best Sellers' wall in the company of Charlotte Church and Andrea Bocelli. The recording went on to appear in 'Best of 1998' listings in several leading newspapers and CBC Radio's In Performance; it was nominated for a Cannes Classical Award, and was listed in the 1999 edition of the Penguin Record Guide as Edward Greenfield's 'Editor's Personal Choice'.

In only a year Georg had gone from obscurity to more fame than we had ever imagined. 'Nothing succeeds like success, Tany,' he said. His recordings were becoming a worldwide triumph, regarded by many as the ideal recordings for winning converts to Bruckner. When Georg filled out a questionnaire in 1976 for a dictionary of wartime émigrés one of the questions was: 'Of what achievements in your life are you most proud?' Georg wrote miserably: 'Of *none*. But perhaps my Violin-Sonata my *Ellipse* for Soprano and Stringquartet are a small justification for my existence, also my missionary work on three continents for the Music of Bruckner.'[4] This ambition, at least, he achieved beyond his wildest dreams. The pity is that he didn't live long enough to see the extent of it.

On 7 September when the recordings were completed, Georg did a number of interviews in London with the leading music magazines and the BBC. Naxos staff took us to dinner in Finsbury Park, and as we left the restaurant I was struck by a chill presentiment. I asked Matthew Freeman, the director of Artists and Repertoire, when Naxos intended to record the Bruckner masses and other choral works, and added, out of Georg's hearing, 'Nobody lasts forever.' Freeman replied that the 1999 recording schedule was already full so it would be at least 2000 before anything could be done. Georg heard this, and though he said nothing I could see that he knew he had just made his last recording.

On 15 September, a week after returning home, Georg consulted Dr Attia about another lump on the right side of his neck. He had noticed it in Glasgow and it was causing him some pain. Dr Attia wasn't unduly worried, as he had removed several similar lumps, all with some melanoma cells encased in hard fibrous material. He arranged for the lump to be excised, and Georg presented himself at Day Surgery on 24 September. It was more than two hours before Dr Attia came to find me. The lump was large, a centimetre in diameter, and this time it wasn't harmless. It was full of a new and aggressive form of melanoma. Dr Attia touched my shoulder and left the room without another word.

The next day I went secretly to the hospital to ask what we could now expect. Dr Attia said that he could not excise all of the lump because it was wrapped around the main nerve to Georg's right arm. The likely progress of the disease was that within six months or so his arm would become paralysed (it occurred to me that Georg should have no trouble conducting with his left arm because he was, after all, originally left-handed). The melanoma could be expected to metastasise, and the usual destinations were the liver, bones or brain. I kept this to myself.

On 22 October Georg was made a Member of the Order of Canada at Rideau Hall in Ottawa. Many of the other recipients, almost as old as Georg, hobbled uncertainly to the front when their names were called. Tears came to my eyes when Georg's name was called and he leapt to his feet, striding quickly and purposefully forward. Despite the tumour eating away at him, he remained courageous, indefatigable.

The next day Matthew Freeman reported that Georg was to be featured on the front cover of *Gramophone* magazine in January – the *ne plus ultra* of publicity and recognition for a classical musician.

But more important to Georg than either of these accolades was a performance of his Violin Sonata, by Philippe Djokic and Lynn Stodola, on 1 November in Halifax. To Georg's great disappointment they played only the first movement because they ran out of rehearsal time, but he was warmed by the audience's enthusiasm. The next day he began rehearsing for a tour of *Der Kaiser von Atlantis*, the opera composed by Viktor Ullmann to a libretto by Petr Kien, while both were incarcerated at Theresienstadt. They were rehearsing the work when they were sent to their deaths at Auschwitz. The tour was the idea of a small group of women in Halifax who were inspired to present the opera after hearing a lecture on it. Georg agreed to conduct on condition they not pay him; he could not take money for it when his own relatives had died in the camps.

*Georg at his investiture as a Member of the Order of Canada in 1998, with the Governor General, the Rt Hon. Roméo LeBlanc, Mrs Diana LeBlanc and Tanya.*

They hired young professional singers, and musicians mostly from Symphony Nova Scotia. They found a producer in Montreal, Tibor Egervari, a Hungarian refugee who had also lost relatives in the camps, who created a minimalist but inspired production. The first performance took place at Dalhousie University on 11 November, Remembrance Day, to a deeply moved capacity audience. The rest were given in Wolfville, Fredericton, Charlottetown and Antigonish. Everyone knew they were participating in something very important; Tibor described it afterwards as 'a life-altering experience'.

In the same month Georg received an invitation to conduct the Yomiuri Orchestra at the Suntory Hall in Tokyo, his first engagement resulting from the Bruckner recordings. Two concerts were arranged for mid-2000, to include Bruckner's Fourth and Seventh symphonies. It was the start of the career Georg had always longed for – his time had come at last.

By then he had severe pain in his right shoulder, and tingling in his right arm. For the first time the disease was detected on the left side of his mouth, in the gums. Palliative care doctors prescribed a series of drugs, each one treating the side effects of the other. Despite still believing that all pain could be controlled by willpower and working harder, Georg did what he was told. But the medication didn't help, and he was worse with it than without. I insisted he give it up, which he did willingly. As none of the treatments seemed to be working, I tried some elements of Gerson Therapy, an alternative treatment that seemed to be based on some reasonable science: that boosting the immune system should assist the body in rejecting melanoma. Freshly pressed organic fruit and vegetable juices had to be drunk every waking hour. Until he died I made him seven or eight each day; they didn't save his life, but the extra 600 or so daily calories caused him to put on weight, and for the first time in his vegetarian life he lost his underfed, ascetic appearance.

Almost the only time I spent away from him now was an hour each morning at a café ('When are you going to your horror?') – my sanity break. As a concession Georg always came to fetch me. If I was still reading the newspaper he would jiggle his knees and fidget and heave mournful sighs. 'Haven't you finished yet?' It was the background music he detested, which for him was always foreground music. Not only could he analyse every chord progression instantly in any piece of music he heard, but he was compelled to do so, and the primitiveness of café music was more than he could stand.

At the end of November we spent a few days in Tübingen visiting Paul and Eva Hoffmann. Paul was ill, and I wanted Georg to see him again before it was too late. While we were there the *New York Times* ran a lengthy article entitled 'A Thinking Man's Bruckner', by Lawrence B. Johnson:

> Through five symphonies, Georg Tintner, an eighty-one-year-old conductor born in Vienna, casts Bruckner's grand, emotionally charged structures in a refreshing light of restraint and proportion. Reflected back is an aura of honest affection and with it a paradoxical exchange: a beguiling intellectual beauty where one often finds a cloistered spirituality.[5]

Recognition in such an august publication was a coup for both Georg and for Naxos.

*Paul Hoffmann and Georg discussing German literature at breakfast (late 1998). Georg, almost never without a score, has brought Sibelius's Seventh Symphony to the table.*

A few weeks later *Gramophone* magazine was published with Georg on the cover. At the same time his Bruckner Fourth, the first recording he was satisfied with, was released to dream reviews. Ates Orga in *BBC Music Magazine* rated it 'the current digital version to have'.[6] Michael Kennedy in the *Sunday Telegraph* said, 'He is clearly a Bruckner interpreter and champion of considerable magnitude...The interpretation and performance will come as a revelation even to devout Brucknerians who already have their preferred version.'[7] Andrew Achenbach, in *Gramophone*, referred to 'the selfless integrity and glowing humanity of Tintner's clear-sighted way with this music,'[8] and Robert McColley in *Fanfare* said: 'This is, by a considerable measure, the most spiritually elevated Bruckner Fourth that I have ever heard.'[9]

In January 1999 Georg conducted Symphony Nova Scotia in a Scandinavian program that included Sibelius's Symphony No. 7 – a work he privately said he was never quite sure how to conduct, but Stephen Pedersen's review said that Georg 'had worked his old magic' and the performance was 'unforgettable'. Nobody noticed anything wrong with him either then or at his Baroque concert on 7 February. Franz came from Cleveland to hear the concerts, one of several visits he made each year. I never looked forward to them, because when they were over Georg would tell me that Franz was a saint. He chose to live in penury, boarding with friends, shopping only at yard sales, and lending his money to persons he considered deserving cases. '*I* would like to give all my money away,' Georg said to me accusingly, ignoring the fact that Franz expected his loans to be repaid, and never forgot a debt even of sixty years' standing – 'but it's *you* who is stopping me!'

Hephzibah, now living in Berlin, also came for a few days. She asked Georg a little about his early life, and about his composing, the first time she had shown interest in the father she had never really known. Georg was intensely, almost pathetically, grateful. A few weeks later, shortly before he left for Australia, Hephzibah phoned him, asking how he was feeling. They chatted for a few minutes, and suddenly Georg said fervently, 'I love you! I love you! I miss you! I think of you all the time!'

His effusion was out of character and I remarked on it, foolishly adding, 'You've never said anything like that to me.' He was taken aback. 'But she's my daughter!' he said. A dreadful thought struck me, and I said, 'Perhaps you haven't said anything like that because you don't love me.' Georg said nothing. He never told lies, not even white ones; he evaded destructive truths with silence. I began to feel sick. 'If you want Eunice or Mercia to come and look after you, then I will go away, if that's what you want,' I said, and I meant it, though I also knew that these women were interested in a famous conductor, not a sick old man. Georg replied, 'I don't love them either.'

It was like an earthquake. I had always taken as given that in spite of everything Georg loved me. Had our life together been all this time a monstrous misunderstanding, a marriage with no foundation? There was nothing more to be said; I left the room. On particularly black and hopeless days during the next few months, as Georg became more and more ill, I wondered what it had all been for. A shameful thought, but one thinks many things in desperate times, and not all of them are kind.

Just after the Baroque concert Robert King's wife Karla called in the middle of the night to tell us he had died of a stroke. The next morning Georg made no comment but wrote on a sheet of paper:

~~Robert~~
Paul
Georg
Franz

He said it was the order in which he and his closest friends would die. He was right.

In March the Bruckner Seventh was released, again to glowing reviews. As they were appearing Georg was consulting a new doctor, Dr Nasser, who was conducting clinical trials for a new treatment for head cancers. Conventional treatments had little to offer Georg and all that remained was experimental. Applications to the hospital Ethics Board, the provincial health board and the drug company had to be made first, which would take some weeks. We spent them in Australia, where on 23 April Georg conducted a concert with the orchestra of the Queensland Conservatorium – Mozart's *Impresario* Overture and Clarinet Concerto, and Bruckner's Fourth Symphony; 115 minutes of music. A film of the performance shows Georg using a minimum of movement, the vigorous arm gestures of the past no longer possible and replaced by an intensity of will reminiscent of the late conducting of Otto Klemperer. The concert had been arranged in conjunction with the conferring of an honorary doctorate by Griffith University. Of all the awards he received, this one meant the most to him: Australia had at last recognised the contribution he had made.

Before leaving Brisbane he sorted out his small collection of manuscripts, some smaller pieces and fragments of completed works. The sight of it reduced him to abject misery and he told me to throw most of it away. I put it in a safe place. We went to visit my parents in Canberra, and it was there that we heard of the death of Paul Hoffmann on 2 May. It was a terrible blow. Georg said nothing, only stood looking out of the kitchen window. He knew he was next. It was important to him to see as many of his children as he could before he left Australia, and in Sydney the following week he managed to see Boris, Paul and Esmeralda. At the last minute, when we were at the airport, Demas arrived. Georg had not seen him for many years. They talked of inconsequential things, and of politics on which they took opposing positions. Demas spoke in his tough-Aussie manner, Georg spoke politely, but there was respect and gentleness between them. Georg never saw any of his children again.

## Thirty-three

By the time we returned to Halifax on 13 May, Georg was inter-
mittently using morphine; he saw it as yet another of his failures.
On 25 May we saw Dr Nasser and Dr Attia about the experimental
treatment, which had now been approved. Georg told them he did
not wish to live at any cost, and that he wanted to live 'only while
I am useful'. Nobody knew what to say. 'Useful' in Georg's view
meant that he could still produce music. His entire sense of identity
was as a musician, and if he wasn't a musician he was nothing. As
we left the consulting room Dr Attia commented on the remarkably slow progression of Georg's illness, which he attributed to
his positive attitude. Out in the street Georg said, 'I *don't* have a
positive attitude. I just keep going.' How true it was. But he had
not lost his old defiance. The offices of the pathologist who had
misdiagnosed him in 1993 were situated between our apartment
and the concert hall, and every so often as we walked past Georg
would say loudly, 'Hullo Spezi!* I'm not dead *yet!*'

The experimental procedure was performed on 25 June. What
we did not know was that the neck tumour was now between
three and five centimetres in diameter; but 'surprisingly he has
quite good function of his right arm and hand'. The predicted
paralysis had not come to pass, and never did. Two hours after the
procedure Georg was discharged. By evening he was in such pain
that he was hallucinating. I made many calls to the resident on
duty but she refused to admit him; just give him more morphine,
more this, more that, she said. Early the next morning I took
Georg to the hospital and said we were not leaving under any
circumstances. They admitted him and gave him a knockout dose
of morphine. That he had this much pain was unexpected, but
equally unexpected was the effect of the treatment itself. In the

---

\*    Austrian nickname form of *Spezialfreund*, bosom buddy.

three days he was in hospital the tumour on his neck appeared to collapse in on itself.

Encouraged by this spectacular success I wrote to Matthew Freeman at Naxos, asking if the recording of the Bruckner Masses could be scheduled as soon as possible. Within a short time he found a suitable choir and orchestra in England. Georg had already been offered more Bruckner concerts: in Berne, Vancouver, more in Tokyo – and now it all looked possible.

While Georg was in hospital I found a review in *Stereophile* magazine by David Patrick Stearns, comparing recordings of Bruckner's Fourth Symphony by Nikolaus Harnoncourt, Otto Klemperer and Georg. He wrote:

> Perhaps the most all-inclusive interpretation yet to appear is that of Vienna-born Georg Tintner, who is having a recording Indian Summer not unlike Günther Wand's. But while Wand always seems like a Kapellmeister whose depth has evolved simply from his having survived so long, Tintner delivers something essential to Bruckner that I've never heard so consistently: a sense of musical narrative...One still senses the long-delayed arrival of a Brucknerian performance outlook that takes the composer for what he is, not what well-meaning interpreters throughout the century have wanted him to be...[1]

I ran to the hospital and read it to him joyfully. He looked out over the treetops and said, 'It's all too late, Tany...'

Georg was sent home on 29 June. Two days later he suddenly stopped eating. I took him to Emergency, and after a six-hour wait he was treated for dehydration. For the next few days he seemed better, and was looking forward to a visit from Franz. But as soon as he arrived Georg took to his bed and stayed there for the duration of the visit. He got up only for a check-up with Dr Nasser, who was delighted with the way Georg's tumour continued to shrink. After a week or so Franz left, and as we walked home from the bus station Georg stopped, and said desperately, 'I feel like I'm dying.' I was stunned. But why? The tumour was shrinking better than anyone had thought possible. Surely there was hope?

Because the treatment had caused damage in his mouth, he was given a gastric feeding tube. Georg hated that I had to clean his wounds, and hated even more that I had to tend to his feeds, and carry home heavy boxes of baby milk. What he had sworn he would never allow to happen had come to pass after all: I was his nurse. I think he was surprised I wanted to look after him – Georg the man, not the artist. He took to saying mournfully, 'I don't think you even like me any more.' But what was the right amount of concern to show in such circumstances? Did I hide my fear too well and act too cheerfully? I did so not to frighten him, but did he think I didn't care? One afternoon, as we were walking to the supermarket, Georg said it again, and I begged him not to because it was both untrue and upsetting. But this time I added, without aforethought, 'Besides, that is funny, coming from you, who doesn't love me,' Georg looked puzzled. 'Don't you remember "I don't love you either"?' I said. Georg stopped dead and said sheepishly, 'I don't think I meant that.' I was so overcome with relief that I didn't think to ask him why he had said it at all.

Day after day he sat slumped in an armchair, gazing listlessly at the television he despised. One day I had to take a bus across the harbour and, trying to be bright and cheery, I suggested Georg wave to me from our balcony as I waited at the bus stop below. Instead of going inside again quickly as I expected, he stood for a long time just looking out. How strange, I thought. What is he thinking about?

What remained of the tumour had become a problem. Poking out of his neck was a very thick black scab several centimetres wide, atop a stem of necrotised tissue that had begun to putrefy. On 9 September Dr Attia removed the tissue and replaced it with a skin graft, taken from Georg's thigh. When he woke two hours later he refused to wear an oxygen monitor and said to the nurses, 'I want to die.'

Back at home, on Sunday 19 September, standing in the hallway, Georg said, 'I want to die. I want to jump over. I want you to help me.' Those words shattered the hope I had clung to for more than six years. I rushed into the bedroom and burst into tears, crouching at my desk so he couldn't see them. Georg blurted out, 'You're a wonderful person.' But after two decades of hearing hardly a loving word, I didn't understand.

'You don't have to be nasty,' I said bitterly.

'What?' he replied, bewildered.

TANYA BUCHDAHL TINTNER

'You don't have to be ironic!' I shouted, but he had already wandered away. I remained at my desk, tears dripping into my lap.

Georg began saying he couldn't breathe through his nose, yet no amount of investigation could find any blockage. His lovely handwriting became almost illegible, and he began to lose words, running out of them mid-sentence, dropping his head in confusion. And then he couldn't tell the time. On 25 September he did a studio interview with Howard Dyck, host of the CBC's *Saturday Afternoon at the Opera*, to be used as an introduction to a broadcast of Pfitzner's *Palestrina*. He was barely able to say a word. Sentences were broken up by agonisingly long pauses, and he seemed not to understand the questions. The heavily edited version played well enough a few days later, but it was a shadow of what he could once have done.

Every couple of days he went to the hospital to have the fragile skin graft dressed with an evil-smelling thick paste. He sat in the waiting room clutching the score of Bruckner's Fifth Symphony, which he was to conduct in Vancouver on 15 October. He was hardly able to read it any more, but keeping Bruckner close to him was a comfort.

He became unusually frightened of what the critics would say about his Bruckner Ninth recording. The reviews were slow to appear and he became convinced that all the critics hated it so much they were postponing saying so in print. On this he was completely mistaken, but he would never know. The first review appeared in the *Guardian* the day before he died, but it was just too late; I only saw it a few hours after he was gone. Tim Ashley called it a 'totally compelling performance' and gave it a five-star rating. A few days later the *Scotsman*'s critic, not realising Georg had died, wrote:

> Perhaps because age has given them the necessary insight and inner strength, the two greatest living Brucknerians are both in their eighties – Günter Wand…and now Georg Tintner… We should, perhaps, also thank Fate for this outstanding reading. Tintner's Bruckner cycle has won much praise, but this disc is its crowning glory.[2]

Those last two weeks of Georg's life were, in retrospect, dreamlike. We were never closer than at that time, though Georg remained almost silent. We went to Point Pleasant Park, and this time took a long walk over most of its paths and hills, not our usual short excursion to a bench overlooking the waters of the Northwest Arm. Every autumn since 1993 I had looked at the leaves making their exuberantly coloured farewell and wondered if Georg would be alive to see them the following year.

We went again to the hospital to have his skin graft dressed and as we walked into the grounds, Georg trailing a little behind me as always, he suddenly reached forward and clutched my hand. In that instant his equanimity, his bravery, deserted him. He was overcome with terror. When the nurses peeled off the dressing they noticed that the skin graft was not taking. It was likely due to the radiation treatment two years before; Georg had been right not to want it.

He continued to claim he couldn't breathe through his nose, and Dr Attia ordered a CT scan for the following week. I returned in secret later that day to ask if the scan could include the rest of his head – Georg was by then very confused and more or less aphasic, and I feared the melanoma had spread to his brain. He began saying, every few days, 'I wish Hephzibah would phone', which struck me as odd because there seemed no reason why he didn't call her himself.

On Monday 27 September he gave a concert in St Andrew's Church with Nova Sinfonia, a local part-amateur group. He made no mistakes and it went well. He even conducted some of it from memory, including a serenely beautiful *Siegfried Idyll*. At the end of the final work Georg turned to the audience and made a few remarks about the piece, his only complete sentences in more than a week. He bowed to the warm applause, then stepped off the podium for the last time.

On the last day of September, a warm and sunny day in an unusually benign autumn, he asked to go to the nearby Public Gardens. Sitting by the flowerbeds in the afternoon sun I discovered Georg knew a lot about dahlias. He seemed resigned, but somehow peaceful. The following day we went to the hospital for a dressing change; I noticed that a lump on the edge of the neck tumour site, left behind when the experiment was done, had started to grow. And the CT scan had to be done again. When it was over Georg rushed into the waiting room, panicked and almost incoherent. 'She pushed me!' he shouted. 'She pushed me down!' The technician had likely only tried to make him lie flat, but he seemed to be hallucinating. He ran from the hospital and went straight to bed.

The next morning, Saturday 2 October, I went to the market alone. Georg was still in a restless sleep from which he seemed unable to wake. By mid-morning he was trying to study a work by Pierre Mercure for a concert in Prince George in a week's time. The piece was simple, but he couldn't understand anything on the page. Finally he said, 'You had better call Paul Mahr and tell him I can't do the concert.' It was the first time Georg had ever cancelled a concert due to illness. I then gave him a haircut, to which he acquiesced without his usual protest. For lunch he ate much better than usual, which I thought a good sign. Afterwards I suggested he listen to the first edit of his Bruckner Third Symphony, which had just arrived. It was hopeless. He could only flip aimlessly through the pages of the score; nothing made any sense to him.

The phone rang at seventeen minutes to four. It was Hephzibah, and Georg spoke to her briefly, only a few words. He handed the phone to me and I spoke with her for a few more minutes. Georg returned to the kitchen, rather agitated, and took the phone again. 'Goodbye,' he said, 'and good luck.' He handed the phone back to me and left the room. I talked with Hephzibah some more, and as I was about to hang up there was a knock at the door. It was about a quarter past four. Two police officers stood there. 'What have I done?' I asked, very surprised. 'You haven't done anything,' the policewoman said. 'Do you live here with anyone?' 'Yes, my husband, he's here,' I said, and took them into the living room. But he wasn't there. And I knew immediately what he had done.

They told me that an elderly man had fallen from the eleventh floor and he was on his way to hospital. As far as they knew he was still alive.

As soon as Georg had said goodbye to Hephzibah he had gone to the balcony, stood on a chair left there for the summer and climbed over the railing. He twisted as he fell and he struck the one-inch-thick metal railing of the balcony beneath, hard enough to bend it. He fell through a small fir tree, narrowly avoiding impaling himself on the trunk, and landed face down in a garden bed. Newspapers reported the next day that he had survived because a branch had broken his fall, but he survived because he had landed on soil, and because, in spite of everything, he had an iron constitution. He was wearing only an old shirt and ragged underpants; at some point the ridiculous thought struck me that it was just like Georg to go out dressed not in the Pierre Cardin seconds I had bought him in Hong Kong but in an old pair full of holes.

The police took me to the hospital, shut me in a small, windowless room and questioned me to find out if I had pushed him. After an agonisingly long time they released me to the emergency room.

There are no words to describe the horror of seeing the broken body of someone you love. Georg's hair was matted with blood and fir needles, his right wrist, which was broken, was in a splint. He had several broken ribs, but he had not ruptured his bladder, spleen or right kidney, although they were not sure about the left. He seemed to be only barely unconscious, moving his left arm in vague gestures as if to fend people off. He looked to be in agony. I hoped from the bottom of my heart that he had never been really conscious, that he was not aware that he had failed in his mission.

Doctors were circling about him, shouting at him, telling him they were going to pierce the side of his chest to reinflate a collapsed lung. They did so and it seemed to cause distress. A resident told me Georg had cracked some bones in his neck, and some sort of decision was needed about what to do, but I had no idea what he was talking about, and nobody explained it. One of the doctors told me they could not get a response from Georg's legs because there was spinal damage. There was no obvious break, but they didn't know whether there was real damage to the spinal cord or merely bruising. For a while I massaged Georg's feet, but his legs remained inert.

Someone asked me what I wanted done. I said I wanted no heroic measures taken to prolong his life. Yet I wondered – Were his injuries treatable? Was I condemning him to death? But how could I wish him to live, however much *I* might want it, when he had wanted so much to end it all? How could I wish him to live when his worst nightmare had come true – that he might end his days in a wheelchair? I told him, in case he could hear me, that I would look after him – Didn't you know I would always look after you?

A resident told me to go to the Emergency waiting room. It seemed icy cold. An aide saw me shivering and brought me a blanket, but it didn't help. Someone brought me inside again. A supervisor asked me what she should tell the press. They had already sniffed out a good story and were hungry for details. I told her not to confirm that Georg was even in the hospital, let alone tell them his condition. Someone else took me to an office lit by a single desk lamp, and a few minutes later the chaplain came to offer me comfort. I said I was not religious and asked him politely to leave me alone. I said that I wanted instead to see Dr Attia, who had promised he would always be there if we needed him. A resident came to say it wasn't possible, but with newfound strength I insisted. At some point a nurse wrote on Georg's chart: 'Wife seems inward with her emotions.' But what did they expect? Screaming, sobbing, hysteria?

Dr Attia arrived, and he told me that the CT scan had shown that the cancer had not gone to Georg's brain. His strange behaviour of the past few weeks, his aphasia, his confusion, even his insistence on being unable to breathe, had been caused by morphine. It had rendered him delusional. But not about his decision to kill himself – that was entirely rational.

It was decided he would be taken to Intensive Care as soon as a bed became free, but first he would be given a CT scan to determine the extent of the spinal damage. I was taken to a small waiting room on the Intensive Care floor and left alone. It was dead silent.

Twenty or so minutes later the emergency doctor came into the room to tell me, I thought, that Georg had now arrived in the ward. Instead he told me Georg had died in the CT scan.

One always thinks that those who bring joy and inspiration to others should have earned the right to immortality, or at least an easeful death, but Georg was not afforded even that. His heart rate and blood pressure had crashed and they had been unable to revive him, despite – as I learned later to my infinite relief – all possible efforts. He was pronounced dead at 9.01 pm. The cause of death: multiple trauma.

The doctor took me to see him. He was back in Emergency but lying alone and forgotten, for the staff was already preparing for the next patient incoming, a road accident victim. A resident hovered close to my elbow as I leant over Georg, and told me I couldn't donate him to medical science because they wouldn't want him, just like his grandmother. I told him to go away and leave us alone.

Georg was already growing cold. There was no repose on his face – far from it. His eyes were half open, and his eyes, which had always been so full of expression, had nothing in them – not anything. I have never seen anything more horrifying. I talked to him for a little while, then I spread a blanket over him to keep him warm, and ran as fast as I could from the hospital.

## Epilogue

When the next day's newspaper splashed 'Tintner Dead in Fall' across the front page, many thought it was a mistake. There are some people who are so vibrantly alive that one can't believe they can ever be anything else. As the news spread around the world there was an outpouring of grief, very personal responses, even from people who knew him only from recordings. Dalhousie University flew the Canadian flag at half-mast for a week. A musician from Orchestra London Ontario wrote to his local newspaper:

> It was with sadness that I heard of the recent passing of the nationally known and respected conductor Georg Tintner, one of the finest musicians in Canada. It is with distress that I note his passing rated nary a mention in the *London Free Press*. On second thought, 'distress' is not strong enough. 'Disgust' is more like it…As conductor of an entire generation of young musicians in eight stints with the National Youth Orchestra, Tintner (it is a measure of the man that he rejected the title 'Maestro') provided an all-too-rare example of unsurpassed artistic integrity and musicianship, yet with exceptional humility. Among Canada's orchestral players, who too often observe the death of a conductor with little more than a feeling of quiet satisfaction, he will be missed.[1]

It may be the only time an orchestral musician has castigated a newspaper for failing to pay enough attention to a conductor.

Georg had said he wanted no funeral and no memorial so I donated his body to Dalhousie University for medical research. So many people wanted to pay their respects, however, that a tribute concert was arranged. Two performances were given on 24 October; over 2000 people filled the hall, more had to be turned away. At the end Symphony Nova Scotia played the piece Georg had wanted performed at his death, Mozart's Minuet and Country Dance K. 463 No. 1, with its 'perfect melody'. The auditorium was in darkness and the stage was lit only by the musicians' sconces. A spotlight fell on the empty podium.

Two years later the university returned Georg's ashes to me, and I took them to Australia and scattered them in the sea at Redcliffe early one morning. When I waded back to the shore I turned to look one more time and the surface of the sea was quivering and trembling in an inexplicable way. People say that such rituals bring comfort, but it brought me nothing of the kind. I felt I was abandoning him.

Many commentators, stunned, questioned in print how someone of Georg's 'vibrancy, enthusiasm and optimism' could have killed himself. Others wondered how such a gentle man could commit such violence. Those who knew him better knew it was entirely in character: a final grand Wagnerian gesture. He did it for two reasons, neither of them because he could not stand the pain. He refused just to 'crumble away', to 'disintegrate'. And he did it for me. He could not bear the idea that I would be only his nurse; he wanted to spare me that. He once said to me that I had given him my youth. He can only have felt guilt for not fulfilling his side of the 'bargain' by writing beautiful music for me. Perhaps he felt he had failed me – an idea I find quite unbearable. He taught me many things, about music and about life. He showed me what was important. I also know, now that I have come to the end of my journey, that it was I who failed him. The difference in our ages – thirty-six years – was just too much. I was too young and short of understanding for someone of his life experience, and it was understanding that he so desperately needed. By the time I had acquired some, it was too late. But, much worse, I failed to do my best, and that is unforgivable. What remains is regret, and the torment of wasted opportunities.

Georg succeeded in only one of his ambitions: to bring Bruckner's music to the masses (his recordings – 'the culminating achievement of his life, a tombstone of blazing intensity'[2] – have sold over 560,000 discs). He became more and more a relic from a vanished Romantic past; he was a survivor in whom something died. But he just kept going, because 'this frail and vulnerable plant' was too proud to do otherwise. In doing so he tried his best to lead a worthwhile and righteous life. He was kind to others, he trod lightly on the earth, he gave pleasure to many, and he served his gods truly.

# Acknowledgments

It was only when I began this book that I realised how little I knew about the first two-thirds of Georg's life. Researching it took me five years of interviews, phone calls, and visits to libraries and archives across several countries and continents. Along the way I was helped by countless people, especially in New Zealand, where Georg is still remembered fondly more than half a century after he left.

I am enormously grateful to the following individuals, who gave me information and/or shared with me their memories of Georg – some of them extremely personal. More than a few extended their generosity to include hospitality. Melodie Alderson, Robert Allman, Neville Amadio, Sam Atlas, Maja Bagley, Peter Baillie, Walter and Corin Fairburn Bass, Malcolm Batty, the late Dame Heather Begg, Jeffrey Bell-Hansen, the late Mizzi Bergel, Valerie Betteridge, the late Tessa Birnie, Rewa Bissett, the late Konny Blumenfeld and Gerti Blumenfeld, David Bollard, James Bonnefin, Sir Richard Bonynge, Gary Brain, Sue Branch, Michael Brimer, Donald and Pearl Britton, Chris Brodrick, Isobel Buchanan, Donald Burstein, the late Sir Frank Callaway, the late Anthony Camden, Joan Carden, Ruth Chick, James Christiansen and Marilyn Richardson, Roger Covell, the late Graeme Craw and Moira Craw, Margaret Crawford, Stephen Cronin, Robert Cuckson, Peter Dart, Robert Dawe, Gregory Dempsey, Grant Dickson, Jozef Drewniak, George Dreyfus, Graeme Edwards, Enid Evans, Megan Evans, Janis Fairburn, Robin Fazakerley,

Betty Fenton, Kevin Findlay, Malcolm Forsyth, Deirdre Foyster, Paul Frère, Clare Galambos-Winter, the late John Germain, Rolf Gjelsten, Barrie Greenwood, Valerie Griffiths, Jordan Grigg, Graeme Gummer, Paul Hawkshaw, David and Gillian Helfgott, William Hennessy, Jim Hessell, Dorothy Hitch, Richard Hoenich, Carl and Christl, Hoffmann, Eva Hoffmann, Frank and the late Joyce Hoffmann, Hugo and Alison Hoffmann, Richard Hoffmann, Michael Hofmann, Stephen Hofmann, Suse Hubscher, the late Anthony Hughes, the late Keith Jacobs, Christine James, Cynthia Johnston, Olwen Jones, Myles Jordan, Simon and Genette Kay, Dr Walter Kemp, Evelyn Klopfer, Gerald Krug, William Lake, Rod Land, Mary Lanigan-O'Keefe, the late Diana Lennard, the late Alan Light, the late Astrid Liljeblad, Doma Lilley, the late Sir Charles Mackerras, the late Paul Mahr and Leslie Mahr, Lloyd Masel, the late John Matheson, George and Connie McAlonan, Rosemary McWhirter-Whitlock, Maureen Meers, Valerie Melrose, the late Dr Elisabeth Mensa, Geoffrey Michaels, the late Felix Millar, Kevin Miller, Erica Munn, Donald Munro, Jean Munro, the late James Murdoch, the late Professor Charles Nalden, Elke Neidhardt, Moffatt Oxenbould, Frank Pam, Marie van Hove Parker, Nicholas Payne, the late Ruth Pearl, Rodney Phillips, Craig Powell, Alan Priestley, Tony Prochazka, Joel Quarrington, the late Harry Quick, the late Christine Rankl, the late Moya Rea, the late Ernst Reinl and Lois Manning, the late Eugene Rittich, Dr Ivan Robertson, the late Franz Röhr, Ivan Ruscoe, Walter Rychtowski, Denis Segond, Wolfgang Simon, Larry Sitsky, the late Jean Snaddon, Althea Bridges Sorring, Pierre Stanislas, Henry Stern, the late Wolf Strauss, Tais Taras, the late Hofrat Dr Walter Tautschnig, Michael Tett, Peter and Jane Tett, June Thom, the late John Thompson, Marjorie Thompson, Rachel Thompson, Radi Tintner, Boris Tintner, Demas and Andrea Tintner, Paul Tintner and Margaret Cooke, Barrie Trussell, Maria Vandamme and Ian Perry, Denise Wadley, Shimon and Peggy Walt, Vincent Warrener, Burt Wathen, Felix Werder, Donald Westlake, Nigel Westlake, Brenda McDermott White, Michael Wieck, Dorothy Wilkinson, Ken and Elizabeth Wilson, John Winther, the late Prier Wintle, Christian Wojtowicz, Yehudi Wyner, Patricia Yates, Jocelyn Young, Ruth Atkinson Young, Gino Zancanaro, 'Raelene' and 'Reg'. To anyone I may have left out in error, I apologise and offer my thanks.

I wish to express my thanks to the following institutions and their dedicated staff, who gave me limitless assistance and made my many hours of research entirely pleasurable: Adelaide Festival Theatre Performing Arts Collection (Jo Peoples); Australasian Performing Right Association; Auckland City Public Library (Kate De Courcy, Marilyn Hayr, Sharyn Palmer); Auckland War Memorial Museum Library; Auckland Philharmonic Orchestra; Australian Broadcasting Corporation (Geoff Harris, Lorna Lander, Barry McKay, John Spence, Peter Taplin, Guy Tranter); BBC Archives, Caversham Park (Karen White); CBC (Barbara Brown), Christchurch Public Library; English National Opera archives (Clare Colvin); Israelitische Kultusgemeinde Wien (Heidrun Weiss); National Archive, Kew and Public Record Office, London; Mount Albert Presbyterian Church (Neil and Pamela McGough); National Archives of Australia, Villawood (Kerrie Jarvis, Eddie Rutlidge) and Canberra; National Archives of New Zealand, Wellington and Auckland; National Library of New Zealand and Alexander Turnbull Library (Barbara Brownlie, Roger Flury, Bronwyn Officer, Jill Palmer); National Library of Australia, Canberra (Robyn Holmes, and the staff of Manuscripts); New South Wales Land Titles Office (Ben Briguglio); New Zealand Symphony Orchestra (Brian Burge, Ian Fraser, Peter Walls); Oesterreichische Nationalbibliothek; Orpheus Trust (Dr Primavera Gruber); Queensland Performing Arts Trust and the QPAT Performing Arts Museum (Beryl Davis); State Library of New South Wales and Mitchell Library; State Library of Queensland; State Library of Victoria and Latrobe Library; State Library of Western Australia and Battye Library; Symphony Nova Scotia; Universität für Musik und Darstellende Kunst (Dr Lynne Heller, Erwin Strouhal); University of Auckland Library (Stephen Innes); Victorian Arts Centre Performing Arts Museum (Catherine O'Donoghue); West Australian Opera Company; Wiener Gebietskrankenkasse; Wiener Sängerknaben (Dr Tina Breckwoldt); Wiener Stadt- und Landesarchiv (MA 8); Wienbibliothek im Rathaus (MA 9); and World Jewish Relief Archive, London (Lilian Levy).

For invaluable research assistance I thank the following: Peter Anderson of the Auckland Choral Society, Graham Badcock, Patrick Brislan, Peter Coates, Paul Cooper, Patrick Day, Georg Gaugusch, Mervyn Keeble, Doug Munro, Rodney Reynolds, Elizabeth Silsbury, Paul Svoboda, Lindis Taylor of the New

Zealand Opera News, the late Dennis Tonks, Joy Tonks, Matthias Wurz and Arthur Zimmerman. I am especially indebted to the late Adrienne Simpson, a writer who shared her own research with me with unparalleled generosity, and Dr Kim Lorenz, who provided me with her PhD thesis on the Wiener Sängerknaben as well as the transcript of her interview with Georg. I am indebted to Corin Fairburn Bass, Edward Benyas, Margaret Cooke and Stephen Pedersen for allowing me access to tapes of unpublished interviews; to Roger Woodward for the transcript of his 1992 interview with Georg; and to Ralph Aldrich for the tape and transcript of Georg's lecture on Mahler at Banff in 1975.

I am most grateful to the Australian Broadcasting Corporation and the ABC's Gordon Williams for allowing me to reproduce certain documents held in their archive at National Archives in Sydney, and I thank the original writers or their heirs for permissions. Derek Watt at Symphony Australia kindly allowed me access to Georg's personnel file 1987–98. The Alexander Turnbull Library allowed me to quote from Georg's letters to Douglas Lilburn, Frederick Page and Helen Shaw, and from Douglas Lilburn's letter to Ron Dellow. Stephen and Michal Hofmann kindly granted me access to their mother's (Helen Shaw) papers there; Rex Hobcroft and the late James Murdoch granted me access to their papers at the National Library in Canberra and Alyn Tilleard granted access to the papers of Kurt and Marea Prerauer at the Mitchell Library.

I am indebted to the following individuals for allowing me to quote them: William Chandler and Norman Lebrecht from the CBC radio documentary *Georg Tintner: A Documentary Tribute*; Rolf Gjelsten, David Quinn and the late Eugene Rittich from their National Youth Orchestra questionnaires; Brent Parker for his letter to Georg; and Jeffrey Wall from his letter to the London Free Press. I thank Corin, Janis and Dinah Fairburn for permission to quote Rex Fairburn's letter to Georg; A. J. North for material by Alfred and Mirrie Hill; the Estate of Yehudi Menuhin for permission to quote from Menuhin's letter to Georg; Beryl Chempin for permission to quote from the letters of Denis Matthews; and Barbara Smith of the National Youth Orchestra of Canada for permission to quote from John Brown's correspondence. Demas, Boris, Radi and Paul Tintner generously allowed me to quote from their mother's letters and gave me access to her photo album.

Personal letters written by Georg proved elusive; several of his main correspondents had not kept, or did not wish to share, his correspondence. I thank the following for granting me access to Georg's letters: Dame Heather Begg, the late Ernst Froehlich, Clara Menuhin-Hauser, Byron Riggan, and especially Marjorie Thompson, without whose collection of several hundred letters my task would have been infinitely more difficult. (All personal letters I have quoted remain in the possession of the addressee unless otherwise noted.) Georg's writing style, especially in earlier years when his English was limited, had a certain charm and I have retained his spelling and punctuation except where obscurity would result.

Photographers George Georgakakos, Arnold Matthews and Ernest McQuillan generously allowed me the use of their images; I am indebted to Stephen and Michal Hofmann who allowed me to include several by their father Frank Hofmann. I thank Judy Barnett who kindly allowed me the use of the photo by Geoffrey Rothwell in the National Library of Australia; the Auckland War Memorial Museum Library for allowing reproduction of the photo on p. 109; the *Sunday Times* in Perth for reproduction of the photo on p. 206; and Rideau Hall in Ottawa for the photo on p. 369.

Several people read sections of the text and offered valuable suggestions and support: Anne French; Hans Kuiper, Peter Kristian Mose, Morty Schiff, Sarah Shieff and Daniel Snowman. I thank also my mother, Pamela Buchdahl, for her superlative proofreading.

Working with University of Western Australia Publishing has been a pleasure. Thanks are due first and foremost to my publisher Melanie Ostell, who took my book on and painstakingly nurtured it from the start, and to Laura Keenan, who shepherded it to publication with care and good humour.

# Notes

## Chapter One

1 Georg Tintner, personal communication.
2 Interview with Kim Lorenz, 28 July 1983, private tape.
3 Ibid.
4 Ibid.
5 Ibid.
6 Lecture on Conductors 1, National Youth Orchestra of Canada, 10 August 1977.
7 Lorenz interview.

## Chapter Two

1 GT interview with Corin Fairburn Bass, 8 January 1994, private tape.
2 GT interview with Kim Lorenz, 28 July 1983, private tape.
3 GT interview with Ken Winters, CBC Radio, 14 March 1991.
4 Letter to Byron Riggan, 25 September 1984, author's collection.
5 GT interview with Eric Friesen, CBC Radio, 23 October 1998.
6 Lecture on Bruckner, National Youth Orchestra of Canada, July 1974.
7 Lecture on Conductors 1, National Youth Orchestra of Canada, 10 August 1977.
8 Podium talk, 4 February 1984.
9 Georg's sister Annemarie Tett, personal communication.
10 Romain Rolland, *Jean-Christophe,* translated by Gilbert Cannan, The Modern Library, New York, 1911.
11 GT interview with Walter Kemp, CKDU Radio, 8 December 1990.
12 Friesen interview.
13 GT interview with Arthur Zimmerman, CFRC-FM, 2 August 1979.
14 Lecture at the Banff Centre, July 1975.
15 GT interview with Roger Woodward, 16 February 1992, unpublished.
16 Zimmerman interview.
17 'Music that is important to me', in 4MBS-FM Radio Guide, July 1996.
18 Lecture on Conductors 2, National Youth Orchestra of Canada, 24 August 1977.
19 Lecture on Conductors 1.
20 Lecture on Conductors 2.
21 4MBS-FM article.
22 Zimmerman interview.

## Chapter Three

1 Letter to Erica Munn, 14 December 1975.
2 Radio Wien (*Illustrierte Wochenschrift der RAVAG*), Vol. 12 No. 20, 20 March 1936.
3 GT interview with Mairi Nicolson, ABC Radio, 11 April 1987.
4 GT interview with Arthur Zimmerman, CFRC-FM Radio, 2 August 1979.
5 GT interview with Roger Woodward, 16 February 1992, unpublished.
6 Letter to Jeanine Trent, 29 July 1996.
7 *International Biographical Dictionary of Central European Émigrés 1933–45*; questionnaire GT completed in 1976 held at Research Foundation for Jewish Immigration, New York. Many biographical details (notably, most

dates) he stated are incorrect.
8    GT interview with Walter Kemp, CKDU Radio, 8 December 1990.
9    Reference by Leo Kraus, director of the Volksoper 1931–33, 22 June 1937,
     author's collection.
10   Kemp interview.
11   GT interview with Edward Benyas, 18 July 1996, private tape.
12   Letter to Les Thompson, 17 March 1966.
13   Letter to Victor Hochhauser, 3 October 1996.
14   Personal communication.
15   Letter to the Franz Schmidt Society (Austria), 1 February 1997.
16   Lecture to Women for Music, Halifax, 4 February 1999, author's tape.
17   Benyas interview.
18   Ibid.
19   GT interview with Ken Winters, CBC Radio, 14 March 1991.

*Chapter Four*
1    GT interview with Ken Winters, CBC Radio, 14 March 1991.

*Chapter Five*
1    Author's interview, 18 November 2000.
2    Maja Bagley, author's interview, 17 November 2004.
3    Archives New Zealand (Wellington), AAAR 493/63 J1941/50/792.

*Chapter Six*
1    Marjorie Thompson, author's interview, 26 February 2000.
2    Carl Hoffmann, unpublished memoir.
3    Letter to author, 19 November 1979.
4    Personal communication.
5    Author's interview, 19 May 2001.
6    Joyce Hoffmann, letter to author, 2 December 1999.
7    Session minutes, 17 March 1944; Auckland War Memorial Museum
     Library, Archives of the Mount Albert Presbyterian Church,
     MS-1501-M924 Box 3.
8    Auckland War Memorial Museum Library, Annual Report 1945,
     MS2002/4, Archives of the Mount Albert Presbyterian Church
9    2 January 1946, Archives New Zealand, AAAC 959 IA1 115/1202,
     Application for Naturalisation.
10   Thompson interview, 17–24 November 2000.
11   Thompson interview, 23–26 February 2000.
12   Marjorie Thompson, letter to author, 18 March 2000.
13   Thompson interview, 23–26 October 2002.
14   Author's interview, 27 October 2001.
15   Thompson interview, 23–26 February 2000.
16   Author's interview, 8 April 2007.
17   Boris Tintner, author's interview, 17 May 2003.
18   Author's interview, 10 July 2001.
19   Author's collection.
20   Letter to Howard Dyck, 3 April 1999.

*Chapter Seven*
1    Archives New Zealand, New Zealand Broadcasting Corporation archive,
     AADL 793 Box 1 pt. 1, Auckland Choral Society.

2    Marjorie Thompson, author's interview, 20–25 November 2001.
3    NZBC archive.
4    12 March 1947.
5    *Christchurch Star-Sun*, 30 August 1951.
6    14 July 1947.
7    14 July 1947.
8    Letter to Corin Fairburn Bass, undated in 1994.
9    NZBC archive.
10   Ibid.
11   Author's interview, 23 May 2003.
12   *New Zealand Herald*, 4 April 1949.
13   Letter to Ron Dellow, 27 August 1949, Alexander Turnbull Library,
     MS-Papers-8123-14, Ronald Dellow archive.
14   Author's interview, 19 May 2001.
15   Eva Hoffmann, author's interview, 11–14 December 1999.
16   Thompson interview, 10 July 2001.
17   Eva Hoffmann, author's interview, 11–14 December 1999.
18   Author's interview, 14 November 2004.
19   Author's interviews, 19 November 2000 and 15 November 2003.
20   Author's interview, 19 May 2001.
21   Letters to author, 16 February 2000 and 2 December 1999.
22   Letter to author, 24 November 2002.

*Chapter Eight*
1    Archives New Zealand (Wellington), New Zealand Broadcasting archive,
     House of Representatives Supplementary Order Paper, AAHT 564/635
     21/2/1 pt 1.
2    Letter to Doug Munro, 25 July 2001.
3    Author's interview, 26 October 2001.
4    11 May 1950, NZBC archive, AADL 793 Box 3 pt. 1, Auckland Music
     Council 1948–50.
5    Author's interview, 23 June 2002.
6    Marjorie Thompson, author's interview, 29 March 2001.
7    Dorothea Turner, *Auckland Star*, 24 September 1951.
8    21 May 1950, NZBC archive, AADL 793 Box 3 pt. 1.
9    Typed copy of original letter in Marjorie Thompson collection.
10   L. C. M. Saunders, 5 May 1952.

*Chapter Nine*
1    3 July 1952.
2    Author's interview, 12 September 2001.
3    Letter to author, 8 March 2002.
4    Interview with Margaret Cooke, 11 April 1987, private tape.
5    Letter to Georg, 18 September 1996.
6    Author's interview, 19 May 2001.
7    Author's interview, 26 October 2002.
8    Author's interview, 28 June 2001.
9    NZBC archive, AADL 793 Box 3 pt. 2.
10   L. C. M. Saunders, 2 July 1952.
11   Author's collection.
12   3 July 1952.

13   18 July 1952.
14   *Listener*, 1 August 1952.
15   Author's interview, 26 October 2004.
16   Marjorie Thompson, author's interview, 23–26 February 2000.
17   L. C. M. Saunders, *New Zealand Herald*, 17 November 1952.
18   24 November 1952.

*Chapter Ten*
1    Feri Hoffmann, author's interview, 29 October 2001.
2    Author's interview, 20 May 2001.
3    Author's interview, 4 September 2000.
4    Author's interview, 26 October 2001.
5    Author's interview, 26 October 2002.
6    Author's interview, 7 January 2002.
7    Letter to author, 8 March 2002.
8    Letter to Les Thompson, 21 January 1953.
9    14 June 1953, State Library of New South Wales, MLMSS 6357, Alfred Hill archive.
10   23 June 1953, author's collection.
11   15 October 1953.
12   H. P., 14 April 1954.
13   Accountant's report, 23 September 1955, National Library of Australia, Australian Elizabethan Theatre Trust archive, MS5908 Box 21 File 56/2.

*Chapter Eleven*
1    L. B., 7 July 1954.
2    GT interview with Vicki Gabereau, CBC Radio, 7 January 1991.
3    GT interview with Corin Fairburn Bass, 8 January 1994, private tape.
4    11 June 1954, author's collection.
5    Christine Rankl, author's interview, 18 November 2003.
6    26 August 1954, Alexander Turnbull Library, MS-Papers-2483-98, Douglas Lilburn Papers.
7    22 September 1954, Ibid.
8    GT interview with Margaret Cooke, 11 April 1987, private tape.
9    Gabereau interview.
10   GT interview with Arthur Kaptainis, *Montreal Gazette*, 31 March 1990.
11   Letter to author, 6 August 2004.
12   Cooke interview.
13   9 January 1955, Lilburn Papers.
14   25 March 1955, Ibid.
15   Personal communication.
16   Mary Lanigan-O'Keefe, author's interview, 13 April 2001.
17   22 May 1955, Lilburn papers.
18   4 October 1956, Lilburn Papers.

*Chapter Twelve*
1    5 December 1955, National Archives of Australia (Sydney), ABC archive, C662/T1 Box 94, Composition files.
2    Letter to Queensland Director-General of Education, 21 October 1955. Copy in Hill's handwriting in author's collection.
3    11 February 1956, Alexander Turnbull Library, MS-Papers-2483-98,

Douglas Lilburn Papers.
4    Personal communication.
5    Maria Vandamme, author's interview, 26 May 2000.
6    Heather Begg, letter to author, 6 December 1999.
7    Mary Lanigan-O'Keefe, author's interview, 13 April 2001.
8    Undated memoir, author's collection.
9    Author's interview, 21 June 2002.
10   4 December 1957, Archives New Zealand (Wellington), NZBC archive, AAHT 564/636 21/2/1 pt. 4, Appointment of Conductor 1957.
11   F. Turnovsky, *Fifty Years in New Zealand*, Allen & Unwin, Wellington, 1990, p. 141.
12   10 May 1958.
13   Unidentified author, June 1958.
14   *Auckland Star*, 13 June 1953.
15   Author's interview, 18 November 2003.
16   Gino Zancanaro, author's interview, 10 October 2001.
17   24 December 1958, Lilburn Papers.
18   Author's interview, 17 May 2003.
19   The words of Gino Zancanaro, who observed the family at the time. Author's interview, 10 October 2001.
20   Pearl Britton, letter to author, 2 January 2000.

*Chapter Thirteen*
1    Podium introduction to a performance in Brisbane on 28 July 1983, private tape.
2    Said to Keith Jacobs; author's interview, 19 May 2001.
3    Interview with Stephen Pedersen, *Halifax Herald*, 26 May 1989, private tape.
4    Letter to Les Thompson, 31 December 1968.
5    Podium introduction.
6    Letter to author, 22 September 1982.
7    Podium introduction, 28 July 1983.
8    J. Devaney, *Poems*, Angus & Robertson, Sydney, 1950.
9    Letter to Les Thompson, 31 December 1968.
10   Letter to author, 31 August 2008.
11   Letter to author, 10 October 2001.
12   Letter to author, 10 October 2001.
13   Letter from Ron Maslyn Williams to John Bishop, 24 January 1960, National Library of Australia, MS7979 Box 5 folder 37, National Music Camp archive.
14   29 April 1960.
15   N. Warren-Smith, *25 Years of the Australian Opera*, OUP, Melbourne, 1983, p. 126.
16   Julian Russell, 6 June 1960.
17   Ramsay Pennicuick, 25 June 1960.
18   Author's interview, 17 June 2000.
19   Author's interview, 13 December 2003.
20   Letter to Heather Begg, 20 December 1960.

*Chapter Fourteen*
1    27 July 1958.

2    Author's interview, 22 January 2005.
3    N. Warren-Smith, *25 Years of the Australian Opera*, OUP, Melbourne, 1983, p. 89.
4    Letter to Marie van Hove Parker, 8 August 2000.
5    GT interview in *The Press*, Christchurch, 28 January 1964.
6    Letter to author, 24 March 2000.
7    Letter to author, 7 March 2002.
8    Letter to author, 6 August 2004.
9    24 December 1987.
10   GT interview with Margaret Cooke, 11 April 1987.
11   Boris Tintner, author's interview, 17 May 2003.
12   Letter to Stefan Haag, 5 January 1961, National Library of Australia, Australian Elizabethan Trust Archive, MS 5908 Box 437.
13   27 April 1967.
14   Author's interview, 1 January 2001.
15   Author's interview, 17 June 2000.
16   Author's interviews, 3 January and 26 June 2001.
17   Author's interviews, 26 January, 3 January and 4 June 2001.
18   12 August 1955, Alexander Turnbull Library, MS-Papers-2483-98, Douglas Lilburn Papers.
19   Author's interview, 17 May 2003.
20   Author's interview, 7 July 2001.
21   Author's interviews with Grant Dickson, 28 May 2003, and Donald Munro, 12 October 2000.

*Chapter Fifteen*

1    K. M. H., *Dominion*, 28 March 1964.
2    GT interview with Corin Fairburn Bass, 8 January 1994, private tape.
3    5 February 1965.
4    Brenda McDermott White (formerly Matthews), author's interview, 30 November 2003.
5    7 September 1964, National Library of Australia, Australian Elizabethan Theatre Trust archive, MS5908 Box 50.
6    10 September 1964, Ibid.
7    *Evening Post*, 1 December 1964.
8    H. L. C., 18 January 1965.
9    GT interview with Howard Ainsworth, 4MBS-FM Radio, 22 May 1997.
10   GT interview with Stephen Pedersen, *Halifax Herald*, 26 May 1989, private tape.
11   M. J., 13 May 1965.
12   Lecture to Women for Music, Halifax, 4 February 1999, author's tape.
13   14 August 1965.
14   Richard Bonynge, author's interview, 11 October 2002.
15   Gerald Krug, author's interview, 7 May 2001.
16   29 July 1965.
17   29 July 1965.
18   Felix Werder, author's interview, 21 June 2000.
19   Author's interview, 20 May 2000.
20   Ibid.
21   Author's interview, 2 December 1999.
22   28 November 1965.

## Chapter Sixteen

1   Noel Storr, 7 January 1966.
2   28 January 1966.
3   *Cape Times*, 18 February 1966.
4   *Cape Times,* 25 February 1966.
5   Author's interview, 7 October 2000.
6   Author's interview, 18 May 2003.
7   Marjorie Thompson, author's interview, 29 March 2001.
8   Georg Tintner, personal communication.
9   Personal communication.
10  Personal communication.
11  Author's interview, 7 July 2001.
12  Letter to Les Thompson, 8 April 1966.
13  Unknown author, *Hawick News and Scottish Border Chronicle*, 27 May 1968.
14  *Cape Times*, 10 February 1967.
15  Letter to author, 11 March 2001.
16  Lecture to Women for Music, Halifax, 4 February 1999, author's tape.
17  31 December 1968.
18  27 April 1967.
19  8 May 1967.
20  1 September 1967.
21  Author's interview, 7 June 2001.

## Chapter Seventeen

1   Letter to author, 24 November 2002.
2   Copy of the letter in Marjorie Thompson collection.
3   Author's interview, 30 November 2003.
4   Undated letter probably in July 1968, author's collection.
5   Letter to Ron and Bev Simmons, 25 September 1968.
6   Donald James, November 1968.
7   Letter to Les Thompson, 30 September 1968.
8   16 January 1969.
9   17 April 1969.
10  17 April 1969.
11  Robert Henderson, 17 April 1969.
12  17 April 1969.
13  Letter to author, 11 May 2002.
14  15 May 1969.
15  Telephone call to Norman Lebrecht, 13 October 1999, reported in Lebrecht letter to author, 14 October 1999.
16  15 May 1969.
17  E. D., *Sunderland Echo*, 7 October 1969.
18  13 November 1969.
19  22 December 1969, Alexander Turnbull Library, MS-Papers-2483-98, Douglas Lilburn papers.
20  Personal communication.
21  Marjorie Thompson, author's interview, 23–26 February 2000.
22  8 March 1970.
23  Author's interview, 24 January 2003, and letter to author, 27 January 2003.
24  *Georg Tintner: A Documentary Tribute*, CBC Radio, 22 November 1999.

*Chapter Eighteen*
1  28 September 1970, National Library of Australia, MS8372 Box 1 Series 1/11, Murdoch Papers.
2  7 May 1970.
3  Interview with Margie van Hattem, 30 June 1970.
4  Author's interviews, 17 June and 31 December 2000, 26 June 2001.
5  Author's interview, 7 February 2008.
6  18 September 1971, National Youth Orchestra of Canada, Georg Tintner personnel file.
7  Letter to author, 3 April 2002.
8  Letter to John Brown, 27 October 1971, personnel file.
9  Letter to author, 23 April 2001.

*Chapter Nineteen*
1  Undated letter, probably late 1971, author's collection.
2  2 February 1972, author's collection.
3  4 June 1972 (erroneously dated 4 August), author's collection.
4  Personal communication.
5  GT interview with Margaret Cooke, 11 April 1987.
6  Author's interview, 19 May 2001.
7  3 June 1972.
8  Letter to the Thompsons, 28 June 1972.
9  Letter to author, 1 August 2000.
10  13 July 1972.
11  14 July 1972.
12  10 August 1972, author's collection.
13  19 August 1972.
14  Personal communication.
15  Valerie Melrose, author's interview, 31 December 2000.
16  1 December 1972, National Archives of Australia (Sydney), ABC archive, C661/T5, Georg Tintner personnel file 1960–80.
17  Letter to John Brown, 25 March 1974, National Youth Orchestra of Canada, Georg Tintner personnel file.
18  Deirdre Foyster, author's interview, 22 April 2000.
19  Author's interviews, 22 and 25 May 2000.
20  Ralph Middenway, 4 June 1973.
21  9 June 1973.
22  22 July 1973.
23  23 July 1973.
24  31 July 1973.
25  29 December 1973.
26  Cooke interview.
27  26 August 1973, ABC archive, C2425/1, Tintner file 1973–87.
28  Handwritten note by unidentified author, 10 September 1973, Ibid.
29  24 December 1973, Ibid.
30  3 January 1974, Ibid.
31  3 January 1974, Ibid.
32  H. T. G., 2 May 1974.

*Chapter Twenty*
1   26 February and 17 December 1973, National Youth Orchestra of Canada, Georg Tintner personnel file.
2   Ian Docherty, 8 August 1974.
3   Violist David Quinn, National Youth Orchestra archives.
4   Undated, around 23 August 1974, NYO Tintner file.
5   30 August 1974, Ibid.
6   Marjorie Thompson, author's interview, 16 April 2004.
7   22 December 1974.
8   13 February 1975.
9   Author's interview, 8 May 2001.
10  Virginia Westbury, 13 January 1975.
11  Letters to the Editor, *Australian*, 18 January 1975.
12  Letter to Maria Prerauer, 16 February 1975, National Library of Australia, MS10040 Series 5 Folder 14, Papers of Kurt and Marea Prerauer.
13  Author's interview, 6 May 2000.
14  National Library of Australia, Australian Elizabethan Theatre Trust archive, MS5908 Box 486, Australian Chamber Orchestra.
15  9 June 1975.
16  11 February 1975, NYO Tintner file.
17  Personal communication.
18  NYO archives.
19  *Opera Opera*, May 2002.
20  Roger Covell, 27 September 1975.
21  Nadine Amadio, 3 October 1975.
22  1 February 1976.
23  *Sydney Morning Herald*, 17 January 1976.
24  8 March 1976.
25  Letters to author, 22 and 30 July 2000.
26  Author's interview, 22 August 2001.
27  7 May 1976.
28  9 May 1976.
29  Frank Harris, 12 May 1976.
30  Georg Tintner, letter to Ruth Atkinson Young, 29 May 1976.
31  12 June 1976.
32  NYO Tintner file.
33  14 June 1976. National Archives of Australia, ABC archive C661/T5, Tintner personnel file 1960–80, Document 76.

*Chapter Twenty-one*
1   26 September 1976.
2   29 September 1976.
3   26 October 1976.
4   Letter to author, 13 November 1999.
5   Author's interview, 8 May 2001.
6   GT interview with Sue Summers, ABC Radio, 8 April 1987.
7   Letter to Les Thompson, 12 June 1976.
8   Undated letter around November 1987.
9   Letter to author, 13 January 1977.
10  Undated letter, November 1976.

11    21 November 1976.
12    Undated letter around 2 December 1987.

*Chapter Twenty-two*
1     Letter to author, 31 December 1976.
2     Undated letter around 26 December 1976.
3     Peter Rorke, 28 February 1977, National Archives of Australia
      (Sydney), ABC archive, C661/T5 Georg Tintner personnel file 1960–80,
      Document 92.
4     4 March 1977, Ibid., Document 95.
5     Undated annotation on Harper's letter of 4 March 1977, Ibid.
6     Letter to John Brown, 21 May 1977, National Youth Orchestra of Canada,
      Georg Tintner personnel file.
7     Letter to John Brown, 16 June 1976, Ibid.
8     Russell Bond, *Dominion*, 28 October 1977.
9     Letter to author, 8 June 1977.
10    12 April 1978.

*Chapter Twenty-three*
1     Said to Les and Marjorie Thompson. Marjorie Thompson, author's
      interview, 26 February 2000.
2     Letter to author, 25 October 1979.
3     GT interview with Margaret Cooke, 11 April 1987.
4     12 August 1955, Alexander Turnbull Library, MS-Papers-2483-98,
      Douglas Lilburn Papers.
5     1 October 1955, Ibid.
6     Author's interview, 19 May 2001.
7     Probably July 1974, National Youth Orchestra of Canada tape.
8     18 June 1955, Lilburn Papers.

*Chapter Twenty-four*
1     2 July 1979, National Youth Orchestra of Canada, Georg Tintner
      personnel file.
2     3 July 1979, Ibid.
3     15 December 1979, Ibid.
4     20 August 1979.
5     Author's interview, 21 December 2000.
6     7 October 1979.
7     Letter to author, 22 December 1979.
8     Author's interview, 17 June 2000.
9     Undated letter in October 1979. John Hopkins was not on the Australian
      Opera board but was chairman of a Programme Advisory Committee.
10    16 January 1980, National Archives of Australia (Sydney), ABC archive,
      C661/T5, Georg Tintner personnel file 1960–80,
      Document 158.
11    B. J. Dempsey, 8 January 1980, Ibid., Document 161.
12    J. Douglas McLean, 8 January 1980, Ibid., Document 162.
13    Ray Irving, 26 November 1979, Ibid., Document 152.
14    N. Wylde, 3 January 1980, Ibid., Document 155.
15    22 November 1979, Ibid., Document 147.
16    Undated note probably early February 1980, Ibid.
17    4 August 1980, ABC archive, C2425/1, Georg Tintner personnel file

1973–87, Document 106.
18   Letter to Georg and Tanya Tintner, 2 September 1980.
19   Kenneth Hince, *Age*, 2 March 1982.
20   John Sinclair, *Herald*, 1 March 1982.
21   7 May 1982, NYO Tintner file.

*Chapter Twenty-five*
1    22 September 1981, National Youth Orchestra of Canada, Georg Tintner
     personnel file.
2    2 November 1981, Ibid.
3    10 August 1982.
4    2 September 1982.
5    22 April 1984, NYO Tintner file.
6    27 May 1984, author's collection.
7    Dr Ivan Roberton, author's interviews, 23 June 2001 and 17 June 2003.
8    15 October 1982.
9    1 March 1983, Auckland Philharmonia Orchestra, Georg Tintner file.
10   20 September 1982.
11   25 September 1983, author's collection.
12   22 September 1983, NYO Tintner file.
13   *Sydney Morning Herald*, 22 February 1984.
14   Musicians' Association letter to the board, 31 August 1984, Queensland
     Performing Arts Museum, Queensland Theatre Orchestra archive.
15   Undated letter around October 1984, Ibid.
16   Report to the board, November 1984, Ibid.
17   Roger Knight, April 1985.
18   Roger Covell, *Sydney Morning Herald*, 19 August 1985.

*Chapter Twenty-six*
1    Anne Boyd, *TV & Entertainment Times*, 14–20 May 1986.
2    Author's interview, 17 June 2000.
3    Author's interview, 17–24 November 2000.
4    19 February 1986, National Youth Orchestra of Canada, Georg Tintner
     personnel file.
5    8 September 1986.
6    8 September 1986.
7    10 October 1986.
8    *Halifax Herald*, 30 October 1986.
9    Fred Blanks, *Sydney Morning Herald*, 13 April 1987.
10   11 April 1987, private tape.
11   30 November 1987.

*Chapter Twenty-seven*
1    *Halifax Herald*, 10 December 1987.
2    Jordan Grigg, letter to author, 3 September 2006.
3    Letter to Hans Buchdahl, 12 February 1984.
4    Lectures on Mahler, Banff Centre, July 1975 and National Youth
     Orchestra of Canada, 3 August 1977.
5    GT interview with Margaret Cooke, 11 April 1987.
6    Ibid.
7    7 August 1989.

8    Myles Jordan (cellist at National Youth Orchestra 1974 and 1975), letter to author, 13 September 2008.
9    *La Presse*, 20 December 1989.
10   20 December 1989.
11   Mostly Mozart Festival concert, Sydney Opera House, 4 January 1991.
12   *Halifax Herald*, 17 May 1990.
13   *Whig-Standard Magazine*, 17 November 1990.
14   *Halifax Herald*, 21 November 1990.
15   Letter to Les Thompson, 22 May 1984.

## Chapter Twenty-eight
1    *The Art of Conducting*, Teldec Video 4509-95038-3.
2    Letters to author, 17 January 2004, 22 and 24 April 2004.
3    GT interview with Stephen Pedersen, *Halifax Herald*, private tape.
4    GT interview with Mairi Nicolson, ABC Radio, 11 April 1987.
5    GT interview with Arthur Zimmerman, CFRC-FM, 2 August 1979.
6    Personal communication.
7    Letter to author, 7 March 2002.
8    GT interview with Sue Summers, ABC Radio, 11 April 1987.
9    Zimmerman interview.
10   Pedersen interview.
11   Author's interview, 19 May 2001.
12   Symphony Nova Scotia board memo, 15 November 1991.
13   Letter to author, 27 April 2004.
14   9 November 1992.
15   Author's interview, 15 May 2004.

## Chapter Twenty-nine
1    *Halifax Herald*, 11 March 1993.
2    GT interview with Vicki Gabereau, CBC Radio, broadcast 7 January 1991.
3    Lecture on Conductors 1, National Youth Orchestra of Canada, 10 August 1977.
4    Ibid.
5    Ibid.
6    GT interview with Stephen Pedersen, *Halifax Herald*, 26 May 1989, private tape.
7    GT interview with Roger Woodward, 16 February 1992, unpublished.
8    Pedersen interview.
9    Kenneth Hince, 5 July 1993.
10   Keith Field, 5 July 1993.
11   26 July 1993, Symphony Australia, Georg Tintner personnel file 1987–98, Document 222.
12   Author's interview, 15 April 2000.
13   26 October 1993, Symphony Australia Tintner file 1987–98.

## Chapter Thirty
1    GT interview with Margaret Cooke, 11 April 1987.
2    21 January 1994.
3    Cooke interview.
4    Anthony Camden, letter to author, 22 June 2001.

5 *Fanfare*, November/December 1995.
6 Letter to author, 13 January 1977.

## Chapter Thirty-one
1 Letter to Judy Voois, Conductors Guild, 14 September 1995.
2 12 November 1997.
3 Georg Tintner, letter to Benjamin Korstvedt, 13 November 1995.
4 19 June 1996.
5 *Georg Tintner: A Documentary Tribute*, CBC Radio, 22 November 1999.
6 Liner notes to his recording of Bruckner Symphony No. 9, Naxos 4.554268.
7 *Hi-Fi News & Record Review*, December 1997.
8 *Irish Times*, 31 October 1997.
9 GT interview with Sue Summers, ABC Radio, 6 April 1987.
10 Richard Osborne, May 1998.
11 Robert McColley, November/December 1998.
12 August 1998.
13 Letters to author, 21 February 2003 and 6 August 2004.

## Chapter Thirty-two
1 Letter to William Carragan, 8 August 1998.
2 Letter to William Carragan, 11 August 1998.
3 Letter to author, 19 August 1998.
4 *International Biographical Dictionary of Central European Émigrés 1933–45*; the questionnaire Georg completed is held at Research Foundation for Jewish Immigration, New York. Many biographical details (notably, most dates) he stated are incorrect.
5 29 November 1998.
6 January 1999.
7 3 January 1999.
8 *Gramophone Awards Issue*, 1999.
9 July/August 1999.

## Chapter Thirty-three
1 *Stereophile*, July 1999.
2 Andrew Clarke, 9 October 1999.

## Epilogue
1 Jeffrey Wall, *London Free Press*, 16 October 1999.
2 Martin Anderson, *Punch*, 21 November 2001.

# Photo Credits

# Index

367, 371

Britten, Benjamin
  *Albert Herring* 216–218,
    220, 278
  *Peter Grimes* 138
Brno, Czech Republic 9
Brown, John 142, 200,
  202–205, 217, 220,
  222–224, 227, 229, 234,
  246–248, 252, 266–267,
  278–281, 285, 292–293,
  304
Browne, Lindsey 233
Bruckner, Anton 20–22,
  30, 35, 52, 119–120,
  146–147, 222, 234,
  267–268, 280, 297, 304,
  307, 344, 351–360, 363,
  365–367, 369–371, 376,
  385
  *Benedictus* 21, 107
  *Die Nullte (Symphony
    No. 0)* 357, 366
  *Eighth Symphony* 30,
    261, 279–280, 323, 351,
    353–357, 365–366
  *Fifth Symphony* 30, 193,
    243, 263, 311, 347, 353,
    359–360, 378
  *First Symphony* 365
  *Fourth Symphony* 42–43,
    97, 108, 126, 146–147,
    169, 177, 202, 261, 263,
    297, 301, 317, 321, 356,
    365, 369, 371, 373, 376
  *Kyrie* 107
  *Mass in E minor* 15
  *Mass in F minor* 21, 106,
    108
  *Ninth Symphony* 233,
    247, 261, 319, 345–346,
    352, 358, 378
  *Second Symphony* 351,
    353, 361–361
  *Seventh Symphony* 30,
    32, 143, 181, 222, 243,
    261, 354, 358, 369, 373
  *Sixth Symphony* 343,
    345, 347, 362
  *Symphony No. 00
    (Study Symphony)* 365

*Te Deum* 288
*Third Symphony* 365,
  380
Brünner, Klara. *See*
  Tintner, Klara
Brünner, Wilhelm 9
Brunner-Orne, Martha 77
Brusey, Harry 164
Brymer, Jack 317
Buchanan, Isobel 230
Buchbinder, Rudolf 232
Bцchdahl, Hans 246
Buchdahl, Kate 315, 324
Budapest 78, 361
Bundaberg, Queensland
  149
Burstein, Joe 75, 97
Busch Quartet 34
Busch, Adolf 34

Cairns, Queensland 131
Callaway, Frank 194, 201
Cambridge Music School
  271
Camden Town, England
  51
Camden, Anthony 193,
  344, 358
Campbell, Elizabeth 297
Canada Council 302
Canadian Brass 303
Canadian Broadcasting
  Corporation (CBC)
  222, 313, 343–344, 367,
  378
Canadian Chamber
  Orchestra 227
Canadian Opera 308
Canadian Youth Orchestra.
  *See* National Youth
  Orchestra (Canada)
Canberra 209, 246, 253,
  282, 315, 324, 373
Canterbury University 75
Cape Town 169, 172, 177,
  179–186, 316
Cape Town Municipal
  Orchestra 173, 177, 179,
  186
Carden, Joan 230
Carmody, John 230

Carr, Edwin
  *Mardi Gras* 92
Carragan, William 351,
  353–355, 365–366
Carter, Brecon 284
Casals, Pablo 33, 35, 320
Casino, New South Wales
  131
Cathedral of St John the
  Divine 303
Cavdarski, Vanco 234, 244
Chandler, Bill 356
Chaplin, Charlie 239
Chard, Geoffrey 110, 159
Charlottetown, Prince
  Edward Island, Canada
  369
Charters Towers,
  Queensland 132
Chausson, Ernest
  *Poème* 280
Chopin, Fryderyk
  Franciszek 28, 38, 58
Christchurch 278
Christchurch Symphony
  Orchestra 275
Christiansen, James 274
Christie, George 189
Church, Charlotte 367
Cillario, Carlo Felice 231
Clare, Maurice 202
Clark, Noel 275
Cleveland, Ohio 372
Cloncurry, Queensland
  149
Cobar, New South Wales
  154
Cocking, Rae 225
Cohrs, Benjanin-Gunnar
  358
Collaroy, New South
  Wales 128, 135
Commemorative
  Medal for the
  125th Anniversary
  of Canadian
  Confederation 326
Concentration Camps 47,
  75, 78, 259, 350, 369
  Auschwitz 78, 368
  Bergen-Belsen 75

353

Stodola, Lynn 368

Sunderland, England 193

Susskind, Walter 200, 202

Sutherland, Joan 165, 168–171, 227

Sutherland–Williamson International Grand Opera Company 169, 172

Sydney 54, 108–111, 115–116, 123, 128, 131, 134–139, 141, 157, 159, 161, 167–168, 172, 200, 216, 218–219, 224, 230, 232–233, 239, 242–244, 252, 258, 274, 283, 288, 294–295, 297, 315, 333, 361, 373

Sydney Festival 275

Sydney Opera House 224, 235, 263, 322, 337–338

Sydney String Orchestra 127, 141

Sydney Symphony Orchestra 125, 127, 129, 137, 142, 145, 148, 167–168, 171, 200, 218, 224, 232, 234, 284, 286, 297

Symphony Nova Scotia 289, 295–296, 301, 311–314, 332, 339, 341, 343, 346, 359, 369, 371, 385

Szymanowski, Karol 319
*Violin Concerto No. 2* 319

Taggart, Michael 161

Tamworth, New South Wales 130, 150, 168, 284, 315

Tanglewood, Massachusetts 303

Taras, Tais 109

Tasmanian Symphony Orchestra 234, 245, 283, 286

Tatura, Victoria 20

Tauber, Richard 34

Tauszky, Rosa 9

Tautschnig, Walther 20, 302–303

Taylor, Coleridge
*Song of Hiawatha* 79–82

Taylor, Florence 142

Tchaikovsky, Pyotr Ilyich 222, 228, 286, 305
*Eugene Onegin* 166, 170, 172
*Sixth Symphony* 219, 228

Tel Aviv 239, 252

Terracini, Paul 218

Tett, Francis William 66, 249, 278

Tett, Michael 72, 162, 293

Thompson, Les 57–60, 64, 66, 69, 85, 93, 102, 104, 116, 118, 145, 156, 159, 173, 178–180, 183–187, 189–191, 193, 198, 203–204, 206, 211, 213–214, 218–219, 223–224, 252, 302, 340, 348

Thompson, Marjorie 58–60, 66–67, 69, 73–75, 85, 97, 106, 145, 156, 179–180, 184, 187, 194–195, 203–204, 206, 211, 213–214, 216, 219, 223, 252, 258, 292, 302, 348

Thompson, Rachel 187

Thompson, Ruth 187

Thorborg, Kerstin 34

Tieck, Ludwig
*Feldeinwärts flog ein Vögelein* (*Into the field flew a little Bird*) 144

Timaru, New Zealand 111

Tintner, Alfons 5, 9–11, 13, 23–24, 37, 42, 45, 48, 51, 67, 69–71, 250

Tintner, Annemarie Rosa 11–12, 24–25, 44, 46–47, 51, 57–60, 62, 66, 72, 74, 78, 99, 106, 116, 139, 162, 188, 248–249,

278, 293

Tintner, Ariadne Georgina 98–99, 168, 315

Tintner, Arthur 9, 77–78

Tintner, Bertha. *See* Weinberger, Bertha

Tintner, Boris Norman 88, 98–100, 132, 139, 144, 156, 160, 168, 188, 258, 374

Tintner, Camilla 9

Tintner, Cecilia. *See* Lawrence, Cecilia (Gretel)

Tintner, Chrysothemis Magdalena 185, 188, 190, 194, 196, 206, 211, 213, 315

Tintner, Elsa 77–78

Tintner, Esmeralda Irit Miriam 190, 194–196, 206, 239, 272, 361, 373

Tintner, Franz Demas 73–74, 84–88, 98–99, 106, 139, 157, 165, 168, 308, 374

Tintner, Georg
composing 23, 52, 53, 65, 71, 74, 96–97, 117, 128, 135, 143, 150, 161, 212–213, 231, 237, 247, 258, 278, 336, 339–341, 349, 372
conducting 23, 29, 38, 41, 48, 79–84, 90–96, 101–102, 106–111, 115, 117, 129, 133, 136, 138, 141, 145–150, 162, 167–168, 173, 179, 189, 193, 196–197, 200, 213, 218, 221–225, 227, 230–234, 238–239, 243, 262–263, 266–268, 274, 276, 280–281, 286–289, 294–297, 301, 303, 307–308, 311, 316–323, 327–331, 336, 345–348, 351, 356, 359–362, 366–369, 373, 378–379
musical works of